W9-ARY-937

Acknowledgments

Before you begin working through the exercises in this book, take a moment to appreciate the long list of contributors and reviewers that collectively labored on this Visual Basic programming course. Although I am the author of record, this book reflects the talents and opinions of a number of interesting people, both inside and outside of Microsoft Corporation. First I'd like to thank the developers of the Visual Basic .NET product for their comments and assistance. Several programmers and product managers offered early glimpses of the Visual Studio software to me and explained the product's inner workings. In particular, Rob Howard, Dennis Angeline, Sam Spencer, Michael Pizzo, Mike Iem, Chris Dias, Omar Khan, and Connie Sullivan deserve special mention. Thanks for creating a great development product for us to use and write about!

At Microsoft Press, my favorite computer book publisher, I would like to acknowledge the contributions of a thoroughly awesome team of professionals. Thanks to Danielle Bird, acquisitions editor; Elizabeth Hansford, principal compositor; Katherine Erickson, compositor; Patty Masserman, principal copy editor; Maria Gargiulo, editorial assistant; Michael Kloepfer, electronic artist; Bill Meyers, indexer; and Bill Teel, publishing support specialist. Your efforts will help numerous readers navigate the complex features of Visual Basic .NET and write their first programs.

In particular, I would like to mention the many contributions and technical insights added by two special Microsoft Press editors. Dick Brown worked on the first version of Visual Basic over ten years ago at Microsoft, and now offers his technical wisdom and organizational skills to authors as a Microsoft Press project editor. Dick really made this book a pleasure to work on, and his editorial fingerprints are on each page of the manuscript. Robert Lyon is a role model technical editor in a group that is really without peer in the computer book industry. Robert tested the code in this book on numerous machines running numerous operating systems; he tracked the changes in each beta and offered technical insights and clever workarounds that I couldn't have written better myself. It was not at all unusual to receive e-mail from Robert early in the morning when he really should have been sleeping or at least relaxing a bit. Every author should be so lucky.

Finally, I would like to thank my wife, Kim, and my sons, Henry and Felix, for their support and patience as this book wore on through the Summer and Autumn of 2001. For the missed trips to the swing set on behalf of Visual Basic .NET, I am truly sorry.

Step by Step

MICROSOFT®
VISUAL BASIC® .NET
STEP BY STEP

Michael Halvorson

PUBLISHED BY
Microsoft Press
A Division of Microsoft Corporation
One Microsoft Way
Redmond, Washington 98052-6399

Library of Congress Cataloging-in-Publication Data
Halvorson, Michael.
    Microsoft Visual Basic .NET Step by Step / Michael Halvorson.
        p. cm.
    ISBN 0-7356-1374-5
    1. Microsoft Visual BASIC.   2. BASIC (Computer program language)   I. Title.

    QA76.73.B3 H3384   2002
    005.2'762--dc21   2001054648

Printed and bound in the United States of America.

1 2 3 4 5 6 7 8 9   QWT   7 6 5 4 3 2

Distributed in Canada by Penguin Books Canada Limited.

A CIP catalogue record for this book is available from the British Library.

Microsoft Press books are available through booksellers and distributors worldwide. For further information about international editions, contact your local Microsoft Corporation office or contact Microsoft Press International directly at fax (425) 936-7329. Visit our Web site at www.microsoft.com/mspress. Send comments to *mspinput@microsoft.com*.

Acquisitions Editor: **Danielle Bird**
Project Editor: **Dick Brown**
Technical Editor: **Robert Lyon**
Manuscript Editor: **Dick Brown**

Body Part No. X08-04499

Contents

Finding Your Best Starting Point

Microsoft Visual Basic .NET Step by Step is a comprehensive introduction to Visual Basic programming using the Microsoft Visual Basic .NET software. I have designed this course with a variety of skill levels in mind so that new programmers can learn software development fundamentals in the context of useful, real world applications and experienced Visual Basic programmers can quickly master the essential tools and programming techniques offered in the Visual Basic .NET upgrade. Complementing this comprehensive approach is the book's structure—six topically organized parts, 22 chapters, and more than 65 step-by-step exercises and sample programs. Using this book, you'll quickly learn how to create professional-quality Visual Basic .NET applications for the Microsoft Windows operating system and a variety of Web browsers. You'll also have fun!

important

Please note that the Microsoft Visual Basic .NET software isn't included with this book—you must purchase it separately and install it before you can complete the exercises that I have created. Visual Basic .NET is available in different editions and product configurations, including Standard Edition. It also is distributed as a component in the Microsoft Visual Studio. NET programming suite, which includes the Microsoft Visual C# .NET and Microsoft Visual C++ .NET compilers and other .NET development tools. Visual Studio .NET is available in several different editions, including Professional Edition, Enterprise Developer Edition, Enterprise Architect Edition, and Academic Edition. I have written this book to be compatible with Visual Basic .NET Standard Edition, Visual Studio .NET Professional Edition, Visual Studio .NET Enterprise Developer Edition, and Visual Studio .NET Enterprise Architect Edition. If a feature works differently in one of the Visual Basic .NET editions, I'll let you know.

Finding Your Best Starting Point in This Book

This book is designed to help you build skills in a number of essential areas. You can use this book if you are new to programming, switching from another programming language, or upgrading from Microsoft Visual Basic 6. Use the following table to find your best starting point in this book.

If you are	Follow these steps
New	
To programming	**1** Install the practice files as described in "About the CD-ROM and Practice Files."
	2 Learn basic skills for using Microsoft Visual Basic .NET by working sequentially through Chapters 1 through 18.
	3 Complete Parts 5 and 6 as your level of interest or experience dictates.

If you are	Follow these steps
Switching	
From Microsoft QuickBasic or an earlier version of the BASIC programming language	**1** Install the practice files as described in "About the CD-ROM and Practice Files."
	2 Complete Chapters 1-4, skim Chapters 5-7, and complete Parts 3 and 4 sequentially.
	3 For specific information about creating database and Internet programs, read Parts 5 and 6, respectively.

If you are	Follow these steps
Upgrading	
From Microsoft Visual Basic 6	**1** Install the practice files as described in "About the CD-ROM and Practice Files."
	2 Read Chapters 1-4 carefully to learn the new features of the Visual Studio .NET development environment.
	3 Pay special attention to the "Upgrade Notes: What's New in Visual Basic .NET?" sidebars at the beginning of each chapter, which highlight the significant differences between Visual Basic 6 and Visual Basic .NET.
	4 Skim through Chapters 5-7 to review the fundamentals of event-driven programming, using variables, and writing decision structures.

If you are	Follow these steps
Upgrading *(continued)*	**5** Work sequentially through Chapters 8 through 22 to learn the new features of Visual Basic .NET. **6** Read Appendix A: "Upgrading Visual Basic 6 Programs to Visual Basic .NET" to learn how to convert Visual Basic 6 programs using the Visual Basic Upgrade Wizard.

If you are	Follow these steps
Referencing This book after working through the chapters	**1** Use the index to locate information about specific topics, and use the table of contents to locate information about general topics. **2** Use the Upgrading Index to see a list of the new features in Visual Basic .NET and how Visual Basic 6 program code should be upgraded. **3** Read the Quick Reference at the end of each chapter for a brief review of the major tasks in the chapter. The Quick Reference topics are listed in the same order as they are presented in the chapter.

New Features in Visual Basic .NET

The following table lists the major new features in Microsoft Visual Basic .NET that are covered in this book. The table shows the chapter in which you can learn how to use each feature. You can also use the index to find specific information about a feature or a task you want to do.

To learn how to	See
Use the new integrated Visual Studio .NET development environment and programming tools	Chapter 1
Use the new Windows Forms Toolbox controls, including DateTimePicker and LinkLabel	Chapters 2–3
Compile your program as debug builds and release builds	Chapter 2
Use the new MainMenu control and new dialog box controls	Chapter 4
Use methods in the new .NET Framework in program code	Chapter 5

(continued)

Corrections, Comments, and Help

Every effort has been made to ensure the accuracy of this book and the contents of the practice files CD-ROM. As corrections or changes are collected for this book, they will be placed on a Web page and any errata will also be integrated into the Microsoft online Help tool known as the Knowledge Base. To view the list of known corrections for this book, visit the following page:

http://support.microsoft.com/support/kb/articles/q314/2/85.asp

To search the Knowledge Base and review your support options for this book or CD-ROM, visit the Microsoft Press Support site:

http://www.microsoft.com/mspress/support/

If you have problems, comments, or ideas regarding this book or the practice files CD-ROM, please send them to Microsoft Press.

Send e-mail to

mspinput@microsoft.com

Or send postal mail to

Microsoft Press
Attn: Microsoft Visual Basic .NET Step by Step Editor
One Microsoft Way
Redmond, WA 98052-6399

Please note that support for the Visual Basic .NET software product itself is not offered through the above addresses.

Visual Basic .NET Software Support

For help using Visual Basic .NET, you can call the Microsoft Professional Support for Developers line at 1-800-936-5800. This service is currently available 24 hours per day and is a charge-based service. (Your version of Visual Basic .NET or Visual Studio .NET may provide free phone support for a limited time.) You will be connected to a real, trained Visual Studio .NET professional when you call the support number, not an endless series of phone recordings. Check your Visual Basic .NET product documentation for the details of your service agreement.

Visit the Microsoft Press World Wide Web Site

You are also invited to visit the Microsoft Press World Wide Web site at the following location:

http://www.microsoft.com/mspress/

You'll find descriptions for the complete line of Microsoft Press books (including others by Michael Halvorson), information about ordering titles, notice of special features and events, world-wide contact information, additional content for Microsoft Press books, and much more.

You can also find out the latest in Visual Basic software developments and news from Microsoft Corporation by visiting the following World Wide Web site:

http://www.microsoft.com/vbasic/

Get online and check it out!

About the CD-ROM and Practice Files

The CD-ROM inside the back cover of this book contains practice files that you'll use as you perform the exercises in the book. For example, when you're learning how to display database records with an ADO.NET dataset, you'll open one of the practice files—an academic database named Students.mdb—and then use ADO.NET commands to access the database. By using the practice files, you won't waste time creating all the samples used in the exercises. Instead, you can concentrate on learning how to master Visual Basic .NET programming techniques. With the files and the step-by-step instructions in the chapters, you'll also learn by doing, which is an easy and effective way to acquire and remember new skills.

important

Before you break the seal on the practice files CD-ROM, be sure that this book matches your version of the software. This book is designed for use with Microsoft Visual Basic .NET and Microsoft Visual Studio .NET for the Microsoft Windows operating system. To find out what software you're running, you can check the product package or you can start the software, open a project, and then on the Help menu at the top of the screen, click About Microsoft Visual Basic .NET.

System Requirements

To compile and run all the practice files on this book's CD-ROM, you will need the following configuration:

■ Microsoft Windows 2000 Professional, Microsoft Windows 2000 Server, Microsoft Windows XP Home Edition, Microsoft Windows XP Professional or later

- Microsoft Visual Basic .NET, which can be one of the following editions:
  - Microsoft Visual Basic .NET Standard
  - Microsoft Visual Studio .NET Professional
  - Microsoft Visual Studio .NET Enterprise Developer
  - Microsoft Visual Studio .NET Enterprise Architect

important

A few features (such as the Setup Wizard discussed in Chapter 14 and the Visual Basic Upgrade Wizard discussed in Appendix A) aren't included in Visual Basic .NET Standard. Also, since Windows XP Home Edition doesn't include Internet Information Services, you can't create local ASP.NET Web applications (discussed in Chapter 22) using Windows XP Home Edition.

This book and practice files were tested using Visual Basic .NET Standard and Visual Studio .NET Professional. You might notice a few differences if you are using other editions of Visual Studio .NET.

Installing the Practice Files on Your Computer

Follow these steps to install the practice files on your computer's hard disk so that you can use them with the exercises in this book.

1   Remove the CD-ROM from the package inside the back cover of this book.

2   Insert the CD-ROM in your CD-ROM drive.

important

On many systems, Windows will automatically recognize that you have inserted a CD-ROM and will display a start window. If this happens, skip to step 5.

Start

Start button

3   On the taskbar at the bottom of your screen, click the Start button, and then click Run.

The Run dialog box appears.

4   In the Open text box, type **d:\startcd**, and then click OK. Don't add spaces as you type. (If your CD-ROM drive is associated with a different drive letter, such as e, type that instead.)

A start window should appear.

5   Click Install Practice Files in the list of options on the left.

     A Setup program appears.

6   Follow the directions on the screen.

     The Setup program will copy the practice files from the CD-ROM to your hard drive and clear the Read-only flag on the files. For best results in using the practice files with this book, accept the preselected installation location, which by default is c:\vbnetsbs. (If you change the installation location, you will need to manually adjust the paths in a few practice files to locate essential components—such as artwork and database files—when you use them.)

7   When the files have been installed, remove the CD-ROM from your CD-ROM drive and replace it in the package inside the back cover of the book.

     A folder named c:\vbnetsbs has been created on your hard disk, and the practice files have been placed in that folder. You'll find one folder in c:\vbnetsbs for each chapter in the book.

Using the Practice Files

Each chapter in this book explains when and how to use any practice files for that chapter. When it's time to use a practice file, the book will list instructions for how to open the file. The chapters are built around scenarios that simulate real programming projects so that you can easily apply the skills you learn to your own work.

For those of you who like to know all the details, here's a list of the Visual Basic projects included on the practice disc. Each project is located in its own folder and has several support files.

Project	Description
Chapter 1	
MusicTrivia	A simple trivia program that welcomes you to the programming course and displays a digital photo.
Chapter 2	
Lucky7	Your first program—a Lucky 7 Slot Machine game that simulates a Las Vegas one-armed bandit.
Chapter 3	
Birthday	A program that uses the DateTimePicker control to pick a date.
CheckBox	A program that demonstrates the CheckBox control and its properties.
Hello	A "Hello, world!" program that demonstrates the Label and TextBox controls.

(continued)

(continued)

Project	Description
Chapter 3 *(continued)*	
Input Controls	The user interface for an electronic shopping program, assembled using several powerful input controls.
WebLink	A demonstration of the new Windows Forms LinkLabel control.
Chapter 4	
Dialog	Demonstrates how to use the Visual Basic .NET dialog box controls.
Menu	Shows how menus and commands are added to a form.
Chapter 5	
Advanced Math	Advanced use of operators for integer division, remainder division, exponentiation, and string concatenation.
Basic Math	Basic use of operators for addition, subtraction, multiplication, and division.
Constant Tester	Uses a constant to hold a fixed mathematical entity.
Data Types	A demonstration of different fundamental data types and their use with variables.
Framework Math	Demonstrates the .NET Framework classes with mathematical methods.
Input Box	Receives input with the InputBox function.
Variable Test	Declares and uses variables to store information.
Chapter 6	
Case Greeting	Uses the Case statement in a program to display an appropriate foreign-language welcome message.
Password Validation	Uses the And logical operator to check for logon password.
User Validation	Uses If...Then...Else to manage the logon process.
Chapter 7	
Celsius Conversion	Converts temperatures by using a Do loop.
Counter Variable	Uses an incremental counter as opposed to a loop to process data.
Digital Clock	A simple digital clock utility.
For Loop	Executing code with a For...Next loop.
For Loop Icons	Demonstrates using the counter in a loop to display icons.
Timed Password	A logon program with a password time-out feature.

Project	Description
Chapter 8	
Debug Test	A simulated debugging problem, designed to be solved using the Visual Studio .NET debugging tools.
Chapter 9	
Disk Drive Error	A program that crashes when a floppy disk drive is used incorrectly. (This project is used as the basis of a Visual Basic .NET error handler.)
Disk Drive Handler	A project with a completed error handler that demonstrates the Try...Catch syntax.
Chapter 10	
Final Track Wins	Uses a public variable to track the number of wins in the Lucky 7 Slot Machine.
Module Test	Creating a new code module in a project.
Text Box Sub	A general-purpose Sub procedure that adds items to a list box.
Track Wins	A clean version of the Lucky7 Slot Machine from Chapter 2 (the basis of the Final Track Wins project).
Chapter 11	
Controls Collection	Uses a Visual Basic .NET collection to move objects on a form.
Dynamic Array	Computes the average temperature for any number of days using a dynamic array.
Fixed Array	Computes the average weekly temperature using a fixed-length array.
URL Collection	Demonstrates a user-defined collection containing a list of Web addresses (URLs) recently visited by the user.
Chapter 12	
Encrypt Text	Encrypts text files by shifting ASCII characters.
Quick Note	A simple note-taking utility.
Sort Text	A text file editor that demonstrates the Shell sort.
Text Browser	Displays the contents of a text file in a Visual Basic .NET program.
Xor Encryption	Encrypts text files by using the Xor operator.
Chapter 13	
Excel Automation	Calls Microsoft Excel 2002 from Visual Basic .NET to compute a loan payment.

(continued)

(continued)

Project	Description
Chapter 13 *(continued)*	
Excel Sheet Tasks	Uses Automation to insert text and execute basic formatting in an Excel 2002 worksheet.
Start App	Starts and controls a Windows application process from within a Visual Basic .NET program.
Chapter 14	
Lucky Seven	Demonstrates how Visual Basic .NET applications are compiled and deployed using the Setup Wizard and other tools.
Chapter 15	
Add Controls	Demonstrates how controls are added to a Windows Form at runtime using program code (not the Windows Forms Designer).
Anchor and Dock	Uses the Anchor and Dock properties of a form to align objects at runtime.
Desktop Bounds	Uses the StartPosition and DesktopBounds properties to position a Windows Form at runtime.
Lucky Seven	Lucky Seven Slot Machine project that is used as the basis of the Multiple Forms project. (Open this project when you start the chapter.)
Multiple Forms	A revision of the Lucky Seven Slot Machine that uses a second form to display online Help.
Startup Form	Demonstrates how the startup (opening) form can be switched between Form1, Form2, and the Sub Main procedure.
Chapter 16	
Draw Shapes	Demonstrates a few of the new graphics methods in the System.Drawing namespace.
Moving Icon	Animates an icon on the form, moving it from the top of the form to the bottom each time that you click.
Transparent Form	Demonstrates how to change the transparency of a form.
Zoom In	Simulates "zooming in" or magnifying an object on a form (in this case, the planet Earth).
Chapter 17	
Class Inheritance	Demonstrates the inheritance feature of the Visual Basic .NET object-oriented programming model.

Project	Description
Chapter 17 *(continued)*	
Form Inheritance	Uses the Visual Studio .NET Inheritance Picker to create a form that inherits its characteristics and functionality from another form.
Person Class	Demonstrates how new classes are created in a Visual Basic .NET project. The new class is called Person, an employee record with first name, last name, and date of birth fields. The class also contains a method that computes the current age of an employee.
Chapter 18	
Print Dialogs	Demonstrates how to create Print Preview and Page Setup dialog boxes.
Print File	A project that handles more sophisticated printing tasks, including printing a multipage text file with wrapping lines.
Print Graphics	Prints graphics from within a Visual Basic .NET program.
Print Text	Demonstrates how simple text is printed in a Visual Basic .NET program.
Chapter 19	
ADO Form	Demonstrates how ADO.NET is used to establish a connection to an Access database and display information from it.
Chapter 20	
DataGrid Sample	Shows how the DataGrid control is used to display an entire record or collection of records on a form.
Chapter 21	
Explorer Objects	A project that demonstrates how a reference is made to the Microsoft Internet Controls library and how a COM "wrapper" is generated within a project. This exercise also instructs readers how to use the Visual Studio .NET Object Browser tool.
Show HTML	Allows the user to pick one of several Web sites from a list box, and then uses Microsoft Internet Explorer to display the selected Web site or HTML document.
Chapter 22	
WebCalculator	Demonstrates using Web Forms controls and ASP.NET to create a car loan calculator that runs in an Internet browser.

(continued)

Project	Description
Appendix A	
AlarmVB6	A sample Visual Basic 6 program.
AlarmVB.NET	A Visual Basic .NET program that was upgraded from Visual Basic 6 using the Visual Basic Upgrade Wizard.

Uninstalling the Practice Files

Use the following steps to delete the practice files added to your hard drive by the Visual Basic .NET Step by Step installation program.

1   Click Start, point to Settings, and then click Control Panel.

2   Double-click the Add/Remove Programs icon.

    The Add/Remove Programs window appears.

3   Select Visual Basic .NET Step by Step from the list, and then click Change/Remove.

    A confirmation message appears.

4   Click Yes.

    The practice files are uninstalled.

5   Close the Add/Remove Programs window.

6   Close the Control Panel window.

Need Help with the Practice Files?

Every effort has been made to ensure the accuracy of this book and the contents of the practice files CD-ROM. As corrections or changes are collected for this book, they will be placed on a Web page and any errata will also be integrated into the Microsoft online Help tool known as the Knowledge Base. To view the list of known corrections for this book, visit the following page:

http://support.microsoft.com/support/kb/articles/q314/2/85.asp

To search the Knowledge Base and review your support options for this book or CD-ROM, visit the Microsoft Press Support site:

http://www.microsoft.com/mspress/support/

If you have problems, comments, or ideas regarding this book or the practice files disc, please send them to Microsoft Press at the follow address:

mspinput@microsoft.com

Conventions and Features in This Book

You can save time when you use this book by understanding, before you start the exercises, how I offer instructions and the elements I use to communicate information about Visual Basic .NET programming. Please take a moment to read the following list, which identifies stylistic issues and discusses helpful features of the book that you might want to use. A few conventions are especially useful for readers who plan to upgrade Visual Basic 6 applications to Visual Basic .NET.

Conventions

- Hands-on exercises for you to follow are given in numbered lists of steps (1, 2, and so on). A round bullet (●) indicates an exercise that has only one step.

- Text that you are to type appears in boldface type.

- As you work through steps, you will occasionally see tables with lists of properties that you will type into Visual Studio. Text properties appear within quotes, but you don't need to type the quotes.

- A plus sign (+) between two key names means that you must press those keys at the same time. For example, "Press Alt+Tab" means that you hold down the Alt key while you press Tab.

- Notes labeled "tip" and text in the left margin provide additional information or alternative methods for a step.

- Control icons and buttons shown in the left margin provide visual hints as to which interface elements you should click in the Visual Studio development environment to create application objects and execute commands.

■   Notes labeled "note" or "important" alert you to essential information that you should check before continuing with the lesson.

tip

important

note

Other Features of This Book

■   You can learn special programming techniques, background information, or features related to the information being discussed by reading the shaded sidebars that appear throughout the chapters. These sidebars often highlight difficult terminology or suggest future areas for exploration.

■   You can learn about options or techniques that build on what you learned in a chapter by trying the optional "One Step Further" exercise at the end of the chapter.

■   You can get a quick reminder of how to perform the tasks you learned by reading the Quick Reference at the end of a chapter.

Upgrading Visual Basic 6 Programs

If you are upgrading from Visual Basic 6 to Visual Basic .NET, you should be aware of three features in this book that are designed to help you evaluate and upgrade your existing projects quickly. Those features are:

■   The Upgrading Index, located before the comprehensive index, which lists in one place the major differences between Visual Basic 6 and Visual Basic .NET, and where you can find information in the book about these differences.

■   "Upgrade Notes" sidebars, near the beginning of each chapter, which provide a basic overview or "executive summary" of the new features in Visual Basic .NET. Use these sidebars if you are interested in how Visual Basic .NET has changed in the context of an individual topic such as variable declaration, Toolbox controls, or database programming.

■   A special appendix, "Appendix A: Upgrading Visual Basic 6 Programs to Visual Basic .NET," which is located immediately after Chapter 22. This appendix describes how to evaluate your existing Visual Basic 6 programs and how to upgrade them to Visual Basic .NET using Internet resources and the new Visual Basic Upgrade Wizard.

PART 1

Getting Started with Microsoft Visual Basic .NET

1

Opening and Running a Visual Basic .NET Program

In this chapter you will learn how to:

✔ *Start Microsoft Visual Studio .NET.*

✔ *Use the Visual Studio development environment.*

✔ *Open and run a Visual Basic program.*

✔ *Change a property setting.*

✔ *Move, resize, dock, and auto hide tool windows.*

✔ *Use online Help and exit Visual Studio.*

Microsoft Visual Basic .NET is an important upgrade and enhancement of the popular Visual Basic development system, a product that enjoys an installed base of more than 3 million programmers worldwide. This chapter introduces you to what's new in Visual Basic .NET and gives you the skills you will need to get up and running with the Visual Studio .NET development environment quickly and efficiently. You should read this chapter whether you are new to Visual Basic programming or you have used previous versions of the Visual Basic compiler. The most important advantage of Visual Basic .NET is that it has been designed to make you even more productive in your daily development work—especially if you need to use information in databases or create solutions for the Internet—but an important additional benefit is that once you become comfortable with the development environment in Visual Studio, you can use the same tools to write programs for Microsoft Visual C++ .NET, Microsoft Visual C# .NET, and other third-party tools and compilers.

In this chapter, you'll learn how to start Visual Basic and how to use the integrated development environment to open and run a simple program. You'll learn the essential Visual Studio menu commands and programming procedures; you'll open and run a simple Visual Basic program named MusicTrivia; you'll change a programming setting called a property; and you'll practice moving, sizing, docking, and auto hiding tool windows. You'll also learn how to get more information by using online Help and how to exit the development environment safely.

Upgrade Notes:
What's New in Visual Basic .NET?

Upgrading from Visual Basic 6 to Visual Basic .NET involves a unique set of challenges—I'm very happy with the new features, but I also notice that more than a few familiar tools and controls have really changed. For this reason, I begin each chapter in this book with a sidebar that highlights the changes. Remember that you don't need *any* programming experience to learn Visual Basic .NET using this book. But if you have some Visual Basic 6 knowledge already, I want to give you a short executive summary. So to begin with, here is my list of Visual Basic .NET upgrade notes for this chapter:

- Visual Basic is now fully part of Visual Studio—it shares the Visual Studio development environment with Microsoft Visual C++ .NET, Microsoft Visual C# .NET, and several other programming tools. Although Visual Basic .NET and Visual C++ .NET are still different programming languages, they share the same development environment.

- As part of its new development environment, Visual Studio offers a new Get Started pane, which shows recently used projects and lets you open new or existing source files. Additional links in the Get Started pane provide you with access to Visual Studio Web sites, profile information, and contacts in the Visual Studio development community.

- The Visual Studio development environment contains several new and modified programming tools. The Project window is now called Solution Explorer, and there is a new context-sensitive help window called Dynamic Help. You'll find that the Toolbox has changed quite a bit—it's now subdivided into several functional categories, from Windows Forms to Web Forms to Data.

- Most of the programming tool windows have an auto hide feature to hide the tool as a tab when it isn't needed.

■ Projects are now saved in a different way. You give your project a name *before* you create it. The project itself now is spread over several files and folders—even more than in Visual Basic 6. In Visual Basic 6, programs that were made up of multiple projects were called *project groups*; now they are called *solutions*.

The Visual Studio .NET Development Environment

Although the programming language you'll be learning in this book is Visual Basic, the development environment you'll be using to write programs is called the Microsoft Visual Studio .NET development environment. Visual Studio is a powerful and customizable programming workshop that contains all the tools you need to build robust programs for Microsoft Windows quickly and efficiently. Most of the features in Visual Studio apply equally to Visual Basic .NET, Visual C++ .NET, and Visual C# .NET. Use the following procedures to start Visual Studio now.

important

If you haven't yet installed this book's practice files, work through "Finding Your Best Starting Point" and "About the CD-ROM and Practice Files" at the beginning of the book. Then return to this chapter.

Start Visual Studio .NET

Start

Start button

1   On the Windows taskbar, click the Start button, point to Programs, and then point to the Microsoft Visual Studio .NET folder. The icons in the Microsoft Visual Studio .NET folder appear in a list.

important

To perform the steps in this book, you must have one of the following Visual Studio .NET editions installed: Visual Basic .NET Standard, Visual Studio .NET Professional, Visual Studio .NET Enterprise Developer, or Visual Studio .NET Enterprise Architect. Also—don't try to use this book if you have an earlier version of the Visual Basic software; if that's your situation, you'll be better served by locating an earlier edition of my book, such as *Microsoft Visual Basic Professional 6.0 Step by Step*.

2   Click the Microsoft Visual Studio .NET program icon.

Visual Studio starts, and you see the development environment on the screen with its many menus, tools, and component windows. (These windows are sometimes called *tool windows*.) If this is a new installation of Visual Studio, you should see a Start Page with a set of links. (If you don't see the Start Page, click Show Start Page on the Help menu.)

The first thing Visual Studio .NET displays when you launch it is the Start Page.

3   On the left side of the Start Page window, click the My Profile link.

Visual Studio displays the My Profile settings. The My Profile pane allows you to configure Visual Studio with your personal preferences. This is an important screen because Visual Studio can be used to build different types of programs (Visual Basic, Visual C++, and so on), so you want to identify yourself as a Visual Basic developer right away.

4   In the Profile drop-down list box, select Visual Basic Developer from the list of choices.

Visual Studio immediately configures the development environment for Visual Basic programming, displays the Toolbox, and makes adjustments to window characteristics and code formatting styles so that your programs will look like standard Visual Basic solutions.

5   In the At Startup drop-down list box, be sure that Show Start Page is selected.

Setting this option will ensure that the Start Page will appear each time you open Visual Studio.

6   Investigate a few of the remaining settings—and notice that Visual Studio changed a few items on the list when you identified yourself as a Visual Basic programmer.

You can come back to My Profile at any time in the future to fine-tune your profile selections. They will mean more to you after you've written a few programs and have looked at some of the Visual Basic code your friends and coworkers have produced.

7   When you're finished with the profile options, click the Get Started link on the left side of the Start Page window.

Now you see the Get Started page in the development environment, the typical "home" page for Visual Studio users and the place you'll begin when you want to open an existing project or create a new one. The following illustration shows some of the common features of the Get Started pane, including a list of recent Visual Studio projects that have been open (although your list might be empty), a button that you can use to open an existing project, and a button that you can use to create a new project.

The regular Start Page (or home page) has buttons and links that allow you to quickly open an existing programming solution or create a new one.

The first thing most developers do when they start Visual Studio is open an existing project—either a completed solution they want to work with again or an ongoing development project. Try opening an existing project now that I created for you—the MusicTrivia program.

Open a Visual Basic project

1   Click the Open Project button on the Get Started pane of the Start Page.

The Open Project dialog box appears on the screen with several options. Even if you haven't used Visual Basic before, the Open Project dialog box will seem straightforward, like the familiar Open box in Microsoft Word or Microsoft Excel.

tip

In the Open Project dialog box, you'll see a number of shortcut icons along the left side of the window. The My Projects icon is particularly useful—it opens the Visual Studio Projects folder inside the My Documents folder on your system. By default, Visual Studio saves your projects in the Visual Studio Projects folder and gives each project its own folder.

2 Browse to the folder c:\vbnetsbs on your hard disk.

The folder c:\vbnetsbs is the default location for this book's extensive sample file collection, and you'll find the files there if you followed the setup instructions in "About the CD-ROM and Practice Files" at the beginning of this book. If you didn't install the sample files, do so now using the CD included with this book.

3 Open the chap01\musictrivia folder, and then double-click the MusicTriva project file (MusicTrivia.vbproj).

Visual Studio loads the MusicTrivia form, properties, and program code for the MusicTrivia project. The Start Page probably will still be visible, but Solution Explorer in the upper right corner of the screen will list some of the files in the project.

tip

If you don't see file name extensions in the Open Project dialog box, the hide file extensions option may be turned on. You can change this option in Windows Explorer. On the Tools menu in Windows Explorer, click Folder Options. On the View tab of the Folder Options dialog box, you can uncheck the Hide File Extensions For Known File Types check box.

Projects and Solutions

In Visual Studio, programs in development are typically called *projects* or *solutions* because they contain many individual components, not just one file. Visual Basic .NET programs include a project file (.vbproj) and a solution file (.sln). A project file contains information specific to a single programming task. A solution file contains information about one or more projects. Solution files are useful to manage multiple related projects and are similar to project group files (.vbg) in Visual Basic 6. The samples included with this book typically have a single project for each solution, so opening the project file (.vbproj) will have the same effect as opening the solution file (.sln). But for a multiproject solution, you will want to open the solution file.

The Visual Studio .NET Tools

At this point, you should take a few moments to study the development environment and identify some of the programming tools and windows that you'll be using as you complete this course. If you've written Visual Basic programs before, you'll recognize many (but not all) of the development tools. Collectively, these features are the components that you use to construct, organize, and test your Visual Basic programs. A few of the programming tools also help you learn more about the resources on your system, including the larger world of databases and Web site connections available to you. There are also several powerful on-line Help tools.

The *menu bar* provides access to most of the commands that control the development environment. Menus and commands work as they do in all Windows-based programs, and you can access them by using the keyboard or the mouse. Located below the menu bar is the *Standard toolbar,* a collection of buttons that serve as shortcuts for executing commands and controlling the Visual Studio development environment. If you've used Excel or Word, the toolbar should be a familiar concept. To activate a button on the toolbar, click the button using the mouse. Along the bottom of the screen is the Windows *taskbar*. You can use the taskbar to switch between various Visual Studio .NET components and to activate other Windows-based programs. You may also see taskbar icons for Microsoft Internet Explorer and other programs.

The following illustration shows some of the tools, windows, and other elements in the Visual Studio development environment. Don't worry that this illustration looks different from your current development environment view. You'll learn more about these elements as you step through the chapter.

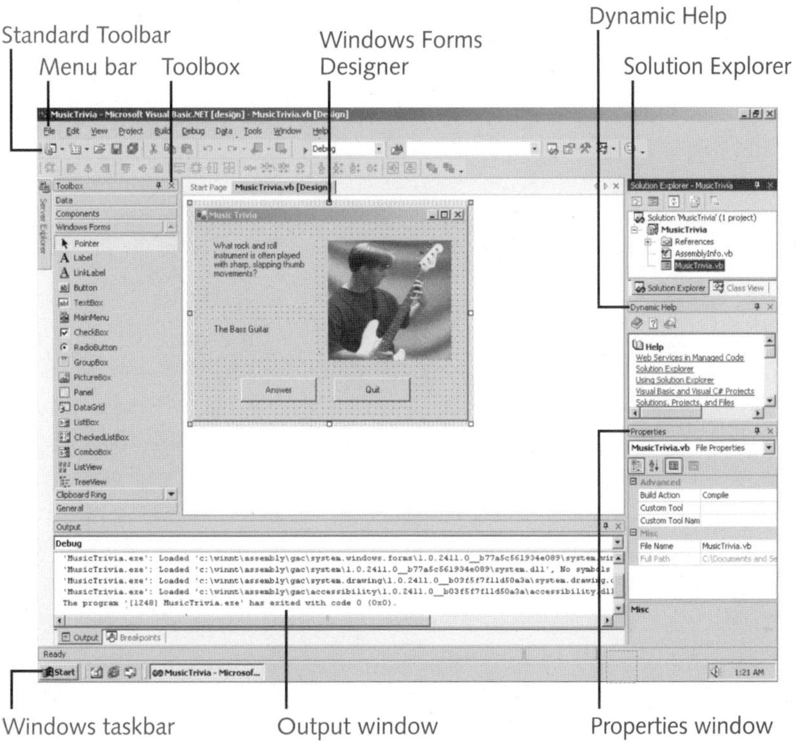

Dynamic Help

Standard Toolbar

Windows Forms
Designer

Solution Explorer

Menu bar Toolbox

Windows taskbar   Output window   Properties window

The main tools that you will see in the Visual Studio development environment are Solution Explorer (formerly called the Project Explorer), the Properties window, Dynamic Help, the Windows Forms Designer, the Toolbox, and the Output window. You may also see more specialized tools such as Server Explorer and Class View, but these are often tabs along the margins of the development environment or at the bottom of tool windows or they aren't visible at all. If a tool isn't visible and you want to see it, click the View menu and select the tool you want to use. The View menu is now pretty full, so Microsoft moved some of the lesser-used tools onto a submenu called (cleverly) Other Windows. Check there if you don't see what you need.

The exact size and shape of the tools and windows depends on how your development environment has been configured. Visual Studio allows you to align and attach, or *dock,* windows to make just the elements that you want visible. You can also hide tools as tabs along the edge of the development environment to move them out of the way until you need them again. Trying to sort out which tools are important to you now and which you can learn about later is a difficult early challenge when you're first learning the busy Visual Studio interface. Your development environment will probably look best if you set your monitor and Windows desktop settings so that they maximize your screen space, but even then things can get a little crowded. (For example, I'm using a desktop property setting of 1024 x 768 for some of the screen shots in this book—an attribute you can change by right-clicking the Windows desktop and clicking Properties.)

What Microsoft is doing with all of this tool complexity is adding many new and useful features to the development environment, while simultaneously providing clever mechanisms for dealing with the clutter. (These mechanisms include features such as docking, auto hiding, and a few other things that I describe later). If you're just starting out with Visual Basic, the best way to resolve this feature tension is to hide the tools that you don't plan to use often and make room for the important ones. The crucial tools for Visual Basic programming— the ones you'll start using right away in this book—are Solution Explorer, Properties window, Windows Forms Designer, Toolbox, Dynamic Help, and the Output window. You won't use the Server Explorer, Class View window, Resource View window, Object Browser, or Debug windows until later in this book.

In the following exercises, you'll start experimenting with the crucial tools in the Visual Studio development environment. You'll also learn to hide the tools you won't use for a while.

The Windows Forms Designer

If you completed the last exercise, the MusicTrivia project will be loaded in the Visual Studio development environment. However, the user interface, or *form,* for the project may not yet be visible in Visual Studio. (More sophisticated projects might contain several forms, but this simple trivia program needs only one.) To make the form of the MusicTrivia project visible in the development environment, you display it by using Solution Explorer.

Display the Windows Forms Designer

1 Locate the Solution Explorer pane near the upper right corner of the Visual Studio development environment. If you don't see Solution Explorer (if it is hidden as a tab in a location that you cannot see or isn't currently visible), click Solution Explorer on the View menu to display it.

When the MusicTrivia project is loaded, Solution Explorer looks like this:

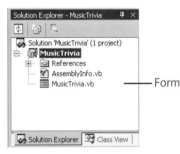 —— Form

2 Click the MusicTrivia.vb form in the Solution Explorer window.

All form files, including this one, have a tiny form icon next to them so that you can easily identify them. When you click the form file, Visual Studio highlights it in Solution Explorer, and some information about the file appears in the Properties window (if you currently have it visible).

View Designer button

3 Click the View Designer button in Solution Explorer to display the program's user interface.

The MusicTrivia form is displayed in the Windows Forms Designer, as shown here:

Click this tab to display the Start Page

    Click this tab to display the MusicTrivia form

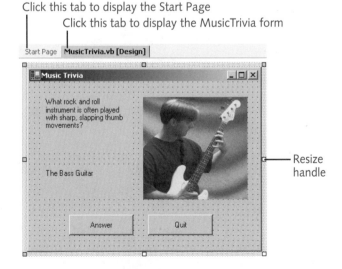 —— Resize handle

Notice that a tab for the Start Page is still visible at the top of the Windows Forms Designer. You can click this tab to display the Start Page, change your profile settings, or open additional project files. To return to Windows Forms Designer view, click the tab labeled "MusicTrivia.vb [Design]" at the top of the MusicTrivia form.

Now try running a Visual Basic program with Visual Studio.

tip

If you don't see the Start Page and MusicTrivia.vb [Design] tabs, your development environment might be in MDI view instead of Tabbed Documents view. To change this option, click Options on the Tools menu. On the left side of the Options dialog box, click the Environment folder and then click General. On the right under Settings, click the Tabbed Documents radio button and then click OK. The next time you start Visual Studio, the various windows that you open will have tabs, and you can switch between them with a simple button click.

Running a Visual Basic Program

MusicTrivia is a simple Visual Basic program designed to get you familiar with the programming tools in Visual Studio. The form you see now has been customized with five objects (two labels, a picture, and two buttons), and I've added three lines of program code to make the trivia program ask a simple question and display the appropriate answer. (The program "gives away" the answer now because it is currently in design mode, but the answer will be hidden when you run the program.) You'll learn more about creating objects and adding program code in the next chapter. For now, try running the program in the Visual Studio development environment.

Run the MusicTrivia program

Start button

1   Click the Start button on the Standard toolbar to run the MusicTrivia program in Visual Studio.

tip

You can also press F5 or click the Start command on the Debug menu to run a program in the Visual Studio development environment. Note that the placement of the Start command is different than it is in the Visual Basic 6 compiler.

Visual Studio loads and compiles the project into an assembly (a structured collection of modules, data, and manifest information for a program) and then runs the program in the development environment. An icon for the program also appears on the Windows taskbar. During compilation, the Output window documents several of the loading and compiling steps and records any errors that occurred so that you can fix them. After a moment, you'll see the MusicTrivia form again, this time with the photograph and answer label hidden from view:

MusicTrivia now asks its important question: What rock and roll instrument is played with sharp, slapping thumb movements?

2 Click the Answer button to reveal the solution to the question.

When you do, the program displays the answer (Bass Guitar) below the question and then displays a photograph of an obscure Seattle bass player demonstrating the technique. The test program works.

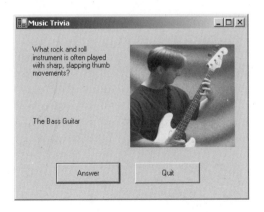

3   Click Quit to close the program.

The form closes, and the Visual Studio development environment becomes active again. Notice that the form looks a little different now in the development environment—a grid of alignment dots is visible on the surface of the form, the two labels are surrounded by some gray space, and resize handles surround the form. These features are visible only when a form is in design mode, and they will help you design and align your user interface. The grid is also a quick giveaway if you're wondering whether a program is running in Visual Studio. (You'll practice using these features in the next chapter.)

The Properties Window

Use the Properties window to change the characteristics, or *property settings,* of the user interface elements on a form. A property setting is a quality of one of the objects in your user interface. For example, the trivia question the MusicTrivia program displays can be modified to appear in a different font or font size or with a different alignment. (With Visual Studio .NET, you can display text in any font installed on your system, just as you would in Excel or Word.) You can change property settings by using the Properties window while you are creating your user interface, or you can add program code via the Code Editor to change one or more property settings while your program is running.

The Properties window contains an Object drop-down list box that itemizes all the user interface elements (objects) on the form; the window also lists the property settings that can be changed for each object. (You can click one of two convenient buttons to view properties alphabetically or by category.) You'll practice changing the Font property of the first label in the MusicTrivia program now.

Change a property

1   Click the Label1 object on the form. (Label1 contains the text "What rock and roll instrument is played with short, slapping thumb movements?")

To work with an object on a form, you must first select the object. When you select an object, resize handles surround it, and the property settings for the object are displayed in the Properties window.

Properties Window button

2   Click the Properties Window button on the Standard toolbar.

The Properties window is another tool that might or might not be visible in Visual Studio, depending on how it has been configured and used on your system. It usually appears below Solution Explorer on the right side of the development environment.

You'll see a window similar to the following:

Font category

The Properties window lists all the property settings for the first label object (Label1) on the form. (In all, 45 properties are available to labels.) Property names are listed in the left column of the window, and the current setting for each property is listed in the right column. Because there are so many properties (and some that are rarely modified), Visual Studio organizes them into categories and displays them in outline view. If a category has a plus sign (+) next to it, you can click the collection title to display all the properties in that category. If a category has a minus sign (−) next to it, the properties are all visible, but you can hide the list under the category name by clicking on the minus sign.

Alphabetic button

Categorized button

tip

The Properties window also has two useful buttons that you can use to further organize properties. The Alphabetic button lists all the properties in alphabetical order and puts them in just a few categories. (Click this button if you know the name of a property and want to locate it quickly.) The Categorized button breaks down the property list into many logical categories. (Click this button if you don't know much about the object you are customizing and would benefit from a more conceptual organization.) If you're new to Visual Studio and Visual Basic, I recommend that you use the Categorized configuration until you get familiar with the most common objects and properties.

3   Scroll in the Properties window list box until the Font property is visible.

The Properties window scrolls like a regular list box.

4   Click the Font property name (in the left column).

The current font (Microsoft Sans Serif) is partially displayed in the right column, and a button with three dots on it appears by the font name. This button is called an ellipsis button and means that a dialog box is available to customize the property setting.

Ellipsis button

5   Click the Font ellipsis button in the Properties window.

Visual Studio displays the Font dialog box, which allows you to specify new formatting characteristics for the text in the selected label on your form. The Font dialog box contains more than one formatting option; for each option you select, a different property setting will be modified.

6   Change the size of the font from 8 point to 10 point, and then change the font style from Regular to Italic. Click OK to confirm your selections.

Visual Studio records your selections and adjusts the property settings accordingly. You can examine the changes that Visual Studio made by viewing your form in the Windows Forms Designer and by expanding the Font category in the Properties window.

Now change a property setting for the Label2 object (the label that contains the text "The Bass Guitar").

7   In the Windows Forms Designer, click the second label object (Label2).

When you select the object, resize handles surround it.

8   Click the Font property again in the Properties window.

The Label2 object has its own unique set of property settings—although the property names are the same as the Label1 object, the values in the property settings are distinct and allow the Label2 object to act independently on the playing field of the form.

9   Click the Font ellipsis button, set the font style to Bold, and then click OK.

10 Scroll to the ForeColor property in the Properties window, and then click it in the left column.

11 Click the ForeColor drop-down arrow in the right column, and then click a dark purple color on the Custom tab.

The text in the Label2 object should now appear bold and in the color purple on the form.

Congratulations! You've just learned how to set properties in a Visual Basic program using the Visual Studio Properties window—one of the important skills in becoming a Visual Basic programmer.

Thinking About Properties

In Visual Basic, each user interface element in a program (including the form itself) has a set of definable properties. You can set properties at design time by using the Properties window. Properties can also be referenced in code to do meaningful work as the program runs. (User interface elements that receive input often use properties to convey information to the program.) At first, you may find properties a difficult concept to grasp. Viewing them in terms of something from everyday life can help.

(continued)

continued

> Consider this bicycle analogy: a bicycle is an object you use to ride from one place to another. Because a bicycle is a physical object, it has several inherent characteristics. It has a brand name, a color, gears, brakes, and wheels, and it's built in a particular style. (It may be a touring bike, a mountain bike, or a bicycle built for two.) In Visual Basic terminology, these characteristics are *properties* of the bicycle object. Most of the bicycle's properties would be defined while the bicycle was being built. But others (tires, travel speed, age, and options such as reflectors and mirrors) could be properties that change as the bicycle is used. As you work with Visual Basic, you'll find object properties of both types.

Moving and Resizing the Programming Tools

With numerous programming tools to contend with on the screen, the Visual Studio development environment can become a pretty busy place. To give you complete control over the shape and size of the elements in the development environment, Visual Studio lets you move, resize, dock, and auto hide most of the interface elements that you use to build programs.

To move one of the tool windows in Visual Studio, simply click the title bar and drag the object to a new location. If you align one window along the edge of another window, it will attach itself, or *dock*, to that window. Dockable windows are advantageous because they always remain visible. (They won't become hidden behind other windows.) If you want to see more of a docked window, simply drag one of its borders to view more content.

If you ever want to completely close a window, click the close button in the upper right corner of the window. You can always open the window again later by clicking the appropriate command on the View menu.

Auto Hide is enabled

If you want an option somewhere between docking and closing a window, you might try "auto hiding" a tool window to the side of the Visual Studio development environment by clicking the tiny Auto Hide pushpin button on the right side of the tool's title bar. This action removes the window from the docked position and places the title of the tool at the edge of the development environment in a tab that is quite unobtrusive. When you perform the auto hide action, you'll notice that the tool window will still be visible as long as you keep the mouse in the area of the window. When you move the mouse to another part of the development environment, the window will slide out of view.

To restore a window that has auto hide enabled, click the tool tab at the edge of the development environment or hold your mouse over the tab. (You can recognize a window that has auto hide enabled because the pushpin in its title bar is pointing sideways.) Holding the mouse over the title allows you to use the tools in what I call "peek-a-boo" mode—in other words, you can quickly display an auto hidden window by clicking its tab, check or set the information you need, and then move the mouse to make the window disappear. If you ever need the tool displayed permanently, click the Auto Hide pushpin button again so that the point of the pushpin faces down, and the window will remain visible.

Auto Hide is disabled

Docking and auto hiding techniques definitely take some practice to master. Use the following exercises to hone your windows management skills and experiment with the features of the Visual Studio development environment along the way. After you complete the exercises here, feel free to configure the Visual Studio tools in a way that seems comfortable for you.

Moving and Resizing Tool Windows in Visual Studio

To move and resize one of the programming tool windows in Visual Studio, follow these steps. This exercise demonstrates how you manipulate the Properties window, but you can move around a different tool window if you want.

Move and resize the Properties window

Properties Window button

1   Click the Properties Window button on the Standard toolbar if the Properties window isn't visible in the development environment.

    The Properties window is activated in the development environment, and its title bar is highlighted.

2   Double-click the Properties window title bar to display the window as a floating (nondocked) window.

    You'll see a Properties window that looks like the following:

3   Using the Properties window title bar, drag the window to a new location in the development environment but don't allow it to be docked.

Moving windows around the Visual Studio development environment gives you some flexibility with the tools and your programming environment. Now resize the Properties window to see more of an object's property settings at once.

4   Move the mouse to the lower right corner of the Properties window until it becomes a resizing pointer.

You resize windows in Visual Studio just as you resize other application windows in the Microsoft Windows operating system.

Resizing pointer

5   Drag the lower right border of the window down and to the right to enlarge the window.

Your Properties window will now look bigger:

Properties	⊠
Label2 System.Windows.Forms.Label	▼

☐ Appearance		▲
BackColor	☐ Control	
BorderStyle	None	
Cursor	Default	
FlatStyle	Standard	
⊞ Font	**Microsoft Sans Serif, 8**	
ForeColor	■ **Purple** ▼	
Image	☐ (none)	
ImageAlign	MiddleCenter	
ImageIndex	☐ (none)	
ImageList	(none)	
RightToLeft	No	
Text	**The Bass Guitar**	
TextAlign	TopLeft	
UseMnemonic	True	
☐ Behavior		
AllowDrop	False	▼

ForeColor
The foreground color used to display text and graphics in the control.

Properties ❷ Dynamic Help

A bigger window lets you work more quickly and with more clarity of purpose. Feel free to move or resize a window when you need to see more of it.

Docking a Tool in Visual Studio

If a tool is floating over the development environment, you can return it to its original docked position by double-clicking the window's title bar. (Notice that this is the same technique that you used in the last exercise to expand a docked window—double-clicking a title bar works like a *toggle*, a state that switches back and forth between two standard positions.) You can also attach or dock a floating tool in a new place when it's in its floating, expanded position. You might want to do this if you need to make more room in Visual Studio for a particular programming task, such as creating a user interface with the Windows Forms Designer. Try docking the Properties window in a new location now.

Dock the Properties window

1   Verify that the Properties window (or another tool that you want to move) is floating over the Visual Studio development environment in an undocked position.

If you completed the last exercise, the Properties window will be in an undocked position now.

2   Drag the title bar of the Properties window to the top, bottom, right, or left edge of the development environment (your choice!) until the border of the window snaps to the window edge you selected.

This snapping behavior signifies that the window will be docked when you release the mouse button. Note that there are several valid docking locations for tool windows in Visual Studio, so you may want to try two or three different spots until you find one that looks right to you. (A window should be located in a place that is handy but not in the way of other needed tools.)

Docking the Properties window

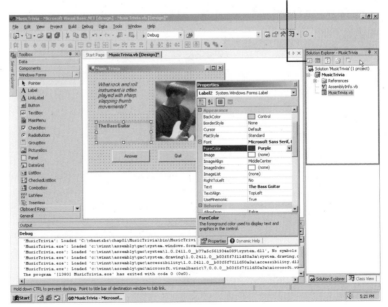

3 Release the mouse button to dock the Properties window.

The window snaps into place in its new home.

> **tip**
>
> To prevent docking as you drag a window, hold down the Ctrl key as you drag. If you want the window you are dragging to be linked to another window by tabs, drag the window directly onto the title bar of the other window. When windows are linked together in this manner, a tab for each window will appear at the bottom of a shared window, and you can switch back and forth between windows by clicking the tabs. Tabbing windows provides an efficient way to use the space of one window for two or more purposes. (Solution Explorer and the Class View window are often tabbed together, for example.)

4 Try docking the Properties window several more times in different places to get the hang of how docking and tabbing works.

I guarantee that a few of these window procedures will seem confusing at first, but after a while they will become routine for you. In general, you want to create window spaces that have enough room for the information you need to see and use while you work on your more important tasks in the Windows Forms Designer and Code Editor.

Hiding a Tool in Visual Studio

Visual Studio .NET includes a mechanism for hiding and displaying tools quickly, called auto hide. The auto hide feature is available for most tool windows. To hide a tool window, click the Auto Hide pushpin button on the right side of the title bar to conceal the window beneath a tool tab on the edge of the development environment, and click it again to restore the window to its docked position. You can also use the Auto Hide command on the Window menu to enable auto hide for a tool window. Note that the auto hide feature and pushpin button are available only for docked windows—you won't see the Auto Hide command or the pushpin for an active window floating on the top of the development environment.

Use the auto hide feature

1 Locate the Toolbox in the development environment (a window that is usually open on the left side of the Windows Forms Designer).

The Toolbox contains many of the controls that you will use to build Visual Basic applications. For example, I used the Label, Button, and PictureBox controls to create the objects you've seen in the MusicTrivia program. There are several different control collections in the Toolbox, and you can access them by clicking on the tabs that you see within the Toolbox.

If you don't see the Toolbox now, click Toolbox on the View menu. The following illustration shows you what it looks like.

2   Locate the Auto Hide pushpin button on the title bar of the Toolbox.

The pushpin is currently in the "down," or "pushed in," position, meaning that the Toolbox is "pinned" open and auto hide is disabled.

3   Click the pushpin button in the Toolbox title bar, and keep the mouse pointer within the Toolbox.

Auto Hide is enabled

The pushpin button changes direction (it now points to the left), indicating that the Toolbox is no longer pinned open and auto hide is enabled, and a tab appears on the left side of the development environment with the word Toolbox on it. You may also notice that the Windows Forms Designer shifted left. However, if your mouse pointer is still resting on the top of the Toolbox, nothing will have changed in the Toolbox itself—the designers of Visual Studio decided that it would be best if a window with auto hide enabled didn't disappear until you move the mouse to another part of the Visual Studio development environment.

4   Move the mouse away from the Toolbox.

As soon as you move the mouse away, the Toolbox slides off the screen and is hidden beneath the small Toolbox tab. (You may also see a Server Explorer tab above the Toolbox tab—an indication that another tool has auto hide enabled. Indeed, depending on how Visual Studio is currently configured, you may now notice that there are other windows in the development environment with auto hide enabled.)

The benefit of enabling auto hide for windows is that they free up considerable work area in Visual Studio but are also quickly accessible.

5   Hold the mouse pointer over the Toolbox tab. (You can also click the Toolbox tab if you wish.)

The Toolbox immediately slides back into view, and you can begin using Toolbox controls to build your user interface. (We'll do this in Chapter 2.)

6   Move the mouse away from the Toolbox, and the tool disappears again.

7   Finally, display the Toolbox again and then click the pushpin button on the Toolbox title bar.

The Toolbox returns to its familiar docked position, and you can use it without worrying about it sliding away.

Spend some time moving, resizing, docking, and auto hiding tool windows in Visual Studio now, to create your version of the perfect work environment. As you work through this book, you'll want to adjust your window settings periodically to adapt your work area to the new tools you're using. When the need arises, come back to this section and practice your skills again.

Auto Hide is disabled

Getting Help

Visual Studio .NET includes an online reference that you can use to learn more about the Visual Studio development environment, the Visual Basic programming language, the resources in the .NET Framework, and the remaining tools in the Visual Studio suite. Take a moment to explore your Help resources before moving to the next chapter, where you will build your first program.

tip

Visual Studio .NET online Help is provided by your Visual Studio .NET CDs. If you have plenty of disk space, you can install all the Visual Studio .NET documentation on your system from these CDs during Setup.

You can access Help information in several ways.

To get Help information	Do this
About the task you're currently working on	Click the Dynamic Help tab in the development environment to see a list of Help topics related to the features you're using, or on the Visual Studio Help menu, click Dynamic Help.
By topic or activity	On the Visual Studio Help menu, click Contents.
While working in the Code Editor	Click the keyword or program statement you're interested in and then press F1.
While working in a dialog box	Click the Help button in the dialog box.
By searching for a specific keyword	On the Help menu, click Search and type the term you're looking for.
In a window separate from Visual Studio	On the Windows taskbar, click the Start button, point to Programs, point to Microsoft Visual Studio .NET, and then click Microsoft Visual Studio .NET Documentation. Use the Contents, Index, and Search tabs to find information.
From Visual Studio Web sites and newsgroups	On the Visual Studio Start Page, click Online Community and then the Web site or newsgroup you're interested in.
About contacting Microsoft for product support	On the Help menu, click Technical Support.

In this section, you'll learn how to use the new Dynamic Help feature in Visual Studio .NET. The goal of this tool is to anticipate the questions you'll ask based on the current context of your work in Visual Studio. I believe you'll find this searching mechanism vastly superior to the general search tools provided with Visual Basic 6 because Dynamic Help uses contextual logic to limit the material you see to the particular compiler or tool that you are using. (In other words, Dynamic Help doesn't bring up Visual C++ or Visual C# topics unless you are working with those tools.)

In this section, you'll also learn how to perform a full-text search of the Visual Studio Help system. Full-text search can be helpful when you want to search for specific keywords.

Because you just completed an exercise on auto hide with the Toolbox in Visual Studio, it is likely that the Dynamic Help system has been gathering information for you about the Toolbox and other recent commands you've issued in Visual Studio. Let's open Dynamic Help now and see.

Running a Program

Get help using Dynamic Help

1   Click the Dynamic Help tab in the development environment, or click Dynamic Help on the Visual Studio Help menu.

The Dynamic Help window appears, as shown here:

The Help menu is your door to the Visual Studio .NET Help system.

The Dynamic Help window is an integrated part of Visual Studio. The window can be moved, resized, docked, or auto hidden to suit your needs, and you can leave it open all the time or open it only when you need it.

2   Click a topic in the Dynamic Help window. It could be about the Toolbox or the Properties window.

The MusicTrivia form is hidden under the MusicTrivia.vb [Design] tab, and the Help topic appears in the main window of the development environment.

tip

If you didn't install the documentation on your system during Setup, the Dynamic Help window won't display any topics. To install the documentation, run the Visual Studio .NET Setup again and select the Documentation item.

3   Browse a few of the other Help topics in the Dynamic Help listing, and see how close these picks are to the actual activities you have been working on.

tip

You can adjust how Dynamic Help comes up with Help information by clicking the Options command on the Tools menu, opening the Environment folder, clicking the Dynamic Help topic, and identifying which topics you want Help to list and how many links there should be. These settings will help you further manage the amount of information Help offers you.

Do a full-text search in Help

1   On the Visual Studio Help menu, click Search.

The Search window appears in the development environment.

2   In the Look For drop-down list box, type "**windows forms designer" and controls** (include the quotes because the name contains spaces).

3   Check the Highlight Search Hits (In Topics) check box, and then click the Search button.

The Search Results window appears with many topics that match your search criteria.

4   In the Search Results window, double-click a topic to see its contents.

The topic appears in the main window, and the text that you searched for is highlighted as shown here:

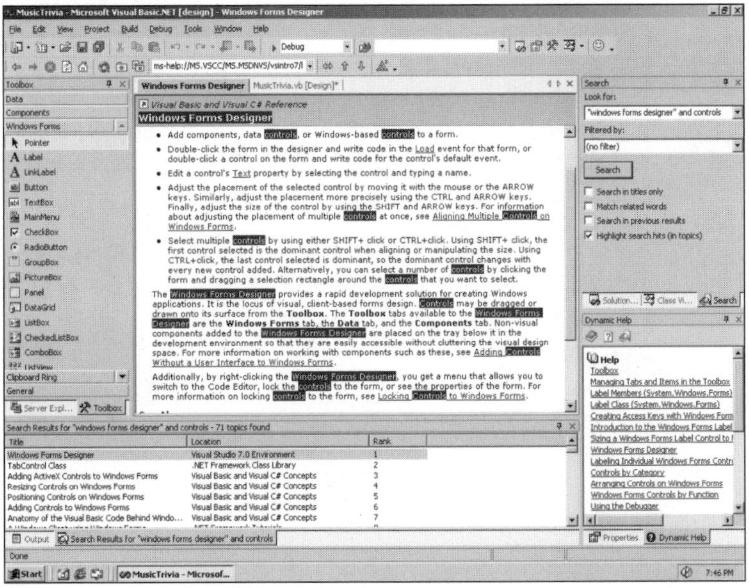

> ### tip
> The Help Contents and Index windows are also integrated into the Visual Studio development environment. You can open these help windows by clicking the Contents or Index command on the Help menu. Keep in mind that you don't have to use the Help features one at a time. (See the Help Information table earlier in this section for other Help suggestions.)

One Step Further: Exiting Visual Studio .NET

Each chapter in this book concludes with a section entitled "One Step Further" that enables you to practice an additional skill related to the topic at hand. After the "One Step Further" tutorial, I've compiled a Quick Reference table that reprises the important concepts discussed in each chapter.

When you're finished using Visual Studio for the day, save any projects that are open and close the development environment. Give it a try.

Exit Visual Studio

Save All button

1 Save any changes you have made to your program by clicking the Save All button on the Standard toolbar.

In contrast with Visual Basic 6, in Visual Studio .NET you give your program a name when you begin the project, not when you're ready to save it, so you won't need to provide any filename information now. As you'll learn, there are also many more folders for projects in Visual Studio .NET than there were in Visual Basic 6. Each project fits in a folder of its own, and several subfolders are created below the main project folder to hold files as the program is built and compiled.

2 On the File menu, click the Exit command.

The Visual Studio .NET program exits. Time to move on to your first program in Chapter 2!

Chapter 1 Quick Reference

To	Do this
Start Visual Studio .NET	Click the Start button on the taskbar, point to Programs, point to the Microsoft Visual Studio .NET folder, and then click the Microsoft Visual Studio .NET program icon.
Open an existing project	Start Visual Studio .NET. Click the File menu, point to Open, and then click Project. *or* On the Start Page, click Open Project.
Run a program	Click the Start button on the Standard toolbar. *or* Press F5.
Set properties	Click the object on the form containing the properties you want to set, and then click the Properties Window button on the Standard toolbar to display the Properties window (if it isn't open).
Display and resize a tool window	Double-click the window's title bar to display it as a floating window. Resize the window by dragging the edges of the window.
Move a tool window	Double-click the window's title bar to display it as a floating window, and then drag the title bar.
Dock a tool window	Double-click the title bar. *or* Drag the tool to the edge of another tool until it snaps into place.
Enable auto hide for a tool window	Click the Auto Hide pushpin button on the right side of the tool's title bar. The tool window hides behind a small tab at the edge of the development environment until you hold the mouse over it.
Disable auto hide for a tool window	Click the tool tab, and then click the Auto Hide pushpin button again.
Quit Visual Studio .NET	On the File menu, click Exit.

Start

Auto Hide enabled

Auto Hide disabled

Running a Program

Writing Your First Program

In this chapter you will learn how to:

✔ *Create the user interface for a new program.*

✔ *Set the properties for each object in your user interface.*

✔ *Write program code.*

✔ *Save and run the program.*

✔ *Build an executable file.*

As you learned in Chapter 1, the Microsoft Visual Studio .NET environment contains several powerful tools to help you run and manage your programs. Visual Studio also contains everything you need to build your own applications for Windows from the ground up. In this chapter, you'll learn how to create a simple but attractive user interface with the controls in the Visual Studio Toolbox. Next you'll learn how to customize the operation of these controls with special characteristics called property settings. Then you'll see how to identify just what your program should do by writing program code. Finally, you'll learn how to save and run your new program (a Las Vegas–style slot machine) and how to compile it as an executable file.

Upgrade Notes:
What's New in Visual Basic .NET?

If you're experienced with Visual Basic 6, you'll notice some new features in Visual Basic .NET, including the following:

■ The Visual Studio .NET development environment provides a few different menus and toolbars with which you can build your programs. For example, Visual Basic 6 included Format, Run, and Add-Ins menus, which aren't included in Visual Studio. Most of the commands have been relocated—you'll find many of the Run menu commands on the Debug menu.

■ The CommandButton control is named the Button control in Visual Studio .NET, and many of its properties and methods have changed. For example, the Caption property is now named the Text property.

■ Some of the properties and methods for the Label control are new or have changed. For example, the Caption property is now named the Text property, and the TextAlign property has more alignment options than the previous Alignment property.

■ The Image control has been removed from Visual Studio. To display pictures, use the PictureBox control.

■ Visual Basic .NET code contains more compiler-generated statements than you saw in Visual Basic 6. In particular, Visual Basic .NET adds to the top of each form a block of code labeled "Windows Forms Designer generated code," which defines important form characteristics and shouldn't be modified. (Add your own program code below this code block.)

■ Visual Studio can create two types of executable files for your project, a *debug build* and a *release build*. Debug builds contain debugging information and are used when testing and debugging your program. Release builds are optimized and smaller and are used when you complete your program.

Lucky Seven: Your First Visual Basic Program

The Windows-based application you're going to construct is Lucky Seven, a game program that simulates a lucky number slot machine. Lucky Seven has a simple user interface and can be created and compiled in just a few minutes using Visual Basic. (If you'd like to run a completed version of Lucky before you start, you can find it in the c:\vbnetsbs\chap02\lucky7 folder on your hard disk.) Here's what your program will look like when it's finished:

Programming Steps

The Lucky Seven user interface contains two buttons, three lucky number boxes, a digital photo depicting your winnings, and the label "Lucky Seven." I produced these elements by creating seven objects on the Lucky Seven form and then changing several properties for each object. After the interface was designed, I added program code for the Spin and End buttons to process the user's button clicks and produce the random numbers. To re-create Lucky Seven, you'll follow three essential programming steps in Visual Basic: create the user interface, set the properties, and write the program code. The following table summarizes the process for Lucky Seven.

Programming step	Number of items
1. Create the user interface.	7 objects
2. Set the properties.	12 properties
3. Write the program code.	2 objects

Creating the User Interface

In this exercise, you'll start building Lucky Seven by creating a new project and then using controls in the Toolbox to construct the user interface.

Create a new project

1   Start Visual Studio.

2   On the Visual Studio Start Page, click the Get Started link and then click the New Project button.

> ## tip
>
> You can also start a new programming project by clicking the File menu, pointing to New, and then clicking Project.

The New Project dialog box appears.

Visual Studio can create operating system components and Web applications, in addition to the standard Windows application that you'll create in this chapter. The New Project dialog box lets you specify the type of program or component that you want to create, the language you'll use to create the program or component, and the name and location you'll use for the files.

3   In the list of Project Types, verify that the Visual Basic Projects folder is selected, and then, in the list of Templates, click the Windows Application icon.

Once these project settings are applied, Visual Studio will set up the development environment for Visual Basic .NET Windows application programming.

4   In the Name text box, type **MyLucky7** and then specify the c:\vbnetsbs\chap02 folder in the Location text box. (If you'd like, click the Browse button to specify the project location.)

Visual Studio assigns the name MyLucky7 to your program and prepares to create a new folder on your hard disk for the project named MyLucky7.

tip

If your copy of Visual Basic .NET didn't come with some of the other tools in the Visual Studio .NET development suite (such as Visual C++ .NET), you'll see a few differences when you work through the procedures in this book. For example, you might not have all the project types and templates shown in the previous illustration. I wrote this book with an installation of the Professional Edition of the Visual Studio .NET suite, which includes Visual C++ .NET, Visual C# .NET, and other development tools. It isn't necessary that you have these extra tools—I won't be using Visual C++ .NET or Visual C# .NET in this book—but I wanted you to see an installation that would be typical in the workplace of a professional software developer.

5   Click OK to create the new project in Visual Studio.

Visual Studio cleans the slate for a new programming project and displays in the center of the screen a blank Windows form (typically called simply "form") you can use to build your user interface.

Now you'll enlarge the form, and then you'll create the two buttons in the interface.

Create the user interface

1   Position the mouse pointer over the lower right corner of the form until the mouse changes into a resizing pointer, and then drag to increase the size of the form to make room for the objects in your program.

As you resize the form, scroll bars may appear in the Windows Forms Designer to give you access to the entire form you're creating. Depending on your screen resolution and the Visual Studio tools you have open, there may not be enough room for you to see the entire form at once. Don't worry about this—your form can be small, or it can fill the entire screen, and the scroll bars will give you access to the entire form.

Size your form so that it is about the size of the form shown here:

Windows Forms Designer   Form

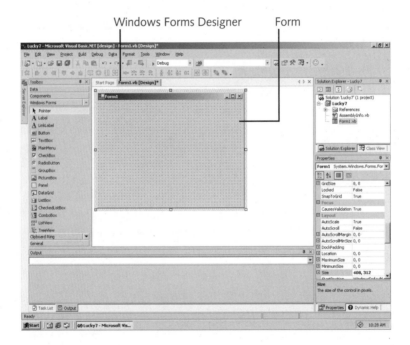

To see the entire form without obstruction, you can resize or close the other programming tools as you learned in Chapter 1. (Return to Chapter 1 if you have questions about resizing windows or tools.)

Now you'll practice adding a button object on the form.

2   Click the Button control in the Toolbox.

Button control

3   Place the mouse pointer over the form.

The mouse pointer changes to crosshairs and a button icon. The crosshairs are designed to help you draw the rectangular shape of a button. When you hold down the left mouse button and drag, the button object takes shape and snaps to the grid formed by the intersection of dots on the form.

Try creating your first button now.

4   Move the mouse pointer close to the upper left corner of the form, hold down the left mouse button, and then drag down and to the right. Stop dragging, and release the mouse button when you've drawn a button similar to the one shown here:

The name of the button is Button1.

Resize handle

A button with resize handles appears on the form. The button is named Button1, the first button in the program. (You might make a mental note of this button name—you'll see it again later when you write your program code.)

You can move buttons by dragging them with the mouse and you can resize them by using the resize handles whenever Visual Basic is in *design mode* (whenever the Visual Studio programming environment is active). When a program is running, however, the user won't be able to move interface elements unless you have changed a special property in the program to allow this. You'll practice moving and resizing the button now.

Move and resize a button

1   Position the mouse pointer over the button so that it changes to a four-headed arrow, and then drag the button down and to the right.

The button snaps to the grid when you release the mouse button. The form grid is designed to help you edit and align different user interface elements. You can change the size of the grid by clicking the Options command on the Tools menu, clicking the Windows Forms Designer folder, and then modifying the GridSize property.

The grid helps you design your user interface.

2   Position the mouse pointer on the lower right corner of the button.

When the mouse pointer rests on a resize handle of a selected object, it changes into a resizing pointer. You can use the resizing pointer to change the size of an object.

3   Enlarge the button by holding down the left mouse button and dragging the pointer down and to the right.

When you release the mouse button, the button changes size and snaps to the grid.

4   Use the resizing pointer to return the button to its original size, and then move the button back to its original location on the form.

Now you'll add a second button to the form, below the first button.

Add a second button

1   Click the Button control in the Toolbox.

Button control

2   Draw a button below the first button on the form. (For consistency, create a button of the same size.)

> ## tip
> To quickly add a control to your form, double-click the control in the Toolbox and a default-size control will be added to your form.

You can delete an object by selecting the object on the form and then pressing Delete.

3   Move or resize the button as necessary after you place it. If you make a mistake, feel free to delete the button and start over.

Now you'll add the labels used to display the numbers in the program. A *label* is a special user interface element designed to display text, numbers, or symbols when a program runs. When the user clicks the Lucky Seven program's Spin button, three random numbers appear in the label boxes. If one of the numbers is a 7, the user hits the jackpot.

Add the number labels

A

Label control

1 Click the Label control in the Toolbox.

2 Place the mouse pointer over the form.

The mouse pointer changes to crosshairs and a letter *A* icon.

3 Draw a small rectangular box like the one shown in the following illustration.

The label object you have created is named Label1, the first label in the program. Now you'll create two more labels, named Label2 and Label3, on the form.

4 Click the Label control in the Toolbox, and then draw a label box to the right of the first label.

Make this label the same size as the first. The text "Label2" will appear in the label.

5 Click the Label control again, and add a third label to the form, to the right of the second label.

The text "Label3" appears in the label.

Now you'll use the Label control to add a descriptive label to your form. This will be the fourth and final label in the program.

6 Click the Label control in the Toolbox.

7 Draw a larger rectangle directly below the two buttons.

When you've finished, your four labels should look like those in the illustration on the following page. (You can resize the label objects if they don't look quite right.)

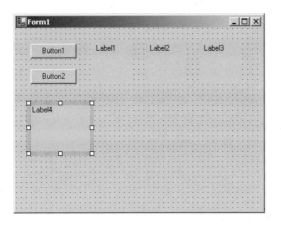

Now you'll add a *picture box* to the form to graphically display the payout you'll receive when you draw a 7 and hit the jackpot. A picture box is designed to display bitmaps, icons, digital photos, and other artwork in a program. One of the best uses for a picture box is to display a JPEG image file.

Add a picture

1   Click the PictureBox control in the Toolbox.

2   Using the PictureBox control, draw a large rectangular box directly beneath the three number labels.

PictureBox control

When you've finished, your picture box object should look like this:

```
┌─ Form1 ──────────────────── _□×┐
│   ┌────────┐   Label1   Label2   Label3 │
│   │ Button1 │                            │
│   └────────┘                            │
│   ┌────────┐                            │
│   │ Button2 │                            │
│   └────────┘                            │
│                    ┌──────────────┐      │
│   Label4           │              │      │
│                    │              │      │
│                    │              │      │
│                    └──────────────┘      │
└──────────────────────────────────┘
```

This object will be named PictureBox1 in your program; you'll use this name later in the program code.

Now you're ready to customize your interface by setting a few properties.

Setting the Properties

As you discovered in Chapter 1, you can change properties by selecting objects on the form and changing their settings in the Properties window. You'll start by changing the property settings for the two buttons.

Set the button properties

1   Click the first button (Button1) on the form.

    The button is selected and is surrounded by resize handles.

2   Double-click the Properties window title bar.

tip

If the Properties window isn't visible, click the Properties Window command on the View menu or press F4.

3   Resize the Properties window so that there is plenty of room to see the property names and their current settings.

    Once you get used to setting properties, it's OK to use the Properties window without enlarging it, but making it bigger helps when you first try it out. The Properties window in the following illustration is a good size for setting properties:

Properties

Button1 System.Windows.Forms.Button

□ **Appearance**	
BackColor	Control
BackgroundImage	(none)
Cursor	Default
FlatStyle	Standard
⊞ Font	Microsoft Sans Serif, 8.25
ForeColor	ControlText
Image	(none)
ImageAlign	MiddleCenter
ImageIndex	(none)
ImageList	(none)
RightToLeft	No
Text	**Button1**
TextAlign	MiddleCenter
□ **Behavior**	
AllowDrop	False

Text
The text contained in the control.

The Properties window lists the settings for the first button. These include settings for the background color, text, font height, and width of the button. Because there are so many properties, Visual Studio organizes them into categories and displays them in outline view. If you want to see the properties in a category, click the plus sign (+) next to the category title.

4   Scroll in the Properties window until you see the Text property, located in the Appearance category.

5   Double-click the Text property in the left column of the Properties window.

   The current Text setting ("Button1") is highlighted in the Properties window.

6   Type **Spin,** and press Enter.

   The Text property changes to "Spin" in the Properties window and on the button on the form. Now you'll change the Text property of the second button to "End". (You'll select the second button in a new way this time.)

7   Open the Object drop-down list box at the top of the Properties window.

   A list of the interface objects in your program appears:

The Object drop-down list box lets you switch from one object to the next

The Object drop-down list box lets you switch from one object to the next.

8   Click Button2 System.Windows.Forms.Button (the second button) in the list box.

   The property settings for the second button appear in the Properties window, and Visual Studio highlights Button2 on the form.

9   Double-click the current Text property ("Button2"), type **End**, and then press Enter.

The text of the second button changes to "End".

> ## tip
>
> Using the Object drop-down list is a handy way to switch between objects in your program. You can also switch between objects on the form by clicking each object.

Now you'll set the properties for the labels in the program. The first three labels will hold the random numbers generated by the program and will have identical property settings. (You'll set most of them as a group.) The descriptive label settings will be slightly different.

Set the number label properties

To select more than one object on a form, hold down the Shift key while clicking the objects.

1   Click the first number label (Label1), and then, holding down the Shift key, click the second and third number labels. (If the Properties window is in the way, move it to a new place.)

A selection rectangle and resize handles appear around each label you click. When you've selected all three labels, release the Shift key. You'll change the TextAlign, BorderStyle, and Font properties now so that the numbers that appear in the labels will be centered, boxed, and identical in font and point size. (Each is located in the Appearance category of the Properties window.)

> ## tip
>
> When more than one object is selected, only those properties that can be changed as a group are displayed in the Properties window.

2   Click the TextAlign property in the Properties window, and then click the drop-down arrow that appears to the right.

A graphical assortment of alignment options appears in the list box; these settings let you align text anywhere within the borders of the label object.

3   Click the center option (MiddleCenter).

The TextAlign property for each of the selected labels changes to MiddleCenter.

Now you'll change the BorderStyle property.

4   Click the BorderStyle property, and then click the drop-down arrow that appears to the right.

A list of the valid property settings (None, FixedSingle, and Fixed3D) appears in the list box.

5   Click FixedSingle in the list box to add a thin border around each label.

Now you'll change the font for the labels by changing settings for the Font property.

Ellipsis button

6   Click the Font property in the Properties window, and then click the ellipsis button (the button with three dots that is located next to the current font setting).

The Font dialog box appears, as shown here:

7   Change the font to Times New Roman, the font style to Bold, and the point size to 24, and then click OK.

The label text appears in the font, style, and size you specified.

Now you'll delete the text for the three labels so that the boxes will be empty when the program starts. (Your font selections will remain with the labels because they're stored as separate properties.) To complete this operation, you'll first need to select each of the labels individually.

8   Click a blank area on the form to remove the selection from the three labels, and then click the first label.

9 Double-click the Text property in the Properties window, press the Delete key, and then press Enter.

The text of the Label1 object is deleted. You'll use program code to put a random "slot machine" number in this property later in this chapter.

10 Delete the text in the second and third labels on the form.

You've finished with the first three labels. Now you'll change the Text, Font, and ForeColor properties of the fourth label.

Set the descriptive label properties

1 Click the fourth label object (Label4) on the form.

2 Change the Text property in the Properties window to **Lucky Seven**.

3 Click the Font property, and then click the ellipsis button.

4 Use the Font dialog box to change the font to Arial, the font style to Bold, and the point size to 18. Click OK.

The font in the label box is updated. Notice that the text in the box wrapped to two lines. This is an important concept: the contents of an object must fit inside the object. If they don't, the contents will wrap or be truncated.

Now you'll change the foreground color of the text.

5 Click the ForeColor property in the Properties window, and then click the drop-down arrow in the second column.

Visual Studio displays a list box with Custom, Web, and System tabs for setting foreground colors (the color of your text) in the label object. The Custom tab contains many of the colors available in your system. The Web tab sets colors for Web pages and lets you pick colors using their common names. The System tab displays the current colors used for user interface elements in your system. (The list reflects the current settings on the Appearance tab of the Display Properties dialog box.)

6 Click the dark purple color on the Custom tab.

The text in the label box changes to dark purple.

Now you're ready to set the properties for the last object.

The Picture Box Properties

The picture box object will contain a picture of a person paying you money when you hit the jackpot (that is, when at least one seven appears in the number labels on the form). This picture is a digitized image from an unpublished fourteenth century German manuscript stored in JPEG format. You need to set the SizeMode property to accurately size the picture and set the Image property to specify the name of the JPEG file that you will load into the picture box. You also need to set the Visible property, which specifies the picture state at the beginning of the program.

Set the picture box properties

1 Click the picture box object on the form.

2 Click the SizeMode property in the Properties window (listed in the Behavior category), click the drop-down arrow, and then click StretchImage.

Setting SizeMode to StretchImage before you open a graphic causes Visual Studio to resize the graphic to the exact dimensions of the picture box. (Typically, you set this property before you set the Image property.)

3 Double-click the Image property in the Properties window, and then click the ellipsis button in the second column.

The Open dialog box appears.

4 In the dialog box, navigate to the c:\vbnetsbs\chap02 folder.

The digital photo PayCoins.jpg appears in the list.

5 Select the file PayCoins.jpg in the dialog box, and then click Open.

The PayCoins photo is loaded into the picture box on the form. Because the photo is relatively small (24KB), it opens quickly on the form.

Now you'll change the Visible property to False so that the image will be invisible when the program starts. (You'll use program code to make it visible later.)

6   Click the Visible property in the Behavior category of the Properties window. Click the Visible drop-down arrow.

   The valid settings for the Visible property appear in a list box.

7   Click False to make the picture invisible when the program starts.

8   The Visible property is set to False. This affects the picture box when the program runs, but not now while you are designing it. Your completed form should look similar to this:

9   Double-click the title bar of the Properties window to return it to the docked position.

Writing the Code

Program code is entered in the Code Editor.

Now you're ready to write the code for the Lucky Seven program. Because most of the objects you've created already "know" how to work when the program runs, they're ready to receive input from the user and process it automatically. The inherent functionality of objects is one of the great strengths of Visual Basic—once objects are placed on a form and their properties are set, they're ready to run without any additional programming. However, the "meat" of the Lucky Seven game—the code that actually calculates random numbers, displays them in boxes, and detects a jackpot—is still missing from the program. This computing logic can be built into the application only by using program statements—code that clearly spells out what the program should do each step of the way. Because the program is driven by the Spin and End buttons, you'll associate the code for the game with those buttons. You enter and edit Visual Basic program statements in the *Code Editor*.

Reading Properties in Tables

In this chapter, you've set the properties for the Lucky Seven program step by step. In future chapters, the instructions to set properties will be presented in table format unless a setting is especially tricky. Here are the properties you've set so far in the Lucky Seven program in table format, as they'd look later in the book.

Object	Property	Setting
Button1	Text	"Spin"
Button2	Text	"End"
Label1, Label2, Label3	BorderStyle	Fixed Single
	Font	Times New Roman, Bold, 24-point
	Text	(empty)
	TextAlign	MiddleCenter
Label4	Text	"Lucky Seven"
	Font	Arial, Bold, 18-point
	ForeColor	Purple
PictureBox1	Image	"c:\vbnetsbs\chap02\paycoins.jpg"
	SizeMode	StretchImage
	Visible	False

In the following steps, you'll enter the program code for Lucky Seven in the Code Editor.

Use the Code Editor

1   Double-click the End button on the form.

After a few moments, the Code Editor appears in the center of the Visual Studio development environment, as shown on the following page.

Inside the Code Editor are program statements associated with the current form. Program statements that are used together to perform some action are typically grouped in a programming construct called a *procedure*. A common type of procedure is a Sub procedure, sometimes called a subroutine. Sub procedures include a Sub keyword in the first line and end with End Sub. Procedures typically get executed when certain events occur, such as when a button is clicked. When a procedure is associated with a particular object and an event, it is called an *event handler* or an *event procedure*.

Code Editor

When you double-clicked the End button (Button2), Visual Studio automatically added the first and last lines of the End button event procedure, as the following code shows. (The first line was wrapped to stay within the book margins.) You will notice other lines of code in the Code Editor, which Visual Studio has added to define important characteristics of the form. (You can recognize these statements by the words, "Windows Form Designer generated code.") Ignore these statements for now and don't modify them. You'll learn about this boilerplate code in later chapters.

```
Private Sub Button2_Click(ByVal sender As System.Object, _
    ByVal e As System.EventArgs) Handles Button2.Click


End Sub
```

The body of a procedure fits between these lines and is executed whenever a user activates the interface element associated with the procedure. In this case, the event is a mouse click, but as you'll see later in the book, it could also be a different type of event.

2   Type **End**, and then press the Down arrow key.

After you type the statement, the letters turn blue, indicating that Visual Basic recognizes it as a valid statement, or *keyword,* in the program.

*The End state-
ment stops the
execution of a
program.*

You use the program statement End to stop your program and remove it from the screen. The Visual Basic programming language contains several hundred unique keywords such as this, complete with their associated operators and symbols. The spelling of and spacing between these items are critical to writing program code that will be accurately recognized by the Visual Basic compiler. As you enter these keywords and perform other edits, the Code Editor will handle many of the formatting details for you, including indents, spacing, and adding parentheses that you need.

tip

Another name for the exact spelling, order, and spacing of keywords in a program is *statement syntax.*

When you pressed the Down arrow key, the End statement was indented to set it apart from the Private Sub and End Sub statements. This indenting scheme is one of the programming conventions you'll see throughout this book to keep your programs clear and readable. The group of conventions regarding how program code is organized in a program is often referred to as *program style*.

Now that you've written the code associated with the End button, you'll write code for the Spin button. These programming statements will be a little more extensive and will give you a chance to learn more about program syntax and style. You'll study each of the program statements later in this book, so you don't need to know everything about them now. Just focus on the general structure of the program code and on typing the program statements exactly as they are printed. (Visual Basic is fussy about spelling and the order in which keywords and operators appear.)

Write code for the Spin button

*View Designer
button*

1   Click the View Designer button in Solution Explorer window to display your form again.

When the Code Editor is visible, you won't be able to see the form you're working on. The View Designer button is one mechanism you can use to display it again. (If more than one form is loaded in Solution Explorer, click the form you want to display first.)

> **tip**
>
> To display the form again, you can also click the tab labeled "Form1.vb [Design]" at the top edge of the Code Editor. If you don't see tabs at the top of the Code Editor, enable Tabbed Documents view in the Options dialog box, as discussed in a Tip in Chapter 1.

2   Double-click the Spin button.

   After a few moments, the Code Editor appears, and an event procedure associated with the Button1 button appears near the Button2 event procedure.

   Although you changed the text of this button to "Spin", its name in the program is still Button1. (The name and the text of an interface element can be different to suit the needs of the programmer.) Each object can have several procedures associated with it, one for each event it recognizes. The click event is the one we're interested in now because users will click the Spin and End buttons when they operate the program.

3   Type the following program lines between the Private Sub and End Sub statements, pressing Enter after each line, indenting with Tab, and taking care to type the program statements exactly as they appear here. (The Code Editor will scroll to the left as you enter the longer lines.) If you make a mistake (usually identified by jagged underline), delete the incorrect statements and try again.

> **tip**
>
> As you enter the program code, Visual Basic formats the text and displays different parts of the program in color to help you identify the various elements. When you begin to type a property, Visual Basic also displays the available properties for the object you're using in a list box, so you can double-click the property or keep typing to enter it yourself. If Visual Basic displays an error message, you may have misspelled a program statement. Check the line against the text in this book, make the necessary correction, and continue typing. (You can also delete a line and type it from scratch.) In addition, Visual Basic might also add code automatically when it is necessary. For example, when you type the following code, Visual Basic will automatically add the End If line. Readers of previous editions of this book have found this first typing exercise to be the toughest part of this chapter—"But Mr. Halvorson, I *know* I typed it just as written!"—so please give this program code your closest attention. I promise you, it works!

```
PictureBox1.Visible = False      ' hide picture
Label1.Text = CStr(Int(Rnd() * 10))     ' pick numbers
Label2.Text = CStr(Int(Rnd() * 10))
Label3.Text = CStr(Int(Rnd() * 10))
' if any caption is 7 display picture and beep
If (Label1.Text = "7") Or (Label2.Text = "7") _
Or (Label3.Text = "7") Then
    PictureBox1.Visible = True
    Beep()
End If
```

When you've finished, the Code Editor should look like this:

4   Click the Save All command on the File menu to save your additions to the program.

The Save All command saves everything in your project—the project file, the form file, any code modules, and other related components in your application. Note that if you want to save just the item you are currently working on (the form, the code module, or something else), you can use the Save command on the File menu. If you want to save the current item with a different name, you can use the Save As command.

A Look at the Button1_Click Procedure

The Button1_Click procedure is executed when the user clicks the Spin button on the form. The procedure uses some pretty complicated statements, and, because I haven't formally introduced them yet, it may look a little confusing. However, if you take a closer look you'll probably see a few things that look familiar. Taking a peek at the contents of the procedures will give you a feel for the type of program code you'll be creating later in this book. (If you'd rather not have a look, feel free to skip to the next section, "Running Visual Basic .NET Applications.")

The Button1_Click procedure performs three tasks: it hides the digital photo, creates three random numbers for the number labels, and displays the photo when the number 7 appears. Let's look at each of these steps individually.

Hiding the photo is accomplished with the following line:

```
PictureBox1.Visible = False    ' hide picture
```

This line is made up of two parts: a program statement and a comment. The program statement (PictureBox1.Visible = False) sets the Visible property of the picture box object (PictureBox1) to False (one of two possible settings). You might remember that you set this property to False once before by using the Properties window. You're doing it again now in the program code because the first task is a spin and you need to clear away a photo that might have been displayed in a previous game. Because the property will be changed at runtime and not at design time, the property must be set by using program code. This is a handy feature of Visual Basic, and we'll talk about it more in Chapter 3.

The second part of the first line (the part displayed in green type on your screen) is called a *comment*. Comments are explanatory notes included in program code following a single quotation mark ('). Programmers use comments to describe how important statements work in a program. These notes aren't processed by Visual Basic when the program runs; they exist only to document what the program does. You'll want to use comments often when you write Visual Basic programs to leave an easy-to-understand record of what you're doing.

The next three lines handle the random number computations. Does this concept sound strange? You can actually make Visual Basic generate unpredictable numbers within specific guidelines—in other words, you can create random numbers for lottery contests, dice games, or other statistical patterns. The Rnd function in each line creates a random number between 0 and 1 (a number with a decimal point and several decimal places), and the Int function rounds the product of the random number and 10 to the nearest decimal place. This computation creates random numbers between 0 and 9 in the program—just what we need for this particular slot machine application.

```
Label1.Text = CStr(Int(Rnd() * 10))    ' pick numbers
```

We then need to jump through a little hoop in our code—we need to copy these random numbers into the three label boxes on the form, but before we do so the numbers need to be converted to text with the CStr (convert to string) function. Notice how CStr, Int, and Rnd are all connected together in the program statement—they work collectively to produce a result like a mathematical formula. After the computation and conversion, the values are then assigned to the Text properties of the first three labels on the form, and the assignment causes the numbers to be displayed in boldface, 24-point, Times New Roman type in the three number labels. The following illustration shows how Visual Basic evaluates one line of code step by step to generate the random number 7 and copy it to a label object. Visual Basic evaluates the expression just like a mathematician solving a mathematical formula.

Example:
```
Label1.Text = CStr(Int(Rnd() * 10))
```

Code	Result
Rnd()	0.7055475
Rnd() * 10	7.055475
Int(Rnd() * 10)	7
CStr(Int(Rnd() * 10))	"7"
Label1.Text = CStr(Int(Rnd() * 10))	7

The last group of statements in the program checks whether any of the random numbers is seven. If one or more of them is, the program displays the medieval manuscript depiction of a payout, and a beep announces the winnings.

```
' if any caption is 7 display picture and beep
If (Label1.Text = "7") Or (Label2.Text = "7") _
Or (Label3.Text = "7") Then
    PictureBox1.Visible = True
    Beep()
End If
```

The complete Lucky 7 program is located in the c:\vbnetsbs\ chap02\lucky7 folder.

Each time the user clicks the Spin button, the Button1_Click procedure is called and the program statements in the procedure are executed again.

Running Visual Basic .NET Applications

Congratulations! You're ready to run your first real program. To run a Visual Basic program from the programming environment, you can click Start on the Debug menu, click the Start button on the Standard toolbar, or press F5. Try running your Lucky Seven program now. If Visual Basic displays an error message, you may still have a typing mistake or two in your program code. Try to fix it by comparing the printed version in this book with the one you typed, or load Lucky7 from your hard disk and run it.

Run the Lucky Seven program

Start button

1   Click the Start button on the Standard toolbar.

The Lucky Seven program compiles and runs in the programming environment. After a few seconds, the user interface appears, just as you designed it.

2   Click the Spin button.

The program picks three random numbers and displays them in the labels on the form, as follows:

Because a seven appears in the first label box, the digital photo appears depicting your payoff and the computer beeps. You win! (The sound you hear depends on your Sounds And Multimedia setting in Windows Control Panel—to make this game sound really cool, change the Default Beep sound to something more dynamic.)

3   Click the Spin button 15 or 16 more times, watching the results of the spins in the number boxes.

About half the time you spin, you hit the jackpot—pretty easy odds. (The actual odds are about 2.8 times out of 10; you're just lucky at first.) Later on you might want to make the game tougher by displaying the photo only when two or three sevens appear, or by creating a running total of winnings.

4   When you've finished experimenting with your new creation, click the End button.

The program stops, and the programming environment reappears on your screen.

> **tip**
>
> If you run this program again, you may notice that Lucky Seven displays exactly the same sequence of random numbers. There is nothing wrong here—the Visual Basic Rnd function was designed to display a repeating sequence of numbers at first so that you can properly test your code using output that can be reproduced again and again. To create truly "random" numbers, use the Randomize function in your code, as shown in the exercise at the end of this chapter.

Building an Executable File

Your last task in this chapter is to complete the development process and create an application for Windows, or an *executable file*. Windows applications created with Visual Basic have the filename extension .exe and can be run on any system that contains Microsoft Windows and the necessary support files. (Visual Basic installs these support files—including the dynamic link libraries and the .NET Framework files—automatically.) If you plan to distribute your applications, see Chapter 14 in this book. In that chapter, you'll learn more about optimizing your Visual Basic .NET applications and how to use *assemblies* to distribute solutions.

At this point, you need to know that Visual Studio has the ability to create two types of executable files for your project, a *debug build* and a *release build*. Debug builds are the default type in Visual Studio, and you'll use them often as you test and debug your program. Debug builds contain debugging information that makes them run slower, but the Visual Basic compiler is able to produce the builds quite quickly. When your project is complete, however, you want to compile your application using a release build, which includes numerous optimizations and doesn't contain unneeded debugging information.

> **tip**
>
> Although there are many similarities, Visual Basic .NET approaches compiling and distributing your applications in a different way than Visual Basic 6. For example, the Make Project.exe command on the Visual Basic 6 File menu has been replaced with the Build Solution command on the Build menu, and assemblies and manifests are now a feature of compilation and deployment. For additional details about this conceptual change, see Chapter 14.

Try creating a release build named MyLucky7.exe now.

Create an executable file

1   On the Build menu, click the Configuration Manager command.

The Configuration Manager dialog box appears. This dialog box lets you switch between debug builds and release builds, and it contains additional program settings such as the operating platform for which you are creating the application.

2   Click Release in the Active Solution Configuration list box, and then click Close.

Your project will now be compiled and optimized as a release build.

> **tip**
>
> You can also specify the debug or release build type using the Solution Configurations drop-down list box on the Standard toolbar.

3   On the Build menu, click the Build Solution command.

The Build Solution command creates a bin folder where your project is located (if the folder doesn't already exist) and compiles the source code in your project. The result is an executable file named MyLucky7.exe. To save you time, Visual Studio often creates these files as you develop your application; however, it is always a good idea to recompile your application manually with the Build Solution command when you reach an important milestone. In particular, you'll need to recompile if you switch from debug build to release build.

Try running this program now by using the Run command on the Start menu.

Start button

4   On the Windows taskbar, click the Start button and then click Run.

The Run dialog box appears.

5   Click the Browse button, and then navigate to the c:\vbnetsbs\chap02\mylucky7\bin folder.

6   Click the MyLucky7.exe application icon, click Open, and then click OK.

7   The Lucky Seven program loads and runs in Windows—you've run the program outside the Visual Studio development environment.

8   Click Spin a few times to verify the operation of the game, and then click End.

tip

You can also run Windows applications, including compiled Visual Basic programs, by opening Windows Explorer and double-clicking the executable file. To create a shortcut icon for MyLucky7.exe on the Windows desktop, right-click the Windows desktop, point to New, and then click Shortcut. When you are prompted for the location of your application file, click Browse and select the MyLucky7.exe executable file. Click the Open, Next, and Finish buttons, and Windows will place an icon on the desktop that you can double-click to run your program.

9   On the File menu, click Exit to close Visual Studio and the MyLucky7 project.

The Visual Studio development environment closes. If you decide later that you want to make extensive changes to this program (more than the changes listed on the following pages), use the Configuration Manager command on the Build menu to change the build type from release build to debug build.

One Step Further: Adding to a Program

You can restart Visual Studio at any time and work on a programming project you have stored on disk. You'll restart Visual Studio now and add a special statement named Randomize to the Lucky Seven program.

Reload Lucky Seven

1 On the Windows taskbar, click the Start button, point to Programs, point to Microsoft Visual Studio .NET, and then click the Microsoft Visual Studio .NET program icon.

A list of the most recent projects that you have worked on appears on the Visual Studio Start Page. Because you just finished working with Lucky Seven, MyLucky7 should be the first project on the list.

2 Click the MyLucky7 link to open the Lucky Seven project.

The Lucky Seven program opens, and the MyLucky7 form appears. (If you don't see the form, click Form1.vb in Solution Explorer and then click the View Designer button.)

Now you'll add the Randomize statement to the Form_Load procedure, a special procedure that is associated with the form and that is executed each time the program is started.

3 Double-click the form (not one of the objects) to display the Form_Load procedure.

The Form_Load procedure appears in the Code Editor, as shown here:

4   Type **Randomize**, and then press the Down arrow key.

The Randomize statement is added to the program and will be executed each time the program starts. Randomize uses the system clock to create a truly random starting point, or "seed," for the Rnd statement used in the Button1_Click procedure. As I mentioned earlier, without the Randomize statement the Lucky Seven program produces the same string of random spins every time you restart the program. With Randomize in place, the program will spin randomly every time it runs. The numbers won't follow a recognizable pattern.

5   Run the new version of Lucky Seven, and then save the project. If you plan to use the new version a lot, you may want to create a new .exe file too.

6   When finished, click Close Solution on the File menu.

The files associated with the Lucky Seven program are closed.

Chapter 2 Quick Reference

To	Do this
Create a user interface	Use Toolbox controls to place objects on your form, and then set the necessary properties. Resize the form and the objects as appropriate.
Move an object	Position the mouse over the object until you get the four-headed arrow, and then drag the object.
Resize an object	Click the object to select it, and then drag the resize handle attached to the part of the object you want to resize.
Delete an object	Click the object, and then press the Delete key.
Open the Code Editor	Double-click an object on the form (or the form itself). *or* Select a form or a module in the Solution Explorer and then click the View Code button.
Write program code	Type Visual Basic program statements associated with the object you want to program in the Code Editor.
Save a program	On the File menu, click the Save All command. *or* Click the Save All button on the Standard toolbar.

To	Do this
Save a form file	Make sure the form is open, and then, on the File menu, click the Save command.
	or
	Click the Save button on the Standard toolbar.
Change the build type from debug build to release build	On the Build menu, click the Configuration Manager command. Click the build type you want (Debug or Release) in the Active Solution Configuration drop-down list box.
	or
	Select the build type from the Solution Configurations drop-down list box on the Standard toolbar.
Create an .exe file	On the Build menu, click the Build command.
Reload a project	On the File menu, point to Open, and then click the Projects command.
	or
	On the File menu, point to Recent Projects, and then click the desired project.
	or
	Click the project in the recent projects list on the Visual Studio Start Page.

CHAPTER

3

Working with Toolbox Controls

In this chapter you will learn how to:

✔ *Use TextBox and Button controls to create a "Hello World" program.*

✔ *Use the DateTimePicker control to display your birth date.*

✔ *Use CheckBox, RadioButton, ListBox, and ComboBox controls to process user input.*

✔ *Use a LinkLabel control to display a Web page on the Internet.*

✔ *Install ActiveX controls.*

Working with Controls

As you learned in Chapters 1 and 2, Microsoft Visual Studio .NET controls are the graphical tools you use to build the user interface of a Visual Basic program. Controls are located in the Toolbox in the development environment, and you use them to create objects on a form with a simple series of mouse clicks and dragging motions. Windows Forms controls are specifically designed for building Windows applications, and you'll find them organized on the Windows Forms tab of the Toolbox. (You used a few of these controls in the previous chapter.) You'll learn about other controls, including the tools you use to build Web Forms and database applications, later in the book.

In this chapter, you'll learn how to display information in a text box, work with date and time information on your system, process user input, and display a Web page within a Visual Basic .NET program. The exercises in this chapter will help you design your own Visual Basic applications and will teach you more about objects, properties, and program code. You'll also learn how to add older ActiveX controls to the Toolbox so that you can extend the functionality of Visual Basic.

Upgrade Notes:
What's New in Visual Basic .NET?

If you're experienced with Visual Basic 6, you'll notice some new features in Visual Basic .NET, including the following:

- A new control named DateTimePicker helps you prompt the user for date and time information. The new LinkLabel control is designed to display and manage Web links on a form.

- The OptionButton control has been replaced with a new RadioButton control.

- The Frame control has been replaced with a new GroupBox control.

- The ListIndex property in the ListBox control has been replaced by a property called SelectedIndex. The same change was made to the ComboBox control.

- There is no longer an Image control. You use the PictureBox control instead.

- Images are added to picture box objects using the System.Drawing.Image.FromFile method (not the LoadPicture function).

- Web browsers and other applications are now started using the System.Diagnostics.Process.Start method.

- ActiveX controls are added to the Toolbox in a new way and are "wrapped" by Visual Studio so that they can be used in Visual Basic .NET applications.

The Basic Use of Controls:
The "Hello World" Program

A great tradition in introductory programming books is the "Hello World" program. Hello World is the name given to a short program that demonstrates how the simplest utility can be built and run in a given programming language. In the days of character-based programming, Hello World was usually a two-line or three-line program typed in a program editor and assembled with a stand-alone compiler. With the advent of graphical programming tools, however, the typical Hello World has grown into a complex program containing dozens of lines and requiring several programming tools for its construction. Fortunately, creating a Hello World program is still quite simple with Visual Basic .NET. You can construct a complete user interface by creating two objects, setting two properties, and entering one line of code. Give it a try.

Create a Hello World program

1 Start Visual Studio if it isn't already open.

2 On the File menu, point to New, and then click Project.

Visual Studio displays the New Project dialog box, which prompts you for the name and location of your project and the template that you want to use to open it. (Unlike previous versions of Visual Basic, you begin a project by specifying a name for your program.)

tip
Use the following instructions each time you want to create a new project on your hard disk.

3 Make sure the Visual Basic Projects folder is selected, and then click the Windows Application template.

These selections indicate that you'll be building a stand-alone Visual Basic Windows application.

4 Type **MyHello** in the Name text box, and then click the Browse button.

The Project Location dialog box opens. You use this dialog box to specify the location of your project and to create new folders for your projects if necessary. Although you can save your projects in any location that you want (the folder \My Documents\Visual Studio Projects is a common location), in this book I will instruct you to save your projects in the c:\vbnetsbs folder, the default location for your Step by Step practice files. If you ever want to remove all of the files associated with this programming course, you will know just where the files are, and you will be able to remove them easily by deleting the entire folder.

tip
Throughout this book, I ask you to create sample projects with the My prefix, to distinguish your own work from the sample files I include on the companion CD.

Working with Controls

3

5   Click the Desktop icon in the Project Location dialog box, double-click the My Computer icon, and then browse to the folder c:\vbnetsbs\chap03.

6   Click the Open button to indicate that the MyHello project and its supporting files will be saved in the c:\vbnetsbs\chap03 folder in a subfolder named MyHello.

The New Project dialog box now looks like this:

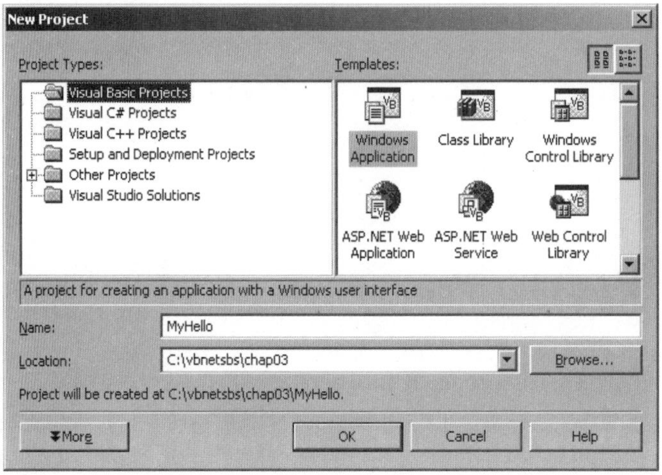

7   Click OK to create your new project.

The new project is created and a blank form appears in the Windows Forms Designer, as shown in the following illustration. The two controls you'll use in this exercise, Button and TextBox, are labeled in the Toolbox. If your programming tools are configured differently now, take a few moments to organize them as shown in the illustration. (Chapter 1 describes how to configure the Visual Studio development environment if you need a refresher course.)

abl	**8**	Click the TextBox control on the Windows Forms tab of the Toolbox.
TextBox control	**9**	Draw a text box similar to this:

A *text box object* is used to display text on a form or to get user input while a Visual Basic program is running. How a text box works depends on how you set its properties and how you reference the text box in the program code. In this simple program, a text box object will be used to display the message "Hello, world!" when you click a button object on the form.

You'll add that button now.

Button control

10   Click the Button control in the Toolbox.

11   Draw a button below the text box on the form.

Your form should look like this:

A *button object* is used to get the most basic input from a user. When a user clicks a button, he or she is requesting that the program perform a specific action immediately. In Visual Basic terms, the user is using the button to create an *event* that needs to be processed in the program. Typical buttons in a program are the OK button, which a user clicks to accept a list of options and indicate that he or she is ready to proceed; the Cancel button, which a user clicks to discard a list of options; and the Quit button, which a user clicks to exit the program. In each case, you should use buttons in a recognizable way so that they work as expected when the user clicks them. A button's characteristics (like those of all objects) can be modified with property settings and references to the object in program code.

For more information about setting properties, see the section "The Properties Window" in Chapter 1.

12   Set the following properties for the text box and button objects, using the Properties window. The setting "(empty)" for TextBox1 means that you should delete the current setting and leave the property blank. Settings you need to type in are shown in quotation marks. You shouldn't type the quotation marks.

Object	Property	Setting
TextBox1	Text	(empty)
Button1	Text	"OK"

The complete Hello World program is located in the c:\vbnetsbs\chap03\hello folder.

13   Double-click the OK button, and type the following program statement between the Private Sub Button1_Click and End Sub statements in the Code Editor:

```
TextBox1.Text = "Hello, world!"
```

tip

After you type the TextBox1 object name and a period, Visual Studio displays a list box containing all the valid properties for text box objects, to jog your memory if you've forgotten the complete list. You can select a property from the list by double-clicking it, or you can continue typing and enter it yourself. (I usually just keep on typing, unless I'm exploring new features.)

The statement you've entered changes the Text property of the text box to "Hello, world!" when the user clicks the button at runtime. (The equal sign assigns everything between the quotation marks to the Text property of the TextBox1 object.) This example changes a property at runtime—one of the most common uses of program code in a Visual Basic program. Your statement is in an *event procedure*—an instruction that is executed when the Button1 object is clicked. It changes the property setting (and therefore the text box contents) immediately after the user clicks the button.

Now you're ready to run the Hello World program.

Run the Hello World program

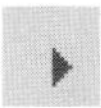

Start button

1   Click the Start button on the Standard toolbar.

The Hello World program compiles and after a few seconds runs in the Visual Studio development environment.

2   Click the OK button.

The program displays the greeting "Hello, world!" in the text box, as shown here:

Working with Controls

When you clicked the OK button, the program code changed the Text property of the empty TextBox1 text box to "Hello, world!" and displayed this text in the box. If you didn't get this result, repeat the steps in the previous section and build the program again. You might have set a property incorrectly or made a typing mistake in the program code. (Syntax errors appear with a jagged underline in the Code Editor.)

3   Click the Close button in the upper right corner of the Hello program window to stop the program.

> ## tip
> To stop a program running in Visual Studio, you can also click the Stop Debugging button on the Visual Studio Debug toolbar to close the program. (In Visual Basic 6, this button was named End.)

Save All button

4   Click the Save All button on the Visual Studio Standard toolbar to save your changes.

Congratulations—you've joined the ranks of programmers who have written a Hello World program. Now let's try another control.

Using the DateTimePicker Control

Some Visual Basic controls display information, and others gather information from the user or process data behind the scenes. In this exercise, you'll work with the DateTimePicker control, which prompts the user for a date or time using a graphical calendar with scroll arrows. Although your use of the control will be rudimentary at this point, experimenting with DateTimePicker will give you an idea of how much Visual Basic controls can do for you automatically and how you process the information that comes from them.

The Birthday Program

The Birthday program uses a DateTimePicker control and a Button control to prompt the user for the date of his or her birthday and displays that information using a message box along with other information. Give it a try now.

Build the Birthday program

1   On the File menu, click Close Solution to close the MyHello project.

The files associated with the Hello World program are closed.

2 On the File menu, point to New, and then click Project.

The New Project dialog box appears.

3 Create a new Visual Basic Windows Application project named **MyBirthday** in the c:\vbnetsbs\chap03 folder.

The new project is created and a blank form appears in the Windows Forms Designer.

DateTimePicker control

4 Click the DateTimePicker control in the Toolbox.

tip

If you don't see the DateTimePicker in the Toolbox, it may be lower in the Toolbox list hidden from your view. To scroll down in the Toolbox list, click the down scroll arrow next to the Clipboard Ring tab. To scroll back up, click the up scroll arrow next to the Windows Forms tab.

Down scroll arrow

Up scroll arrow

5 Draw a date time picker object in the middle of the form, as shown in the following:

```
┌─ Form1 ──────────────── _ □ ×
│
│
│   ┌─────────────────────────┐
│   │ Thursday ,  June  20, 2002 ▼│
│   └─────────────────────────┘
│
│
│
│
│
│
│
│
└────────────────────────────────
```

The date time picker object by default displays the current date, but you can adjust the date displayed by changing the object's Value property. Displaying the date is a handy design guide—it lets you size the date time picker object correctly when you are creating it.

Button control

6 Click the Button control in the Toolbox, and then add a button object below the date time picker.

You'll use this button to display your birth date and verify that the date time picker works correctly.

3

Working with Controls

7 In the Properties window, change the Text property of the button object to **Show My Birthday**.

Now you'll add a few lines of program code to a procedure associated with the button object. This procedure is called an *event procedure* because it runs when an event, such as a mouse click, occurs in the object.

Double-click an object to display its default event procedure.

8 Double-click the button object on the form, and then type the following program statement between the Private Sub and End Sub statements in the Button1_Click event procedure:

```
MsgBox("Your birth date was " & DateTimePicker1.Text)
MsgBox("Day of the year: " & _
   DateTimePicker1.Value.DayOfYear.ToString())
MsgBox("Today is " & DateTimePicker1.Value.Now.ToString())
```

These program statements display three successive message boxes (small dialog boxes) with information from the date time picker object. The first line uses the Text property of the date time picker to display the birth date information you select when using the object at runtime. The MsgBox function displays the string value "Your birth date was" in addition to the textual value held in the date time picker's Text property. These two pieces of information are joined together by the string concatenation operator (&). You'll learn more about the MsgBox function and the string concatenation operator in Chapter 5.

The second and third lines collectively form one program statement and have been broken by the line continuation character (_) because the statement was a bit too long to print in our book. (See Tip box below for an explanation of this useful convention for breaking longer lines.) The statement DateTimePicker1.Value.DayOfYear.ToString() uses the date time picker object to calculate the day of the year in which you were born, counting from January 1. This is accomplished by the DayOfYear property and the ToString method, which converts the numeric result of the date calculation to a textual value that is more easily displayed by the MsgBox function.

Methods are special statements that perform an action or a service for a particular object, such as converting a number to a string or adding items to a list box. Methods differ from properties, which contain a value, and event procedures, which execute when a user manipulates an object. Methods can also be shared among objects, so when you learn how to use one method, you'll often be able to apply it to several circumstances. We'll discuss several important methods as you work through this book.

The fourth line in the program code uses the Now property to check your computer's system clock for the current date and time and displays that information in a message box after converting it to a string, or textual, value.

> # tip
> Program lines can be more than 65,000 characters long in the Visual Studio Code Editor, but it is usually easiest to work with lines of 80 or fewer characters. You can divide long program statements among multiple lines by using a space and a line continuation character (_) at the end of each line in the statement, except the last line. (You cannot use a line continuation character to break a string that is in quotation marks, however.) I use the line continuation character in this exercise to break the second line of code into two parts.

After you enter the code for the Button1_Click event procedure, the Code Editor should look similar to the following illustration.

The complete Birthday program is located in the c:\vbnetsbs\chap03\birthday folder.

```
Start Page | Form1.vb [Design]* | Form1.vb* |
Form1 (Birthday)                    ▼   Button1_Click                    ▼
□ Public Class Form1
     Inherits System.Windows.Forms.Form

  ⊞  Windows Form Designer generated code

     Private Sub Button1_Click(ByVal sender As System.Object, ByVal e A
         MsgBox("Your birth date was " & DateTimePicker1.Text)
         MsgBox("Day of the year: " & _
           DateTimePicker1.Value.DayOfYear.ToString())
         MsgBox("Today is " & DateTimePicker1.Value.Now.ToString())

     End Sub
  └ End Class
```

9 Click the Save All button to save your changes to disk.

Save All button

Now you're ready to run the Birthday program.

Run the Birthday program

Start button

1 Click the Start button on the Standard toolbar.

The Birthday program starts to run in the development environment. The current date is displayed in the date time picker.

2 Click the drop-down arrow in the date time picker to display the object in calendar view.

Your form will look like the illustration on the following page. (You'll see a different date.)

Working with Controls   3

3   Click the left scroll arrow to look at previous months on the calendar.

Notice that the text box portion of the object also changes as you scroll the date. The "today" value at the bottom of the calendar doesn't change, however.

Although you could scroll all the way back to your exact birthday, you may not have the patience to scroll month by month. To move to your birth year faster, select the year value in the date time picker text box and enter a new date.

4   Select the four-digit year in the date time picker text box.

When you select the date, the date time picker will close.

5   Type your birth year in place of the year that is currently selected, and then click the drop-down arrow again.

The calendar reappears in the year of your birth.

6   Click the scroll arrows again to locate the month in which you were born, and then click the exact day on which you were born.

If you didn't know the day of the week you were born on, now you can find out!

When you select the final date, the date time picker closes, and your birth date is displayed in the text box. Now click the button object to see how this information is made available to other objects on your form.

7   Click the Show My Birthday button.

Visual Basic executes your program code and displays a message box containing the day and date of your birth. Notice how the two dates match:

8   Click OK in the message box.

A second message box appears indicating which day of the year you were born on.

9   Click OK to display the final message box.

The current date and time are displayed—the program works!

You'll find the date time picker object to be quite capable—not only does it remember the new date or time information that you enter, but it keeps track of the current date and time as well, and it can display this date and time information in a variety of useful formats.

tip
To configure the date time picker object to display times instead of dates, set the object's Format property to Time.

10   Click OK to close the message box, and then click the Close button on the form.

You're finished using the DateTimePicker control for now.

A Word About Terminology

So far in this book I've used several different terms to describe items in a Visual Basic program. Although I haven't defined each of them formally, it's worth listing several of them now to clear up any confusion. Can you tell the difference yet?

Program statement A program statement is a keyword in the code that does the work of the program. Visual Basic program statements create storage space for data, open files, perform calculations, and do several other important tasks. Most keywords are shown in blue type in the Code Editor.

Variable A variable is a special container used to hold data temporarily in a program. The programmer creates variables using the Dim statement to store the results of a calculation, create filenames, process input, and so on. Numbers, names, and property values can be stored in variables.

Control A control is a tool you use to create objects on a Visual Basic form. You select controls from the Toolbox and use them to draw objects on a form with the mouse. You use most controls to create user interface elements, such as buttons, picture boxes, and list boxes.

Object An object is the name of a user interface element you create on a Visual Basic form with a Toolbox control. You can move, resize, and customize objects by using property settings. Objects have what is known as *inherent functionality*—they know how to operate and can respond to certain situations on their own. (A list box "knows" how to scroll, for example.) And objects are the members of *classes*, which serve as the blueprints for defining what an object does. You can program Visual Basic objects by using customized event procedures for different situations in a program. In Visual Basic, the form itself is also an object.

Property A property is a value, or characteristic, held by an object. For example, a button object has a Text property to specify the text that appears on the button and an Image property to specify the path to an image file that should appear on the button face. In Visual Basic, properties can be set at design time by using the Properties window or at runtime by using statements in the program code. In code, the format for setting a property is

```
Object.Property = Value
```

where *Object* is the name of the object you're customizing, *Property* is the characteristic you want to change, and *Value* is the new property setting. For example,

```
Button1.Text = "Hello"
```

could be used in the program code to set the Text property of the Button1 object to "Hello".

Event procedure   An event procedure is a block of code that is executed when an object is manipulated in a program. For example, when the Button1 object is clicked, the Button1_Click event procedure is executed. Event procedures typically evaluate and set properties and use other program statements to perform the work of the program.

Method   A method is a special statement that performs an action or a service for a particular object in a program. In program code, the notation for using a method is

```
Object.Method(Value)
```

where *Object* is the name of the object you want to work with, *Method* is the action you want to perform, and *Value* is an optional argument to be used by the method. For example, the statement

```
ListBox1.Items.Add("Check")
```

uses the Add method to put the word *Check* in the ListBox1 list box. Methods and properties are often identified by their position in a collection or object library, so don't be surprised if you see very long references such as System.Drawing.Image.FromFile, which would be read as "the FromFile method, which is a member of the Image class, which is a member of the System.Drawing object library (or *namespace*)."

Controls for Gathering Input

Visual Basic provides several mechanisms for gathering input in a program. *Text boxes* accept typed input, *menus* present commands that can be clicked or chosen with the keyboard, and *dialog boxes* offer a variety of elements that can be chosen individually or selected in a group. In this exercise, you'll learn to use four important controls that will help you gather input in several different situations. You'll learn about the RadioButton, CheckBox, ListBox, and ComboBox controls. You will explore each of these objects as you use a Visual Basic program called Input Controls, the user interface for a graphical ordering system. As you run the program, you'll get some hands-on experience with the input objects. In the next chapter, I'll discuss how these objects can be used along with menus in a full-fledged program.

As a simple experiment, try using the CheckBox control now to see how user input is processed on a form and in program code. Follow these steps:

Experiment with the CheckBox control

1 On the File menu, click Close Solution to close the Birthday project.

2 On the File menu, point to New, and then click Project.

   The New Project dialog box appears.

3 Create a new Visual Basic Windows Application project named **MyCheckBox** in the c:\vbnetsbs\chap03 folder.

   The new project is created and a blank form appears in the Windows Forms Designer.

CheckBox control

4 Click the CheckBox control in the Toolbox.

5 Draw two check box objects on the form, one above the other.

   Check boxes appear like objects on your form just as other objects do.

PictureBox control

6 Click the PictureBox control and draw two square picture box objects beneath the two check boxes.

7 Set the following properties for the check box and label objects:

Object	Property	Setting
CheckBox1	Checked	True
	Text	"Calculator"
CheckBox2	Text	"Copy machine"
PictureBox1	Image	c:\vbnetsbs\chap03\calcultr.bmp
	SizeMode	StretchImage
PictureBox2	SizeMode	StretchImage

In this demonstration program, you'll use the check boxes to display and hide images of a calculator and a copy machine. The Text property of the check box object determines the contents of the check box label in the user interface. The Checked property lets you set a default value for the check box. Setting Checked to True will place a check mark in the box, and setting Checked to False (the default setting) will remove the check mark. I use the SizeMode properties in the picture boxes to size the images so that they stretch to fit in the picture box.

Your form should look like this:

8   Double-click the first check box object to open the Code Editor for the CheckBox1_CheckedChanged event procedure, and then enter the following program code:

```
If CheckBox1.CheckState = 1 Then
    PictureBox1.Image = System.Drawing.Image.FromFile _
      ("c:\vbnetsbs\chap03\calcultr.bmp")
    PictureBox1.Visible = True
Else
    PictureBox1.Visible = False
End If
```

The CheckBox1_CheckChanged event procedure runs only if the user clicks in the first check box object. The event procedure uses an If...Then decision structure (described in Chapter 6) to check the current status, or "state," of the first check box, and it displays a calculator picture from the c:\vbnetsbs\chap03 folder if a check mark is in the box. The CheckState property holds a value of 1 if there is a check mark present and 0 if there is no check mark present. I use the Visible property to display the picture if a check mark is present or hide the picture if a check mark isn't present.

Notice that I wrapped the long line that loads the image into the picture box object by using the line continuation (_) character.

View Designer button

9 Click the View Designer button in Solution Explorer to display the form again, and then double-click the second check box and add the following code to the CheckBox2_CheckedChanged event procedure:

```
If CheckBox2.CheckState = 1 Then
    PictureBox2.Image = System.Drawing.Image.FromFile _
        ("c:\vbnetsbs\chap03\copymach.bmp")
    PictureBox2.Visible = True
Else
    PictureBox2.Visible = False
End If
```

The complete CheckBox program is located in the c:\vbnetsbs\ chap03\checkbox folder.

This event procedure is almost identical to the one that you just entered; only the names of the image (copymach.bmp), the check box object (CheckBox2), and the picture box object (PictureBox2) are different.

10 Click the Save All button on the Standard toolbar to save your changes.

Save All button

Run the CheckBox program

Start button

1 Click the Start button on the Standard toolbar.

Visual Basic runs the program in the development environment. Because you placed a check mark in the first check box, the calculator image appears on the form.

2 Click the Copy machine check box.

Visual Basic displays the copy machine image, as shown here:

![Form1 window showing Calculator and Copy Machine check boxes both checked, with a calculator image and a copy machine image displayed below them]

3 Experiment with different combinations of check boxes, clicking the boxes several times to test the program. The program logic you added with a few short lines of Visual Basic code manages the boxes perfectly. (You'll learn much more about program code in upcoming chapters.)

4   Click the Close button on the form to end the program.

The Input Controls Demo

Now that you've had a little experience with check boxes, run and examine the Input Controls demonstration program that I created to simulate an electronic ordering environment that makes more extensive use of check boxes, radio buttons, a list box, and a combo box. If you work in a business that does a lot of order entry, you might want to expand this into a full-featured graphical order entry program. After you experiment with Input Controls, spend some time learning how the four input controls work in the program. They were created in a few short steps by using Visual Basic and the techniques you just learned.

Run the Input Controls program

1   On the File menu, point to Open, and then click Project.

The Open Project dialog box appears.

2   Open the c:\vbnetsbs\chap03\input controls folder, and then double-click the Input Controls project file (Input Controls.vbproj).

The Input Controls project opens in the development environment.

View Designer button

3   If the project's form isn't visible, click the Form1.vb form in Solution Explorer and then click the View Designer button.

4   Move or close the windows that block your view of the form so that you can see how the objects are laid out.

You'll see a form similar to this:

The Online Shopper

Outfit your office now by choosing the office products you need using radio buttons, check boxes, a list box, and a combo box.

Products Ordered

Computer (required)
- PC
- Macintosh
- Laptop

Peripherals (one only)
ListBox1

Office Equipment (0-3)
- Answering Machine
- Calculator
- Copy machine

Payment Method

Quit

The Input Controls form contains radio button, check box, list box, combo box, picture box, button, and label objects. These objects work together to create a simple order entry program that demonstrates how the Visual Basic input objects work. When the Input Controls program is run, it loads images from the \vbnetsbs\chap03\input controls folder on drive C and displays them in the six picture boxes on the form.

tip

If you installed the practice files in a location other than the default c:\vbnetsbs folder, the statements in the program that load the artwork from the disk will contain an incorrect path. (Each statement begins with c:\vbnetsbs\chap03\input controls, as you'll see soon.) If this is the case, you can make the program work by renaming your practice files folder \vbnetsbs or by changing the paths in the Code Editor using the editing keys or the Find And Replace submenu on the Edit menu.

5   Click the Start button on the Standard toolbar.

The program runs in the development environment.

Start button

6   Click the Laptop radio button in the Computer box.

The image of a laptop computer appears in the Products Ordered area on the right side of the form. The user can click various options and the current choice is depicted in the order area on the right. In the Computer box, a group of *radio buttons* is used to gather input from the user. (Note: Radio buttons were called option buttons in Visual Basic 6.) Radio buttons force the user to choose one (and only one) item from a list of possibilities.

Radio buttons allow the user to select only one item from a list.

When radio buttons are placed inside a group box object on a form, the radio buttons are considered to be part of a group and only one option can be chosen. To create a group box, click the GroupBox control on the Windows Forms tab of the Toolbox, and then draw the control on your form. (The GroupBox control replaces the Frame control in Visual Basic 6.) You can give the group of radio buttons a title (as I have) by setting the Text property of the group box object. When you move a group box object on the form, the controls within it also move.

7   Click the Answering Machine, Calculator, and Copy Machine check boxes in the Office Equipment box.

Check boxes let the user select any number of items.

Check boxes are used in a program so that the user can select more than one option at a time from a list. Click the Calculator check box again, and notice that the picture of the calculator disappears from the order area. Because each user interface element is live and responds to click events as they occur, order choices are reflected immediately. The code that completes these tasks is nearly identical to the code you entered earlier in the CheckBox program.

8 Click Satellite Dish in the Peripherals list box.

List boxes let the user select one item from a variable-length list of choices.

A picture of a satellite dish is added to the order area. A *list box* is used to get a user's single response from a list of choices. List boxes are created with the ListBox control, and may contain many items to choose from (scroll bars appear if the list of items is longer than the list box). Unlike radio buttons, a default selection isn't required in a list box. In a Visual Basic program, items can be added to, removed from, or sorted in a list box while the program is running. If you would like to see check marks next to the items in your list box, use the CheckedListBox control in the Toolbox instead of the ListBox control.

9 Now choose U.S. Dollars (sorry, no credit) from the payment list in the Payment Method combo box.

Combo boxes take up less space than list boxes.

A *combo box,* or drop-down list box, is similar to a regular list box, but it takes up less space. (The "combo" in a combo box basically comes from a "combination" of an editable text box and a drop-down list.) Visual Basic automatically handles the opening, closing, and scrolling of the list box. All you do as a programmer is create the combo box using the ComboBox control in the Toolbox, set the Text property to provide directions or a default value, and then write code to add items to the combo box and to process the user's combo box selection. You'll see examples of each task in the program code for the Input Controls demonstration.

After you make your order selections, your screen should look something like this:

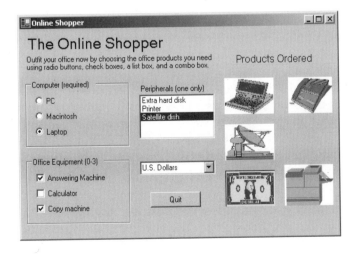

10 Practice making a few more changes to the order list in the program (try different computers, peripherals, and payment methods), and then click the Quit button in the program to exit.

The program closes when you click Quit, and the programming environment appears.

Looking at the Input Controls Program Code

Chapters 5, 6, and 7 discuss program code in detail.

Although you haven't had much formal experience with program code yet, it's worth taking a quick look at a few event procedures in Input Controls to see how the program processes input from the user interface elements. In these procedures, you'll see the If...Then and Select Case statements at work. You'll learn about these and other decision structures in Chapter 6. For now, concentrate on the CheckState property, which changes when a check box is selected, and the SelectedIndex property, which changes when a list box is selected.

Examine the check box code and the list box code

1 Be sure the program has stopped running, and then double-click the Answering Machine check box in the Office Equipment box to display the CheckBox1_CheckedChanged event procedure in the Code Editor.

You'll see the following program code:

```
'If the CheckState property for a check box is 1, it has a mark in it
If CheckBox1.CheckState = 1 Then
    PictureBox2.Image = System.Drawing.Image.FromFile _
      ("c:\vbnetsbs\chap03\input controls\answmach.bmp")
    PictureBox2.Visible = True
Else
    'If there is no mark, hide the image
    PictureBox2.Visible = False
End If
```

The first line of this event procedure is called a comment. Comments are displayed in green type and are simply notes written by the programmer to describe what is important or interesting about this particular piece of program code. (Comments are also occasionally generated by automated programming tools that compile programs or insert code snippets.) I wrote this comment to remind myself that the CheckState property contains a crucial value in this routine—a value of 1 if the first check box was checked.

The rest of the event procedure is nearly identical to the one you just wrote in the CheckBox program. If you scroll down in the Code Editor, you'll see a similar event procedure for the CheckBox2 and CheckBox3 objects.

2   At the top edge of the Code Editor, click the tab labeled "Form1.vb [Design]" to display the form again, and then double-click the Peripherals list box on the form.

The ListBox1_SelectedIndexChanged event procedure appears in the Code Editor. You'll see the following program statements:

```
'The item you picked (0-2) is held in the SelectedIndex property
Select Case ListBox1.SelectedIndex
    Case 0
        PictureBox3.Image = System.Drawing.Image.FromFile _
            ("c:\vbnetsbs\chap03\input controls\harddisk.bmp")
    Case 1
        PictureBox3.Image = System.Drawing.Image.FromFile _
            ("c:\vbnetsbs\chap03\input controls\printer.bmp")
    Case 2
        PictureBox3.Image = System.Drawing.Image.FromFile _
            ("c:\vbnetsbs\chap03\input controls\satedish.bmp")
End Select
```

Here you see code that executes when the user clicks an item in the Peripherals list box in the program. In this case, the important keyword is ListBox1.SelectedIndex, which is read "the SelectedIndex property of the first list box object." After the user clicks an item in the list box, the SelectedIndex property returns a number that corresponds to the location of the item in the list box. (The first item is numbered 0, the second item is numbered 1, and so on.)

In the previous code, SelectedIndex is evaluated by the Select Case decision structure, and a different image is loaded depending on the value of the SelectedIndex property. If the value is 0, a picture of a hard disk is loaded; if the value is 1, a picture of a printer is loaded; if the value is 2, a picture of a satellite dish is loaded. You'll learn more about how the Select Case decision structure works in Chapter 6.

3   At the top edge of the Code Editor, click the Form1.vb [Design] tab to display the form again, and then double-click the form (not any of the objects) to display the code associated with the form itself.

Statements in the Form1_Load event procedure run when the program starts.

The Form1_Load event procedure appears in the Code Editor. This is the procedure that is executed each time the Input Controls program starts, or *loads*. Programmers put program statements in this special procedure when they want them executed every time a form loads. (Your program can display more than one form, or none at all, but the default behavior is that Visual Basic loads and runs the Form1_Load event procedure each time the

3

Working with Controls

user runs the program.) Often, as in the Input Controls program, these statements define an aspect of the user interface that couldn't be created by using Toolbox controls or the Properties window.

Here is what the Form1_Load event procedure looks like for this program:

```
'These program statements run when the form loads
PictureBox1.Image = System.Drawing.Image.FromFile _
  ("c:\vbnetsbs\chap03\input controls\pcomputr.bmp")
'Add items to a list box like this:
ListBox1.Items.Add("Extra hard disk")
ListBox1.Items.Add("Printer")
ListBox1.Items.Add("Satellite dish")
'Combo boxes are also filled with the Add method:
ComboBox1.Items.Add("U.S. Dollars")
ComboBox1.Items.Add("Check")
ComboBox1.Items.Add("English Pounds")
```

Three lines in this event procedure are comments displayed in green type. The second line in the event procedure loads the personal computer image into the first picture box. (This line is broken in two using a space and the line continuation character, but the compiler still thinks of it as one line.) Loading an image establishes the default setting reflected in the Computer radio button group box. The next three lines add items to the Peripherals list box (ListBox1) in the program. The words in quotes will appear in the list box when it appears on the form. Below the list box program statements, the items in the Payment Method combo box (ComboBox1) are specified. The important keyword in both these groups is Add, which is a special function, or method, to add items to list box and combo box objects.

You're finished using the Input Controls program. Take a few minutes to examine any other parts of the program you're interested in, and then move on to the next exercise.

Using the LinkLabel Control

Providing access to the Web is now a standard feature of many Windows applications, and Visual Studio .NET makes adding this functionality easier than ever before. You can create sophisticated Web-aware applications using Web Forms and other technologies in Visual Studio, or you can open a simple Web page using your computer's Web browser using just a few lines of program code.

In this exercise, you'll learn to use the LinkLabel control to display text on a Visual Basic form that looks and acts just like an Internet link. The LinkLabel control is a new addition to Visual Basic, and when you combine it with the

Process.Start method, you can quickly open links on your form using Internet Explorer, Netscape Navigator, or another browser. Use the LinkLabel control now to connect to the Microsoft Press home page on the Internet.

> **tip**
> To learn more about writing Web-aware Visual Basic .NET applications, read Chapters 21-22.

Create the WebLink program

1   On the File menu, click Close Solution to close the Input Controls project.

2   On the File menu, point to New, and then click Project.

     The New Project dialog box appears.

3   Create a new Visual Basic Windows Application project named **MyWebLink** in the c:\vbnetsbs\chap03 folder.

     The new project is created and a blank form appears in the Windows Forms Designer.

LinkLabel control

4   Click the LinkLabel control in the Toolbox, and draw a rectangular link label object on your form.

     Link label objects look like label objects, except that all label text is displayed in blue underlined type on the form.

5   Set the Text property of the link label object to **www.microsoft.com/ mspress/** (the Web site for Microsoft Press).

     Your form will look like this:

     ![Form1 showing a link label with text www.microsoft.com/mspress/]

Working with Controls

3

6   Click the form in the development environment to select it. (The form itself, not the link label object.)

This is the technique you use to view the properties of the default form or Form1 in the Properties window. Like other objects in your project, the form also has properties that you can set.

7   Set the Text property of the form object to **Web Link Test**.

The Text property for a form controls what appears on the form's title bar when the program runs. Although this isn't customization related exclusively to the Web, I thought you'd enjoy picking up that skill now, before we move on to other projects. (We'll customize the title bar in most of the programs we build.)

8   Double-click the link label object, and type the following program code in the LinkLabel1_LinkClicked event procedure:

```
' Change the color of the link by setting LinkVisited to True.
LinkLabel1.LinkVisited = True
' Use the Process.Start method to open the default browser
' using the Microsoft Press URL:
System.Diagnostics.Process.Start _
  ("http://www.microsoft.com/mspress/")
```

I've included comments in the program code to give you some practice entering them. As soon as you enter the single quote character ('), Visual Studio changes the color of the line to green, identifying the line as a comment. Comments are for documentation purposes only—they aren't evaluated or executed by the compiler.

The two program statements that aren't comments actually control how the link works. Setting the LinkVisited property to True gives the link that dimmer color of purple which indicates in many browsers that the HTML document associated with the link has already been viewed. Although setting this property isn't necessary to display a Web page, it is good programming practice to provide the user with information that is consistent in other applications.

The second program statement (that was broken into two lines) runs the default Web browser (such as Internet Explorer) if the browser isn't already running. (If the browser is running, the URL just loads immediately.) The Start method in the Process class performs the important work, by starting a *process* or executable program session in memory for the browser. The Process class, which manages many other aspects of program execution, is a member of the System.Diagnostics object library, which Visual Basic .NET programmers called the System.Diagnostics namespace. By including an Internet address or *URL* along with the Start method, I'm letting Visual Basic know that I want to view a Web site, and Visual Basic is clever enough to know that the default system browser is the tool that would best display that URL, even though we didn't identify the browser by name.

An exciting feature of the Process.Start method is that it can be used to run other Windows applications, too. If I did want to identify a particular browser by name to open the URL, I could have specified one using the following syntax. (Here I'll request the Internet Explorer browser.)

```
System.Diagnostics.Process.Start("IExplore.exe", _
   "http://www.microsoft.com/mspress/")
```

Two arguments are used here with the Start method, separated by a comma. The exact location for the program named IExplore.exe on my system isn't specified, but Visual Basic will search the current system path for it when the program runs.

Or if I had wished to run a different application with the Start method, such as the application Microsoft Word (and open the document c:\myletter.doc), I could have used the following syntax:

```
System.Diagnostics.Process.Start("Winword.exe", _
   "c:\myletter.doc")
```

The complete WebLink program is located in the c:\vbnetsbs\ chap03\weblink folder.

Save All button

As you can see, the Start method in the Process class is very useful, and we'll make use of it again in this book. Now that you've entered your code, save your project and run it. (If you experimented with the Start syntax as I showed you, restore the original code shown at the beginning of step 8.)

9   Click the Save All button on the Standard toolbar to save your changes.

Run the WebLink program

Start button

1   Click the Start button on the Standard toolbar to run the WebLink program.

The form opens and runs, showing its Web site link and handsome title bar text.

2   Click the link to open the Web site shown (*www.microsoft.com/mspress/*).

Recall that it is only a happy coincidence that the link label Text property contains the same URL as the site you named in the program code. You may enter any text you like in the link label. You can also use the Image property for a link label to specify a picture to display in the background of the link label. Look on the following page to see what the Microsoft Press Web page looks like (in English) when the WebLink program displays it using Internet Explorer.

3   Display the form again. (Click the Web Link Test form icon on the Windows task bar if the form isn't visible.)

Notice that the link now appears in a dimmed style. Like a standard Web link, your link label communicates that it has been used (but is still active) by the color and intensity that it appears in.

4   Click the Close button on the form to quit the test utility.

You're finished writing code in this chapter.

One Step Further: Installing ActiveX Controls

Visual Studio .NET is a new product, so many developers will find that the current list of Windows Forms controls isn't as extensive as the ActiveX controls that were available to Visual Basic 6 programmers. If you want to expand the collection of controls that you have access to in Visual Studio .NET, you can load and use older ActiveX (COM) components and controls. These customizable programming tools were provided by Visual Basic 6, Visual C++ 6, Microsoft Office, and other third-party products. When you add older ActiveX controls to your Toolbox, Visual Studio displays them with the .NET controls, and you can use the ActiveX controls on your forms with few limitations. The only technical qualification is that Visual Studio must create a *wrapper* for the control, which makes the objects in the control usable in a .NET program. In most cases, Visual Studio .NET handles the creation of a control wrapper automatically when the ActiveX control is loaded.

> ## tip
> ActiveX controls on your computer typically have an .ocx or .dll filename extension. These library files are routinely added to your system when you install a new application program, and you can reuse them in your own programs if you can figure out how to use the objects, methods, and properties that they provide, or *expose*. Visual Studio .NET "learns" about the presence of new ActiveX controls when they are cataloged in the Windows system registry.

The Microsoft Chart Control

You probably have numerous ActiveX controls on your system now, especially if you have a previous version of Visual Basic or Microsoft Office on your system. Try installing one of the ActiveX controls now, even if you're not sure how to use it yet. (You'll start putting ActiveX controls to work later in the book, so you should learn the installation technique now.) The control you'll open in this exercise is the Microsoft Chart control, which allows you to build charts on your forms. The Microsoft Chart control is included in several versions of Microsoft Office. If you don't have Office or this control, pick another one.

Install the Chart control

1   If you still have the Code Editor open for the WebLink project, display the form.

2   Click the Toolbox, and open the tab to which you would like to add an ActiveX control. For example, click the Windows Forms tab.

   ActiveX controls are added to individual tabs in the Toolbox so that you can remember where they are. Once on a Toolbox tab, they look just like regular controls in Visual Studio .NET.

3   Click the Windows Forms tab again with the right mouse button, and then click the Customize Toolbox command on the pop-up menu.

   The Customize Toolbox dialog box opens.

4   Click the COM Components tab in the Customize Toolbox dialog box.

   You'll see a long list of ActiveX components and controls that is unique to your system. The components appear in alphabetical order.

5   Scroll to the Microsoft Office Chart 9.0 control, or another control that looks interesting, and then click the check box next to the control.

   Your dialog box will look similar to the illustration on the following page.

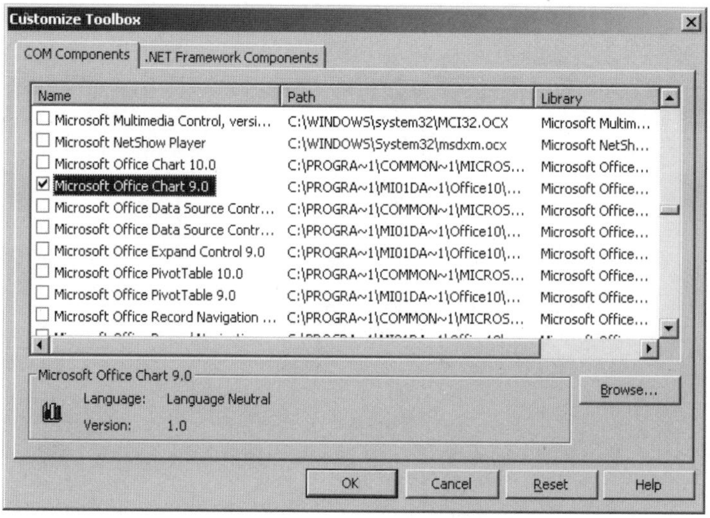

6   To add additional controls to the Toolbox, simply click check boxes next to the controls that you want.

> ## note
>
> Not all the components listed in the Customize Toolbox dialog box are designed to work in the Toolbox, so they may not work properly when you try to use them.

7   Click OK to add the selected ActiveX control (or controls) to this project's Toolbox.

The control will appear at the bottom of the Toolbox list. The control will appear for this project only and won't appear in other projects.

Down scroll arrow

8   Click the down scroll arrow in the Toolbox to see the newly added control as shown here:

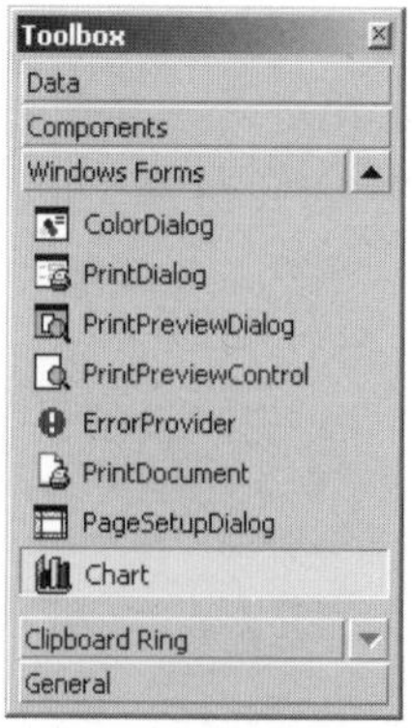

The Microsoft Office Chart ActiveX control is available in several different versions and is included with applications such as Office 2000 and Office XP. You'll find that most ActiveX controls work just like the standard controls in the Visual Basic .NET Toolbox. In fact, if you didn't know they were ActiveX controls, it would be difficult to tell them apart from the default controls in Visual Studio .NET. Each ActiveX control has adjustable property settings and methods that you can call just like the other controls you've used in this chapter.

Chapter 3 Quick Reference

To	Do this
Create a text box	Click the TextBox control, and draw the box.
Create a button	Click the Button control, and draw the button.
Change a property at runtime	Change the value of the property by using program code. For example: `Label1.Text = "Hello!"`
Create a radio button	Use the RadioButton control. To create multiple radio buttons, place more than one button object inside a box that you create by using the GroupBox control.
Create a check box	Click the CheckBox control, and draw a check box.
Create a list box	Click the ListBox control, and draw a list box.
Create a drop-down list box	Click the ComboBox control, and draw a drop-down list box.
Add items to a list box	Include statements with the Add method in the Form1_Load event procedure of your program. For example: `ListBox1.Items.Add "Printer"`
Display a Web page	Create a link to the Web page using the LinkLabel control, and then open the link in a browser using the Process.Start method in program code.
Install ActiveX controls	Right click the Toolbox tab that you want to place the control in, and then click the Customize Toolbox command. Click the COM Components tab, place a check mark next to the ActiveX control that you want to install, and then click OK.

Working with Menus and Dialog Boxes

In this chapter you will learn how to:

✔ *Add menus to your programs by using the MainMenu control.*

✔ *Process menu choices by using program code.*

✔ *Use the OpenFileDialog and ColorDialog controls to display special-purpose dialog boxes.*

In Chapter 3, you used several Microsoft Visual Studio controls to gather input from the user while he or she was using a program. In this chapter, you'll learn to present choices to the user by using professional-looking menus and dialog boxes. A *menu* is located on the menu bar and contains a list of related commands. When you click a menu title, a list of the menu commands appears in a drop-down list. Most menu commands are executed immediately after they are clicked; for example, when the user clicks the Copy command on the Edit menu, information is copied to the Clipboard immediately. If a menu command is followed by an ellipsis (…), however, Visual Basic displays a dialog box requesting more information before the command is carried out. In this chapter, you'll learn to use the MainMenu control and two dialog box controls to add menus and standard dialog boxes to your programs.

Upgrade Notes: What's New in Visual Basic .NET?

If you're experienced with Visual Basic 6, you'll notice some new features in Visual Basic .NET, including the following:

- Menus are no longer created using the Visual Basic 6 Menu Editor tool. Instead, you create a main menu object on your form using the MainMenu control, and then customize the object using property settings and the Menu Designer. However, menu choices are still processed with program code.

- Standard dialog boxes are no longer created using the Common-Dialog control. Instead, you use one of seven Windows Forms controls that add standard dialog boxes to your project. These controls include OpenFileDialog, SaveFileDialog, FontDialog, ColorDialog, PrintDialog, PrintPreviewDialog, and PageSetupDialog.

- Forms now feature the ShowDialog method and the DialogResult property, making it easier to create custom forms that look and act like standard dialog boxes.

Adding Menus Using the MainMenu Control

The MainMenu control is a tool that adds menus to your programs and allows you to customize them with property settings in the Properties window. With the control, you can add new menus, modify and reorder existing menus, and delete old menus. You also can add special effects to your menus, such as access keys, check marks, and keyboard shortcuts. After you have added menus to your form, you can use event procedures to process the menu commands. In the following exercise, you'll use the MainMenu control to create a Clock menu containing commands that display the current date and time.

Create a menu

1   Start Visual Studio.

2   On the File menu, point to New, and then click Project.

The New Project dialog box appears.

3   Create a new Visual Basic Windows Application project named **MyMenu** in the c:\vbnetsbs\chap04 folder.

MainMenu control

4   Click the MainMenu control on the Windows Forms tab of the Toolbox, and draw a menu control on your form.

Don't worry about the location—Visual Studio will move the control and resize it automatically. Your screen will look like this:

Menu Designer

Component tray

The main menu object doesn't appear on your form, but below it. That's different from previous versions of Visual Basic, which in one way or another displayed all objects on the form itself—even ones that didn't have a visual representation when the program ran, such as the Timer control. But in Visual Studio .NET, non-visible objects such as menus and timers are displayed on a separate pane, named the component tray, in the development environment, and you can select them, set their properties, or delete them right from this pane.

In addition to the main menu object in the component tray, Visual Studio .NET displays a visual representation of the menu you created at the top of the form. The tag "Type Here" encourages you to click the tag and enter the title of your menu right now. After you enter the first menu title, you can enter submenu titles and other menu names by pressing the arrow keys and typing additional names. Best of all, you can come back to this in-line Menu Designer later and edit what you have done or add additional menu items—the main menu object is fully customizable and allows you to create an exciting menu-driven user interface like the ones you've seen in the best Windows applications.

5   Click the Type Here tag, type **Clock**, and then press Enter.

The word "Clock" is entered as the name of your first menu, and two additional Type Here tags appear, allowing you to create submenu items below the new Clock menu or additional menu titles. The submenu item is currently selected.

tip

If the menu disappears from the form, click MainMenu1 in the component tray and the menu on the form should reappear.

6   Type **Date** to create a new Date command for the Clock menu, and then press Enter.

Visual Studio adds the Date command to the menu and selects the next submenu item.

7   Type **Time** to create a new Time command for the menu, and then press Enter.

You now have a Clock menu with two menu commands, Date and Time. You could continue to create additional menus or commands, but what you've done is sufficient for this example program. Your form will look like this:

8   Click the form to close the Menu Designer.

The Menu Designer closes, and your form appears in the development environment with no Clock menu. So where did the Clock menu go? The Clock menu is there, but it isn't currently visible—you need to click the Clock menu again to see the menus and work with them.

9 Click the Clock menu on the form.

The Clock menu appears again, along with the familiar Type Here tags. You're ready to start customizing the menu now.

Adding Access Keys to Menu Commands

Most applications allow you to access and execute menu commands using the keyboard. For example, in Visual Studio you can open the File menu by pressing the Alt key and then pressing the F key. Once the File menu is open, you can execute the Print command by pressing the P key. The key that you press in addition to the Alt key and the key that you press to execute a command in an open menu is called the *access key*. You can identify the access key in a menu item because it is underlined.

You define an access key by placing an ampersand (&) before the letter.

Visual Studio makes it easy to provide access key support. To add an access key to a menu item, activate the Menu Designer and type an ampersand (&) before the appropriate letter in the menu name. When you open the menu at runtime (when the program is running), your program will automatically support the access key.

> **tip**
>
> By default, Windows 2000 doesn't display the underline for access keys for a program until you press the Alt key for the first time. You can turn off this option on the Effects tab of the Display control panel.

Try adding access keys to the Clock menu now.

Menu Conventions

By convention, each menu title and menu command in an application for Microsoft Windows has an initial capital letter. File and Edit are often the first two menu names on the menu bar, and Help is the last. Other common menu names are View, Format, and Window. No matter what menus and commands you use in your applications, take care to be clear and consistent with them. Menus and commands should be easy to use and should have as much in common with those in other Windows-based applications as possible. As you create menu items, use the following guidelines:

- Use short, specific captions consisting of one or two words at most.
- Assign each menu item an access key. Use the first letter of the item if possible.
- Menu items at the same level must have a unique access key.
- If a command is used as an on/off toggle, place a check mark next to the item when it is active. You can add a check mark by setting the Checked property of the menu command to True using the Properties window.
- Place an ellipsis (…) after a menu command that requires the user to enter more information before the command can be executed. The ellipsis indicates that you will open a dialog box if the user selects this item.

Add access keys

1 Click the Clock menu name on the form, and then click it again.

   A blinking text-editing cursor appears in the Clock menu name. The text-editing cursor allows you to edit your menu name or add the ampersand character (&) for an access key.

2 Press the Left Arrow key to move the text-editing cursor to the beginning of the Clock menu name.

   The cursor blinks before the letter "C" in *Clock*.

3 Type **&** to define the letter "C" as the access key for the Clock menu.

   An ampersand appears in the text box in front of the word Clock.

4 Click the Date command in the menu list, and then click Date a second time to display the text-editing cursor.

5   Type an ampersand before the letter "D".

The letter "D" is now defined as the access key for the Date command.

6   Click the Time command in the menu list, and then click the command a second time to display the text-editing cursor.

7   Type an ampersand before the letter "T".

The letter "T" is now defined as the access key for the Time command.

8   Press Enter.

Pressing Enter locks in your text-editing changes. Your form will look like this:

Now you'll practice using the Menu Designer to switch the order of the Date and Time commands on the Clock menu. Changing the order of menu items is an important skill to have; at times you'll think of a better way to define your menus.

Change the order of menu items

1   Click the Clock menu on the form to display its menu items.

Changing the order of menu items is very easy. You simply drag the menu item that you want to move to a new location on the menu. Try it now.

2   Drag the Time menu on top of the Date menu, and then release the mouse button.

Dragging one menu item on top of a second menu item means that you want to place the first menu item ahead of the second menu item on the menu. As quick as that, Visual Studio moved the Time menu item ahead of the Date item.

You've finished creating the user interface for the Clock menu. Now you'll use the menu event procedures to process the user's menu selections in the program.

tip
To delete an unwanted menu item from a menu, click the unwanted item in the menu list and then press the Delete key.

Processing Menu Choices

After menus and commands are configured using the main menu object, they also become new objects in your program. To make the menu objects do meaningful work, you need to write event procedures for them. Menu event procedures typically contain program statements that display or process information on the user interface form and modify one or more menu properties. If more information is needed from the user to process the selected command, an event procedure will often display a dialog box by using one of the Windows Forms dialog box controls or one of the input controls you used in Chapter 3.

In the following exercise, you'll add a label object to your form to display the output of the Time and Date commands on the Clock menu.

Add a label object to the form

Label control

1 Click the Label control in the Toolbox.

2 Draw a medium-sized label in the middle area of the form.

The label object appears on the form and will bear the name Label1 in the program code.

3 Set the following properties for the label:

Object	Property	Setting
Label1	BorderStyle	FixedSingle
	Font	Microsoft Sans Serif, Bold, 14-point
	Text	(empty)
	TextAlign	MiddleCenter

Set Label1 properties by using the Properties window.

Your form should look like this:

tip

In the following exercises, you'll enter program code to process menu choices. It's OK if you're still a bit hazy on what program codes does and how you use it—you'll learn much more about program statements in Chapters 5 through 7.

Now you'll add program statements to the Time and Date event procedures to process the menu commands.

Edit the menu event procedures

1   Click the Clock menu on the form to display its submenus.

2   Double-click the Time command in the menu to open an event procedure for the command in the Code Editor.

The MenuItem3_Click event procedure appears in the Code Editor. The name MenuItem3_Click means that Time was the third menu item you created in this project (following Clock and Date), and the _Click syntax means that this is the event procedure that runs when a user clicks the menu item. We'll keep this menu name for now, but I wanted to point out to you that it isn't really that intuitive to use. You can create your own names for objects that describe their function in the program a little more specifically by using the Name property. Although I don't bother with that extra step in the first few exercises, later in the chapter you'll create menu names to establish more understandable and professional programming practices.

3   Type the following program statement:

```
Label1.Text = TimeString
```

This program statement displays the current time (from the system clock) in the Text property of the Label1 object, replacing the previous Label1 text (if any). TimeString is a property that contains the current time formatted for display or printing; you can use TimeString at any time in your programs to display the time accurately down to the second. (TimeString is essentially a replacement for the older QuickBASIC TIME$ statement.)

tip

Visual Basic's TimeString property returns the current system time. You can set the system time by using the Date/Time icon in Windows Control Panel; you can change the system time format by using Control Panel's Regional Settings (or Regional Options) icon.

4   Press the Down Arrow key.

Visual Basic interprets the line and adjusts capitalization and spacing, if necessary. (Visual Basic checks each line for syntax errors as you enter it. You can enter a line by pressing Enter, Up Arrow, or Down Arrow.)

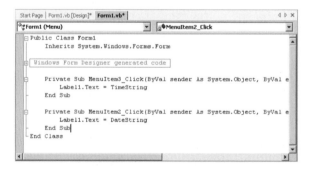

View Designer button

5   Click the View Designer button in Solution Explorer, and then double-click the Date command on the Clock menu.

The MenuItem2_Click event procedure appears in the Code Editor. This event procedure is executed when the user clicks the Date command on the Clock menu.

6   Type the following program statement:

```
Label1.Text = DateString
```

This program statement displays the current date (from the system clock) in the Text property of the Label1 object, replacing the previous Label1 text. The DateString property is also available for general use in your programs. Assign DateString to the Text property of an object whenever you want to display the current date on a form.

tip
Visual Basic's DateString property returns the current system date. You can set the system date by using the Date/Time icon in Control Panel; you can change the system date format by using Control Panel's Regional Settings (or Regional Options) icon.

7   Press the Down Arrow key to enter the line.

Your screen should look like this:

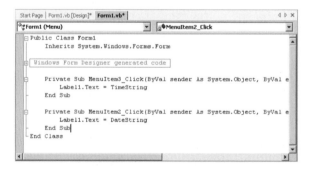

You've finished entering the menu demonstration program. Now you'll save your changes to the project and prepare to run it.

Save All button

8   Click the Save All button on the Standard toolbar.

Run the Menu program

Start button

1   Click the Start button on the Standard toolbar.

The Menu program runs in the development environment.

The complete Menu program is located in the c:\vbnetsbs\ chap04\menu folder.

2   Click the Clock menu on the menu bar.

The Clock menu appears.

3   Click the Time command.

The current system time appears in the label box, as shown here:

```
Form1                    _ □ ×
Clock


        ┌─────────────────┐
        │    13:01:11     │
        └─────────────────┘
```

Now you'll try displaying the current date by using the access keys on the menu.

4   Press and release the Alt key.

The Clock menu on the menu bar is highlighted.

5   Press C to display the Clock menu.

The contents of the Clock menu appear.

6   Press D to display the current date.

The current date appears in the label box.

7   Click the Close button on the program's title bar to stop the program.

Congratulations! You've created a working program that makes use of menus and access keys. In the next exercise, you'll learn how to use menus to display standard dialog boxes.

System Clock Properties and Functions

You can use various properties and functions to retrieve chronological values from the system clock. You can use these values to create custom calendars, clocks, and alarms in your programs. The following table lists the most useful system clock functions. For more information, check the Visual Studio online Help.

Property or Function	Description
TimeString	This property returns the current time from the system clock.
DateString	This property returns the current date from the system clock.
Now	This property returns an encoded value representing the current date and time. This property is most useful as an argument for other system clock functions.
Hour (*time*)	This function returns the hour portion of the specified time (0 through 23).
Minute (*time*)	This function returns the minute portion of the specified time (0 through 59).
Second (*time*)	This function returns the second portion of the specified time (0 through 59).
Day (*date*)	This function returns a whole number representing the day of the month (1 through 31).
Month (*date*)	This function returns a whole number representing the month (1 through 12).
Year (*date*)	This function returns the year portion of the specified date.
Weekday (*date*)	This function returns a whole number representing the day of the week (1 is Sunday, 2 is Monday, and so on).

Using Dialog Box Controls

Visual Studio contains seven standard dialog box controls on the Windows Forms tab of the Toolbox. These are provided ready-made so that you don't need to create your own custom dialog boxes for the most common tasks in

Windows applications, such as opening files, saving files, and printing. In many cases, you'll still need to write the program code that connects these dialog boxes to your program, but the user interfaces are built for you and conform to the standards for common use among Windows applications.

The seven standard dialog box controls available to you are listed in the following table. In many respects they are parallel to the objects provided by the CommonDialog control in Visual Basic 6, with a few important exceptions. The PrintPreviewControl control isn't listed here, but you'll find it useful if you use the PrintPreviewDialog control.

Control Name	Purpose
OpenFileDialog	Get the drive, folder name, and filename for an existing file
SaveFileDialog	Get the drive, folder name, and filename for a new file
FontDialog	Let the user choose a new font type and style
ColorDialog	Let the user select a color from a palette
PrintDialog	Let the user set printing options
PrintPreviewDialog	Display a print preview dialog box like Microsoft Word does
PageSetupDialog	Let the user control page setup options, such as margins, paper size, and layout

In the following exercises, you'll add a new menu to the Menu program and practice using the OpenFileDialog and ColorDialog controls. You may either use your existing Menu project or load the Menu project from the practice files folder if you didn't create it from scratch. (The completed version I've named Dialog, to preserve both projects on disk.)

Add OpenFileDialog and ColorDialog controls

1   If you didn't create the Menu project, click the File menu, point to Open, and then click Project, select the Menu project in the c:\vbnetsbs\chap04\menu folder, and then click Open. If the form isn't open, double-click Form1.vb in Solution Explorer to display the form.

Start your upgrades to this program by adding two dialog box controls to the component tray that contains the main menu object. The OpenFileDialog control will let your program open bitmap files, and the ColorDialog control will enable your program to change the color of the clock output. Dialog box controls appear in the component tray because they don't appear on the form at runtime.

OpenFileDialog control

2 Click the OpenFileDialog control on the Windows Forms tab of the Toolbox, and then click the component tray containing the main menu object.

> **tip**
> If you don't see the OpenFileDialog in the Toolbox, it may be lower in the Toolbox list hidden from your view. To scroll down in the Toolbox list, click the down scroll arrow next to the Clipboard Ring tab.

Down scroll arrow

An open file dialog object appears in the component tray.

ColorDialog control

3 Click the ColorDialog control on the Windows Forms tab of the Toolbox, and then click the component tray below the form again.

The component tray now looks like this:

Just like the main menu object, the open file dialog and color dialog objects can be customized with property settings.

Now you'll create a picture box object by using the PictureBox control. As you've seen, the picture box object displays artwork on a form. This time, you'll display artwork in the picture box by using the open file dialog box.

Add a picture box object

PictureBox control

1 Click the PictureBox control in the Toolbox.

2 Draw a picture box object on the form, below the label.

3 Use the Properties window to set the SizeMode property of the picture box to StretchImage.

Now you'll use the Menu Designer to add a File menu to the program.

Add a File menu

1 Click the Clock menu on the form, and then click the Type Here tag to the right of the menu.

Now you'll add to the program a File menu that includes Open, Close, and Exit commands.

2 Type **&File** to create a File menu with the letter "F" as an access key.

3   Press the Down Arrow key, and then type **&Open...** to create an Open... command with the letter "O" as an access key.

The Open command will be used to open Windows bitmaps. Because the command will display a dialog box, you added an ellipsis to the command name.

4   Press the Down Arrow key, and then type **&Close** to create a Close command with the letter "C" as an access key.

The Close command will be used to close open bitmap files in your program.

5   Press the Down Arrow key, and then type **E&xit** to create an Exit command with the letter "x" as an access key.

The Exit command will be used to close the program. Notice that in this case the second letter of the Exit command was used as an access key, which matches how Exit is used in most Windows applications (such as Microsoft Word).

6   Drag the File menu on top of the Clock menu to move it to the first position.

You can move entire menus, as well as menu commands, with the Menu Designer. It makes sense to have the File menu be the first menu in your program.

Your form should look like this:

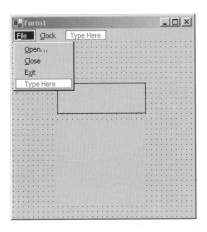

Changing the Object Names for Items on the File Menu

As I mentioned earlier in the chapter, you can change the name of objects on your form, including the names of menu item objects, by changing the Name property for each object that you want. The Name property doesn't change how an object looks at runtime, or what it displays for the user to see, but it does make objects more readable and recognizable in your program code. Practice changing the names of the objects on the new File menu now so that you can recognize them more clearly in your program code. In future chapters, you'll routinely change the names of the objects you use often.

Change the object names

1 Click the File menu item, open the Properties window, and change the Name property to **mnuFile**. (The Name property appears in the Design category and is surrounded with parentheses.)

Most programmers begin the names of their objects with a three-character extension that identifies what control or object library the object is related to or derived from. I've used *mnu* here to identify this object as a menu item, and I've used the word *File* to remind myself that the object is the File menu on the menu bar. Later you'll use other three-character extensions to identify different types of objects.

2 Click the Open… menu item, and change its Name property to **mnuOpenItem**.

3 Click the Close menu item, and change its Name property to **mnuCloseItem**.

4 Click the Exit menu item, and change its Name property to **mnuExitItem**.

5 Click the Save All button on the Standard toolbar to save your changes.

Save All button

These names will make your program easier to understand, and you can name the other objects in your project now if you like. (Good candidates would be the label object, the picture box object, and the other menu items.) But as I indicated, naming objects is optional, and the three-character prefix I recommended for menus is just an industry convention that some Visual Basic programmers follow.

Disabling a Menu Command

In a typical application for Windows, not all menu commands are available at the same time. In a typical Edit menu, for example, the Paste command is available only when there is data on the Clipboard. You can disable a menu item by setting the Enabled property for the menu object to False. When a command is disabled, it appears in dimmed type on the menu bar.

In the following exercise, you'll disable the Close command on the File menu. (Close is a command that can be used only after a file has been opened in the program.) Later in the chapter, you'll include a statement in the Open command event procedure that enables the Close command at the proper time.

Disable the Close command

1   Click the Close command on the Menu program's File menu.

2   Open the Properties window, and set the Enabled property for the
mnuCloseItem object to False.

Now you'll add a Text Color command to the Clock menu to demonstrate how
the color dialog box works. The color dialog box returns a color setting to the
program through the Color property. You'll use that property to change the
color of the text in the Label1 object.

Add the Text Color command to the Clock menu

1   Click the Clock menu, and then click the Type Here tag at the bottom of it.

2   Type **Text Co&lor...** to add a Text Color command to the menu with an
access key of "l".

The command Text Color is added to the Clock menu. The command contains a trailing ellipsis to indicate that it will display a dialog box when the
user clicks it. The access key chosen for this command is "L" because "T" is
already used in the menu, for Time. Your access keys won't behave correctly
if you use duplicate keys at the same level within a particular menu or duplicate keys at the menu bar level.

3   Use the Properties window to change the Name property of the Text Color
command to **mnuTextColorItem**.

Event Procedures That
Manage Common Dialog Boxes

To display a dialog box in a program, you need to type the dialog box name
with the ShowDialog method in an event procedure associated with the menu
command. If necessary, you must also set one or more dialog box properties using
program code before opening the dialog box. Finally, you need to use program
code to respond to the user's dialog box selections after the dialog box has been
manipulated and closed.

In the following exercise, you'll type in the program code for the mnuOpenItem_
Click event procedure, the routine that executes when the Open command is
clicked. You'll set the Filter property in the OpenFileDialog1 object to define the
file type in the Open common dialog box. (You'll specify Windows bitmaps.)
Then you'll use the ShowDialog method to display the open file dialog box. After
the user has selected a file and closed this dialog box, you'll display the file he or

she selects in a picture box by setting the Image property of the picture box object to the filename the user selected. Finally you'll enable the Close command so that the user can unload the picture if he or she wants.

Edit the Open command event procedure

1   Double-click the Open command on the Menu project's File menu.

The mnuOpenItem_Click event procedure appears in the Code Editor.

2   Type the following program statements in the event procedure, between the Private Sub and End Sub statements. Be sure to type each line exactly as it is printed here, and press the Down arrow key after the last line.

```
OpenFileDialog1.Filter = "Bitmaps (*.bmp)|*.bmp"
If OpenFileDialog1.ShowDialog() = DialogResult.OK Then
    PictureBox1.Image = System.Drawing.Image.FromFile _
        (OpenFileDialog1.FileName)
    mnuCloseItem.Enabled = True
End If
```

Your screen should look like the illustration shown here:

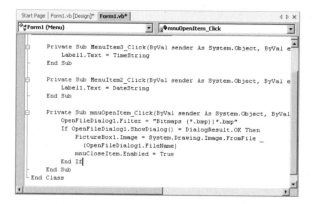

The first three statements in the event procedure refer to three different properties of the open file dialog object. The first statement uses the Filter property to define a list of valid files. (In this case, the list has only one item: *.bmp.) This is important for the Open dialog box because a picture box object is designed for six types of files: bitmaps (.bmp files), Windows metafiles (.emf and .wmf files), icons (.ico files), Joint Photographic Experts Group format (.jpg and .jpeg files), Portable Network Graphics format (.png files), and Graphics Interchange Format (.gif files). (Attempting to display a .txt file in an image object would cause a runtime error, for example.)

The Filter property defines the file types that will be listed in the Open dialog box.

To add additional items to the Filter list, you can type a pipe symbol (|) between items. For example,

```
OpenFileDialog1.Filter = "Bitmaps (*.bmp)|*.bmp|Metafiles (*.wmf)|*.wmf"
```

allows both bitmaps and Windows metafiles to be chosen in the Open dialog box.

The second statement in the event procedure displays the Open dialog box in the program. ShowDialog is a new method in Visual Basic .NET—it is similar to the Show method in Visual Basic 6, but it can be used with any Windows Form. The ShowDialog method returns a result, named DialogResult, which indicates the button on the dialog box the user clicked. To determine whether the user clicked the Open button, an If...Then decision structure is used to check whether the returned result equals DialogResult.OK. If it does, then a valid bmp file path should be stored in the FileName property of the open file dialog object. (You'll learn more about the syntax of If...Then decision structures in Chapter 6.)

The third statement uses the filename selected in the dialog box by the user. When the user selects a drive, folder, and filename and then clicks Open, the complete path is passed to the program through the OpenFileDialog1.FileName property. The System.Drawing.Image.FromFile method, a method that loads electronic artwork, is then used to copy the specified Windows bitmap into the picture box object. (I wrapped this statement with the line continuation character because it was rather long.)

The fourth statement in the procedure enables the Close command on the File menu. Now that a file has been opened in the program, the Close command should be available so that users can close the file.

Now you'll type in the program code for the mnuCloseItem_Click event procedure, the routine that runs when the Close command on the File menu is clicked.

Edit the Close command event procedure

1   Display the form again, and then double-click the Close command on the File menu.

    The event procedure for the Close command appears in the Code Editor.

2   Type the following program statements in the event procedure, between the Private Sub and End Sub statements.

Use the Nothing keyword to clear the Image property of the picture box object.

```
PictureBox1.Image = Nothing
mnuCloseItem.Enabled = False
```

The first statement closes the open Windows bitmap by clearing the picture box object's Image property. The Nothing keyword is used here to disassociate the current bitmap object from the Image property—in other words, Nothing sets the property to zero, and the picture disappears. (You'll use Nothing later in this book to reset other object variables and properties too.) The second statement dims the Close command on the File menu because there is no longer an open file. This program statement is the equivalent to using the Properties window to change the Enabled property from True to False.

Now you'll type in the program code for the mnuExitItem_Click event procedure, the routine that stops the program when the Exit command on the File menu is clicked.

Edit the Exit command event procedure

1   Display the form again, and then double-click the Exit command on the File menu.

    The event procedure for the Exit command appears in the Code Editor.

2   Type the following program statement in the event procedure, between the Private Sub and End Sub statements:

```
End
```

    The End statement stops the program when the user is finished. (It might look familiar by now.)

Edit the Text Color command event procedure

1   Display the form again, and then double-click the new Text Color command on the Clock menu.

    The event procedure for the Text Color command appears in the Code Editor.

2   Type the following program statements in the event procedure:

```
ColorDialog1.ShowDialog()
Label1.ForeColor = ColorDialog1.Color
```

tip

The Color dialog box can be used to set the color of any user interface element that supports color. Other possibilities include the form background color, the colors of shapes on the form, and the foreground and background colors of objects.

The first program statement uses the ShowDialog method to open the color dialog box. As you learned earlier in this chapter, ShowDialog is the method you use to open any form as a dialog box, including a form created by one of the standard dialog box controls that Visual Studio provides. The second statement in the event procedure assigns color that the user selected in the dialog box to the ForeColor property of the Label1 object. You might remember Label1 from earlier in this chapter—it's the label box you used to display the current time and date on the form. You'll use the color returned from the color dialog box to set the color of the text in the label.

3   Click the Save All button on the Standard toolbar to save your changes.

Save All button

Controlling Color Choices by Setting Color Dialog Box Properties

If you want to further customize the color dialog box, you can control just what color choices the dialog box presents to the user when the dialog box opens. You can adjust these color settings by using the Properties window, or by setting properties using program code before you display the dialog box with the ShowDialog method. The following table describes the most useful properties of the ColorDialog control. Each property should be set with a value of True to enable the option, or False to disable the option.

Property	Meaning
AllowFullOpen	Set to True to enable the Define Custom Colors button in the dialog box.
AnyColor	Set to True if the user can select any color shown in the dialog box.
FullOpen	Set to True if you want to display the Custom Colors area when the dialog box first opens.
ShowHelp	Set to True if you want to enable the Help button in the dialog box.
SolidColorOnly	Set to True if you only want the user to select solid colors (dithered colors will be disabled).

Now you'll run the Menu program and experiment with the menus and dialog boxes you've created.

Run the Menu program

▶

Start button

1   Click the Start button on the Standard toolbar.

The program runs, and both the File and Clock menus appear on the menu bar.

The complete program is named Dialog, and is located in the c:\vbnetsbs\ chap04\dialog folder.

2   On the form's File menu, click Open.

The Open dialog box appears. It looks great, doesn't it? Notice the Bitmaps (*.bmp) entry in the Files Of Type box. You defined this entry with the statement

```
OpenFileDialog1.Filter = "Bitmaps (*.bmp)|*.bmp"
```

in the mnuOpenItem_Click event procedure. The first part of the text in quotes—Bitmaps (*.bmp)—specifies which items are listed in the Files Of Type box. The second part—*.bmp—specifies the filename extension of the files that are to be listed in the dialog box.

3   Open the c:\windows folder (or c:\winnt folder) on your hard disk, and browse through the long list of folders to get to the bitmap files.

A standard collection of bitmaps appears. Most of these files were included with Windows, and you may have added to the collection yourself.

4   Select one of the bitmap files and then click the Open button.

A picture of the bitmap appears in the picture box. (I've selected the FeatherTexture.bmp file.) Your form looks like this:

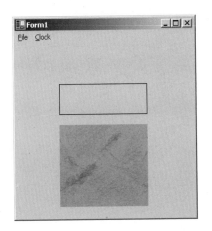

Now you'll practice using the Clock menu.

5   On the Clock menu, click the Time command.

The current time appears in the label box.

6   On the Clock menu, click the Text Color command.

The Color dialog box appears, as shown here:

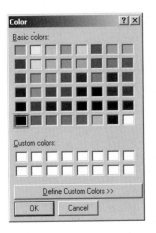

The Color dialog box contains elements that let you change the color of the clock text in your program. The current color setting, black, is selected.

7   Click the blue box, and then click the OK button.

The Color dialog box closes, and the color of the text in the clock label changes to blue.

8   On the Clock menu, click the Date command.

The current date is displayed in blue type. Now that the text color has been set in the label, it will remain blue until the color is changed again or the program closes.

9   Click the File menu.

Notice that the Close command is now enabled. (You enabled it in the mnuOpenItem_Click event procedure by using the statement mnuCloseItem.Enabled = True.)

10   Press **C** (the access key for Close) to close the bitmap image.

The file closes, and the Windows bitmap is removed. (This is the Nothing keyword at work.)

11   Click the File menu.

The Close command is now dimmed because there is no bitmap in the picture box.

12   Click the Exit command.

The program closes, and the Visual Studio development environment appears.

Adding Nonstandard Dialog Boxes to Programs

What if you need to add a dialog box to your program that isn't provided by one of the seven dialog box controls in Visual Studio? No problem—but you'll need to do a little extra design work. As you'll learn in future chapters, a Visual Basic program can use more than one form to receive and display information. To create nonstandard dialog boxes, you'll need to add new forms to your program, add input and output objects, and process the dialog box clicks in your program code. (These techniques will be discussed in Chapter 15.) In the next chapter, you'll learn how to use two handy dialog boxes that are specifically designed for receiving text input (InputBox) and displaying text output (MsgBox). These dialog boxes will help bridge the gap between the dialog box controls and the dialog boxes that you need to create on your own.

That's it! You've learned several important commands and techniques for creating menus and dialog boxes in your programs. After you learn more about program code, you'll be able to put these skills to work in your own programs.

One Step Further: Assigning Shortcut Keys to Menus

The MainMenu control also lets you assign *shortcut keys* to your menus. Shortcut keys are key combinations that a user can press to activate a command without using the menu bar. For example, on a typical Edit menu in an application for Windows (Microsoft Word), you can copy selected text to the Clipboard by pressing Ctrl+C. The MainMenu control's Shortcut property allows you to customize this setting. Try assigning two shortcut keys to the Clock menu in the Menu program now.

Assign shortcut keys to the Clock menu

1   Make sure that your program has stopped running, and is in design mode.

     You can modify a program only when it isn't running.

2   Click the Clock menu, and then click the Time command to highlight it.

Before you set the shortcut key for a menu command, you must select it. You assign a shortcut key by setting the Shortcut property for the command using the Properties window. The main menu object provides many standard shortcut key settings for you automatically.

You'll assign Ctrl+T as the shortcut key for the Time command.

3   Open the Properties window, click the Shortcut property, click the drop-down arrow in second column, scroll down the list of shortcut key settings, and then click CtrlT.

The Properties window will look like this:

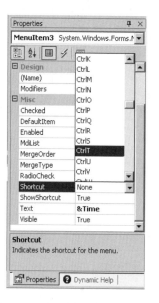

> ## tip
> Visual Basic normally displays the shortcut key combination in the menu when you run the program, to give users a hint about which keys to press. To hide shortcut key combinations from the user (if you are running out of space), set the ShowShortcut property to False. The shortcut key will still work, but users won't see a visual reminder for it.

4 Click the Date command, and then change its Shortcut property setting to CtrlD.

Now you'll run the program and try the shortcut keys.

5 Click the Start button on the Standard toolbar.

6 Press Ctrl+T to run the Time command.

The current time appears in the program.

7 Press Ctrl+D to run the Date command.

The current date appears in the program.

8 Click the Clock menu.

The shortcut keys are listed beside the Time and Date commands, as shown in the following illustration. Visual Basic adds these key combinations when you define the shortcuts by using the Shortcut property.

Start button

9 On the program's File menu, click the Exit command.

The program stops, and the development environment appears.

Chapter 4 Quick Reference

To	Do this
Create a menu item	Click the MainMenu control, and draw a menu on your form. Click the Type Here tag on your form, and type the name of the menu.
Add an access key to a menu item	Click the menu item twice to display the text editing cursor, and then type an ampersand (&) before the letter you want to use as an access key.
Assign a shortcut key to a menu item	Set the Shortcut property of the menu item using the Properties window. A list of common shortcut keys is provided.
Change the order of menu items	Drag the menu item you want to move to a new location.
Use a standard dialog box in your program	Add one of the seven standard dialog box controls to your form, and then customize it with property settings and program code.
Display an open file dialog box	Add the OpenFileDialog control to your form. Display the dialog box with the ShowDialog method. The FileName property contains the name of the file selected.
Display a Color dialog box	Add the ColorDialog control to your form. Display the dialog box with the ShowDialog method. The Color property contains the color the user selected.
Disable a menu	Set the Enabled property of a menu item to False using the Properties window.
Enable a menu command by using program code	Use the program statement `mnuCloseItem.Enabled = True` but substitute your command name for *mnuCloseItem*.
Clear an image from a picture box	Use the program statement `PictureBox1.Image = Nothing`

PART 2

Programming Fundamentals

5

Visual Basic .NET Variables and Operators

In this chapter you will learn how to:

- ✔ *Use variables to store data in your programs.*
- ✔ *Get input by using the InputBox function.*
- ✔ *Display messages by using the MsgBox function.*
- ✔ *Work with different data types.*
- ✔ *Use mathematical operators and functions in formulas.*
- ✔ *Use the math methods in the System.Math class of the .NET Framework.*

In Part 1, you learned how to create the user interface of a Microsoft Visual Basic .NET program and how to build and run a program in the Visual Studio development environment. In the next five chapters, you'll learn more about Visual Basic program code—the statements and keywords that form the core of a Visual Basic program. After you complete Part 2, you'll be ready for more advanced topics.

In this chapter, you'll learn how to use variables to store data temporarily in your program and how to use mathematical operators to perform tasks such as addition and multiplication. You'll also learn how to use mathematical functions to perform calculations involving numbers, and you'll use the InputBox and MsgBox functions to gather and present information by using dialog boxes. Finally, you'll get your first real look at using classes in the .NET Framework to perform useful work in a program.

Upgrade Notes:
What's New in Visual Basic .NET?

If you're experienced with Visual Basic 6, you'll notice some new features in Visual Basic .NET, including the following:

- To encourage better programming practices and cleaner program code, all Visual Basic .NET variables must be declared before they are used. The implicit declaration of variables (using variables without declaring them) is allowed only if you use the Option Explicit Off statement—a practice that is discouraged.

- Visual Basic no longer supports the Variant data type. You should declare all variables using Dim and the keyword "As" to identify the type of data that they will hold.

- There are several new fundamental data types, and some of the older data types now support different ranges. For example, there is a 16-bit Short data type, a 32-bit Integer data type, and a 64-bit Long data type. The Visual Basic 6 Currency data type has been replaced with the Decimal data type.

- Visual Basic .NET includes a new statement named Option Strict. When Option Strict is turned on, variables usually need to be the same type if they are added, compared, or combined. (Sometimes variables can be different types, as long as there won't be any data loss.) This means that type conversion is more important in Visual Basic .NET than in Visual Basic 6, and you'll need to become familiar with type conversion functions such as CInt, CLng, and CType to make different types of data compatible. As you upgrade your applications, you can use the Option Strict Off statement to continue combining data types as you did in Visual Basic 6 (permitting what is known as automatic type coercion), but this feature should be used sparingly and not relied on for future versions of Visual Basic .NET.

- There are now shortcuts for mathematical operations with some arithmetic operators, such as addition (+), subtraction (-), and multiplication (*). These shortcuts allow you to write a formula such as $X = X + 2$ using the syntax $X += 2$.

- Visual Basic .NET no longer provides built-in keywords (such as Abs or Cos) for mathematical operations. Instead, you must use the methods in the System.Math class library of the .NET Framework for mathematical functions. The functionality of these methods is similar to the familiar Visual Basic 6 functions, although a few names have changed (for example, Sqr is now Sqrt).

- Visual Studio includes a MessageBox object, which is an alternative to the MsgBox function for displaying message boxes. To display a message box, you use the MessageBox.Show method.

A program statement is a valid instruction for the Visual Basic compiler.

The Anatomy of a Visual Basic Program Statement

As you learned in Chapter 2, a line of code in a Visual Basic program is called a *program statement*. A program statement is any combination of Visual Basic keywords, properties, functions, operators, and symbols that collectively create a valid instruction recognized by the Visual Basic compiler. A complete program statement can be a simple keyword, such as

```
End
```

which halts the execution of a Visual Basic program, or it can be a combination of elements, such as the following statement, which uses the TimeString property to assign the current system time to the Text property of the Label1 object:

```
Label1.Text = TimeString
```

The rules of construction that must be used when you build a programming statement are called statement *syntax*. Visual Basic shares many of its syntax rules with earlier versions of the BASIC programming language and with other language compilers. The trick to writing good program statements is learning the syntax of the most useful language elements and then using those elements correctly to process the data in your program. Fortunately, Visual Basic does a lot of the toughest work for you, so the time you spend writing program code will be relatively short, and the results can be used again in future programs.

In the following chapters, you'll learn the most important Visual Basic keywords and program statements, as well as many of the objects, properties, and methods provided by Visual Studio controls and the .NET Framework. You'll find that these keywords and objects will complement nicely the programming skills you've already learned and will help you to write powerful programs in the future. Variables and data types, the first topics, are critical features of nearly every program.

Using Variables to Store Information

A *variable* is a temporary storage location for data in your program. You can use one or many variables in your code, and they can contain words, numbers, dates, or properties. Variables are useful because they let you assign a short and easy-to-remember name to each piece of data you plan to work with. Variables can hold information entered by the user at runtime, the result of a specific calculation, or a piece of data you want to display on your form. In short, variables are handy containers that you can use to store and track almost any type of information.

Using variables in a Visual Basic .NET program requires some planning. Before you can use a variable, you must set aside memory in the computer for the variable's use. This process is a little like reserving a seat at the theatre or a baseball game. I'll cover the process of making reservations for, or *declaring,* a variable in the next section.

Setting Aside Space for Variables: The Dim Statement

In Visual Basic .NET, you must explicitly declare your variables before using them. This is a change from earlier versions of Visual Basic, where (under certain circumstances) you could declare variables implicitly—in other words, simply by using them and without a Dim statement. This was a flexible but rather dangerous practice—it created the potential for variable confusion and misspelled variable names, which introduced potential bugs into the code that would be discovered only later.

To declare a variable in Visual Basic .NET, type the variable name after the Dim statement. (Dim stands for *dimension*.) This declaration reserves room in memory for the variable when the program runs, and it lets Visual Basic know what type of data it should expect to see later. Although this declaration can be done at any place in the program code (as long as the declaration happens before the variable is used), most programmers declare variables in one place at the top of their event procedures or code modules.

For example, the following statement creates space for a variable named LastName in a program that will hold a textual, or string, value:

Dim reserves space for a variable.

```
Dim LastName As String
```

Note that in addition to identifying the variable by name, I have used the "As" keyword to give the variable a particular type, and I have identified the type using the keyword String. (You'll learn about other data types later in the lesson.) A string variable contains textual information: words, letters, symbols—even numbers. I find myself using string variables a lot; they hold names, places, lines from a poem, the contents of a file, and many other "wordy" data.

Why do you need to declare variables? Visual Basic wants you to identify the name and the type of your variables in advance so that the compiler can set aside the memory the program will need to store and process the information held in variables. Memory management might not seem like a big deal to you (after all, modern personal computers have lots of RAM and gigabytes of free hard disk space), but in some programs, memory usage can be consumed quickly, and it is a good practice to take memory allocation seriously even as you take your first steps as a programmer. As you'll soon see, different types of variables have different space requirements and size limitations.

tip

In some earlier versions of Visual Basic, specific variable types (such as String or Integer) were not required—information was simply held using a generic (and memory hungry) data type called Variant, which could hold data of any size or format. Variants are no longer supported in Visual Basic .NET. Although they were handy for beginning programmers, the way they were designed made them slow and inefficient, and they allowed variables to be converted from one type to another too easily—causing unexpected results.

After you declare a variable, you are free to assign information to it in your code. For example, the following program statement assigns the last name "Jefferson" to the LastName variable:

You store data in a variable by using the assignment operator (=).

```
LastName = "Jefferson"
```

Note that I was careful to assign a textual value to the LastName variable, because it is of the type String. I could also assign values with spaces, symbols, or numbers to the variable, such as

```
LastName = "1313 Mockingbird Lane"
```

but the variable would still be considered a string value. The number portion could only be used in a mathematical formula if it were first converted to an integer or floating-point value using one of a handful of conversion functions I'll discuss later in this book.

After the LastName variable is assigned a value, it can be used in place of the name "Jefferson" in your code. For example, the assignment statement

```
Label1.Text = LastName
```

would display *Jefferson* in the first label (Label1) on your form.

> ## tip
>
> If you really want to declare variables "the old way" in Visual Basic .NET, in other words, without explicitly declaring them using the Dim statement, you can place the statement
>
> Option Explicit Off
>
> at the very top of your form or module's program code (before any event procedures), and it will defeat Visual Basic's default requirement that variables be declared before they are used. I don't recommend this statement as a permanent addition to your code, but you may find it useful temporarily as you convert older Visual Basic programs to Visual Studio .NET.

Using Variables in a Program

Variables can maintain the same value throughout a program or they can change values several times, depending on your needs. The following exercise demonstrates how a variable named LastName can contain different text values and how the variable can be assigned to object properties.

Change the value of a variable

1 Start Visual Studio.

2 On the File menu, point to Open, and then click Project.

   The Open Project dialog box appears.

3 Open the Variable Test project in the c:\vbnetsbs\chap05\variable test folder.

View Designer button

4 If the project's form isn't visible, click Form1.vb in Solution Explorer and then click the View Designer button.

   The Variable Test form appears in the Windows Forms Designer. Variable Test is a skeleton program—it contains a form with labels and buttons for displaying output, but little program code. You'll add code in this exercise.

The Variable Test form looks like this:

The form contains two labels and two buttons. You'll use variables to display information in each of the labels.

> **tip**
> The label objects look like boxes because I set their BorderStyle properties to Fixed3D.

5 Double-click the Show button.

The Button1_Click event procedure appears in the Code Editor.

6 Type the following program statements to declare and use the LastName variable:

```
Dim LastName As String


LastName = "Luther"
Label1.Text = LastName


LastName = "Bodenstein von Karlstadt"
Label2.Text = LastName
```

Variables can transfer information to a property.

The program statements are arranged in three groups. The first statement declares the LastName variable by using the Dim statement and the String type. The second and third lines assign the name "Luther" to the LastName variable and then display this name in the first label on the form. This example demonstrates one of the most common uses of variables in a program—transferring information to a property.

The fourth line assigns the name Bodenstein von Karlstadt to the LastName variable (in other words, it changes the contents of the variable). Notice that the second string is longer than the first and contains a few blank spaces. When you assign text strings to variables, or use them in other places, you need to enclose the text within quotation marks. (You don't need to do this with numbers.)

Finally, keep in mind another important characteristic of the variables being declared in this event procedure—they maintain their *scope*, or hold their value, only within the event procedure you are using them in. Later in this chapter you'll learn how to declare variables so that they can be used in any of your form's event procedures.

7   Click the Form1.vb [Design] tab to display the form again.

8   Double-click the Quit button.

The Button2_Click event procedure appears in the Code Editor.

9   Type the following program statement to stop the program.

```
End
```

Your screen should look like this:

```
Start Page  Form1.vb [Design]*  Form1.vb*                          ◁ ▷ ✕
Form1 (Variable_Test)                ▼    Button2_Click                     ▼
Public Class Form1
    Inherits System.Windows.Forms.Form

   Windows Form Designer generated code

    Private Sub Button1_Click(ByVal sender As System.Object, ByVal e
        Dim LastName As String

        LastName = "Luther"
        Label1.Text = LastName

        LastName = "Bodenstein von Karlstadt"
        Label2.Text = LastName
    End Sub

    Private Sub Button2_Click(ByVal sender As System.Object, ByVal e
        End
    End Sub
End Class
```

Save All button   **10**   Click the Save All button to save your changes.

11   Click the Start button on the Standard toolbar to run the program.

Start button   The program runs in the development environment.

12   Click the Show button.

The program declares the variable, assigns two values to it, and copies each value to the appropriate label on the form. The program produces the following output:

Variable Naming Conventions

Naming variables can be a little tricky because you need to use names that are short but intuitive and easy to remember. To avoid confusion, use the following conventions when naming variables:

■ Begin each variable name with a letter. With the exception of the underscore, this is a Visual Basic requirement. Variable names can contain only letters, numbers, and underscores.

■ Although variable names can be virtually any length, try to keep them under 33 characters to make them easier to read. (Variable names were limited to 255 characters in Visual Basic 6, but that is no longer a constraint.)

■ Make your variable names descriptive by combining one or more words when it makes sense to do so. For example, the variable name SalesTaxRate is much clearer than Tax or Rate.

■ Use a combination of uppercase and lowercase characters and numbers if you wish. An accepted convention is to capitalize the first letter of each word in a variable; for example, DateOfBirth. However, some programmers prefer to use so-called "camel casing" (making the first letter of a variable name lowercase) to distinguish variable names from functions and module names (which usually do begin with an uppercase letter). Examples of "camel casing" include dateOfBirth, employeeName, and counter.

(continued)

(continued)

■ Don't use Visual Basic keywords, objects, or properties as variable names. If you do, you'll get an error when you try to run your program.

■ (Optional) Begin each variable name with a two- or three- character abbreviation corresponding to the type of data that is stored in the variable. For example, use strName to show that the Name variable contains string data. Although you don't need to worry too much about this detail now, you might make a note of this convention for later—you'll see it in the Visual Studio online Help and many of the advanced books about Visual Basic programming. (This convention and abbreviation scheme was originally created by Microsoft Distinguished Engineer Charles Simonyi and is sometimes called the Hungarian Naming Convention.)

13   Click the Quit button to stop the program.

The program stops, and the development environment returns.

Using a Variable to Store Input

You can get input from the user effectively by using the InputBox function and a variable.

One practical use for a variable is to hold information input from the user. Although you can often use an object such as a list box or a text box to retrieve this information, at times you may want to deal directly with the user and save the input in a variable rather than in a property. One way to retrieve input is to use the InputBox function to display a dialog box on the screen and then use a variable to store the text the user types. You'll try this approach in the following example.

Get input by using InputBox

1   On the File menu, point to Open, and then click Project.

The Open Project dialog box appears.

2   Open the Input Box project in the c:\vbnetsbs\chap05\input box folder.

The Input Box project opens in the development environment. InputBox is a skeleton program—it contains a form with buttons and a label for displaying output, but it contains little program code.

View Designer button

3   If the project's form isn't visible, click Form1.vb in Solution Explorer, and then click the View Designer button.

The form contains one label and two buttons. You'll use the InputBox function to get input from the user, and then you'll display the input in the label on the form.

4   Double-click the Input Box button.

The Button1_Click event procedure appears in the Code Editor.

5   Type the following program statements to declare two variables and call the InputBox function:

```
Dim Prompt, FullName As String
Prompt = "Please enter your name."

FullName = InputBox(Prompt)
Label1.Text = FullName
```

This time you're declaring two variables by using the Dim statement: Prompt and FullName. Both variables are declared using the String type. (You can declare as many variables as you want on the same line, as long as they are of the same type. Note that in Visual Basic 6, this same syntax would have produced different results. Dim would create the Prompt variable using the Variant type (because no type was specified), and Dim would create the second variable using the String type. But this logical inconsistency has been fixed in Visual Basic .NET.

The second line in the event procedure assigns a text string to the Prompt variable. This message will be used as a text argument for the InputBox function. (An argument is a value or an expression passed to a procedure or a function.) The next line calls the InputBox function and assigns the result of the call (the text string the user enters) to the FullName variable. InputBox is a special Visual Basic function that displays a dialog box on the screen and prompts the user for input. In addition to a prompt string, the InputBox function supports other arguments you may want to use occasionally. Consult the Visual Basic online Help for details.

After InputBox has returned a text string to the program, the fourth statement in the procedure places the user's name in the Text property of the Label1 object, which displays it on the form.

tip
In older versions of BASIC, the InputBox function was spelled with a $ character at the end to help programmers remember that the function returned information in the string ($) data type. String variables were also identified with the $ symbol on occasion. These days we don't use type character abbreviations. String ($), Integer (%), and the other type abbreviations are relics of the past.

Variables and Operators   5

6   Save your changes.

Do you remember which toolbar button to click to save your project? See step 10 of the previous exercise if you have forgotten.

Start button

7   Click the Start button on the Standard toolbar to run the program.

The program runs in the development environment.

8   Click the Input Box button.

Visual Basic executes the Button1_Click event procedure, and the Input Box dialog box appears on your screen:

9   Type your full name, and then click OK.

The InputBox function returns your name to the program and places it in the FullName variable. The program then uses the variable to display your name on the form as shown here:

Use the InputBox function in your programs anytime you want to prompt the user for information. You can use this function in combination with the other input controls to regulate the flow of data into and out of a program. In the next exercise, you'll learn how to use a similar function to display text in a dialog box.

10   Click the Quit button on the form to stop the program.

The program stops, and the development environment returns.

What Is a Function?

InputBox is a special Visual Basic keyword known as a *function*. A function is a statement that performs meaningful work (such as prompting the user for information or calculating an equation) and then returns a result to the program. The value returned by a function can be assigned to a variable, as it was in the Input Box program, or it can be assigned to a property or another statement or function. Visual Basic functions often use one or more arguments to define their activities. For example, the InputBox function you just executed used the Prompt variable to display dialog box instructions for the user. When a function uses more than one argument, the arguments are separated by commas, and the whole group of arguments is enclosed in parentheses. The following statement shows a function call that has two arguments:

```
FullName = InputBox(Prompt, Title)
```

Using a Variable for Output

The MsgBox function can display text in a dialog box and has multiple optional arguments.

You can display the contents of a variable by assigning the variable to a property (such as the Text property of a label object) or by passing the variable as an argument to a dialog box function. One useful dialog box function for displaying output is the MsgBox function. When you call the MsgBox function it displays a dialog box, sometimes called a message box, with various options that you can specify. Like InputBox, it takes one or more arguments as input, and the results of the function call can be assigned to a variable. The syntax for the MsgBox function is

```
ButtonClicked = MsgBox(Prompt, Buttons, Title)
```

where *Prompt* is the text to be displayed in the message box, *Buttons* is a number that specifies the buttons, icons, and other options to display for the message box, and *Title* is the text displayed in the message box title bar. The variable *ButtonClicked* is assigned the result returned by the function, which indicates which button the user clicked in the dialog box.

If you're just displaying a message using the MsgBox function, the *Button-Clicked* variable, the assignment operator (=), the *Buttons* argument, and the *Title* argument are optional. You will be using the *Title* argument, but the others you won't be using in the following exercise; for more information about them (including the different buttons you can include in MsgBox and a few more options), search for *MsgBox* in Visual Basic online Help.

tip

Visual Basic .NET provides both the MsgBox function and the MessageBox class for displaying text on a form using a dialog box. The MessageBox class is part of the System.Windows.Forms namespace, takes arguments much like MsgBox, and is displayed using the Show method. I'll use both MsgBox and MessageBox in this book.

Now you'll add a MsgBox function to the Input Box program to display the name the user enters in the InputBox dialog box.

Display a message by using MsgBox

1   If the Code Editor isn't visible, double-click the Input Box button on the Input Box form.

The event procedure for the Button1_Click procedure appears in the Code Editor. (This is the code you entered in the last exercise.)

2   Select the following statement in the event procedure (the last line):

```
Label1.Text = FullName
```

This is the statement that displays the contents of the FullName variable in the label.

3   Press the Delete key to delete the line.

The statement is removed from the Code Editor.

4   Type the following line into the event procedure as a replacement:

```
MsgBox(FullName, , "Input Results")
```

This new statement will call the MsgBox function, display the contents of the FullName variable in the dialog box, and place the words *Input Results* in the title bar. (The optional *Buttons* argument and the *ButtonClicked* variable are irrelevant here and have been omitted.) Your event procedure should look like this:

```
Start Page | Form1.vb [Design]* | Form1.vb* |                          ◁ ▷ ×
Form1 (Input_Box)                    ▼ | Button1_Click                ▼
  Windows Form Designer generated code                                 ▲
        Private Sub Button2_Click(ByVal sender As System.Object, ByVal e
            End
        End Sub

        Private Sub Button1_Click(ByVal sender As System.Object, ByVal e
            Dim Prompt, FullName As String
            Prompt = "Please enter your name."

            FullName = InputBox(Prompt)
            MsgBox(FullName, , "Input Results")
        End Sub
    End Class
```

Start button

5 Click the Start button on the Standard toolbar.

6 Click the Input Box button, type your name in the input box, and then click OK.

Visual Basic stores the input in the program in the FullName variable and then displays it in a message box. Your screen should look similar to this:

```
Input Box                              _ □ ×

   Input Box          Label1


      Quit         Input Results    X

                   Hugo Fernandez

                        OK
```

7 Click OK to close the message box. Then click Quit to close the program.

The program closes, and the development environment returns.

tip

You may have noticed that when you run a Visual Basic program, Visual Studio .NET automatically saves your project before it starts the compiler and displays your opening form. This is a safety feature that should prevent data loss if something unexpected were to happen during the compilation.

Working with Specific Data Types

The String data type is useful for managing text in your programs, but what about numbers, dates, and other types of information? To allow for the efficient memory management of all types of data, Visual Basic provides several additional data types that you can use for your variables. Many of these are familiar data types from earlier versions of BASIC or Visual Basic, and some of the data types are new or have been changed in Visual Studio .NET to allow for the efficient processing of data in newer 64-bit computers.

The following table lists the fundamental (or elementary) data types in Visual Basic .NET. You'll gain a performance advantage in your programs if you choose the right data type for your variables—a size that is neither too big nor too small. In the next exercise, you'll see how several of these data types work.

tip

Variable storage size is measured in bits. The amount of space required to store one standard (ASCII) keyboard character in memory is eight bits, which equals one byte.Data

Data type	Size	Range	Sample usage
Short	16-bit	−32,768 through 32,767	`Dim Birds As Short` `Birds = 12500`
Integer	32-bit	−2,147,483,648 through 2,147,483,647	`Dim Insects As Integer` `Insects = 37500000`
Long	64-bit	−9,223,372,036,854,775,808 to 9,223,372,036,854,775,807	`Dim WorldPop as Long` `WorldPop = 4800000004`
Single	32-bit floating point	−3.4028235E38 through 3.4028235E38	`Dim Price As Single` `Price = 899.99`
Double	64-bit floating point	−1.79769313486231E308 through 1.79769313486231E308	`Dim Pi As Double` `Pi = 3.1415926535`
Decimal	128-bit	values up to $+/-79,228 \times 10^{24}$	`Dim Debt As Decimal` `Debt = 7600300.50`
Byte	8-bit	0–255 (no negative numbers)	`Dim RetKey As Byte` `RetKey = 13`
Char	16-bit	Any Unicode symbol in the range 0–65,535	`Dim UnicodeChar As Char` `UnicodeChar = "Ä"`

Data type	Size	Range	Sample usage
String	Usually 16-bits per character	0 to approximately 2 billion 16-bit Unicode characters	`Dim Dog As String` `Dog = "pointer"`
Boolean	16-bit	True or False (during conversions, 0 is converted to False, other values to True)	`Dim Flag as Boolean` `Flag = True`
Date	64-bit	January 1, 0001, through December 31, 9999	`Dim Birthday as Date` `Birthday = #3/1/1963#`

Object	32-bit	Any type can be stored in a variable of type Object	`Dim MyApp As Object`
			`MyApp = CreateObject _`
			`("Word.Application")`

The Data Types program demonstrates fundamental data types in program code.

View Designer button

Use fundamental data types in code

1 On the File menu, point to Open, and then click Project.

The Open Project dialog box appears.

2 Open the Data Types project in the c:\vbnetsbs\chap05\data types folder.

3 If the project's form isn't visible, click Form1.vb in Solution Explorer and then click the View Designer button.

Data Types is a complete Visual Basic program that demonstrates how several fundamental data types work. You'll run the program to see what the data types look like, and then you'll look at how the variables are declared and used in the program code. You'll also learn where to place variable declarations so that they are available to all of the event procedures in your program.

Start button

4 Click the Start button on the Standard toolbar.

The following application window appears:

The Data Types program lets you experiment with 11 data types, including integer, single-precision floating point, and date. The program displays an example of each type when you click its name in the list box.

5　Click the Integer type in the list box.

The number 37,500,000 appears in the Sample Data box, as shown in the following illustration. Note that neither the Short, Integer, nor Long data types allow you to insert or display commas in them. To display commas, you'll need to use the Format function.

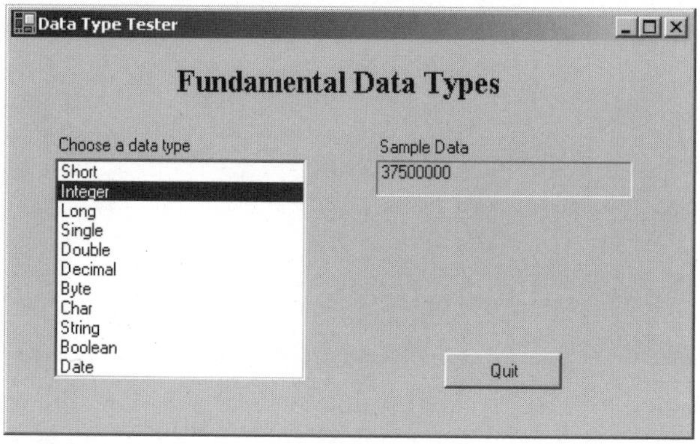

6　Click the Date type in the list box.

The date 3/1/1963 appears in the Sample Data box.

7　Click each data type in the list box to see how Visual Basic displays it in the Sample Data box.

8　Click the Quit button to stop the program.

Now you'll examine how the fundamental data types are declared at the top of the form and how they are used in the ListBox1_SelectedIndexChanged event procedure.

9　Double-click the form itself (not any objects on the form), and enlarge the Code Editor to see more of the program code.

The Code Editor will look like this:

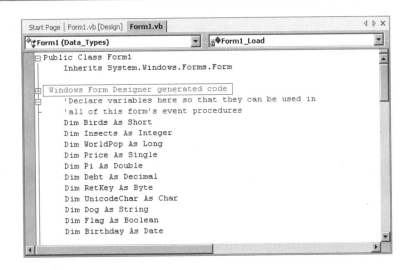

At the top of the Code Editor you'll see a line that says "Windows Form Designer generated code". If you click the plus sign next to this line, you will see statements that Visual Basic adds to your project so that the objects placed on the form contain the correct properties and the form loads correctly. In previous versions of Visual Basic, this "setup" code wasn't accessible, but now it exists in each form file so that you can examine the inner workings of your forms and fine tune them if you wish. (I don't recommend customizing the Windows Forms Designer generated code until you have completed this book and feel very comfortable with Visual Basic programming!)

Below the Windows Forms Designer generated code you'll see the dozen or so program statements I added to declare 11 variables in your program—one for each of the fundamental data types in Visual Basic. (I didn't create an example for the Object type, but we'll experiment with that in later chapters.) By placing each Dim statement here, at the top of the form's code initialization area, I'm insuring that the variables will be valid, or will have scope, in all of the form's event procedures. That way, I can set the value of a variable in one event procedure and read it in another. Normally, variables are valid only in the event procedure in which they are declared. To make them valid across the form, you need to declare variables at the top of your form's code.

tip

I've given each variable the same name as I did in the data types table earlier in the chapter so that you can see the examples I showed you in actual program code.

10   Scroll down in the Code Editor and examine the Form1_Load event procedure.

You'll see the following statements that add items to the list box object in the program. (You may remember this syntax from Chapter 3—I used some similar statements there.)

```
Start Page   Form1.vb [Design]   Form1.vb                                      ◁ ▷ ✕
Form1 (Data_Types)                    ▼   ♦ Form1_Load                          ▼
      Private Sub Form1_Load(ByVal sender As System.Object, ByVal e As
          'add names to the list box (see chapter 3)
          ListBox1.Items.Add("Short")
          ListBox1.Items.Add("Integer")
          ListBox1.Items.Add("Long")
          ListBox1.Items.Add("Single")
          ListBox1.Items.Add("Double")
          ListBox1.Items.Add("Decimal")
          ListBox1.Items.Add("Byte")
          ListBox1.Items.Add("Char")
          ListBox1.Items.Add("String")
          ListBox1.Items.Add("Boolean")
          ListBox1.Items.Add("Date")
      End Sub

      Private Sub ListBox1_SelectedIndexChanged(ByVal sender As System
          Select Case ListBox1.SelectedIndex
```

11   Scroll down and examine the ListBox1_SelectedIndexChanged event procedure.

The ListBox1_SelectedIndexChanged event procedure processes the selections you make in the list box and looks like this:

```
Start Page   Form1.vb [Design]   Form1.vb                                      ◁ ▷ ✕
Form1 (Data_Types)                    ▼   ♦ ListBox1_SelectedIndexChanged       ▼
      Private Sub ListBox1_SelectedIndexChanged(ByVal sender As System
          Select Case ListBox1.SelectedIndex
              Case 0
                  Birds = 12500
                  Label4.Text = Birds
              Case 1
                  Insects = 37500000
                  Label4.Text = Insects
              Case 2
                  WorldPop = 4800000004
                  Label4.Text = WorldPop
              Case 3
                  Price = 899.99
                  Label4.Text = Price
              Case 4
                  Pi = 3.1415926535
                  Label4.Text = Pi
              Case 5
```

The heart of the event procedure is a Select Case decision structure. In the next chapter, we'll discuss how this group of program statements selects one choice from many. For now, notice how each section of the Select Case block assigns a sample value to one of the fundamental data type variables and then assigns the variable to the Text property of the Label4 object on the form. I used code like this in Chapter 3 to process list box choices, and you can also use these techniques to work with list boxes and data types in your own programs.

tip

If you have more than one form in your project, you need to declare variables in a slightly different way (and place) to give them scope throughout your program (i.e. in each form that your project contains). The type of variable that you will declare is a *public*, or global, variable, and it is declared in a *code module* (a special file that contains declarations and procedures not associated with a particular form.) For information about creating public variables in code modules, see Chapter 10, "Using Modules and Procedures."

12   Scroll through the ListBox1_SelectedIndexChanged event procedure and examine each of the variable assignments closely.

Try changing the data in a few of the variable assignment statements and running the program again to see what the data looks like. In particular, you might try assigning values to variables that are *outside their accepted range*, as shown in the data types table presented earlier. If you make such an error, Visual Basic will add a jagged underline below the incorrect value in the Code Editor, and the program won't run until you change it. To learn more about your mistake, you can hold the mouse over the jagged underlined value and read a short tooltip error message about the problem.

13   If you made any changes you want to save to disk, click the Save All button on the Standard toolbar.

Variables and Operators 5

User-Defined Data Types

Visual Basic also lets you create your own data types. This feature is most useful when you're dealing with a group of data items that naturally fit together but fall into different data categories. You create a *user-defined type* (UDT) by using the Structure statement, and you declare variables associated with the new type by using the Dim statement. (The Structure statement cannot be located in an event procedure—it must be located at the top of the form, along with other variable declarations, or in a code module.)

For example, the following declaration creates a user-defined data type named Employee that can store the name, date of birth, and hire date associated with a worker:

```
Structure Employee
    Dim Name As String
    Dim DateOfBirth As Date
    Dim HireDate As Date
End Structure
```

After you create a new data type, you can use it in the program code for the form or module's event procedures. The following statements use the new Employee type. The first statement creates a variable named ProductManager, of the Employee type, and the second statement assigns the name "Erick Cody" to the Name component of the variable:

```
Dim ProductManager As Employee
ProductManager.Name = "Erick Cody"
```

This looks a little like setting a property, doesn't it? Visual Basic uses the same notation for the relationship between objects and properties as it uses for the relationship between user-defined data types and component variables.

Constants: Variables That Don't Change

If a variable in your program contains a value that never changes (such as π, a fixed mathematical entity), you might consider storing the value as a *constant* instead of as a variable. A constant is a meaningful name that takes the place of a number or text string that doesn't change. Constants are useful because they increase the readability of program code, they can reduce programming mistakes, and they make global changes easier to accomplish later. Constants operate a lot like variables, but you can't modify their values at runtime. They are declared with the Const keyword, as shown in the following example:

```
Const Pi As Double = 3.14159265
```

The previous statement creates a constant named Pi that can be used in place of the value of π in the program code. To make a constant available to all the objects and event procedures in your form, place the statement at the top of your form along with other variable and structure declarations that will have scope in all the form's event procedures. To make the constant available to all the forms and modules in a program (not just Form1), create the constant in a code module, with the Public keyword in front of it. For example:

```
Public Const Pi As Double = 3.14159265
```

The following exercise demonstrates how you can use a constant in an event procedure.

Use a constant in an event procedure

1   On the File menu, point to Open, and then click Project.

   The Open Project dialog box appears.

2   Open the Constant Tester project in the c:\vbnetsbs\chap05\constant tester folder.

3   If the project's form isn't visible, click Form1.vb in Solution Explorer and then click the View Designer button.

View Designer button

   The Constant Tester form appears in the Windows Forms Designer. Constant Tester is a skeleton program. The user interface is finished, but you need to type in the program code.

4   Double-click the Show Constant button on the form.

   The Button1_Click event procedure appears in the Code Editor.

5   Type the following statements in the Button1_Click event procedure:

```
Const Pi As Double = 3.14159265
Label1.Text = Pi
```

> **tip**
> The location you choose for your declarations should be based on how you plan to use the constants or the variables. Programmers typically keep the scope for declarations as small as possible, while still making them available for code that needs to use them. For example, if a constant is needed only in a single event procedure, you should put the constant declaration within that event procedure. However, you could also place the declaration at the top of the form code, which would give all the event procedures in your form access to it.

Start button

6 Click the Start button on the Standard toolbar to run the program.

7 Click the Show Constant button.

The Pi constant appears in the label box, as shown here:

8 Click the Quit button to stop the program.

Visual Basic operators link the parts of a formula.

Constants are useful in program code, especially in involved mathematical formulas, such as Area = πr^2. The next section describes how you can use operators and variables to write similar formulas.

Working with Visual Basic Operators

A *formula* is a statement that combines numbers, variables, operators, and keywords to create a new value. Visual Basic contains several language elements designed for use in formulas. In this section, you'll practice working with mathematical operators, the symbols used to tie together the parts of a formula. With a few exceptions, the mathematical symbols you'll use are the ones you use in everyday life, and their operations are fairly intuitive. You'll see each demonstrated in the following exercises.

Visual Basic includes the following operators:

Operator	Description
+	Addition
−	Subtraction
*	Multiplication
/	Division
\	Integer (whole number) division
Mod	Remainder division
^	Exponentiation (raising to a power)
&	String concatenation (combination)

Basic Math: The +, −, *, and / Operators

The operators for addition, subtraction, multiplication, and division are pretty straightforward and can be used in any formula where numbers or numeric variables are used. The following exercise demonstrates how you can use them in a program.

Work with basic operators

1   On the File menu, point to Open, and then click Project.

2   Open the Basic Math project in the c:\vbnetsbs\chap05\basic math folder.

3   If the project's form isn't visible, click Form1.vb in Solution Explorer and then click the View Designer button.

View Designer button

The Basic Math form appears in the Windows Forms Designer. The Basic Math program demonstrates how the addition, subtraction, multiplication, and division operators work with numbers you type. It also demonstrates how you can use text box, radio button, and button objects to process user input in a program.

4   Click the Start button on the Standard toolbar.

Start button

The Basic Math program runs in the development environment. The program displays two text boxes in which you enter numeric values, a group of operator radio buttons, a box that displays results, and two button objects (Calculate and Quit).

A text box object is a useful tool for getting keyboard input from the user.

5   Type **100** in the Variable 1 text box, and then press Tab.

The cursor moves to the second text box.

6   Type **17** in the Variable 2 text box.

You can now apply any of the mathematical operators to the values in the text boxes.

7   Click the Addition radio button, and then click the Calculate button.

The operator is applied to the two values, and the number 117 appears in the Result box, as shown here:

8   Practice using the subtraction, multiplication, and division operators with the two numbers in the variable boxes. (Click Calculate to calculate each formula.)

The results appear in the Result box. Feel free to experiment with different numbers in the variable text boxes. (Try a few numbers with decimal points if you like.) I used the Double data type to declare the variables, so you can use very large numbers if you like.

Now try the following test to see what happens:

9   Type **100** in the Variable 1 text box, type **0** in the Variable 2 text box, click the Division radio button, and then click Calculate.

Dividing by zero is a no-no in mathematical calculations, because it produces an infinite result. But Visual Basic is able to handle this calculation, and displays a value of *Infinity* in the Result text box. Being able to handle some divide-by-zero conditions is a new feature automatically provided by Visual Basic .NET.

10   When you've finished contemplating this and other tests, click the Quit button.

The program stops, and the development environment returns.

Now take a look at the program code to see how the results were calculated. Basic Math uses a few of the standard input controls you experimented with in Chapter 3 and an event procedure that uses variables and operators to process the simple mathematical formulas. The program declares its variables at the top of the form so that they can be used in all of the Form1 event procedures.

Examine the Basic Math program code

1   Double-click the Calculate button on the form.

The Code Editor displays the Button1_Click event procedure. At the top of the form code, you'll see the following statement that declares two variables of type Double:

```
'Declare FirstNum and SecondNum variables
Dim FirstNum, SecondNum As Double
```

I used the Double type because I wanted a large, general purpose variable type that could handle many different numbers—integers, numbers with decimal points, very big numbers, small numbers, and so on. The variables are declared on the same line using the shortcut notation. Both FirstNum and SecondNum are of type Double, and they will be used to hold the values input in the first and second text boxes, respectively.

2   Scroll down in the Code Editor to see the contents of the Button1_Click event procedure.

Your screen will look like this:

```
Start Page | Form1.vb [Design] | Form1.vb                               ◁ ▷ ✕

Form1 (Basic_Math)              ▼    Button1_Click                 ▼

    Private Sub Button1_Click(ByVal sender As System.Object, ByVal e
        'Assign text box values to variables
        FirstNum = TextBox1.Text
        SecondNum = TextBox2.Text

        'Determine checked button and calculate
        If RadioButton1.Checked = True Then
            TextBox3.Text = FirstNum + SecondNum
        End If
        If RadioButton2.Checked = True Then
            TextBox3.Text = FirstNum - SecondNum
        End If
        If RadioButton3.Checked = True Then
            TextBox3.Text = FirstNum * SecondNum
        End If
        If RadioButton4.Checked = True Then
            TextBox3.Text = FirstNum / SecondNum
        End If
    End Sub

End Class
```

The first two statements in the event procedure transfer data entered into the text box objects into the FirstNum and SecondNum variables.

```
'Assign text box values to variables
FirstNum = TextBox1.Text
SecondNum = TextBox2.Text
```

The TextBox control handles the transfer with the Text property—a property that accepts text entered by the user and makes it available for use in the program. I'll make frequent use of the TextBox control in this book. When it is set to multiline and resized, it can display many lines of text—even a whole file!

After the text box values are assigned to the variables, the event procedure determines which radio button has been checked, calculates the mathematical formula, and displays the result in a third text box. The first radio button test looks like this:

```
'Determine checked button and calculate
If RadioButton1.Checked = True Then
    TextBox3.Text = FirstNum + SecondNum
End If
```

Remember from Chapter 3 that only one radio button object in a group box object can be selected at once. You can tell whether a radio button has been selected by evaluating the Checked property. If it is True, the button has been selected. If the Checked property is False, then the button has not been selected. After this simple test, you're ready to compute the result and display it in the third text box object. That's all there is to using basic mathematical operators. (You'll learn more about the syntax of If...Then tests or decision structures in Chapter 6.)

You're done using the Basic Math program.

Using Advanced Operators: \, Mod, ^, and &

In addition to the four basic mathematical operators, Visual Basic includes four advanced operators, which perform integer division (\), remainder division (Mod), exponentiation (^), and string concatenation (&). These operators are useful in special-purpose mathematical formulas and text processing applications. The following utility (a slight modification of the Basic Math program) shows how you can use each of these operators in a program.

New Shortcut Operators

An interesting new feature of Visual Basic .NET is that you can use shortcut operators for mathematical and string operations that involve changing the value of an existing variable. For example, if you combine the "+" symbol with the "=" symbol, you can add to a variable without repeating the variable name twice in the formula. Thus, you can write the formula X = X + 6 using the syntax X += 6. The following table shows examples of these shortcut operators:

Operation	Long-form syntax	Shortcut syntax
Addition (+)	X = X + 6	X += 6
Subtraction (-)	X = X – 6	X -= 6
Multiplication (*)	X = X * 6	X *= 6
Division (/)	X = X / 6	X /= 6
Integer division (\)	X = X \ 6	X \= 6
Exponentiation (^)	X = X ^ 6	X ^= 6
String concatenation (&)	X = X & "ABC"	X &= "ABC"

Work with advanced operators

1   On the File menu, point to Open, and then click Project.

    The Open Project dialog box appears.

2   Open the Advanced Math project in the c:\vbnetsbs\chap05\advanced math folder.

View Designer button

3   If the project's form isn't visible, click Form1.vb in Solution Explorer and then click the View Designer button.

    The Advanced Math form appears in the Windows Forms Designer. The Advanced Math program is identical to the Basic Math program, with the exception of the operators shown in the radio buttons and in the program.

Start button

4   Click the Start button on the Standard toolbar.

    The program displays two text boxes in which you enter numeric values, a group of operator radio buttons, a text box that displays results, and two buttons.

5   Type **9** in the Variable 1 text box, and then press Tab.

6   Type **2** in the Variable 2 text box.

You can now apply any of the advanced operators to the values in the text boxes.

7   Click the Integer Division radio button, and then click the Calculate button.

The operator is applied to the two values, and the number 4 appears in the Result box, as shown here:

Integer division produces only the whole number result of the division operation. Although 9 divided by 2 equals 4.5, the integer division operation returns only the first part, an integer (the whole number 4). You might find this result useful if you're working with quantities that can't easily be divided into fractional components, such as the number of adults that can fit in a car.

8   Click the Remainder radio button, and then click the Calculate button.

The number 1 appears in the Result box. Remainder division (modulus arithmetic) returns the remainder (the part left over that won't evenly divide) after two numbers are divided. Because 9 divided by 2 equals 4 with a remainder of 1 ($2 \times 4 + 1 = 9$), the result produced by the Mod operator is 1. In addition to adding an early-seventies quality to your code, the Mod operator can help you track "leftovers" in your calculations, such as the amount of change left over after a financial transaction.

9   Click the Exponentiation radio button, and then click the Calculate button.

The number 81 appears in the Result box. The exponentiation operator ($\wedge$) raises a number to a specified power. For example, $9 \wedge 2$ equals 9^2 or 81. In a Visual Basic formula, 9^2 is written $9 \wedge 2$.

10   Click the Concatenation radio button, and then click the Calculate button.

The number 92 appears in the Result box. The string concatenation operator (&) combines two strings in a formula, but not through addition. The result is a combination of the "9" character and the "2" character. String concatenation can be performed on numeric variables—for example, if you are displaying the inning by inning score of a baseball game as they do in old-time score boxes—but concatenation is more commonly performed on string values or variables.

Because I declared the FirstNum and SecondNum variables as type Double, you can't combine words or letters using the program code as written. Try the following test, for example, which will cause an error and end the program.

11 Type **birth** in the Variable 1 text box, type **day** in the Variable 2 text box, verify that Concatenation is selected, and then click Calculate.

Visual Basic is unable to process the text values you entered; the program stops running and an error message appears on the screen, as shown here:

This type of error is called a *runtime error*—an error that surfaces not during the design and compilation of the program, but later, when the program is running and encounters a condition it doesn't know how to process. If this seems odd, you might imagine that Visual Basic is simply offering you a modern rendition of the robot plea "Does not compute!" from the best science fiction films of the 1950s. The updated computer-speak message *Cast from string ('birth') to Double is not valid* means that the words you entered in the text boxes ('birth' and 'day') could not be assigned or *cast* by Visual Basic to variables of the type Double. Double types can only contain numbers. Period.

12 Click the Continue button in the Microsoft Development Environment dialog box.

If another Microsoft Development Environment dialog box is displayed indicating that no source code is available for the current location, click OK.

Your program ends and returns you to the development environment. The Break button, which you'll learn about in Chapter 8, allows you to use the debugging tools in Visual Studio to learn more about the defects or *bugs* in your program code.

Now take a look at the program code to see how variables were declared and how the advanced operators were used.

13   Scroll to the code at the top of the Code Editor. You'll see the following comment and program statement:

```
'Declare FirstNum and SecondNum variables
Dim FirstNum, SecondNum As Double
```

As you may recall from the previous exercise, FirstNum and SecondNum are the variables that hold numbers coming in from the TextBox1 and TextBox2 objects.

14   Change the data type from Double to String now so that you can properly test how the String Concatenation (&) operator works.

15   Now scroll down in the Code Editor to see how the advanced operators are used in the program code. You'll see the following code:

```
'Assign text box values to variables
FirstNum = TextBox1.Text
SecondNum = TextBox2.Text

'Determine checked button and calculate
If RadioButton1.Checked = True Then
    TextBox3.Text = FirstNum \ SecondNum
End If
If RadioButton2.Checked = True Then
    TextBox3.Text = FirstNum Mod SecondNum
End If
If RadioButton3.Checked = True Then
    TextBox3.Text = FirstNum ^ SecondNum
End If
If RadioButton4.Checked = True Then
    TextBox3.Text = FirstNum & SecondNum
End If
```

Like the Basic Math program, this program loads data from the text boxes and places it in the FirstNum and SecondNum variables. The program then checks to see which radio button the user checked and computes the requested formula. In this event procedure, the Integer Division (\), Remainder (Mod), Exponentiation (^), and String Concatenation (&) operators are used. Now that you have changed the data type of the variables to String, run the program again to see how the & operator works on text.

16   Click the Start button.

17 Type **birth** in the Variable 1 text box, type **day** in the Variable 2 text box, click Concatenation, and then click Calculate.

The program now concatenates the string values and doesn't produce a runtime error, as shown here:

18 Click the Quit button to close the program.

You're finished working with the Advanced Math program.

> **tip**
>
> Runtime errors are difficult to avoid completely—even the most sophisticated application programs, such as Microsoft Word or Microsoft Excel, run into error conditions they can't handle sometimes, producing runtime errors or *crashes*. Designing your programs to handle many different data types and operating conditions will help you to produce solid or *robust* applications. In Chapter 9, you'll learn about another helpful tool for preventing runtime error crashes— the structured error handler.

Working with Math Methods in the .NET Framework

Now and then you'll want to do a little extra number crunching in your programs. You may need to round a number, calculate a complex mathematical expression, or introduce randomness to your programs. The math methods shown in the table below can help you work with numbers in your formulas. These methods are provided by the .NET Framework, a class library that lets you tap the power of the Windows operating system and accomplish many of the common programming tasks that you need to create your projects. The .NET Framework is a new feature of Visual Studio .NET that is shared by Visual Basic, Visual C++, Visual C#, and other tools in Visual Studio. It is an underlying interface that becomes part of the Windows operating system itself. The .NET Framework is organized into classes that you can include by name in your programming projects using the Imports statement. The process is quite simple, and you'll experiment with how it works now by using a math method in the System.Math class of the .NET Framework.

The following table offers a partial list of the math methods in the System.Math class. The argument n in the table represents the number, variable, or expression you want the method to evaluate. If you use any of these methods, be sure that you put the statement

```
Imports System.Math
```

at the very top of your form code in the Code Editor.

Method	Purpose
Abs(n)	Returns the absolute value of n.
Atan(n)	Returns the arctangent, in radians, of n.
Cos(n)	Returns the cosine of the angle n. The angle n is expressed in radians.
Exp(n)	Returns the constant e raised to the power n.
Sign(n)	Returns −1 if n is less than 0, 0 if n is 0, and +1 if n is greater than 0.
Sin(n)	Returns the sine of the angle n. The angle n is expressed in radians.
Sqrt(n)	Returns the square root of n.
Tan(n)	Returns the tangent of the angle n. The angle n is expressed in radians.

Use the System.Math class to compute square roots

1 On the File menu, point to New, and then click Project.

The New Project dialog box appears.

2 Create a new Visual Basic Windows Application project named **My Framework Math** in the c:\vbnetsbs\chap05 folder.

The new project is created and a blank form appears in the Windows Forms Designer.

ab|

Button control

|abl|

TextBox control

3 Click the Button control on the Windows Forms tab of the Toolbox, and create a button object at the top of your form.

4 Click the TextBox control in the Toolbox, and draw a text box below the button object.

5 Set the Text property of the button object to **Square Root**, and set the Text property of the text box object to blank (empty).

6 Double-click the button object to display the Code Editor.

7 At the very top of the Code Editor, above the Public Class Form1 statement, type the following program statement:

```
Imports System.Math
```

The Imports statement adds a library of objects, properties, and methods to your project. This statement must be the first statement in your program—it must even come before the variables that you declare for the form and the Public Class Form1 statement that Visual Basic automatically provides. The particular library you've chosen is the System.Math class, a collection of objects, properties, and methods provided by the .NET Framework for mathematical operations.

8 Move down in the Code Editor, and add the following code to the Button1_Click event procedure between the Private Sub and End Sub statements.

```
Dim Result As Double
Result = Sqrt(625)
TextBox1.Text = Result
```

These three statements declare a variable of the double type named Result, use the Sqrt method to compute the square root of 625, and assign the Result variable to the Text property of the text box object so that the answer will be displayed.

9 Click the Save All button on the Standard toolbar to save your changes.

10 Click the Start button on the Standard toolbar.

The Framework Math program runs in the development environment.

▶

Start button

11 Click the Square Root button.

Visual Basic calculates the square root of 625 and displays the result (25) in the text box, as shown on the following page. The Sqrt method works!

12   Click the Close button on the form to end the program.

To use a particular .NET Framework class in your program, include the Imports statement and specify the appropriate class library. You can use this technique to use any class in the .NET Framework. You'll see several more examples of this skill as you work through the book.

Operator Precedence

In the past few exercises, you experimented with several mathematical operators and one string operator. Visual Basic lets you mix as many mathematical operators as you like in a formula, as long as each numeric variable and expression is separated from another by one operator. For example, this is an acceptable Visual Basic formula:

```
Total = 10 + 15 * 2 / 4 ^ 2
```

The formula processes several values and assigns the result to a variable named Total. But how is such an expression evaluated by Visual Basic? In other words, which mathematical operators does Visual Basic use first when solving the formula? You might not have noticed, but the order of evaluation matters a great deal in this example.

The operator order of evaluation is important when you are building mathematical formulas.

Visual Basic solves this dilemma by establishing a specific *order of precedence* for mathematical operations. This list of rules tells Visual Basic which operators to use first when evaluating an expression that contains more than one operator. The following table lists the operators from first to last in the order in which they will be evaluated. (Operators on the same level in this table are evaluated from left to right as they appear in an expression.)

Operator(s)	Order of precedence
( )	Values within parentheses are always evaluated first.
^	Exponentiation (raising a number to a power) is second.
–	Negation (creating a negative number) is third.
* /	Multiplication and division are fourth.
\	Integer division is fifth.
Mod	Remainder division is sixth.
+ –	Addition and subtraction are last.

Given the order of precedence in the table above, the expression

```
Total = 10 + 15 * 2 / 4 ^ 2
```

would be evaluated by Visual Basic in the following steps. (Boldface type is used to show each step in the order of evaluation and its result.)

```
Total = 10 + 15 * 2 / 4 ^ 2
Total = 10 + 15 * 2 / 16
Total = 10 + 30 / 16
Total = 10 + 1.875
Total = 11.875
```

One Step Further: Using Parentheses in a Formula

Parentheses clarify and influence the order of evaluation.

You can use one or more pairs of parentheses in a formula to clarify the order of precedence. For example, Visual Basic would calculate the formula

```
Number = (8 - 5 * 3) ^ 2
```

by determining the value within the parentheses (–7) before doing the exponentiation—even though exponentiation is higher in order of precedence than subtraction and multiplication. You can further refine the calculation by placing nested parentheses in the formula. For example,

```
Number = ((8 - 5) * 3) ^ 2
```

directs Visual Basic to calculate the difference in the inner set of parentheses first, perform the operation in the outer parentheses next, and then determine the exponentiation. The result produced by the two formulas is different: the first formula evaluates to 49 and the second to 81. Parentheses can change the result of a mathematical operation, as well as make it easier to read.

Chapter 5 Quick Reference

To	Do this
Declare a variable	Type Dim followed by the variable name, the "As" keyword, and the variable data type in the program code. To make the variable valid in all the form's event procedures, place this statement at the top of the code for a form, before any event procedures. For example: `Dim Country As String`
Change the value of a variable	Assign a new value with the assignment operator of (=). For example: `Country = "Japan"`
Get input with a dialog box	Use the InputBox function, and assign the result to a variable. For example: `UserName = InputBox("What is your name?")`

Display output in a dialog box	Use the MsgBox function. (The string to be displayed in the dialog box can be stored in a variable.) For example:
	`Forecast = "Rain, mainly on the plain."`
	`MsgBox(Forecast, , "Spain Weather Report")`

Create a constant	Type the Const keyword followed by the constant name, the assignment operator (=), the constant data type, and the fixed value. For example: `Const JackBennysAge As Short = 39`
Create a formula	Link together numeric variables or values with one of the seven mathematical operators, and then assign the result to a variable or a property. For example: `Result = 1 ^ 2 * 3 \ 4   'this equals 0`
Combine text strings	Use the string concatenation operator (&). For example: `Msg = "Hello" & "," & " world!"`
Include a class library from the .NET Framework	Place an Imports statement at the very top of the form's code that identifies the class library. For example: `Imports System.Math`
Make a call to a method from an included class library	Use the method name, and include any necessary arguments so that it can be used in a formula or program statement. For example, to make a call to the Sqrt method in the System.Math class library: `Hypotenuse = Sqrt(x ^ 2 + y ^ 2)`

Control the evaluation order in a formula	Use parentheses in the formula. For example:
	`Result = 1 + 2 ^ 3 \ 4         'this equals 3`
	`Result = (1 + 2) ^ ( 3 \ 4)  'this equals 1`

Using Decision Structures

In this chapter you will learn how to:

✔ *Write conditional expressions.*

✔ *Use an If...Then statement to branch to a set of program statements based on a varying condition.*

✔ *Short-circuit an If...Then statement.*

✔ *Use a Select Case statement to select one choice from many options in program code.*

✔ *Detect and manage mouse events.*

In the past few chapters, you used several features of Microsoft Visual Basic .NET to process user input. You used menus, objects, and dialog boxes to display choices for the user, and you processed input by using properties and variables. In this chapter, you'll learn how to branch conditionally to a specific program code section based on input you receive from the user. You'll also learn how to evaluate one or more properties or variables by using conditional expressions and then execute one or more program statements based on the results.

Upgrade Notes:
What's New in Visual Basic .NET?

If you're experienced with Visual Basic 6, you'll notice some new features in Visual Basic .NET, including the following:

■   Visual Basic .NET includes two new logical operators named AndAlso and OrElse. In a conditional statement that contains multiple conditions, such as an If...Then structure, it might not be necessary to always evaluate all the conditions. Passing over conditions is sometimes called "short-circuiting" and can be specified by using the AndAlso and OrElse operators.

Event-Driven Programming

The programs you have written so far in this book have displayed menus, objects, and dialog boxes on the screen, and these programs have encouraged users to manipulate the screen elements in whatever order they saw fit. The programs put the user in charge, waited patiently for a response, and then processed the input predictably. In programming circles, this methodology is known as *event-driven programming*. You build a program by creating a group of "intelligent" objects that know how to respond when the user interacts with them, and then you process the input by using event procedures associated with the objects. The following diagram shows how an event-driven program works in Visual Basic:

Visual Basic programs are event-driven.

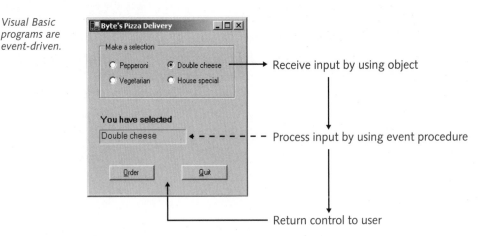

Program input can also come from the computer system itself. For example, your program might be notified when a piece of electronic mail arrives or when a specified period of time has elapsed on the system clock. These events are triggered by the computer, not by the user. Regardless of how an event is triggered, Visual Basic reacts by calling the event procedure associated with the object that recognized the event. So far, you've dealt primarily with the Click, CheckedChanged, and SelectedIndexChanged events. However, Visual Basic objects also can respond to several other types of events.

Events Supported by Visual Basic Objects

Each object in Visual Basic has a predefined set of events it can respond to. These events are listed when you select an object name in the Class Name drop-down list box at the top of the Code Editor and then click the Method Name drop-down list box. (Events are visually identified in Visual Studio by a lightning bolt icon.) You can write an event procedure for any of these events, and if that event occurs in the program, Visual Basic will execute the event procedure that is associated with it. For example, a list box object supports more than 60 events, including Click, DoubleClick, DragDrop, DragOver, GotFocus, KeyDown, KeyPress, KeyUp, LostFocus, MouseDown, MouseMove, MouseUp, MouseWheel, TextChanged, and Validated. You probably won't need to program for more than three or four of these events in your applications, but it's nice to know that you have so many choices when you create elements in your interface. The following illustration shows a partial listing of the events for a list box object in the Code Editor:

Class Name   Method Name

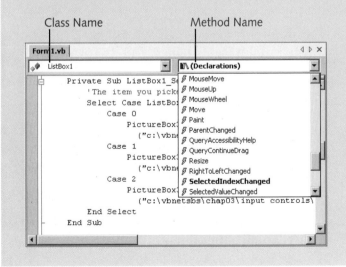

The event-driven nature of Visual Basic means that most of the computing done in your programs will be accomplished by event procedures. These event-specific blocks of code process input, calculate new values, display output, and handle other tasks. In the previous chapter, you learned how to use variables, operators, and mathematical formulas to perform calculations in your event procedures. In this chapter, you'll learn how to use *decision structures* to compare variables, properties, and values, and you'll learn how to execute one or more statements based on the results. In the next chapter, you'll use *loops* to execute a group of statements over and over until a condition is met. Together, these powerful flow-control structures will help you build your event procedures so that they can respond to almost any situation.

Using Conditional Expressions

One of the most useful tools for processing information in an event procedure is a *conditional expression*. A conditional expression is a part of a complete program statement that asks a True-or-False question about a property, a variable, or another piece of data in the program code. For example, the conditional expression

Conditional expressions ask True-or-False questions.

```
Price < 100
```

evaluates to True if the Price variable contains a value that is less than 100, and it evaluates to False if Price contains a value that is greater than or equal to 100. You can use the following comparison operators in a conditional expression.

Comparison operator	Meaning
=	Equal to
<>	Not equal to
>	Greater than
<	Less than
>=	Greater than or equal to
<=	Less than or equal to

tip

Expressions that can be evaluated as True or False are also known as *Boolean expressions*, and the True or False result can be assigned to a Boolean variable or property. You can assign Boolean values to certain object properties or Boolean variables that have been created by using the Dim statement and the As Boolean keywords.

The following table shows some conditional expressions and their results. In an exercise later in this chapter, you'll work with conditional expressions.

Conditional expression	Result
10 <> 20	True (10 is not equal to 20)
Score < 20	True if Score is less than 20; otherwise, False
Score = Label1.Text	True if the Text property of the Label1 object contains the same value as the Score variable; otherwise, False
Text1.Text = "Bill"	True if the word "Bill" is in the first text box; otherwise, False

If...Then Decision Structures

If...Then decision structures let you add logic to your programs.

Conditional expressions used in a special block of statements called a *decision structure* control whether other statements in your program are executed and in what order they are executed. You can use an If...Then decision structure to evaluate a condition in the program and take a course of action based on the result. In its simplest form, an If...Then decision structure is written on a single line:

```
If condition Then statement
```

where *condition* is a conditional expression and *statement* is a valid Visual Basic program statement. For example,

```
If Score >= 20 Then Label1.Text = "You win!"
```

is an If...Then decision structure that uses the conditional expression

```
Score >= 20
```

to determine whether the program should set the Text property of the Label1 object to "You win!" If the Score variable contains a value that is greater than or equal to 20, Visual Basic sets the Text property; otherwise, it skips the assignment statement and executes the next line in the event procedure. This sort of comparison always results in a True or False value. A conditional expression never results in maybe.

Testing Several Conditions in an If...Then Decision Structure

ElseIf and Else clauses let you set several conditions in an If...Then structure.

Visual Basic also supports an If...Then decision structure that allows you to include several conditional expressions. This block of statements can be several lines long and contains the important keywords ElseIf, Else, and End If.

```
If condition1 Then
    statements executed if condition1 is True
ElseIf condition2 Then
    statements executed if condition2 is True
[Additional ElseIf clauses and statements can be placed here]
Else
    statements executed if none of the conditions is True
End If
```

In this structure, *condition1* is evaluated first. If this conditional expression is True, the block of statements below it is executed, one statement at a time. (You can include one or more program statements.) If the first condition isn't True, the second conditional expression (*condition2*) is evaluated. If the second condition is True, the second block of statements is executed. (You can add additional ElseIf conditions and statements if you have more conditions to evaluate.) If none of the conditional expressions is True, the statements below the Else keyword are executed. Finally, the whole structure is closed by the End If keywords.

The following code shows how a multiple-line If...Then structure could be used to determine the amount of tax due in a hypothetical progressive tax return. (The income and percentage numbers are from the United States Internal Revenue Service 2001 Tax Rate Schedule for single filing status.)

Multiple-line If...Then structures are perfect for calculating values that fall in different ranges, such as numbers in a tax return.

```
Dim AdjustedIncome, TaxDue As Double
AdjustedIncome = 32000

If AdjustedIncome <= 27050 Then          '15% tax bracket
    TaxDue = AdjustedIncome * 0.15
ElseIf AdjustedIncome <= 65550 Then      '28% tax bracket
    TaxDue = 4057.5 + ((AdjustedIncome - 27050) * 0.28)
ElseIf AdjustedIncome <= 136750 Then     '31% tax bracket
    TaxDue = 14837.5 + ((AdjustedIncome - 65550) * 0.31)
ElseIf AdjustedIncome <= 297350 Then     '36% tax bracket
    TaxDue = 36909.5 + ((AdjustedIncome - 136750) * 0.36)
Else                                     '39.6% tax bracket
    TaxDue = 94725.5 + ((AdjustedIncome - 297350) * 0.396)
End If
```

important

The order of the conditional expressions in your If...Then and ElseIf clauses is critical. What if you reversed the order of the conditional expressions in the tax computation example and listed the rates in the structure from highest to lowest? Taxpayers in the 15 percent, 28 percent, and 31 percent tax brackets would all be placed in the 36 percent tax bracket, because they all would have an income that is less than or equal to 297,350. (Visual Basic stops at the first conditional expression that is True, even if others are also True.) Because all the conditional expressions in this example test the same variable, they need to be listed in ascending order to get the taxpayers to fall out at the right spots. Moral: When you use more than one conditional expression, consider their order carefully.

This useful decision structure tests the double-precision variable Adjusted-Income at the first income level and subsequent income levels until one of the conditional expressions evaluates to True, and then determines the taxpayer's income tax accordingly. With some simple modifications, it could be used to compute the tax owed by any taxpayer in a progressive tax system such as the one in the United States. Provided that the tax rates are complete and up-to-date and that the value in the AdjustedIncome variable is correct, the program as written will give the correct tax for single U.S. taxpayers for 2001. If the tax rates change, it is a simple matter to update the conditional expressions. With an additional decision structure to determine taxpayers' filing status, the program readily extends itself to include all U.S. taxpayers.

In the next exercise you'll use an If...Then decision structure to validate users as they log in to a program. You might use similar program logic to write a network application that includes user validation.

Validate users by using If...Then

1   Start Visual Studio and create a new Visual Basic Windows Application project named **My User Validation** in the c:\vbnetsbs\chap06 folder.

     The new project is created and a blank form appears in the Windows Forms Designer.

2   Use the Button control on the Windows Forms tab of the Toolbox to create a button object in the upper left of the form.

Button control

3   Set the Text property of the button to **Sign In**.

PictureBox control

4   Use the PictureBox control to create a large rectangular picture box object on the form below the button object.

Your form should look like this:

5   Double-click the Sign In button.

The Button1_Click event procedure appears in the Code Editor.

By convention, statements below If...Then, ElseIf, and Else clauses are indented.

6   Type the following program statements in the event procedure:

```
Dim UserName As String
UserName = InputBox("Enter your first name.")
If UserName = "Henry" Then
    MsgBox("Welcome, Henry!  How are you today?")
    PictureBox1.Image = System.Drawing.Image.FromFile _
      ("c:\vbnetsbs\chap06\henry photo.jpg")
ElseIf UserName = "Felix" Then
    MsgBox("Welcome, Felix!  Ready to play?")
    PictureBox1.Image = System.Drawing.Image.FromFile _
      ("c:\vbnetsbs\chap06\felix photo.jpg")
Else
    MsgBox("Sorry, I don't recognize you.")
    End    'quit the program
End If
```

The space and the line continuation character (_) used after the Picture-Box1.Image properties break two long program statements into four lines so that they can be printed in this book. If you choose, you can type each of these long statements on one line; the Code Editor will scroll to the right.

tip

Program lines can be more than 65,000 characters long in the Visual Studio Code Editor, but it is usually easiest to work with lines of 80 or fewer characters. You can divide long program statements among multiple lines by using a space and a line continuation character (_) at the end of each line in the statement except the last line. (You cannot use a line continuation character to break a string that is in quotation marks, however.)

The complete User Validation program is available on disk in the c:\vbnetsbs\ chap06\user validation folder.

When you've finished, your screen should look like this:

```
Public Class Form1
    Inherits System.Windows.Forms.Form

    Windows Form Designer generated code

    Private Sub Button1_Click(ByVal sender As System.Object, ByVal e .
        Dim UserName As String
        UserName = InputBox("Enter your first name.")
        If UserName = "Henry" Then
            MsgBox("Welcome, Henry!  How are you today?")
            PictureBox1.Image = System.Drawing.Image.FromFile _
                ("c:\vbnetsbs\chap06\henry photo.jpg")
        ElseIf UserName = "Felix" Then
            MsgBox("Welcome, Felix!  Ready to play?")
            PictureBox1.Image = System.Drawing.Image.FromFile _
                ("c:\vbnetsbs\chap06\felix photo.jpg")
        Else
            MsgBox("Sorry, I don't recognize you.")
            End    'quit the program
        End If
    End Sub
End Class
```

7   Click the Save All button on the Standard toolbar to save your changes.

8   Click the Start button on the Standard toolbar.

Start button

The program runs in the development environment. A blank form appears on the screen, with a Sign In button in the upper left.

9   Click the Sign In button.

The InputBox function in the Button1_Click event procedure displays a dialog box that asks you to enter your first name.

10   Type **Henry**, and then click OK.

Using Decision Structures

6

tip
The conditional checks in this program are case sensitive, so be sure to type "Henry" instead of "henry".

The If...Then decision structure compares the name you typed with the text "Henry" in the first conditional expression. The expression evaluates to True and the If...Then statement displays a welcome message by using the MsgBox function.

11   Click OK in the message box.

The message box closes, and a JPEG photo image appears in the picture box, as shown here:

The procedure used to load the picture is the same as I showed you in Chapters 3 and 4 of this book—I use the System.Drawing.Image.FromFile method, which is part of the System.Drawing namespace (or object library). This method is specially designed for loading pictures from files.

12   Click the Sign In button, type **Felix**, and then click OK.

This time the decision structure selects the ElseIf clause and admits Felix to the program. A welcome message is displayed on the screen again by the MsgBox function.

13   Click OK in the message box.

A JPEG photo image associated with this user is loaded into the picture box object.

14   Click the Sign In button, type **Sally**, and then click OK.

The Else clause in the decision structure is executed, and the following message appears in a message box:

15   Click OK to close the message box.

The message box closes, and the program closes. Your code has prevented an unauthorized user from using the program.

Using Logical Operators in Conditional Expressions

Logical operators let you add tests to your expressions.

You can test more than one conditional expression in If...Then and ElseIf clauses if you want to include more than one selection criterion in your decision structure. The extra conditions are linked together by using one or more of the logical operators listed in the table on the following page:

Logical operator	Meaning
And	If both conditional expressions are True, then the result is True.
Or	If either conditional expression is True, then the result is True.
Not	If the conditional expression is False, then the result is True. If the conditional expression is True, then the result is False.
Xor	If one and only one of the conditional expressions is True, then the result is True. If both are True or both are False, then the result is False. (Xor stands for exclusive Or.)

tip

When your program evaluates a complex expression that mixes different operator types, it evaluates mathematical operators first, comparison operators second, and logical operators third.

The following table lists some examples of the logical operators at work. In the expressions, it is assumed that the string variable Vehicle contains the value "Bike" and the integer variable Price contains the value 200.

Logical expression	Result
Vehicle = "Bike" And Price < 300	True (both conditions are True)
Vehicle = "Car" Or Price < 500	True (one condition is True)
Not Price < 100	True (condition is False)
Vehicle = "Bike" Xor Price < 300	False (both conditions are True)

In the following exercise, you'll modify the My User Validation program to prompt the user for a password during the validation process. An input box gets the password from the user, and you modify the If...Then and ElseIf clauses in the decision structure so that they use the And operator to verify the password.

Add password protection by using the And operator

1   Display the Button1_Click event procedure in the Code Editor.

2   Modify the Dim statement at the top of the event procedure so that it also declares a variable named Pass of the String type. Use this syntax:

```
Dim UserName, Pass As String
```

3 Insert the following statement between the InputBox statement and the If...Then statement in the procedure (between the second and third lines):

```
Pass = InputBox("Enter your password.")
```

4 Modify the If...Then statement to the following:

```
If UserName = "Henry" And Pass = "flower" Then
```

The statement now includes the And logical operator, which verifies the user name and password before Henry is admitted to the program.

5 Modify the ElseIf statement to the following:

```
ElseIf UserName = "Felix" And Pass = "sand" Then
```

The complete Password Validation application is available in the c:\vbnetsbs\ chap06\ password validation folder.

The And logical operator adds a check for the "sand" password in Felix's account.

6 Click the Start button on the Standard toolbar.

The program runs in the development environment.

7 Click the Sign In button, type **Henry**, and then click OK.

The program prompts you for a password.

8 Type **flower**, and then click OK.

The And conditional expression evaluates to True, and Henry is welcomed to the program.

9 Click OK to close the message box.

10 Click the Sign In button, type **Felix**, and then click OK.

The program prompts you for a password.

11 Type **sand**, and then click OK.

Felix is welcomed to the program—the passwords work!

12 Now try the Henry and Felix usernames with an incorrect or blank password.

You'll find that they don't work, the program ends, and the development environment returns.

tip

If you are writing a full-featured version of the Password Validation program, consider using a text box object on a form to receive the password input in the program. Text box objects support the PasswordChar property, which you can use to display a placeholder character such as an asterisk (*) as the user types, and the MaxLength property, which lets you limit the number of characters entered.

Short-Circuiting Using AndAlso and OrElse

Visual Basic .NET offers two new logical operators that you can use in your conditional statements, AndAlso and OrElse. These operators work the same way as And and Or respectively, but offer an important subtlety in the way they are evaluated that will be new to programmers experienced with earlier versions of Visual Basic.

Consider an If statement that has two conditions that are connected by an AndAlso operator. For the statements of the If structure to be executed, both conditions must evaluate to True. If the first condition evaluates to False, Visual Basic .NET will skip to the next line or Else statement immediately, without testing the second condition. This partial or "short-circuiting" evaluation of an If statement may make logical sense—why should Visual Basic continue to evaluate the If statement if both conditions cannot be True?

The OrElse operator works in a similar fashion. Consider an If statement that has two conditions that are connected by an OrElse operator. For the statements of the If structure to be executed, at least one condition must evaluate to True. If the first condition evaluates to True, Visual Basic .NET will begin to execute the statements in the If structure immediately, without testing the second condition.

Here's an example of the "short-circuit" situation in Visual Basic .NET, a simple routine that uses an If statement and an AndAlso operator to test two conditions and display the message *Inside If* if both conditions are True:

```
Dim Number As Integer = 0
If Number = 1 AndAlso MsgBox("Second condition test") Then
    MsgBox("Inside If")
Else
    MsgBox("Inside Else")
End If
```

The MsgBox function itself is used as the second conditional test, which is somewhat unusual, but the strange syntax is completely valid and gives us a perfect opportunity to see how "short-circuiting" works up close. The text *Second condition test* will only appear in a message box if the Number variable is set to 0; otherwise, the AndAlso operator "short-circuits" the If statement and the second condition isn't evaluated. If you actually try this code, remember that it is for demonstration purposes only—you wouldn't want to use MsgBox with this syntax as a test because it doesn't really test anything. But by changing the Number variable from 0 to 1 and back, you can get a good idea of how the AndAlso statement and "short-circuiting" works.

Here's a second example of how "short-circuiting" functions in Visual Basic .NET when two conditions are evaluated using the AndAlso operator. This time, a more complex conditional test (7 / HumanAge <= 1) is used after the AndAlso operator to determine the "dog age" of a person:

```
Dim HumanAge As Integer
HumanAge = 7
'One year for a dog is seven years for a human
If HumanAge <> 0 AndAlso 7 / HumanAge <= 1 Then
    MsgBox("You are at least one dog year old")
Else
    MsgBox("You are less than one dog year old")
End If
```

This bare-bones routine tries to determine whether the value in the HumanAge integer variable is at least 7. It is part of a larger program that determines the so-called "dog age" of a person by dividing their current age by 7. (If you haven't heard the concept of "dog age" before, bear with me—following this logic, a 28-year-old person would be 4 dog years old.) The code uses two If statement conditions, and can be used in a variety of different contexts—I used it in the Click event procedure for a button object. The first condition checks to see if a non-zero number has been placed in the HumanAge variable—I've assumed momentarily that the user has enough sense to place a positive age into HumanAge, because a negative number would produce incorrect results. The second condition checks to see whether the person is at least 7 years old. If both conditions evaluate to True, the message *You are at least one dog year old* is displayed in a message box. If the person is less than 7, the message *You are less than one dog year old* is displayed.

Now, imagine that I've changed the value of the HumanAge variable from 28 to 0. What happens? The first If statement condition is evaluated as False by the Visual Basic .NET compiler, and that evaluation prevents the second condition from being evaluated, thus halting or "short-circuiting" the If statement, and saving us from a nasty "divide by zero" error that could result if we divided 7 by 0 (the new value of the HumanAge variable). But although we get a benefit from the "short-circuiting" behavior in Visual Studio .NET, we don't have the same luck in Visual Basic 6. Setting the HumanAge variable to 0 in Visual Basic 6 produces a runtime error and crash because the entire If statement is evaluated, and division by zero isn't permitted in Visual Basic 6.

In summary, the AndAlso and OrElse operators in Visual Basic .NET open up a few new possibilities for Visual Basic programmers, including the potential to prevent runtime errors and other unexpected results. It's also possible to

6

Using Decision Structures

improve performance by placing conditions that are time consuming to calculate at the end of the condition statement. Visual Basic .NET won't perform these expensive condition calculations unless it is necessary. However, you need to think carefully about all the possible conditions that your If statements might encounter as variable states change during program execution.

Select Case Decision Structures

Select Case decision structures base branching decisions on one key variable.

Visual Basic also lets you control the execution of statements in your programs by using Select Case decision structures. You used Select Case structures in Chapters 3 and 5 of this book when you wrote event procedures to process list box and combo box choices. A Select Case structure is similar to an If...Then...ElseIf structure, but it is more efficient when the branching depends on one key variable, or *test case*. You can also use Select Case structures to make your program code more readable.

The syntax for a Select Case structure looks like this:

```
Select Case variable
    Case value1
        program statements executed if value1 matches variable
    Case value2
        program statements executed if value2 matches variable
    Case value3
        program statements executed if value3 matches variable
    ⋮
    Case Else
        program statements executed if no match is found
End Select
```

A Select Case structure begins with the Select Case keywords and ends with the End Select keywords. You replace *variable* with the variable, property, or other expression that is to be the key value, or test case, for the structure. You replace *value1*, *value2*, and *value3* with numbers, strings, or other values related to the test case being considered. If one of the values matches the variable, the statements below the Case clause are executed, and then Visual Basic jumps to the line after the End Select statement and picks up execution there. You can include any number of Case clauses in a Select Case structure, and you can include more than one value in a Case clause. If you list multiple values after a case, separate them with commas.

The example below shows how a Select Case structure could be used to print an appropriate message about a person's age in a program. Since the Age variable contains a value of 18, the string "You can vote now!" is assigned to the Text property of the label object.

```
Dim Age As Integer
Age = 18

Select Case Age
    Case 16
        Label1.Text = "You can drive now!"
    Case 18
        Label1.Text = "You can vote now!"
    Case 21
        Label1.Text = "You can drink wine with your meals."
    Case 65
        Label1.Text = "Time to retire and have fun!"
End Select
```

The organization of a Select Case structure can make it clearer than an equivalent If...Then structure.

A Select Case structure also supports a Case Else clause that you can use to display a message if none of the earlier cases matches. Here's how Case Else would work in the following example—note that I've changed the value of Age to 25 to trigger the Case Else clause.

```
Dim Age As Integer
Age = 25

Select Case Age
    Case 16
        Label1.Text = "You can drive now!"
    Case 18
        Label1.Text = "You can vote now!"
    Case 21
        Label1.Text = "You can drink wine with your meals."
    Case 65
        Label1.Text = "Time to retire and have fun!"
    Case Else
        Label1.Text = "You're a great age! Enjoy it!"
End Select
```

Using Comparison Operators with a Select Case Structure

A Select Case structure supports comparison operators just like an If...Then structure does.

You can use comparison operators to include a range of test values in a Select Case structure. The Visual Basic comparison operators that can be used are =, <>, >, <, >=, and <=. To use the comparison operators, you need to include the Is keyword or the To keyword in the expression to identify the comparison you're making. The Is keyword instructs the compiler to compare the test variable to the expression listed after the Is keyword. The To keyword identifies a range of values. The following structure uses Is, To, and several comparison operators to test the Age variable and to display one of five messages:

```
Select Case Age
    Case Is < 13
        Label1.Text = "Enjoy your youth!"
    Case 13 To 19
        Label1.Text = "Enjoy your teens!"
    Case 21
        Label1.Text = "You can drink wine with your meals."
    Case Is > 100
        Label1.Text = "Looking good!"
    Case Else
        Label1.Text = "That's a nice age to be."
End Select
```

If the value of the Age variable is less than 13, the message "Enjoy your youth!" is displayed. For the ages 13 through 19, the message "Enjoy your teens!" is displayed, and so on.

A Select Case decision structure is usually much clearer than an If...Then structure and is more efficient when you're making three or more branching decisions based on one variable or property. However, when you're making two or fewer comparisons, or when you're working with several different values, you'll probably want to use an If...Then decision structure.

In the following exercise, you'll see how you can use a Select Case structure to process input from a list box. You'll use the ListBox1.Text and ListBox1-.SelectedIndexChanged properties to collect the input, and then you'll use a Select Case structure to display a greeting in one of four languages.

Use a Select Case structure to process a list box

1   On the File menu, point to New, and then click Project.

The New Project dialog box appears.

2 Create a new Visual Basic Windows Application project named **My Case Greeting** in the c:\vbnetsbs\chap06 folder.

The new project is created and a blank form appears in the Windows Forms Designer.

Label control

3 Click the Label control on the Windows Forms tab of the Toolbox, and then draw a large label across the top of the form to display a title for the program.

4 Draw a small label just below the title label.

ListBox control

5 Click the ListBox control in the Toolbox, and then draw a list box below the two existing labels.

6 Draw two small labels below the list box to display program output.

Button control

7 Click the Button control in the Toolbox, and then draw a small button on the bottom of the form.

Properties window button

8 Click the Properties window button on the Standard toolbar, and then set the object properties as shown in the following table. You'll assign Name properties too, since you have a number of objects to keep track of on your form.

Object	Property	Setting
Form1	Text	Case Greeting
Label1	Font	Times New Roman, Bold, 12-point
	Name	lblTitle
	Text	"International Welcome Program"
Label2	Name	lblTextBoxLabel
	Text	"Choose a country"
Label3	Font	10-point
	Name	lblCountry
	Text	(empty)
Label4	BorderStyle	Fixed3D
	ForeColor	Red
	Name	lblGreeting
	Text	(empty)
ListBox1	Name	lstCountryBox
Button1	Name	btnQuit
	Text	"Quit"

When you've finished setting properties, your form should look similar to this:

Now you'll enter the program code to initialize the list box.

9   Double-click the form.

The Form1_Load event procedure appears in the Code Editor.

You load values in a list box by using the Add method.

10   Type the following program code to initialize the list box:

```
lstCountryBox.Items.Add("England")
lstCountryBox.Items.Add("Germany")
lstCountryBox.Items.Add("Mexico")
lstCountryBox.Items.Add("Italy")
```

These lines use the Add method of the list box object to add entries to the list box on your form.

11   Click the Form1.vb tab [Design] at the top of the Code Editor to switch back to the Windows Forms Designer, and then double-click the list box object on your form to edit its event procedure.

The lstCountryBox_SelectedIndexChanged event procedure appears in the Code Editor.

12   Type the following lines to process the list box selection made by the user:

```
lblCountry.Text = lstCountryBox.Text
Select Case lstCountryBox.SelectedIndex
    Case 0
        lblGreeting.Text = "Hello, programmer"
    Case 1
        lblGreeting.Text = "Hallo, programmierer"
    Case 2
        lblGreeting.Text = "Hola, programador"
```

```
Case 3
        lblGreeting.Text = "Ciao, programmatore"
End Select
```

The SelectedIndex property contains the number of the selected list item.

The first line copies the name of the selected list box item to the Text property of the third label on the form (which you renamed lblCountry). The most important property used in the statement is lstCountryBox.Text, which contains the exact text of the item selected in the list box. The remaining statements are part of the Select Case decision structure. The structure uses the lstCountryBox.SelectedIndex property as a test case variable and compares it to several values. The SelectedIndex property always contains the number of the item selected in the list box; the item at the top is 0 (zero), the second item is 1, the next item is 2, and so on. Using SelectedIndex, the Select Case structure can quickly identify the user's choice and display the correct greeting on the form.

13 Display the form again, and double-click the Quit button (btnQuit).

The btnQuit_Click event procedure appears in the Code Editor.

14 Type **End** in the event procedure.

The complete Case Greeting project is located in the c:\vbnetsbs\ chap06\case greeting folder.

15 Click the Save All button on the Standard toolbar to save your changes.

Now run the program and see how the Select Case statement works.

16 Click the Start button on the Standard toolbar to run the program.

17 Click each of the country names in the Choose A Country list box.

The program displays a greeting for each of the countries listed. The illustration below shows the greeting for Italy:

18 Click the Quit button to stop the program.

The program stops, and the development environment returns.

You've finished working with If...Then and Select Case decision structures in this chapter. You'll have several additional opportunities to work with them in this book, however. If...Then and Select Case are two of the crucial decision making mechanisms in the Visual Basic programming language, and you'll find that you use them in almost every program that you write.

One Step Further: Detecting Mouse Events

I began this chapter by discussing a few of the events that Visual Basic .NET programs can respond to, and as the chapter progressed you learned how to manage different types of events using the If and Select Case decision structures. In this section, you'll add an event handler to the Case Greeting program that detects when the mouse pointer "hovers" over the country list box for a moment or two. You'll write the special routine or *event handler* by building a list box event procedure for the MouseHover event, one of several mouse-related activities that Visual Basic .NET can monitor and process. This event procedure will display the message "Please click the country name" if the user holds the mouse over the country list box for a moment or two but doesn't make a selection, perhaps because they don't know how to or have become engrossed with another task.

Adding a mouse event handler

1   Open the Code Editor if it isn't already open.

You can use the ToolTip feature to help identify elements in Visual Studio.

2   At the top of the Code Editor, click the drop-down arrow in the Class Name list box, and then click the lstCountryBox object.

3   Click the drop-down arrow in the Method Name list box, and then click the MouseHover event.

Visual Basic opens the lstCountryBox_MouseHover event procedure in the Code Editor as shown here:

```
        Class Name                    Method Name

Start Page | Form1.vb [Design]*  Form1.vb*                          ◁ ▷ ×
 lstCountryBox              ▼    MouseHover                    ▼
          End Sub

          Private Sub lstCountryBox_MouseHover(ByVal sender /

          End Sub
     End Class
```

Each object on the form has one event procedure that opens automatically when you double-click the object on the form. The remaining event procedures need to be opened using the Method Name list box. When you build an event procedure to manage one of an object's events, it is called an event handler.

4   Type the following program statements in the lstCountryBox_MouseHover event procedure:

```
If lstCountryBox.SelectedIndex < 0 Or _
lstCountryBox.SelectedIndex > 4 Then
    lblGreeting.Text = "Please click the country name"
End If
```

This If statement evaluates the SelectedIndex property of the list box object using two conditional statements and the Or operator. The event handler assumes that if there is a value between 1 and 4 in the SelectedIndex property, the user doesn't need help picking the country name (they have already selected a country!). But if the SelectedIndex property is outside that range, then the event handler displays the message "Please click the country name" in the Greeting label at the bottom of the form. This message appears when the user "hovers" the mouse over the list box and disappears when a country name is selected.

5   Click the Start button to run the program.

6   Hold the mouse over the country list box and wait a few moments.

The message "Please click the country name" appears in red type in the label as shown here:

7   Click a country name in the list box.

The translated greeting appears in the label, and the help message disappears.

8   Click the Quit button to stop the program.

You've learned how to process mouse events in a program! In Chapter 16, you'll continue developing this skill by adding animation effects to a Visual Basic application.

Chapter 6 Quick Reference

To	Do this
Write a conditional expression	Use one of the following comparison operators between two values: =, <>, >, <, >=, <=

Use an If...Then decision structure	Use the following syntax:
	```If condition1 Then```
	``` Statements executed if condition1 True```
	```ElseIf condition2 Then```
	``` Statements executed if condition2 True```
	```Else```
	``` Statements executed if none are True```
	```End If```

Use a Select Case decision structure	Use the following syntax:
	```Select Case variable```
	```Case value1```
	``` Statements executed if value1 matches```
	```Case value2```
	``` Statements executed if value2 matches```
	```Case Else```
	``` Statements executed if none match```
	```End Select```

Make two comparisons in a conditional expression	Use a logical operator between comparisons (And, Or, Not, or Xor).
Short-circuit an If...Then statement	In Visual Basic .NET, If...Then statements can be short-circuited when the AndAlso and OrElse operators are used and two or more conditional expressions are given. Depending on the result of the first condition, Visual Basic .NET might not evaluate the additional conditions and the statement is "short-circuited".
Write an event handler	In the Code Editor, click an object name in the Class Name drop-down list box, and then click an event name in the Method Name drop-down list box. Add program statements to the event procedure (or event handler) that perform useful work when the event is executed.

CHAPTER

7.

Using Loops and Timers

In this chapter you will learn how to:

✔ *Use a For...Next loop to execute statements a set number of times.*

✔ *Display output in a multi-line text box using string concatenation.*

✔ *Use a Do loop to execute statements until a specific condition is met.*

✔ *Use a timer object to execute code at specific times.*

✔ *Create your own digital clock and timed password utility.*

In Chapter 6, you learned how to use the If...Then and Select Case decision structures to choose which statements to execute in a program. In this chapter, you'll learn how to execute a block of statements over and over again by using a *loop*. You'll use a For...Next loop to execute statements a set number of times, and you'll use a Do loop to execute statements until a conditional expression is met. You'll also learn how to display more than one line of text in a text box object using the string concatenation (&) operator. Finally, you'll learn how to use a timer object to execute code at specific intervals in your program.

Upgrade Notes: What's New in Visual Basic .NET?

If you're experienced with Visual Basic 6, you'll notice some new features in Visual Basic .NET, including the following:

- In Visual Basic 6, you could display text directly on your form using the Print method, a holdover from the Print statement in GW-BASIC and Microsoft QuickBasic. In Visual Basic .NET, the Print method can be used only to send data to a file on disk. The chapter shows you an alternative method for displaying large amounts of text on a form—appending text to a multi-line text box object using the string concatenation operator (&).

- In Visual Basic 6, a While loop was specified with the following syntax: While...Wend. In Visual Basic .NET, the closing statement has changed to While...End While to parallel other similar structures.

- The Timer control in Visual Basic .NET is similar but not identical to the Timer control in Visual Basic 6. For example, the Timer1_Timer event procedure (which is executed at each pre-set timer interval) has been renamed Timer1_Tick in Visual Studio .NET. In addition, you can no longer disable a Timer by setting the Interval property to 0.

Writing For...Next Loops

With a For...Next loop you can execute a specific group of program statements a set number of times in an event procedure or code module. This approach can be useful if you are performing several related calculations, working with elements on the screen, or processing several pieces of user input. A For...Next loop is really just a shorthand way of writing out a long list of program statements. Because each group of statements in such a list would do essentially the same thing, Visual Basic lets you define just one group of statements and request that it be executed as many times as you want.

The syntax for a For...Next loop looks like this:

```
For variable = start To end
    statements to be repeated
Next [variable]
```

In a For...Next loop, start *and* end *determine how long the loop runs.*

In this syntax statement, For, To, and Next are required keywords and the equal-to operator (=) also is required. You replace *variable* with the name of a numeric variable that keeps track of the current loop count (the variable after Next is optional), and you replace *start* and *end* with numeric values representing the starting and stopping points for the loop. (Note that you must declare *variable* before it is used in the For...Next statement.) The line or lines between the For and Next statements are the instructions that are repeated each time the loop is executed.

For example, the following For...Next loop sounds four beeps in rapid succession from the computer's speaker (although the result might be difficult to hear):

```
Dim i As Integer
For i = 1 To 4
    Beep()
Next i
```

This loop is the functional equivalent of writing the Beep statement four times in a procedure. The compiler treats it the same as

```
Beep()
Beep()
Beep()
Beep()
```

The variable used in the loop is i, a single letter that, by convention, stands for the first integer counter in a For...Next loop, and is declared as an Integer type. Each time the loop is executed, the counter variable is incremented by one. (The first time through the loop, the variable contains a value of 1, the value of *start*; the last time through, it contains a value of 4, the value of *end*.) As you'll see in the following examples, you can use this counter variable to great advantage in your loops.

Displaying a Counter Variable in a TextBox Control

A counter variable is just like any other variable in an event procedure. It can be assigned to properties, used in calculations, or displayed in a program. One of the practical uses for a counter variable is to display output in a TextBox control. You used the TextBox control earlier in this book to display a single line of output, but in this chapter you'll display many lines of text using a TextBox control. The trick to displaying more than one line is simply to set the Multiline property of the TextBox control to True and to set the ScrollBars property to Vertical. Using these simple settings, the one-line text box object becomes a multi-line text box object with scroll bars for easy access.

Display information by using a For...Next loop

1   Start Visual Studio and create a new Visual Basic Windows Application project named **My For Loop** in the c:\vbnetsbs\chap07 folder.

   The new project is created and a blank form appears in the Windows Forms Designer. Your first programming step is to add a Button control to the form, but this time you'll do it in a new way.

2   Double-click the Button control on the Windows Forms tab of the Toolbox.

Button control

   Visual Studio places a button object in the upper left corner of the form. With the Button control and many others, double-clicking is a quick way to create a standard-size object on the form. Now you can drag the button object to the place that you want, and customize it with property settings.

3   Drag the button object to the right and center it near the top of the form.

4   Open the Properties window, and then set the Text property of the button to **Loop**.

5   Double-click the TextBox control in the Toolbox.

TextBox control

   Visual Studio creates a small text box object on the form.

6   Set the Multiline property of the text box object to True, and then set the ScrollBars property of the text box object to Vertical.

   These settings prepare the text box for displaying more than one line of text.

7   Set the Text property of the text box object to blank (empty).

8   Move the text box below the button and enlarge it so that it takes up most of the form.

9   Double-click the Loop button on the form.

   The Button1_Click event procedure appears in the Code Editor.

10   Type the following program statements in the procedure:

```
Dim i As Integer
Dim Wrap As String
Wrap = Chr(13) & Chr(10)
For i = 1 To 10
    TextBox1.Text = TextBox1.Text & "Line " & i & Wrap
Next i
```

   This event procedure declares two variables, one of type Integer (i) and one of type String (Wrap), and then assigns the second variable a string value representing the carriage return character. (In programmer terms, a carriage return character is the equivalent of pressing the Enter key on the keyboard. I created a special variable for this character, which is made up of return and linefeed elements, to make using it less cumbersome.)

After the variable declaration and assignment, I use a For...Next loop to display Line *X* ten times in the text box object, where X is the current value of the counter variable (in other words, Line 1 through Line 10). The string concatenation characters (&) join the component parts of each line together in the text box. First, the entire value of the text box, which is stored in the Text property, is added to the object so that previous lines aren't discarded when new ones are added. Next, the string "Line", the current line number, and the carriage return character (Wrap) are combined to display a new line and move the cursor to the left margin and down one line. The Next statement completes the loop.

Note that Visual Studio automatically adds the Next statement to the bottom of the loop when you type For to begin the loop. In this case, I edited the Next statement to include the i variable name—this is an optional syntax clarification that I like to use. (The variable name makes it clear which variable is being updated, especially in nested For...Next loops.)

Save All button

11 Click the Save All button on the Standard toolbar to save your changes.

Now you're ready to run the program.

12 Click the Start button on the Standard toolbar.

Start button

13 Click the Loop button.

The For...Next loop displays 10 lines in the text box, as shown here:

The complete For Loop program is available in the c:\vbnetsbs\ chap07\for loop folder.

14 Click the Loop button again.

The For...Next loop displays another 10 lines on the form, and you can see any nonvisible lines by using the vertical scroll bar to scroll down. Each time the loop is repeated, it will add 10 more lines to the text box object.

> **tip**
>
> Worried about running out of room in the text box object? It won't happen fast if you're displaying only simple text lines. A multi-line text box object has a practical limit of 32 KB of text. (For even more space and formatting options, try the RichTextBox control.)

15   Click the Close button on the form to stop the program.

> **tip**
>
> If you need to execute a set of statements multiple times, a For…Next loop can considerably simplify your code and reduce the total number of statements that you need to type. In the previous example, a For…Next loop three lines long processed the equivalent of 10 program statements.

Creating Complex For…Next Loops

You can create a different sequence of numbers for your For…Next counter variable by using the Step keyword.

The counter variable in a For…Next loop can be a powerful tool in your programs. With a little imagination, you can use it to create several useful sequences of numbers in your loops. To create a loop with a counter pattern other than 1, 2, 3, 4, and so on, you can specify a different value for *start* in the loop and then use the Step keyword to increment the counter at different intervals. For example, the code

```
Dim i As Integer
Dim Wrap As String
Wrap = Chr(13) & Chr(10)

For i = 5 To 25 Step 5
    TextBox1.Text = TextBox1.Text & "Line " & i & Wrap
Next i
```

would display the following sequence of line numbers in a text box:

```
Line 5
Line 10
Line 15
Line 20
Line 25
```

You can use the Step keyword with decimal values.

You can also specify decimal values in a loop if you declare i as a single or double-precision type. For example, the For...Next loop

```
Dim i As Single
Dim Wrap As String
Wrap = Chr(13) & Chr(10)


For i = 1 To 2.5 Step 0.5
    TextBox1.Text = TextBox1.Text & "Line " & i & Wrap
Next i
```

would display the following line numbers in a text box:

```
Line 1
Line 1.5
Line 2
Line 2.5
```

In addition to displaying the counter variable, you can use the counter to set properties, calculate values, or process files. The following exercise shows how you can use the counter to open Visual Basic icons that are stored on your hard disk in files that have numbers in their names. You'll find many files like this in the c:\program files\microsoft visual studio .net\common7\graphics\icons\misc folder.

Open files by using a For...Next loop

1   On the File menu, point to New, and then click Project.

The New Project dialog box appears.

2   Create a new Visual Basic Windows Application project named **My For Loop Icons** in the c:\vbnetsbs\chap07 folder.

The new project is created and a blank form appears in the Windows Forms Designer.

PictureBox control

3   Click the PictureBox control on the Windows Forms tab of the Toolbox, and then draw a medium-sized picture box object centered on the top half of the form.

4   Click the Button control in the Toolbox, and then draw a very wide button below the picture box (you'll put a longer than usual label on the button).

5   Set the following properties for the two objects:

Object	Property	Setting
PictureBox1	BorderStyle	Fixed3D
	SizeMode	StretchImage
Button1	Text	"Display four faces"

6   Double-click the Display four faces button on the form to display the event procedure for the button object.

The Button1_Click event procedure appears in the Code Editor.

7   Type the following For...Next loop:

```
Dim i As Integer
For i = 1 To 4
    PictureBox1.Image = System.Drawing.Image.FromFile _
      ("c:\vbnetsbs\chap07\face0" & i & ".ico")
    MsgBox("Click here for next face.")
Next
```

tip
The FromFile method in this event procedure is too long to fit on one line in this book, so I broke it into two lines by using a space and the line continuation character (_). You can use this character anywhere in your program code except within a string expression.

The loop uses the FromFile method to load four icon files from the c:\vbnetsbs\chap07 folder on your hard disk. The filename is created by using the counter variable and the concatenation operator you used earlier in this chapter. The code

```
PictureBox1.Image = System.Drawing.Image.FromFile _
  ("c:\vbnetsbs\chap07\face0" & i & ".ico")
```

combines a path, a filename, and the .ico extension to create four valid filenames of icons on your hard disk. In this example, you're loading face01.ico, face02.ico, face03.ico, and face04.ico into the picture box. This statement works because several files in the c:\vbnetsbs\chap07 folder have the filename pattern facexx.ico. Recognizing the pattern lets you build a For...Next loop around the filenames.

tip
The message box function (MsgBox) is used primarily to slow the action down and allow you to see what is happening in the For...Next loop. In a normal application, you probably wouldn't use such a function (but you are welcome to do so).

8   Click the Save All button on the toolbar to save your changes.

*The complete
For Loop Icons
program is
available in the
c:\vbnetsbs\
chap07\for
loop icons
folder.*

9   Click the Start button on the Standard toolbar to start the program, and
then click the Display four faces button.

The For…Next loop loads the first face into the picture box, and then displays this message box:

> ## tip
>
> If Visual Basic displays an error message, check your program code for typos
> and then verify that the icon files are in the path you specified in the program.
> If you installed the Step by Step practice files in a folder other than the default
> folder or if you moved your icon files after installation, the path in the event
> procedure may not be correct.

10   Click the OK button to display the next face.

Your screen will look like this:

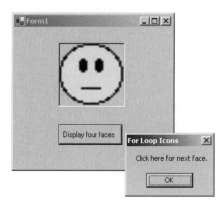

11   Click the OK button three more times to see the entire face collection.

You can repeat the sequence if you like.

12   When you're finished, click the Close button on the form to quit the program.

The program stops, and the development environment returns.

Opening Files Using a Counter That Has Greater Scope

Are there times when using a For...Next loop isn't that efficient or elegant? Sure. In fact, the preceding example, while useful as a demonstration, was a little hampered by the intrusive behavior of the message box, which opened four times in the For...Next loop and distracted the user from the form, where we want their attention to be. Is there a way we can do away with that intrusive message box?

One solution is to remove both the MsgBox function and the For...Next loop and substitute in their place a counter variable that has greater scope throughout the form. As you learned in Chapter 5, you can declare a variable that has scope (or maintains its value) throughout the entire form by placing a Dim statement for the variable at the top of the form in the Code Editor—a special location above the event procedures and just below the Windows Forms Designer generated code section. In the following exercise, you'll use an Integer variable named Counter that will maintain its value between calls to the Button1_Click event procedure, and you'll use that variable to open the same icon files without using the MsgBox function to pause the action.

Use a global Counter

1   In the Code Editor, locate the Button1_Click event procedure in the For Loop Icons project.

2   Move the cursor above the Button1_Click event procedure, and directly below the Windows Forms Designer generated code section, declare an Integer variable named Counter using this syntax:

```
Dim Counter As Integer = 1
```

You've done something unusual here—in addition to declaring the variable Counter, you've also assigned the variable a value of 1. This is a new syntax option in Visual Studio .NET, and now and then you'll find it very handy to use. (Declaring and assigning at the same time isn't permitted in Visual Basic 6.)

3 Within the Button1_Click event procedure, change the code so that it precisely matches the following group of program statements (delete the statements that aren't here):

```
PictureBox1.Image = System.Drawing.Image.FromFile _
    ("c:\vbnetsbs\chap07\face0" & Counter & ".ico")
Counter += 1
If Counter = 5 Then Counter = 1
```

As you can see, I've deleted the declaration for the i integer, the For and Next statements, and the MsgBox function, and I've changed the way the FromFile method works (I've replaced the i variable with the Counter variable). I've also added two new statements that use the Counter variable. The first statement adds 1 to Counter (Counter += 1), and the second statement resets the Counter variable if the value has been incremented to 5. ("Resetting" the variable in this way will allow the list of icon files to cycle indefinitely.) The Counter += 1 syntax is a new shortcut feature in Visual Basic .NET also—it is the functional equivalent of the statement

```
Counter = Counter + 1
```

The complete Counter Variable program is located in the c:\vbnetsbs\ chap07\counter variable folder.

4 Click the Start button to run the program.

The program runs in the development environment.

5 Click the Display four faces button several times (notice how the mood of the faces develops from glum to cheery).

6 When you're finished, click the Close button on the form to stop the program.

As you can see, this solution is a little more elegant than the previous example I used because it allows the user to click just one button, not a form button and a message box button. The shortcoming of the interface in the first program was not the fault of the For...Next loop, however, but rather the limitation I had imposed that the Button1_Click event procedure use only local variables (in other words, variables that were declared within the event procedure itself). Between button clicks, these local variables lost their value, and the only way I was able to increment the counter was to build a loop. Using an Integer variable with a greater scope, we were able to preserve the value of the Counter variable between clicks and use that numeric information to display files within the Button1_Click event procedure.

The Exit For Statement

Most For...Next loops run to completion without incident, but now and then you'll find it useful to end the computation of a For...Next loop if a particular "exit condition" comes up. Visual Basic allows for this possibility by providing the Exit For statement, a special statement that you use to terminate the execution of a For...Next loop early and move execution to the first statement after the loop.

For example, the following For...Next loop prompts the user for 10 names and displays them one by one in a text box unless the user enters the word "Done":

```
Dim i As Integer
Dim InpName As String
For i = 1 To 10
    InpName = InputBox("Enter your name or type Done to quit.")
    If InpName = "Done" Then Exit For
    TextBox1.Text = InpName
Next i
```

If the user does enter "Done", the Exit For statement terminates the loop and execution picks up with the statement after Next.

Writing Do Loops

Do loops execute code until a specific condition is met.

As an alternative to a For...Next loop, you can write a Do loop that executes a group of statements until a certain condition is True. Do loops are valuable because often you can't know in advance how many times a loop should repeat.

For example, you might want to let the user enter names in a database until the user types the word "Done" in an input box. In that case, you can use a Do loop to cycle indefinitely until the text string "Done" is entered.

A Do loop has several formats, depending on where and how the loop condition is evaluated. The most common syntax is:

```
Do While condition
    block of statements to be executed
Loop
```

For example, the following Do loop will prompt the user for input and display that input in a text box until the word "Done" is typed in the input box:

```
Dim InpName As String
Do While InpName <> "Done"
    InpName = InputBox("Enter your name or type Done to quit.")
    If InpName <> "Done" Then TextBox1.Text = InpName
Loop
```

The placement of the conditional test affects how a Do loop runs.

The conditional statement in this loop is InpName <> "Done", which the Visual Basic compiler translates to mean "loop as long as the InpName variable doesn't contain the word *Done*." This brings up an interesting fact about Do loops: if the condition at the top of the loop isn't True when the Do statement is first evaluated, the Do loop is never executed. Here, if the InpName string variable did contain the value "Done" before the loop started (perhaps from an earlier assignment in the event procedure), Visual Basic would skip the loop altogether and continue with the line below the Loop keyword.

If you always want the loop to run at least once in a program, put the conditional test at the bottom of the loop. For example, the loop

```
Dim InpName As String
Do
    InpName = InputBox("Enter your name or type Done to quit.")
    If InpName <> "Done" Then TextBox1.Text = InpName
Loop While InpName <> "Done"
```

is essentially the same as the previous Do loop, but here the loop condition is tested after a name is received from the InputBox function. This has the advantage of updating the InpName variable before the conditional test in the loop so that a preexisting "Done" value won't cause the loop to be skipped. Testing the loop condition at the bottom ensures that your loop will be executed at least once, but often it will force you to add a few extra statements to process the data.

tip

The previous code samples asked the user to type "Done" to quit. Note that the test of the entered text is case-sensitive, which means that typing "done" or "DONE" doesn't end the program. You can do a case-insensitive test of the entered text by using the StrComp function. I'll discuss the StrComp function in Chapter 12.

Avoiding an Endless Loop

Because of the relentless nature of Do loops, it's very important to design your test conditions so that each loop has a true exit point. If a loop test never evaluates to False, the loop will execute endlessly and your program might not respond to input. Consider the following example:

```
Dim Number as Double
Do
    Number = InputBox("Enter a number to square. Type -1 to quit.")
    Number = Number * Number
    TextBox1.Text = Number
Loop While Number >= 0
```

In this loop the user enters number after number, and the program squares each number and displays it in the text box. Unfortunately, when the user has had enough, he or she can't quit because the advertised exit condition doesn't work. When the user enters –1, the program squares it and the Number variable is assigned the value 1. (The problem can be fixed by setting a different exit condition.) Watching for endless loops is essential when you're writing Do loops. Fortunately, they're pretty easy to spot if you test your programs thoroughly.

important

Be sure that each loop has a legitimate exit condition.

The following exercise shows how you can use a Do loop to convert Fahrenheit temperatures to Celsius temperatures. The simple program prompts the user for input by using the InputBox function, converts the temperature, and displays the output in a message box.

Convert temperatures by using a Do loop

1 On the File menu, point to New, and then click Project.

The New Project dialog box appears.

2 Create a new Visual Basic Windows Application project named **My Celsius Conversion** in the c:\vbnetsbs\chap07 folder.

The new project is created and a blank form appears in the Windows Forms Designer. This time you'll place all the code for your program in the Form1_Load event procedure so that Visual Basic immediately prompts you for the Fahrenheit temperature when you start the application. You'll use an InputBox function to request the Fahrenheit data, and you'll use a MsgBox function to display the converted value.

The Form1_ Load event procedure is executed when a program starts running.

3 Double-click the form.

The Form1_Load event procedure appears in the Code Editor.

4 Type the following program statements in the Form1_Load event procedure:

```
Dim FTemp, Celsius As Single
Dim strFTemp As String
Dim Prompt As String = "Enter a Fahrenheit temperature."
Do
    strFTemp = InputBox(Prompt, "Fahrenheit to Celsius")
    If strFTemp <> "" Then
        FTemp = CSng(strFTemp)
        Celsius = Int((FTemp + 40) * 5 / 9 - 40)
        MsgBox(Celsius, , "Temperature in Celsius")
    End If
Loop While strFTemp <> ""
End
```

tip

Be sure to include the "End" statement at the bottom of the Form1_Load event procedure.

This code handles the calculations for the utility. The first line declares two single-precision variables, FTemp and Celsius, to hold the Fahrenheit and Celsius temperatures, respectively. The second line declares a string variable named strFTemp that holds a string version of the Fahrenheit temperature. The third line declares a string variable named Prompt, which will be used in the InputBox function, and assigns it an initial value. The Do loop repeatedly prompts the user for a Fahrenheit temperature, converts the number to Celsius, and then displays it on the screen by using the MsgBox function.

The value that the user enters in the input box is stored in the strFTemp variable. The InputBox function always returns a value of type string, even if the user enters in numbers. Since we want to perform mathematical calculations on the entered value, strFTemp must be converted to a number. The CSng function is used to convert a string into a Single. CSng is one of many conversion functions to convert a string to a different data type. The converted single value is then stored in the FTemp variable.

The loop executes until the user clicks the Cancel button or until the user presses Enter or clicks OK with no value in the input box. Clicking the Cancel button or entering no value returns an empty string (""). The loop checks for the empty string by using a While conditional test at the bottom of the loop. The program statement

```
Celsius = Int((FTemp + 40) * 5 / 9 - 40)
```

handles the conversion from Fahrenheit to Celsius in the program. This statement employs a standard conversion formula, but it uses the Int function to return to the Celsius variable a value that contains no decimal places. (Everything to the right of the decimal point is discarded.) This cutting sacrifices accuracy, but it helps you avoid long, unsightly numbers, such as 21.11111, the Celsius value for 70 degrees Fahrenheit.

The complete Celsius Conversion program is available in the c:\vbnetsbs\ chap07\celsius conversion folder.

5   Click the Save All button on the toolbar to save your changes.

Now try running the program.

6   Click the Start button on the Standard toolbar.

The program starts, and the InputBox function prompts you for a Fahrenheit temperature.

7   Type **212**.

Your screen should look like this:

8 Click OK.

The temperature 212 degrees Fahrenheit is converted to 100 degrees Celsius, as shown in this message box:

9 Click OK. Type **72** in the input box, and click OK.

The temperature 72 degrees Fahrenheit is converted to 22 degrees Celsius.

10 Click OK, and then quit the program by clicking Cancel in the input box.

The program quits, and the development environment returns.

Using the Until Keyword in Do Loops

The Do loops you have worked with so far have used the While keyword to execute a group of statements as long as the loop condition remains True. Visual Basic also lets you use the Until keyword in Do loops to cycle *until* a certain condition is True. You can use the Until keyword at the top or bottom of a Do loop to test a condition, just like the While keyword. For example, the following Do loop uses the Until keyword to loop repeatedly until the user enters the word "Done" in the input box:

```
Dim InpName As String
Do
    InpName = InputBox("Enter your name or type Done to quit.")
    If InpName <> "Done" Then TextBox1.Text = InpName
Loop Until InpName = "Done"
```

As you can see, a loop that uses the Until keyword is similar to a loop that uses the While keyword, except that the test condition usually contains the opposite operator—the = (equal to) operator versus the <> (not equal to) operator, in this case. If using the Until keyword makes sense to you, feel free to use it with test conditions in your Do loops.

The Timer Control

The Timer control works like an invisible stopwatch in a program.

You can execute a group of statements at a specific time by using the Timer control. The Timer control is an invisible stopwatch that gives you access to the system clock in your programs. It can be used like an egg timer to count down from a preset time, to cause a delay in a program, or to repeat an action at prescribed intervals.

Although timer objects aren't visible at runtime, each timer is associated with an event procedure that runs every time the timer's preset *interval* has elapsed. You set a timer's interval by using the Interval property, and you activate a timer by setting the timer's Enabled property to True. Once a timer is enabled, it runs constantly—executing its event procedure at the prescribed interval—until the user stops the program or the timer is disabled.

Creating a Digital Clock Using a Timer Control

The Interval property sets the tick rate of a timer.

One of the most practical uses for a Timer control is creating a digital clock. In the following exercise, you'll create a simple digital clock that keeps track of the current time down to the second. In the example, you'll set the Interval property for the timer to 1000, directing Visual Basic to update the clock time every 1000 milliseconds, or once a second. Because the Windows operating system is a multitasking environment and other programs will also require processing time, Visual Basic may not always get a chance to update the clock each second, but it will always catch up if it falls behind. To keep track of the time at other intervals (such as once every tenth of a second), simply adjust the number in the Interval property.

Create the Digital Clock program

1   On the File menu, point to New, and then click Project.

    The New Project dialog box appears.

2   Create a new Visual Basic Windows Application project named **My Digital Clock** in the c:\vbnetsbs\chap07 folder.

    The new project is created and a blank form appears in the Windows Forms Designer.

3   Resize the form to a small rectangular window (a window that is wider than it is tall).

    You don't want the clock to take up much room.

Timer control

4 Double-click the Timer control on the Windows Forms tab of the Toolbox.

Visual Studio creates a small timer object in the component tray beneath your form, as shown here:

Recall that certain Visual Studio controls don't have a visual representation on the form, and when objects for these controls are created, they appear in the component tray beneath the form. (This was also the case for the MainMenu control that you used in Chapter 4.) However, you can still select controls in this special pane and set properties for them, as you'll do for the timer object in this exercise.

A

Label control

5 Click the Label control in the Toolbox, and then draw a very large label object on the form—a label that is almost the size of the entire form itself.

You'll use the label to display the time in the clock, and you want to create a very big label to hold the 24-point type you'll be using.

6 Open the Properties window, and set the following properties for the form and two objects in your program.

Object	Property	Setting
Label1	Text	(empty)
	Font	Times New Roman, Bold, 24-point
	TextAlign	MiddleCenter
Timer1	Enabled	True
	Interval	1000
Form1	Text	"Digital Clock"

tip

If you would like to put some artwork in the background of your clock, set the BackgroundImage property of the Form1 object to the path of a graphics file.

Now you'll write the program code for the timer.

7   Double-click the timer object in the component tray.

The Timer1_Tick event procedure appears in the Code Editor. Experienced Visual Basic 6 programmers will notice that this event procedure has been renamed from Timer1_Timer to Timer1_Tick, clarifying what this event procedure does in the program (i.e. the event procedure runs each time that the timer clock ticks).

8   Type the following statement:

```
Label1.Text = TimeString
```

This statement gets the current time from the system clock and assigns it to the Text property of the Label1 object. (If you would like to have the date displayed in the clock as well as the time, use the System.DateTime.Now property instead of the TimeString property.) Only one statement is required in this program because you set the Interval property for the timer by using the Properties window. The timer object handles the rest.

The complete Digital Clock program is available in the c:\vbnetsbs\ chap07\digital clock folder.

9   Click the Save All button on the toolbar to save your changes.

10   Click the Start button on the Standard toolbar to run the clock.

The clock appears, as shown in the following illustration. (Your time will be different, of course.)

If you used the System.DateTime.Now property, you'll see the date in the clock also, as shown here:

11   Watch the clock for a few moments.

Visual Basic updates the time every second.

12   Click the Close button in the title bar to stop the clock.

The Digital Clock program is so handy that you might want to compile it into an executable file and use it now and then on your computer. Feel free to customize it by using your own artwork, text, and colors.

One Step Further:
Using a Timer Object to Set a Time Limit

Another interesting use of a timer object is to set it to wait for a given period of time and then either to enable or prohibit an action. This is a little like setting an egg timer in your program—you set the Interval property with the delay you want, and then you start the clock ticking by setting the Enabled property to True.

The following exercise shows how you can use this approach to set a time limit for entering a password. (The password for this program is "secret".) The program uses a timer to close its own program if a valid password isn't entered in 15 seconds. (Normally, a program like this would be part of a larger application.) You can also use this timer technique to display a welcome message or a copyright message on the screen, or to repeat an event at a set interval, such as saving a file to disk every 10 minutes.

Set a password time limit

1   On the File menu, point to New, and then click Project.

    The New Project dialog box appears.

2   Create a new Visual Basic Windows Application project named **My Timed Password** in the c:\vbnetsbs\chap07 folder.

    The new project is created and a blank form appears in the Windows Forms Designer.

3   Resize the form to a small rectangular window about the size of an input box.

TextBox control

4   Click the TextBox control on the Windows Forms tab of the Toolbox, and then draw a text box for the password in the middle of the form.

Label control

5   Click the Label control in the Toolbox, and then draw a long label above the text box.

Button control

6   Click the Button control in the Toolbox, and then draw a button below the text box.

Timer control

7   Double-click the Timer control in the Toolbox.

    Visual Studio adds a timer object to the component tray below the form.

8   Set the properties in the table below for the program.

Object	Property	Setting
Label1	Text	"Enter your password within 15 seconds"
TextBox1	PasswordChar	"*"
	Text	(empty)
Button1	Text	"Try Password"
Timer1	Enabled	True
	Interval	15000
Form1	Text	"Password"

The PasswordChar setting will display asterisk (*) characters in the text box as the user enters a password. Setting the timer Interval property to 15000 will give the user 15 seconds to enter a password and click the Try Password button. Setting the Enabled property to True will start the timer running when the program starts. (You could also disable this property and then enable it in an event procedure if your timer was not needed until later in the program.)

Your form should look like this:

9   Double-click the timer object in the component tray, and then type the following statements in the Timer1_Tick event procedure.

```
MsgBox("Sorry, your time is up.")
End
```

The first statement displays a message indicating that the time has expired, and the second statement stops the program. Visual Basic executes this event procedure if the timer interval reaches 15 seconds and a valid password hasn't been entered.

10   Display the form, double-click the button object, and then type the following statements in the Button1_Click event procedure:

```
If TextBox1.Text = "secret" Then
    Timer1.Enabled = False
    MsgBox("Welcome to the system!")
    End
Else
    MsgBox("Sorry, friend, I don't know you.")
End If
```

This program code tests whether the password entered in the text box is "secret." If it is, the timer is disabled, a welcome message is displayed, and the program ends. (A more useful program would continue working rather than ending here.) If the password entered isn't a match, the user is notified with a message box and is given another chance to enter the password. But the user has only 15 seconds to do so!

The complete Timed Password program is available in the c:\vbnetsbs\chap07\timed password folder.

11   Click the Save All button on the toolbar to save your changes.

Test the Timed Password program

1   Click the Start button to run the program.

The program starts, and the 15-second clock starts ticking.

2   Type **open** in the text box.

The text of your input is hidden by the asterisk characters, as shown here:

3   Click the Try Password button.

The following message box appears on the screen, noting your incorrect response:

4   Click OK, and then wait patiently until the sign-on period expires.

The program displays the time up message shown in this message box:

5   Click OK to end the program.

6   Run the program again, type **secret** (the correct password) in the text box, and then click Try Password.

7   The program displays this message:

8   Click OK to end the program.

The Visual Basic development environment appears.

As you can see, there are many practical uses for timer objects. Like For...Next loops and Do loops, you can use timer objects to repeat commands and procedures as many times as you need in a program.

Chapter 7 Quick Reference

To	Do This

Execute a group of program statements a set number of times	Insert the statements between For and Next statements in a loop. For example:
	```Dim i As Integer```
	```For i = 1 To 10```
	``` MsgBox("Press OK already!")```
	```Next i```

Use a specific sequence of numbers with statements	Insert the statements in a For...Next loop and use the To and Step keywords to define the sequence of numbers. For example:
	```Dim i As Integer```
	```For i = 2 To 8 Step 2```
	``` TextBox1.Text = TextBox1.Text & i```
	```Next i```

Avoid an endless Do loop	Be sure the loop has a test condition that can evaluate to False.

Exit a For...Next loop prematurely	Use the Exit For statement. For example:
	```Dim InpName As String```
	```Dim i As Integer```
	```For i = 1 To 10```
	``` InpName = InputBox("Name?")```
	``` If InpName = "Trotsky" Then Exit For```
	``` TextBox1.Text = InpName```
	```Next i```

To	Do This

Execute a group of program statements until a specific condition is met	Insert the statements between Do and Loop statements. For example:
	`Dim Query As String = ""`
	`Do While Query <> "Yes"`
	`    Query = InputBox("Trotsky?")`
	`    If Query = "Yes" Then MsgBox("Hi")`
	`Loop`

Loop until a certain condition is True	Use a Do loop with the Until keyword. For example:
	`Dim GiveIn As String`
	`Do`
	`    GiveIn = InputBox("Say 'Uncle'")`
	`Loop Until GiveIn = "Uncle"`

Loop for a specific period of time in your program	Use the Timer control.

Debugging Visual Basic .NET Programs

In this lesson you will learn how to:

✔ *Identify different types of errors in your programs.*

✔ *Use Visual Studio .NET debugging tools to set breakpoints and correct mistakes.*

✔ *Use a Watch window to examine variables during program execution.*

✔ *Use the Command window to change the value of variables and execute commands in Visual Studio.*

In the past few chapters, you've had plenty of opportunity to make programming mistakes in your code. Unlike human conversation, which usually works well despite occasional grammatical mistakes and mispronunciations, communication between a software developer and the Visual Basic compiler is successful only when the precise rules and regulations of the Visual Basic programming language are followed. In this chapter, you'll learn more about the software defects, or *bugs*, that stop Visual Basic programs from running. You'll learn about the different types of errors that turn up in programs, and how to use the Visual Studio .NET debugging tools to detect and correct these defects. What you learn will be useful to you as you experiment with the programs in this book, and when you write longer programs in the future.

Upgrade Notes:
What's New in Visual Basic .NET?

If you're experienced with Visual Basic 6, you'll notice some new features in Visual Basic .NET, including the following:

■ Visual Basic .NET includes several new tools for finding and correcting errors. Many of the familiar Visual Basic 6 debugging commands are still a part of Visual Studio (Start, Break, End, Next, Step Into, Step Over), but there are also new debugging tools and commands, including a revised Debug toolbar, menu commands that manage processes and exceptions, and tools that support the debugging of multilanguage solutions.

■ Several new debugging windows have been added to the Visual Studio .NET user interface, including Autos, Command, Call Stack, Threads, Memory, Disassembly, and Registers. You won't use these tools for each debugging session, but you may find them useful in more sophisticated applications.

Finding and Correcting Errors

The defects you have encountered in your programs so far have probably been simple typing mistakes or syntax errors. But what if you discover a nastier problem in your program—one you can't find and correct by a simple review of the objects, properties, and statements you've used? The Visual Studio development environment contains several tools that will help you track down and fix errors in your programs. These tools won't stop you from making mistakes, but they'll often ease the pain when you encounter one.

Three Types of Errors

Three types of errors can occur in a Visual Basic program: syntax errors, runtime errors, and logic errors.

■ A *syntax error* (or *compiler error*) is a programming mistake (such as a misspelled property or keyword) that violates the rules of Visual Basic. Visual Basic points out several types of syntax errors in your programs while you type program statements, and won't let you run a program until each syntax error is fixed.

■ A *runtime error* is a mistake that causes a program to stop unexpectedly during execution. Runtime errors occur when an outside event or an undiscovered syntax error forces a program to stop while it is running. For instance, if you misspell a filename when you use the System.Drawing.Image.FromFile method or if you try to read the diskette drive and it doesn't contain a disk, your code will generate a runtime error.

■ A *logic error* is a human error—a programming mistake that makes the program code produce the wrong results. Most debugging efforts are focused on tracking down logic errors introduced by the programmer.

The Code Editor identifies incorrect statements with a blue, jagged line.

If you encounter a syntax error, you often can solve the problem by using Visual Basic online Help to learn more about the error message, and you can fix the mistake by paying close attention to the exact syntax of the functions, objects, methods, and properties that you use. In the Code Editor, incorrect statements are underlined with a blue, jagged line, and you can learn more about the error by holding the mouse pointer over the statement. The following illustration shows the error message that appears in Visual Studio when I type the keyword Case incorrectly ("Csae" instead of "Case"), and then hold the mouse pointer over the error. This error message is just like a ToolTip.

Syntax error identified by the Visual Basic compiler

Runtime errors require a code fix or a more extensive structured error handler.

```
Private Sub lstCountryBox_SelectedIndexChanged(ByVal s
    lblCountry.Text = lstCountryBox.Text
    Select Case lstCountryBox.SelectedIndex
        Csae 0
        The name 'Csae' is not declared.  "Hello, programmer"
        Case 1
            lblGreeting.Text = "Hallo, programmierer"
        Case 2
            lblGreeting.Text = "Hola, programador"
        Case 3
            lblGreeting.Text = "Ciao, programmatore"
    End Select
End Sub
```

If you encounter a runtime error, you often can address the problem by correcting your typing. For example, if a bitmap loads incorrectly into a picture box object, the problem might simply be a misspelled path. However, many runtime errors require a more thorough solution—the structured error handler, which is a special block of program code that recognizes a runtime error when it happens, suppresses any error messages, and adjusts program conditions to handle the problem. I discuss the new syntax for structured error handlers in Chapter 9.

Identifying Logic Errors

The process of finding and correcting errors in programs is called debugging.

Logic errors in your programs are often the most difficult to fix. They are the result of faulty reasoning and planning, not a misunderstanding about Visual Basic syntax. Consider the following If...Then decision structure, which evaluates two conditional expressions and then displays one of two messages based on the result:

```
If Age > 13 And Age < 20 Then
    TextBox2.Text = "You're a teenager"
Else
    TextBox2.Text = "You're not a teenager"
End If
```

Can you spot the problem with this decision structure? A teenager is a person who is between 13 and 19 years old, inclusive, yet the structure fails to identify the person who is exactly 13. (For this age, the structure erroneously displays the message "You're not a teenager.") This type of mistake isn't a syntax error (the statements follow the rules of Visual Basic); it is a mental mistake, or logic error. The correct decision structure contains a greater than or equal to operator (>=) in the first comparison after the If...Then statement:

```
If Age >= 13 And Age < 20 Then
```

Believe it or not, this type of mistake is the most common problem in a Visual Basic program. Code that works most of the time—but not all of the time—is the hardest to test and to fix.

Debugging 101: Using Break Mode

Break mode lets you see how your program executes.

One way to identify a logic error is to execute your program code one line at a time and examine the content of one or more variables or properties as they change. To do this, you can enter *break mode* while your program is running and then view your code in the Code Editor. Break mode gives you a close-up look at your program while the Visual Basic compiler is executing it. It's kind of like pulling up a chair behind the pilot and copilot and watching them fly the airplane. But in this case, you can touch the controls.

While you are debugging your application, you'll need to use the Debug toolbar, a special toolbar with buttons devoted entirely to tracking down errors. The following illustration shows this toolbar, which you can open by pointing to the Toolbars command on the View menu and then clicking Debug.

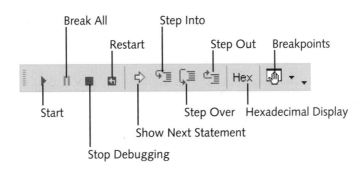

In the following exercise, you'll set a breakpoint and use break mode to find and correct the logic error you discovered earlier in the If…Then structure. (The error is part of an actual program.) To isolate the problem, you'll use the Step Into button on the Debug toolbar to execute program instructions one at a time, and you'll use the Autos window to examine the value of key program variables and properties. Pay close attention to this debugging strategy. You can use it to correct many types of glitches in your own programs.

Debug the Debug Test program

1   Start Visual Studio.

2   On the File menu, point to Open, and then click Project.

     The Open Project dialog box appears.

3   Open the Debug Test project in the c:\vbnetsbs\chap08\debug test folder.

     The project opens in the development environment.

4   If the form isn't visible, display it now.

     The Debug Test program prompts the user for his or her age. When the user clicks the Test button, the program lets the user know whether he or she is a teenager. The program still has the problem with 13-year-olds that we identified earlier in the chapter, however. You'll open the Debug toolbar now, and set a breakpoint to find the problem.

5   If the Debug toolbar isn't visible, click the View menu, point to the Toolbars, and then click Debug.

     The Debug toolbar appears below the Standard toolbar.

6   Click the Start button on the Debug toolbar.

     The program runs and displays the Debug Test form.

Start button

7   Remove the 0 from the age text box, type **14**, and then click the Test button.

     The program displays the message, "You're a teenager". So far, the program displays the correct result.

8   Type **13** in the age text box, and then click the Test button.

The program displays the message, "You're not a teenager", as shown here:

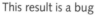

This result is a bug

This answer is incorrect, and you need to look at the program code to fix the problem.

9   Click the Quit button on the form, and then open the Code Editor.

10   Move the mouse pointer to the Margin Indicator bar (the gray bar just beyond the left margin of the Code Editor window), next to the statement Age = TextBox1.Text in the Button1_Click event procedure, and then click the bar to set a breakpoint.

The breakpoint immediately appears in red. A *breakpoint* is the place in your program where execution will stop so that you can use the Visual Studio development tools. See the following illustration for the breakpoint's location and shape:

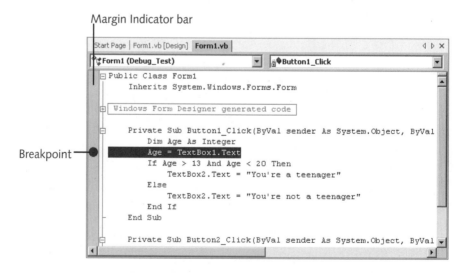

11   Click the Start button to run the program again.

The form appears just like before, and you can continue your tests.

12 Type **13** in the age text box, and then click Test.

Visual Basic opens the Code Editor again and displays the Button1_Click event procedure—the program code currently being executed by the compiler. The statement that you selected as a breakpoint is highlighted with yellow and an arrow appears in the Margin Indicator bar, as shown in the following illustration. Visual Studio is now in break mode, and you can tell because the text "[break]" appears in the Visual Studio title bar. In break mode you have an opportunity to see how the logic in your program is evaluated.

Break mode

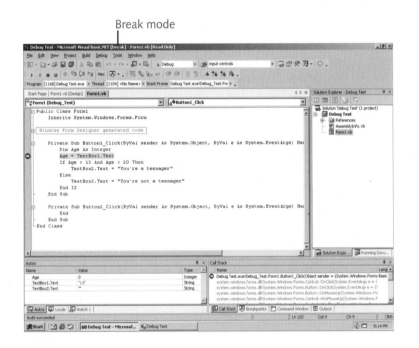

tip

You can also enter break mode in a Visual Basic program by placing the Stop statement in your program code where you would like to pause execution. This is an older, but still reliable, method for entering break mode in a Visual Basic program.

13 Place the mouse pointer over the Age variable in the Code Editor.

Visual Studio displays the message "Age = 0". While you are in break mode, you can display the value of variables or properties by simply holding the mouse over the value in the program code. Age currently holds a value of 0 because it has not yet been filled by the TextBox1 text box—that statement is the next statement to be evaluated by the compiler.

Step Into button

14   Click the Step Into button on the Debug toolbar to execute the next program statement.

The Step Into button executes the next program statement in the event procedure (the line that is currently highlighted); it allows you to see how the program state changes when just one more program statement is evaluated. If you hold the mouse pointer over the Age variable now, it will contain a value of 13.

15   From the Debug menu, point to Windows, and then click Autos.

The Debug Windows submenu gives you access to the entire set of debugging windows in Visual Studio. The Autos window is an automatic window that shows the state of variables and properties currently being used. As you can see in the following illustration, the Age variable holds a value of 13, the TextBox1.Text property holds a string of 13, and the TextBox2.Text property is currently an empty string.

Breakpoint   Step Into button

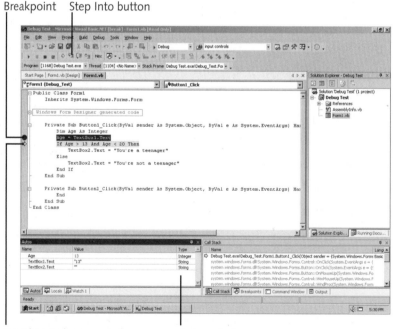

Next line to be executed   Autos window

Step Into button

16 Click the Step Into button twice more.

The If statement evaluates the conditional expression to False, and moves to the Else statement in the decision structure. Here is our bug—the decision structure logic is somehow incorrect, because a 13-year old is a teenager.

17 Select the conditional test **Age > 13**, and then hold the mouse pointer over the selected text.

Visual Studio evaluates the condition and displays the message, "Age > 13 = False".

18 Select the conditional test **Age < 20**, and then hold the mouse pointer over the selected text.

Visual Studio displays the message, "Age < 20 = True". The mouse pointer has given us an additional clue—only the first conditional test is producing an incorrect result! Because a 13-year-old is a teenager, Visual Basic should evaluate the test to True, but the Age > 13 condition returns a False value. And this forces the Else clause in the decision structure to be executed. Do you recognize the problem? The first comparison needs the >= operator to specifically test for this boundary case of 13. Stop debugging now and fix this logic error.

Stop Debugging button

19 Click the Stop Debugging button on the Debug toolbar.

20 In the Code Editor, add the = operator to the first condition in the If statement, so that it reads

If Age >= 13 And Age < 20 Then

21 Run the program again and test your solution, paying particular attention to the numbers 12, 13, 19, and 20—the boundary, or "fringe," cases that are likely to cause problems.

Use the Step In button to watch the program flow around the crucial If statement, and use the Autos window to track the value of your variables as you complete the tests. When the form appears, enter a new value and try the test again. In addition, you may find that selecting certain expressions and holding the mouse over them, such as the conditional tests, gives you a better understanding of how they are being evaluated.

Stop Debugging button

22 When you're finished experimenting with break mode, click the Stop Debugging button on the Debug toolbar to end the program.

Congratulations! You've successfully used break mode to find and correct a logic error in a program.

Tracking Variables Using a Watch Window

The Autos window is useful for examining the state of certain variables and properties as they are evaluated by the compiler, but items in the Autos window persist, or maintain their values, only for the current statement (the statement highlighted in the debugger) and the previous statement (the statement just executed). When your program goes on to execute code that doesn't use the variables, they disappear from the Autos window.

To view the contents of variables and properties *throughout* the execution of a program, you need to use a Watch window, a special Visual Studio tool that tracks important values for you as long as you are working in break mode. In Visual Basic 6, you had access to one Watch window to examine variables as they changed. In Visual Studio .NET, you can open up to four Watch windows. These windows are numbered Watch 1, Watch 2, Watch 3, and Watch 4 on the Watch submenu, which you open by choosing the Windows command on the Debug menu. You can also add expressions, such as Age >= 13, to a Watch window.

Open a Watch window

The Debug Test project is located in the c:\vbnetsbs\ chap08\debug test folder.

1   Click the Start button to run the Debug Test program again.

I'm assuming that the breakpoint you set on the line *Age = TextBox1.Text* in the previous exercise is still present. If that breakpoint isn't set, stop the program now and set the breakpoint by clicking in the Margin Indicator bar next to the statement, as shown in step 10 of the previous exercise, and then start the program again.

2   Type **20** in the age text box, and then click Test.

The program stops at the breakpoint, and Visual Studio enters break mode. To add variables, properties, or expressions to a Watch window, you need to be in break mode. Adding items is as simple as selecting the values in the Code Editor, right-clicking the selection, and then clicking the Add Watch command.

3   Select the **Age** variable, right click it, and then click the Add Watch command.

Visual Studio opens the Watch 1 window and adds the Age variable to it. The value for the variable is currently 0, and the Type column in the window identifies the Age variable as an Integer type.

4   Select the **TextBox2.Text** property and then drag it to the empty row in the Watch 1 window.

You can also drag items from the Code Editor into the Watch window. When you release the mouse button, Visual Studio adds the property and displays its value (right now the property is an empty string).

5 Select the expression **Age < 20**, and add it to the Watch window.

Age < 20 is a conditional expression, and you can use the Watch window to display its logical, or Boolean, value, much like you did by holding the mouse over a condition earlier in this chapter. Your Watch window will look like this:

Name	Value	Type
Age	0	Integer
TextBox2.Text	""	String
Age < 20	True	Boolean

Autos | Locals | Watch 1

Now step through the program code to see how the values in the Watch 1 window change.

Step Into button

6 Click the Step Into button on the Debug toolbar.

tip
Instead of clicking the Step Into button on the Debug toolbar, you can also press the F8 key on the keyboard.

The Age variable is set to 20 and the Age < 20 condition evaluates to False. These values are displayed in red type in the Watch window, because they have just been updated.

7 Click the Step Into button three more times.

The Else clause is executed in the decision structure, and the value of the TextBox2.Text property in the Watch window changes to "You're not a teenager". This conditional test is operating correctly. Because you're satisfied with this condition, you may remove the test from the Watch window.

8 Click the Age < 20 row in the Watch window, and then press Delete.

Visual Studio removes the value from the Watch window. As you can see, adding and removing values from the Watch window is a speedy process.

Leave Visual Studio running in break mode for now. You'll continue using the Age variable in the next section.

Using the Command Window

So far you have used the Visual Studio debugging tools that allow you to enter break mode, execute code one statement at a time, and examine the value of important variables, properties, and expressions in your program. Now you'll learn how to change the value of a variable and run other commands using the Command window, a dual-purpose tool in the Visual Studio development environment. When the Command window is in Immediate mode, you can use it to interact with the code in a Visual Basic program that you are debugging. When the Command window is in Command mode, you can use it to execute commands in Visual Studio, such as Save All or Print. If you execute more than one command, you can use the arrow keys to scroll through previous commands and see their results.

The following exercises demonstrate how the Command window works; they assume that you are currently debugging the Debug Test program, and that the program is now in break mode.

Open the Command window in Immediate mode

1   From the Debug menu, point to Windows, and then click Immediate.

Visual Studio opens the Command window in Immediate mode, a special state that allows you to interact with a program in break mode. Because the Command window has two modes (Immediate and Command), it is important that you learn to recognize the different modes to avoid issuing the wrong commands. In Immediate mode, the window title bar contains the text "Command Window - Immediate".

tip
If the Command window is in Command mode, you can switch to Immediate mode by typing the immed command. If the Command window is in Immediate mode, you can switch to Command mode by typing the >cmd command (the > symbol is required).

2   In the Command window, type **Age = 17**, and then press Enter.

You've just changed the value of a variable with the Command window. The value of the Age variable in the Watch window immediately changes to 17, and the next time the If statement is executed, the value in the TextBox2.Text property will change to "You're a teenager". Your Command window will look like this:

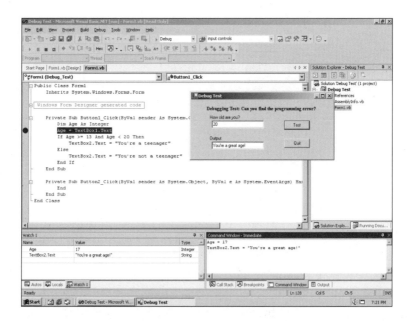

3 Type the following statement in the Command window, and then press Enter:

```
TextBox2.Text = "You're a great age!"
```

The Text property of the TextBox2 object is immediately changed to "You're a great age!" In Immediate mode, the Command window lets you change the value of properties, as well as variables.

4 Click the Step Into button two times to display the Debug Test form again.

Notice that the Text property of the TextBox2 object has been changed, as you directed, but the Text property of the TextBox1 object still holds a value of 20 (not 17). This is because you changed the Age variable in the program, not the property that assigned a value to Age. Your screen will look like this:

The Immediate mode of the Command window has many uses—it provides an excellent companion to the Watch window, and it can help you experiment with specific test cases that might otherwise be very difficult to enter into your program.

Switching to Command Mode in the Command Window

The Command window can also be used to run interface commands in the Visual Studio development environment. For example, the command File.SaveAll will save all the files in the current project (the command is the equivalent to the Save All command on the File menu). However, you must first switch to Command mode in the Command window before you can execute development environment commands. Practice using Command mode in the following exercise.

Run the File.SaveAll command

1   In the Command window, type **>cmd**, and then press Enter to switch to Command mode.

    The Command window title bar changes to "Command Window", and the ">" prompt now appears in the window (a visual clue that the window is in Command mode).

2   Type **File.SaveAll** in the window, and then press Enter.

    Visual Studio saves the current project, and the command prompt returns.

tip

Did you see all the commands that appeared when you typed the word "File" in the Command window? The Command window uses the statement completion feature to show you all the menu commands that match the letters you're typing. This is a powerful feature, and you can use it to discover most of the menu commands that you can execute using the Command window.

3   Click the Close button on the Command window; you're finished using it for now.

One Step Further: Removing Breakpoints

If you've been following the instructions in this chapter carefully, the Debug Test program will still be running and will have a breakpoint in it. Follow these steps to remove the breakpoint and end the program. You're finished debugging the Debug Test utility.

Remove a breakpoint

1   In the Code Editor, click the round red circle associated with the breakpoint in the Margin Indicator bar.

The breakpoint disappears. That's all there is to it! Note that if you have more than one breakpoint in a program, you can remove them all by clicking the Clear All Breakpoints command on the Debug menu. Visual Studio saves breakpoints with your project, so it is important to know how to remove them—they'll still be there in your program, even if you close Visual Studio and restart it!

2   Click the Stop Debugging button on the Debug toolbar.

The Debug Test program ends.

Stop Debugging button

3   On the View menu, point to Toolbars, and then click Debug.

The Debug toolbar closes.

You've learned the fundamental techniques of debugging Visual Basic programs with Visual Studio .NET. Place a bookmark in this chapter so that you can return to it as you encounter problems later in the book. In the next chapter, you'll learn how to handle runtime errors using structured error handling techniques.

Lesson 8 Quick Reference

To	Do this
Display the Debug toolbar	From the View menu, point to Toolbars, and then click Debug.
Set a breakpoint	In the Code Editor, click in the Margin Indicator bar next to the statement that you want to stop program execution at. When the compiler reaches the breakpoint, it will enter break mode.
	or
	Place a Stop statement in the program code where you want to enter break mode.
Execute one line of code in the Code Editor	Click the Step Into button on the Debug toolbar.
Examine a variable, property, or expression in the Code Editor	Select the value in the Code Editor, and then hold the mouse over it.

(continued)

Debugging Programs

8

continued

To	Do this
Use the Autos window to examine a variable on the current or previous line	In break mode, click the Debug menu, point to Windows, and then click Autos.
Add a variable, property, or expression to a Watch window	In break mode, select the value in the Code Editor, right-click the value, and then click Add Watch.
Display a Watch window	In break mode, click the Debug menu, point to Windows, and then click Watch.
Open the Command window in Immediate mode	Click the Debug menu, point to Windows, and then click Immediate.
Switch between Command mode and Immediate mode in the Command window	To switch to Command mode in the Command window, type ">cmd" and then press Enter. To switch to Immediate mode in the Command window, type "immed" and then press Enter.
Remove a breakpoint	Click the breakpoint in the Margin Indicator bar of the Code Editor, or click the Clear All Breakpoints command on the Debug menu.
Stop debugging	Click the Stop Debugging command on the Debug toolbar.

9

Trapping Errors Using Structured Error Handling

In this chapter you will learn how to:

✔ *Manage runtime errors using the new Try...Catch error handler.*

✔ *Test specific error conditions using the Catch When statement.*

✔ *Use Err.Number and Err.Description properties to identify exceptions.*

✔ *Build nested Try...Catch statements.*

✔ *Use error handlers in combination with defensive programming techniques.*

✔ *Leave error handlers prematurely using the Exit Try statement.*

In Chapter 8, you learned how to recognize runtime errors in a Visual Basic .NET program and how to locate logic errors and other defects in your program code using the Visual Studio .NET debugging tools. In this chapter, you'll learn how to build blocks of code that handle runtime errors, also referred to as *exceptions*, which occur as a result of normal operating conditions—for example, errors due to a disk not being in the drive or an offline printer. These routines are called *structured error handlers* (or *structured exception handlers*), and you can use them to recognize runtime errors as they occur in a program, suppress unwanted error messages, and adjust program conditions so that your application can regain control and run again.

Visual Basic .NET includes the Try...Catch code block, a new syntax for handling errors. In this chapter, you'll learn how to trap runtime errors using Try...Catch code blocks, and you'll learn how to use the Err.Number and Err.Description properties to identify specific runtime errors. You'll also learn how to use multiple Catch statements to write more flexible error handlers, build nested Try...Catch code blocks, and use the Exit Try statement to exit a Try...Catch code block prematurely. The programming techniques you'll learn are similar to the On Error Goto syntax from earlier versions of Visual Basic, and to the structured error handlers currently provided by the Java and C++ programming languages. The most seaworthy or *robust* Visual Basic programs make use of several error handlers to handle unforeseen circumstances and provide users with consistent and trouble-free computing experiences.

Upgrade Notes: What's New in Visual Basic .NET?

If you're experienced with Visual Basic 6, you'll notice some new features in Visual Basic .NET, including the following:

- The Try...Catch code block is a new mechanism for writing structured error handlers. Although you can still use Visual Basic 6 error-handling keywords, including On Error Goto, Resume, and Resume Next, the Try...Catch syntax avoids the potential complications of Goto constructions and offers a very efficient way to manage runtime errors.

- The Catch When statement allows you to test specific program conditions and handle more than one runtime error in a Try...Catch code block.

- The Exit Try statement offers a new way to exit structured error handlers.

- Visual Basic .NET continues to provide the Err.Number and Err.Description properties to identify runtime errors. In addition, you can use the new Err.GetException method to return information about the underlying error condition, or *exception*, that halted program execution.

Processing Errors Using Try...Catch

A runtime error, or program crash, is an unexpected problem that occurs in a Visual Basic program from which it can't recover. You may have experienced your first program crash when Visual Basic couldn't load artwork from a file, or in the previous chapter when you intentionally introduced errors into your program code during debugging. A runtime error happens anytime Visual Basic executes a statement that for some reason can't be completed "as dialed" while the program is running. It's not that Visual Basic isn't smart enough to handle the glitch; it's just that Visual Basic hasn't been told what to do when something goes wrong.

An error han-
dler helps your
program
recover from
runtime errors.

Fortunately, you don't have to live with occasional errors that cause your programs to crash. You can write special Visual Basic routines, called structured error handlers, to respond to runtime errors. An error handler *handles* a runtime error by telling the program how to continue when one of its statements doesn't work. Error handlers are placed in the event procedures where there is a potential for trouble, or in generic functions or subprograms that handle errors for you systematically. (You'll learn more about writing functions and subprograms in Chapter 10.) As their name implies, error handlers handle, or *trap,* a problem by using the Try...Catch statement and a special error handling object named Err. The Err object has a Number property that identifies the error number and a Description property that allows you to print a description of the error. For example, if the runtime error is associated with loading a file from disk, your error handler might display a custom error message that identifies the problem and disables disk operations until the user fixes the problem.

When to Use Error Handlers

Most runtime
errors are
caused by
external events.

You can use error handlers in any situation in which an expected or unexpected action might result in an error that stops program execution. Typically, error handlers are used to process external events that influence a program—for example, events caused by a failed network or Internet connection, a disk not being in the floppy drive, or a printer that is offline. The table on the following page lists potential problems that can be addressed by error handlers.

Problem	Description
Network/Internet problems	Network servers, modems, or resources that fail, or "go down," unexpectedly
Disk drive problems	Unformatted or incorrectly formatted disks, disks that aren't properly inserted, bad disk sectors, disks that are full, problems with a CD-ROM drive, and so on.
Path problems	A path to a necessary file is missing or incorrect.
Printer problems	Printers that are offline, out of paper, out of memory, or otherwise unavailable
Software not installed	A file or component that your application relies on is not installed on the user's computer, or there is an operating system incompatibility.
Permissions problems	The user doesn't have the appropriate permissions to perform a task.
Overflow errors	An activity that exceeds the allocated storage space
Out-of-memory errors	Application or resource space that is not available in Windows
Clipboard problems	Problems with data transfer or the Windows Clipboard
Logic errors	Syntax or logic errors undetected by the compiler and previous tests (such as an incorrectly spelled filename)

Setting the Trap: The Try...Catch Statement

The Try statement identifies the beginning of an error handler

The code block used to handle a runtime error is called Try...Catch. You place the Try statement in an event procedure right before the statement you're worried about, and the Catch statement follows immediately with a list of the statements that you want to run if a runtime error actually occurs. A number of optional statements, such as Catch When, Finally, Exit Try, and nested Try...Catch code blocks can also be included, as the examples in this chapter will demonstrate. However, the basic syntax for a Try...Catch exception handler is simply:

```
Try
    Statements that might produce a runtime error
Catch
    Statements to run if a runtime error occurs
Finally
    Optional statements to run whether an error occurs or not
End Try
```

where Try, Catch, and End Try are required keywords, and Finally (and the statements that follow) are optional. Note that programmers sometimes call the statements between the Try and Catch keywords *protected code*, because any runtime errors resulting from these statements won't cause the program to crash. (Instead, Visual Basic executes the error handling statements in the Catch code block.)

Path and Disk Drive Errors

The following example demonstrates a common runtime error situation—a problem with a path or floppy disk drive. To complete this exercise, you'll load a sample Visual Basic project that I created to show how artwork files are opened in a picture box object on a Windows Form. To prepare for the exercise, insert a floppy disk into drive A and copy the file fileopen.bmp to it. (You can find a copy of this file, along with the Disk Drive Error project, in the c:\vbnetsbs\chap09\disk drive error folder.) You'll use the disk throughout the chapter to force runtime errors and recover from them.

Experiment with disk drive errors

1   Insert a blank floppy disk in drive A (your primary floppy drive), and copy the file fileopen.bmp to it.

You'll find the fileopen.bmp file in the c:\vbnetsbs\chap09\disk drive error folder. Use Windows Explorer or another tool to copy the file.

2   Start Visual Studio and open the Disk Drive Error project in the c:\vbnetsbs\chap09\disk drive error folder.

The Disk Drive Error project opens in the development environment.

3   If the project's form isn't visible, display it now.

The disk drive error project is a skeleton program that displays the fileopen.bmp file in a picture box when the user clicks the Check Drive button. I designed the project as a convenient way to create and trap runtime errors, and you can use it throughout this chapter to build error handlers using the Try...Catch code block.

4   Double-click the Check Drive button on the form to display the Button1_Click event procedure.

You'll see the following line of program code between Private Sub and End Sub statements:

```
PictureBox1.Image = _
    System.Drawing.Bitmap.FromFile("a:\fileopen.bmp")
```

As you've learned in earlier chapters, the FromFile method opens the specified file. This particular use of FromFile opens the fileopen.bmp file on drive A and displays it in a picture box. However, if the disk isn't fully inserted or there is a problem with the file path, the statement will produce a "File Not Found" error in Visual Basic. This is the runtime error we want to trap.

5   With your floppy disk still in drive A, click the Start button to run the program.

The form for the project appears, as shown here:

6   Click the Check Drive button on the form.

The program loads the fileopen.bmp file from the floppy disk, and displays it in the picture box, as shown here:

The SizeMode property of the picture box object is set to StretchImage, so the file fills the entire picture box object. Now see what happens when the floppy disk isn't in the disk drive when the program attempts to load the file.

7   Remove the floppy disk from the drive.

8   Click the Check Drive button on the form.

The program can't find the file, and Visual Basic issues a runtime error or *unhandled exception*, which causes the program to crash. You'll see the following dialog box:

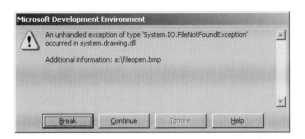

9   Click the Continue button to close the program.

The development environment returns.

Writing a Disk Drive Error Handler

The problem with the Disk Drive Error program isn't that it somehow defies the inherent capabilities of Visual Basic to process errors—we just haven't specified what Visual Basic should do when it encounters an exception that it doesn't know how to handle. The solution to this problem is to write a Try...Catch code block that recognizes the error and tells Visual Basic what to do about it. You'll add this error handler now.

Use Try...Catch to trap the error

1   Display the Button1_Click event procedure if it isn't visible in the Code Editor.

You need to add an error handler to the event procedure that is causing the problems. As you'll see in this example, you actually build the Try...Catch code block around the code that is the potential source of trouble, protecting the rest of the program from the runtime errors it might produce.

2   Modify the event procedure so that the existing FromFile statement fits between Try and Catch statements, as shown in the following code block:

```
Try
    PictureBox1.Image = _
        System.Drawing.Bitmap.FromFile("a:\fileopen.bmp")
Catch
    MsgBox("Please insert the disk in drive A!")
End Try
```

You don't need to retype the FromFile statement—just type the Try, Catch, MsgBox, and End Try statements above and below it.

This program code demonstrates the most basic use of a Try...Catch code block. It places the problematic FromFile statement in a Try code block so that if it produces an error, the statements in the Catch code block will be executed. The Catch code block simply displays a message box asking the user to insert the required disk in drive A so that the program can continue. This Try...Catch code block contains no Finally statement, so the error handler ends with the keywords End Try.

3   Make sure the floppy disk is removed from drive A, and then click the Start button to run the program.

4   Click the Check Drive button.

Instead of stopping program execution, Visual Basic invokes the Catch code block, which displays the following message box:

5   Click OK, and then click the Check Drive button again.

The program displays the message box again, asking you to insert the disk properly in drive A. Each time there is a problem loading the file, this message box will appear.

6   Insert the disk in drive A, click OK, and then click the Check Drive button again.

The file appears in the picture box, as expected. The error handler has completed its work effectively—rather than crashing the program inadvertently, the program has told you how to correct your mistake, and you can now continue working with the application.

7   Click the Close button on the form to stop the program.

It's time to learn some of the variations of the Try...Catch error handler.

Using the Finally Clause to Perform Cleanup Tasks

As the syntax description for Try...Catch noted earlier in the chapter, you can use the optional Finally clause with Try...Catch to execute a block of statements regardless of how the Try or Catch blocks are executed by the compiler. In other words, whether or not the Try statements produced a runtime error, there might be some code that you need to run each time an error handler is finished. For example, you might want to update variables or properties, display the results of a computation using a message box or other mechanism, or perform "cleanup" operations by clearing variables or disabling unneeded objects on a form.

The following exercise demonstrates how the Finally clause works, by displaying a second message box whether or not the FromFile method produces a runtime error.

Use Finally to display a message box

1   Display the Button1_Click event procedure, and then edit the Try...Catch code block so that it contains two additional lines of code above the End Try statement. The complete error handler should look like this:

```
Try
    PictureBox1.Image = _
        System.Drawing.Bitmap.FromFile("a:\fileopen.bmp")
Catch
    MsgBox("Please insert the disk in drive A!")
Finally
    MsgBox("Error handler complete")
End Try
```

The Finally statement indicates to the compiler that a final block of code should be executed whether or not a runtime error is processed. To help you learn exactly how this feature works, I've inserted a MsgBox function to display a test message below the Finally statement. Although this simple use of Finally is useful for testing purposes, in a real program you'll probably want to use the Finally code block to update important variables or properties, display data, or perform other cleanup operations.

2   Remove the floppy disk from drive A, and then click the Start button to run the program.

3   Click the Check Drive button.

The error handler displays a dialog box asking you to insert the disk in drive A.

4   Click OK.

The program executes the Finally clause in the error handler, and the following message box appears:

Disk Drive Error
Error handler complete
OK

9

Trapping Errors

5   Click OK, insert the disk in drive A, and then click the Check Drive button again.

The file appears in the picture box as expected. In addition, the Finally clause is executed, and the "Error handler complete" message box appears again. As I noted above, Finally statements are executed at the end of a Try...Catch block whether or not there is an error.

6   Click OK, and then click the Close button on the form to stop the program.

More Complex Try...Catch Error Handlers

As your programs become more sophisticated, you may find it useful to write more complex Try...Catch error handlers that manage a variety of runtime errors and unusual error-handling situations. Try...Catch provides for this complexity by:

- Permitting multiple lines of code in each Try, Catch, or Finally code block

- Offering the Catch When syntax, which tests specific error conditions

- Allowing nested Try...Catch code blocks, which can be used to build sophisticated and robust error handlers

In addition, a special error-handling object named Err allows you to identify and process specific runtime errors and conditions in your program. You'll investigate each of these error-handling features in the following section.

The Err Object

The Err.Number and Err.Description properties contain information about the most recent runtime error.

Err is a special Visual Basic object that is assigned detailed error handling information each time a runtime error occurs. The most useful Err properties for identifying runtime errors are Err.Number and Err.Description. Err.Number contains the number of the most recent runtime error, and Err.Description contains a short error message that matches the runtime error number. By using the Err.Number and Err.Description properties together in an error handler, you can recognize specific errors and respond to them, and you can give the user useful information about how they should respond.

The Err object can be cleared using the Err.Clear method (which discards previous error information), but if you use the Err object within a Catch code block, clearing the Err object isn't usually necessary, because Catch blocks are entered only when a runtime error has just occurred in a neighboring Try code block.

The following table lists many of the runtime errors that Visual Basic applications can encounter. (For more information on a particular error, search the Visual Studio online Help.) In addition to these error codes, you'll find that some Visual Basic libraries and other components (such as database and system components) provide their own unique error messages, which often can be discovered by using the online Help. Note that despite the error message descriptions, some errors don't appear as you might expect them to, so you will need to specifically test the error numbers (when possible) by observing how the Err.Number property changes during program execution. Unused error numbers in the range 1–1000 are reserved for future use by Visual Basic .NET.

Error Number	Default Error Message
5	Procedure call or argument is not valid
6	Overflow
7	Out of memory
9	Subscript out of range
11	Division by zero
13	Type mismatch
48	Error in loading DLL
51	Internal error
52	Bad file name or number
53	File not found
55	File already open
57	Device I/O error
58	File already exists
61	Disk full
62	Input past end of file
67	Too many files
68	Device unavailable
70	Permission denied
71	Disk not ready
74	Can't rename with different drive
75	Path/File access error
76	Path not found
91	Object variable or With block variable not set
321	File format is not valid
322	Cannot create necessary temporary file

(continued)

continued

Error Number	Default Error Message
380	Property value is not valid
381	Property array index is not valid
422	Property not found
423	Property or method not found
424	Object required
429	Cannot create ActiveX component
430	Class does not support Automation or does not support expected interface
438	Object does not support this property or method
440	Automation error
460	Clipboard format is not valid
461	Method or data member not found
462	The remote server machine does not exist or is unavailable
463	Class not registered on local machine
481	Picture is not valid
482	Printer error

The following exercise uses the Err.Number and Err.Description properties in a Try...Catch error handler to test for more than one runtime error condition. This capability is made possible by the Catch When syntax, which allows you to test for specific error conditions in a Try...Catch code block.

Test for multiple runtime error conditions

1   In the Button1_Click event procedure, edit the Try...Catch error handler so that it looks like the following code block. (The original FromFile statement is the same as the code you used in the previous exercises, but the Catch statements are all new.)

The Catch When syntax allows you to test specific values in an error handler.

```
Try
    PictureBox1.Image = _
        System.Drawing.Bitmap.FromFile("a:\fileopen.bmp")
Catch When Err.Number = 53 'if File Not Found error
    MsgBox("Check pathname and disk drive")
Catch When Err.Number = 7  'if Out Of Memory error
    MsgBox("Is this really a bitmap?", , Err.Description)
Catch
    MsgBox("Problem loading file", , Err.Description)
End Try
```

The Catch When syntax is used twice in the error handler, and each time it is used with the Err.Number property to test whether the Try code block produced a particular type of runtime error. If the Err.Number property contains the number 53, the File Not Found runtime error has occurred during the file open procedure, and the message "Check pathname and disk drive" is displayed in a message box. If the Err.Number property contains the number 7, an Out of Memory error has occurred—probably the result of loading a file that doesn't actually contain artwork. (I get this error if I accidentally try to open a Microsoft Word document in a picture box object using the FromFile method.)

The final Catch statement handles all other runtime errors that could potentially occur during a file opening process—it is a general "catch-all" code block that prints a general error message inside a message box, and a specific error message from the Err.Description property in the title bar of the message box.

2   Click the Start button to run the program.

3   Remove the floppy disk from drive A.

4   Click the Check Drive button.

The error handler displays the error message "Check pathname and disk drive" in a message box. The first Check When statement works.

5   Click OK, and then click the Close button on the form to end the program.

6   Insert the floppy disk again, and then use Windows Explorer or another tool to copy a second file to the disk that isn't an artwork file. For example, copy a Word document or Excel spreadsheet to the disk.

You won't open this file in Word or Excel—it is only for testing purposes.

7   In the Code Editor, change the name of the fileopen.bmp file in the FromFile program statement to the name of the file you just copied to the disk in drive A.

Using a file with a different format will give you an opportunity to test a second type of runtime error—an Out of Memory exception, which occurs when Visual Basic attempts to load a file that isn't a graphic or has too much information for a picture box.

8   Run the program again, and click the Check Drive button.

The error handler displays the following error message:

9   Click OK, and then click the Close button on the form to stop the program.

10   Change the filename back to fileopen.bmp in the FromFile method. (You'll use it in the next exercise.)

The Catch When statement is very powerful. In combination with the Err.Number and Err.Description properties, Catch When allows you to write very sophisticated error handlers that recognize and respond to several types of exceptions.

Raising Your Own Errors

For testing purposes and other specialized uses, you can artificially generate your own runtime errors in a program, a technique called "throwing" or "raising" exceptions. To accomplish this, you use the Err.Raise method with one of the error numbers in the table presented earlier. For example, the following syntax uses the Raise method to produce a Disk Full runtime error, and then handles the error using a Catch When statement:

```
Try
    Err.Raise(61) 'raise Disk Full error
Catch When Err.Number = 61
    MsgBox("Error: Disk is full")
End Try
```

When you learn how to write your own procedures, this technique will allow you to generate your own errors and return them to the calling routine.

Specifying a Retry Period

Another strategy you can use in an error handler is to try an operation a few times and then disable it if the problem isn't resolved. For example, in the following exercise a Try...Catch block employs a counter variable named Retries to track the number of times the message "Please insert the disk in drive A!" is displayed, and after the second time, the error handler disables the Check Drive command button. The trick to this technique is declaring the Retries variable at the top of the form's program code, so that it has scope throughout all of the form's event procedures. The Retries variable is then incremented and tested in the Catch code block. The number of retries can be modified by simply changing the "2" in the statement:

```
If Retries <= 2
```

Use a variable to track runtime errors

1　In the Code Editor, scroll to the top of the form's program code, and directly below the tag "Windows Form Designer generated code," type the following variable declaration:

```
Dim Retries As Short = 0
```

Retries is declared as a Short integer variable because it won't contain very big numbers. It is assigned an initial value of 0 so that it resets properly each time the program runs.

2　In the Button1_Click event procedure, edit the Try...Catch error handler so that it looks like the following code block:

```
Try
    PictureBox1.Image = _
        System.Drawing.Bitmap.FromFile("a:\fileopen.bmp")
Catch
    Retries += 1
    If Retries <= 2 Then
        MsgBox("Please insert the disk in drive A!")
    Else
        MsgBox("File Load feature disabled")
        Button1.Enabled = False
    End If
End Try
```

The Try block tests the same file-opening procedure, but this time if an error occurs the Catch block increments the Retries variable and tests the variable to be sure that it is less than or equal to 2. The number 2 could be changed to allow any number of retries—currently it allows only two runtime errors. After two errors, the Else clause is executed, and a message box appears indicating that the file loading feature has been disabled. The Check Drive button is then disabled—in other words, grayed out and rendered unusable for the remainder of the program.

The complete Disk Drive Handler program is located in the c:\vbnetsbs\ chap09\disk drive handler folder.

3　Click the Start button to run the program.

4　Remove the floppy disk from drive A.

5　Click the Check Drive button.

The error handler displays the error message "Please insert the disk in drive A!" in a message box. Behind the scenes, the Retries variable is also incremented to 1.

6   Click OK, and then click the Check Drive button again.

The Retries variable is set to 2, and the message "Please insert the disk in drive A!" appears again.

7   Click OK, and then click the Check Drive button a third time.

The Retries variable is incremented to 3, and the Else clause is executed. The message "File Load feature disabled" appears:

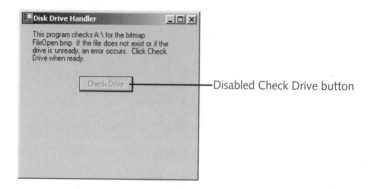

8   Click OK in the message box.

The Check Drive button is disabled on the form, as shown here:

—Disabled Check Drive button

The error handler has responded to the disk drive problem by allowing the user a few tries to fix the problem, and then it has disabled the problematic button. This disabling action will stop future runtime errors, although the program may no longer function exactly as it was originally designed.

9   Click the Close button to stop the program.

Using Nested Try...Catch Blocks

You can also use nested Try...Catch code blocks in your error handlers. For example, the following disk drive error handler uses a second Try...Catch block to retry the file open operation a single time if the first attempt fails and generates a runtime error:

```
Try
    PictureBox1.Image = _
      System.Drawing.Bitmap.FromFile("a:\fileopen.bmp")
```

```
Catch
    MsgBox("Insert the disk in drive A, then click OK!")
    Try
        PictureBox1.Image = _
            System.Drawing.Bitmap.FromFile("a:\fileopen.bmp")
    Catch
        MsgBox("File Load feature disabled")
        Button1.Enabled = False
    End Try
End Try
```

If the user inserts the disk in the drive as a result of the message prompt, the second Try block will open the file without error. However, if a file-related runtime error still appears, the second Catch block displays a message saying that the file load feature is being disabled, and the button is disabled.

In general, nested Try...Catch error handlers work well as long as you don't have too many tests or retries to manage. If you do need to retry a problematic operation many times, use a variable to track your retries or develop a function containing an error handler that can be called repeatedly from your event procedures. (See the next chapter for more information about creating functions.)

Comparing Error Handlers to Defensive Programming Techniques

Error handlers aren't the only mechanism for protecting a program against runtime errors. For example, the following program code uses the File.Exists method in the System.IO namespace of the .NET Framework class library to check whether a file exists on disk before it is opened:

```
If File.Exists("a:\fileopen.bmp") Then
    PictureBox1.Image = _
        System.Drawing.Bitmap.FromFile("a:\fileopen.bmp")
Else
    MsgBox("Cannot find fileopen.bmp on drive A.")
End If
```

This If...Then statement isn't an actual error handler, because it doesn't prevent a runtime error from halting a program. Instead, it is a validation technique that some programmers call *defensive programming*. It uses a handy method in the .NET Framework class library to verify the intended file operation *before* it is actually attempted in the program code. And in this particular case, testing to see whether the file exists with the .NET Framework method is actually faster than waiting for Visual Basic to issue an exception and recover from a runtime error using an error handler.

> **note**
>
> To get this particular program logic to work, the following statement must be included at the very top of the form's program code, to make reference to the .NET Framework class library that is being invoked:
>
> ```
> Imports System.IO
> ```
>
> For more information about using the Imports statement to use the objects, properties, and methods in the .NET Frameworks class libraries, see Chapter 5.

When should you use defensive programming techniques and when should you use error handlers? The answer depends on how often you think a problem will occur with the statements that you plan to use. If an exception or runtime error will occur relatively rarely, say less than 25 percent of the time a particular piece of code is executed, using an error handler is probably the most efficient way to go. Error handlers are also essential if you have more than one condition to test, and if you want to provide the user with numerous options for responding to the error. However, if there is real likelihood that a piece of code will produce a runtime error—say more than 25 percent of the time—defensive programming logic is usually the most efficient way to manage potential problems. As I mentioned when discussing the If...Then code block above, the File.Exists method is actually faster than using a Try...Catch error handler, so it also makes sense to use a defensive programming technique if there are performance issues involved. In the end, it probably makes the most sense to use a combination of defensive programming and structured error handling techniques in your code.

One Step Further: The Exit Try Statement

You've learned a lot about error handlers in this chapter; now you're ready to put them to work in your own programs. But before you move on to the next chapter, here's one more syntax option for Try...Catch code blocks that you might find very useful—the Exit Try statement. Exit Try is a quick and slightly abrupt technique for exiting a Try...Catch code block prematurely; if you have written Visual Basic programs before, you may notice its similarity to the Exit For or Exit Sub statements, which allow you to leave a structured routine early.

Using the Exit Try syntax, you can jump completely out of the current Try or Catch code block. If there is a Finally code block, this code will be executed, but Exit Try lets you jump over any remaining Try or Catch statements you don't want to execute.

The following sample routine shows how the Exit Try statement works. It first checks to see whether the Enabled property of the PictureBox1 object is set to False, a flag that might indicate that the picture box isn't yet ready to receive input. If the picture box isn't yet enabled, the Exit Try statement skips to the end of the Catch code block, and the file load operation isn't attempted.

```
Try
    If PictureBox1.Enabled = False Then Exit Try
    PictureBox1.Image = _
        System.Drawing.Bitmap.FromFile("a:\fileopen.bmp")
Catch
    Retries += 1
    If Retries <= 2 Then
        MsgBox("Please insert the disk in drive A!")
    Else
        MsgBox("File Load feature disabled")
        Button1.Enabled = False
    End If
End Try
```

The example builds on the last error handler you experimented with in this chapter (the Disk Drive Handler project). If you would like to test the Exit Try statement in the context of that program, load the Disk Drive Handler project again, and enter the If statement that contains the Exit Try in the Code Editor. You'll also need to use the Properties window to disable the picture box object on the form (in other words, set its Enabled property to False).

Congratulations! You've learned a number of important fundamental programming techniques in Visual Basic .NET, including how to write error handlers. Now you're ready to move on to more advanced programming topics.

9

Trapping Errors

Lesson 9 Quick Reference

To	Do this

Detect and process runtime errors	Build an error handler using one or more Try...Catch code blocks. For example, the following error handler code tests for path or disk drive problems:
	
	``
	Try
	    PictureBox1.Image = _
	        System.Drawing.Bitmap.FromFile _
	        ("a:\fileopen.bmp")
	Catch
	    MsgBox("Check path or insert disk")
	Finally
	    MsgBox("Error handler complete")
	End Try
	``

Test for specific error conditions in an event handler	Use the Catch When syntax and the Err.Number property. For example:
	
	``
	Try
	    PictureBox1.Image = _
	        System.Drawing.Bitmap.FromFile _
	        ("a:\fileopen.bmp")
	Catch When Err.Number = 53 'if File Not Found
	    MsgBox("Check pathname and disk drive")
	Catch When Err.Number = 7 'if Out Of Memory
	    MsgBox("Is this really a bitmap?", , _
	        Err.Description)
	Catch
	    MsgBox("Problem loading file", , _
	        Err.Description)
	End Try
	``

Create your own errors in a program	Use the Err.Raise method. For example, the following code generates a Disk Full error and handles it:
	
	``
	Try
	    Err.Raise(61) 'raise Disk Full error
	Catch When Err.Number = 61
	    MsgBox("Error: Disk is full")
	End Try
	``

To	Do this

Write nested Try...Catch error handlers	Place one Try...Catch code block within another. For example:
	
	``
	Try
	    PictureBox1.Image = _
	      System.Drawing.Bitmap.FromFile _
	      ("a:\fileopen.bmp")
	Catch
	    MsgBox("Insert the disk in drive A!")
	    Try
	        PictureBox1.Image = _
	          System.Drawing.Bitmap.FromFile _
	          ("a:\fileopen.bmp")
	    Catch
	        MsgBox("File Load feature disabled")
	        Button1.Enabled = False
	    End Try
	End Try
	``

Exit the current Try or Catch code block	Use the Exit Try statement in the Try or Catch code block. For example: ``` If PictureBox1.Enabled = False Then Exit Try ```

PART 3
Managing Corporate Data

10

Using Modules and Procedures

In this chapter you will learn how to:

✔ *Create standard modules.*

✔ *Declare and use public variables that have a global scope.*

✔ *Create user-defined functions and Sub procedures, known collectively as procedures.*

✔ *Call user-defined procedures.*

After studying the programs and completing the exercises in Chapters 1 through 9, you can safely call yourself an intermediate Visual Basic programmer. You've learned the basics of programming in Microsoft Visual Basic .NET, and you have the skills necessary to create a variety of useful utilities. In Part 3, you'll learn what it takes to write more complex programs in Visual Basic. You'll start by learning how to create standard modules.

A standard module is a separate container in a program that contains global, or *public,* variables and Function and Sub procedures. In this chapter, you'll learn how to declare and use public variables. You'll also learn how to create your own procedures and how to call them. The skills you'll learn will be especially applicable to larger programming projects and team development efforts.

Upgrade Notes:
What's New in Visual Basic .NET?

If you're experienced with Visual Basic 6, you'll notice some new features in Visual Basic .NET, including the following:

- Standard modules are still supported in Visual Basic .NET, but there are now Module and End Module keywords that wrap the module content within the Code Editor. Public variables are declared in standard modules as they were in Visual Basic 6.

- Visual Basic .NET continues to support the Function and Sub keywords, allowing you to create your own procedures. However, the syntax for declaring and calling procedures has changed a little.

- If you are using the default Option Explicit setting to control variable declaration, a specific type declaration is also recommended for functions when you declare them. It is also recommended that you specifically declare all types in your procedure argument lists. If you don't assign a type using the As keyword, Visual Basic will use the default Object type for the parameter, a data type that is often less efficient than a specific data type.

- Visual Basic .NET has changed the way that arguments are passed to procedures. In Visual Basic 6, the default mechanism for passing arguments was by reference (ByRef), meaning that changes to arguments in the procedure were passed back to the calling routine. In Visual Basic .NET, the default way to pass arguments is by value (ByVal), meaning that changes to arguments within a procedure aren't passed back to the calling routine. You can explicitly specify the behavior for argument passing by using the ByRef and ByVal keyword in your argument declarations. If necessary you can specify ByRef to achieve the same functionality you have in Visual Basic 6.

- When you call procedures in Visual Basic .NET, parentheses are now required around all argument lists. The Visual Studio development environment will add these for you—even if your procedures don't require any arguments. (If no arguments are required, parentheses will be inserted.)

- Programmers now have the option of using the Return statement to send the result of a function calculation back to the calling routine. The older method—assigning a value to the function name— is also supported.

Working with Standard Modules

As you write longer programs, you're likely to have several forms and event procedures that use some of the same variables and routines. By default, variables are *local* to an event procedure, meaning that they can be read or changed only in the event procedure in which they were created. You can also declare variables at the top of a form's program code and give the variables a greater scope throughout the form. However, if you create multiple forms in a project, the variables declared at the top of a form will be valid only in the form in which they were declared. Likewise, event procedures are by default declared as private and are only local to the form in which they are created. For example, you can't call the Button1_Click event procedure from a second form named Form2 if the event procedure is declared to be private to Form1.

> **note**
>
> You'll learn how to add additional forms to your project in Chapter 15.

Standard modules let you share variables and procedures throughout a program.

To share variables and procedures among all the forms and event procedures in a project, you can declare them in one or more *standard modules* for that project. A standard module, or code module, is a special file that has the filename extension .vb and contains variables and procedures that can be used anywhere in the program. (Note that in previous versions of Visual Basic, modules had the file extension .bas.) Just like forms, standard modules are listed separately in Solution Explorer, and a standard module can be saved to disk by using the Save Module1 As command on the File menu. Unlike forms, however, standard modules contain only code and don't have a user interface.

Creating a Standard Module

To create a new standard module in a program, you click the Add New Item button on the Standard toolbar, or you click the Add New Item command on the Project menu. A dialog box opens that allows you to select the Module template, prompts you for the name of the module, and then a new, blank module appears in the Code Editor. The first standard module in a program is named Module1.vb by default, but you can change the name by right-clicking the module in Solution Explorer, or with the Save Module1.vb As command on the File menu. Try creating an empty standard module in a project now.

Create and save a standard module

1   Start Visual Studio and create a new Visual Basic Windows Application project named **My Module Test** in the c:\vbnetsbs\chap10 folder.

The new project is created and a blank form appears in the Windows Forms Designer.

2   Click the Add New Item command on the Project menu.

The Add New Item dialog box appears.

3   Select the Module template.

The default name of Module1.vb appears in the Name text box.

tip

The Add New Item dialog box has multiple containers that you can use in your projects. Each of these containers has different characteristics and includes starter code to help you use them. The containers you'll primarily use are modules, Windows Forms, and classes. Modules are where you can place general-purpose procedures and variable declarations that are available throughout your project. You already have experience using Windows Forms, because each new project includes a form. You'll learn more about forms in Chapter 15. Classes are a way to design your own objects with properties, methods, and events. You'll learn more about classes in Chapter 17.

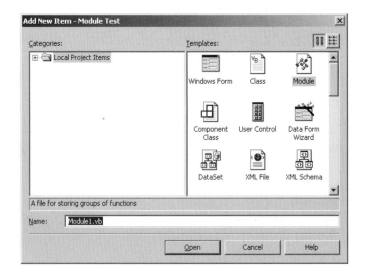

4   Click the Open button.

Visual Basic adds a standard module named Module1 to your project. The module appears in the Code Editor, as shown here:

Method Name

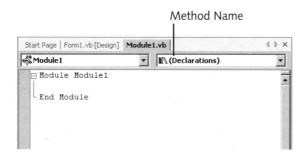

The Method Name list box indicates that the general declarations section of the standard module is open. Variables and procedures declared here will be available to the entire project. (You'll try declaring variables and procedures later.)

5   Double-click Solution Explorer title bar to see the entire Solution Explorer window, and then select Module1.vb.

Solution Explorer appears, as shown here:

Standard modules have the filename extension .vb.

Solution Explorer lists the standard module you added to the program in the list of components for the project. The name Module1 identifies the default filename of the module. (Visual Studio created the file on disk when you first created the new module.) You'll change this filename in the following steps.

6   Double-click the Properties window title bar to see the window full size.

The Properties window displays the properties for Module1.vb:

Because a standard module contains just code, it only has a few properties. Its most significant property is File Name. The File Name property lets you create a custom filename for the module that describes its purpose. It makes sense to give this identifying label some thought, because later on you may want to incorporate your module into another solution. The remaining properties for the module are useful for more sophisticated projects—you don't need to worry about them now.

7   Change the File Name property to **Math Functions.vb** or another filename that sounds impressive, and then press Enter. (I'm granting you considerable leeway here, because this project is simply for testing purposes—you won't actually create math function or any other "content" for the module.)

You use the File Name property to set the name of the module.

The filename for your standard module is updated in the Properties window, Solution Explorer, the Code Editor, and on disk.

8   Return the Properties window and Solution Explorer to their regular docked positions by double-clicking their title bars.

As you can see, working with standard modules in a project is a lot like working with forms. In the next exercise, you'll add a public variable to a standard module.

tip

To remove a standard module from a project, click the module in Solution Explorer, and then click the Exclude From Project command on the Project menu. Exclude From Project doesn't delete the module from your hard disk, but it does remove the link between the specified module and the current project. You can reverse the effects of this command by clicking the Add Existing Item command on the File menu, selecting the file that you want to add to the project, and then clicking Open.

Working with Public Variables

Public variables in a standard module can be used by all the procedures in a program.

Declaring a global, or public, variable in a standard module is simple—you type the keyword *Public* followed by the variable name and a type declaration. After you declare the variable, you can read it, change it, or display it in any procedure in your program. For example, the program statement

```
Public RunningTotal As Integer
```

declares a public variable named RunningTotal of type Integer.

Lucky Seven is the slot machine program from Chapter 2.

The following exercises demonstrate how you can use a public variable named Wins in a standard module. You'll revisit Lucky Seven, the first program you wrote in this book, and you'll use the Wins variable to record how many spins you win as the slot machine runs.

Revisit the Lucky Seven project

1   Click the Save All button on the Standard toolbar to save your changes, and then click the Close Solution command on the File menu.

    The Close Solution command clears the current solution and projects from the development environment.

2   Open the **Track Wins** project in the c:\vbnetsbs\chap10\track wins folder.

    The project opens in the development environment.

3   If the form isn't visible, display it now.

You'll see the following user interface:

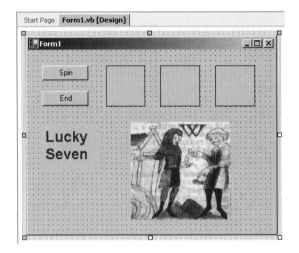

The Track Wins solution is the same slot machine program you created in Chapter 2. It allows the user to click a spin button to display "random" numbers in three number boxes, and if the number 7 appears in one of the boxes, the computer beeps and displays a bitmap showing an enticing, though quite dated, cash payout. I've simply renamed the Lucky7 solution in this chapter so that you won't modify the original version.

4   Click the Start button on the Standard toolbar to run the program.

5   Click the Spin button six or seven times, and then click the End button.

You win the first five spins (a 7 appears each time), and then your luck goes sour. As you might recall, the program uses the Rnd function to generate three random numbers each time you click the Spin button. If one of the numbers is a 7, the event procedure for the Spin button (Button1_Click) displays a cash payout picture and sounds a beep.

Now you'll edit the form, and add a standard module to enhance the program.

Add a standard module

1   Display the form in the Track Wins project.

Label control

2   Click the Label control in the Toolbox, and then create a new rectangular label below the Lucky Seven label.

3   Set the properties shown in the following table for the new label and the form. To help identify the new label in the program code, you'll change the new label object's name to lblWins.

Object	Property	Setting
Label5	Font	Arial, Bold Italic, 12-point
	ForeColor	Green (on Custom tab)
	Name	lblWins
	Text	"Wins: 0"
	TextAlign	MiddleCenter
Form1	Text	"Lucky Seven"

When you've finished, your form should look similar to this:

Now you'll add a new standard module to the project.

4 Click the Add New Item command on the Project menu, select the Module template, and then click Open.

A module named Module1.vb appears in the Code Editor.

5 Move the cursor to the blank line between the Module and End Module statements, type **Public Wins As Short**, and then press Enter.

This program statement declares a public variable of the Short integer type in your program. It is identical to a normal variable declaration you might make in your program code, except the Public keyword has been substituted for the Dim keyword. When your program runs, each event procedure in the program will have access to this variable. Your standard module should look like this:

```
Start Page | Form1.vb [Design]* | Module1.vb*

Module1 (TrackWins)           (Declarations)

Module Module1
    Public Wins As Short

End Module
```

6   In Solution Explorer, click Form1.vb, click the View Designer button, and then double-click the Spin button.

The Button1_Click event procedure for the Spin button appears in the Code Editor.

7   Type the following statements below the Beep() statement in the event procedure:

```
Wins = Wins + 1
lblWins.Text = "Wins: " & Wins
```

The public variable Wins is updated in an event procedure.

This is the part of the program code that increments the Wins public variable if a 7 appears during a spin. The second statement uses the concatenation operator (&) to assign a string to the lblWins object in the format *Wins: X*, where *X* is the number of wins. The completed event procedure should look like this:

```
Start Page | Form1.vb [Design]* | Module1.vb* | Form1.vb*                    ◁ ▷ ×
Form1 (TrackWins)                          ▼   Button1_Click               ▼

        Private Sub Button1_Click(ByVal sender As System.Object, By
            PictureBox1.Visible = False     ' hide picture
            Label1.Text = CStr(Int(Rnd() * 10))     ' pick numbers
            Label2.Text = CStr(Int(Rnd() * 10))
            Label3.Text = CStr(Int(Rnd() * 10))
            ' if any caption is 7 display picture and beep
            If (Label1.Text = "7") Or (Label2.Text = "7") _
            Or (Label3.Text = "7") Then
                PictureBox1.Visible = True
                Beep()
                Wins = Wins + 1
                lblWins.Text = "Wins: " & Wins
            End If
        End Sub
    End Class
```

The complete program is named Final Track Wins and is located in the c:\vbnetsbs\ chap10\final track wins folder.

8   Click the Save All button on the Standard toolbar to save all your changes to disk.

Save All saves your module changes as well as the changes on your form and in your event procedures.

9   Click the Start button to run the program.

10   Click the Spin button 10 times.

The Wins variable keeps a running total of your jackpots.

The Wins label keeps track of your jackpots. Each time you win, it increments the total by 1. After 10 spins, you'll have won six times, as shown here:

11 Click End to quit the program.

The public variable Wins was useful here because it maintained its value through 10 calls to the Button1_Click event procedure. If you had declared Wins locally in the Button1_Click event procedure, the variable would have reset each time, just as the trip odometer in your car does when you reset it. Using a public variable in a standard module lets you avoid "hitting the reset." Public variables have more in common with the main odometer in your car.

Public Variables vs. Form Variables

In this exercise, you used a public variable to track the number of wins in the slot machine program. Alternatively, you could have declared the Wins variable within the form at the top of the form's program code. Both techniques would produce the same result, as both a public variable and a variable declared in the general declarations area of a form have scope throughout the entire form. Public variables are unique, however, in that they maintain their values in *all* the forms and standard modules you use in a project (in other words, all the components that share the same project *namespace*). The project namespace keyword is set automatically when you first save your project, and you can view or change the namespace text by selecting the project in Solution Explorer, clicking the Properties command on the Project menu, and then examining or changing the text in the Root Namespace text box.

Creating Procedures

Procedures are a way to group a set of related statements to perform a task. In Visual Basic .NET, there are primarily two types of procedures: function procedures and Sub procedures. *Function procedures* are called by name from event procedures or other procedures. They can receive arguments, and they always return a value in the function name. They are typically used for calculations.

Sub procedures are called by name from event procedures or other procedures. They can receive arguments, and they also can return values. Unlike functions, however, Sub procedures don't return values associated with their particular Sub procedure names (although they can return values through the arguments). Sub procedures are typically used to receive or process input, display output, or set properties.

Function procedures and Sub procedures can be defined in a form's program code, but for many users it's most useful to create procedures in a standard module so that they have scope throughout the entire project. This is especially true for procedures that might be called *general-purpose procedures*—blocks of code that are flexible and useful enough to be used in a variety of programming contexts.

For example, imagine a program that has three mechanisms for printing a bitmap: a menu command named Print, a Print toolbar button, and a drag-and-drop printer icon. You could place the same printing statements in each of the three event procedures, or you could handle printing requests from all three sources by using one procedure in a standard module. General-purpose procedures save you typing time, reduce the possibility of errors, make programs smaller and easier to handle, and make event procedures easier to read.

Advantages of General-Purpose Procedures

General-purpose procedures provide the following benefits:

- Enable you to associate an often-used group of program statements with a familiar name.
- Eliminate repeated lines. You can define a procedure once and have your program execute it any number of times.
- Make programs easier to read. A program divided into a collection of small parts is easier to take apart and understand than is a program made up of one large part.

- Simplify program development. Programs separated into logical units are easier to design, write, and debug. Plus, if you're writing a program in a group setting, you can exchange procedures and modules instead of entire programs.

- Can be reused in other projects and solutions. You can easily incorporate standard-module procedures into other programming projects.

- Extend the Visual Basic language. Procedures often can perform tasks that can't be accomplished by individual Visual Basic keywords.

Writing Function Procedures

A function performs a service, such as a calculation, and returns a value.

A *Function procedure* is a group of statements located between a Function statement and an End Function statement. The statements in the function do the meaningful work—typically processing text, handling input, or calculating a numeric value. You execute, or *call*, a function in a program by placing the function name in a program statement along with any required arguments. *Arguments* are the data used to make functions work, and they must be included between parentheses and separated by commas. Basically, using a Function procedure is exactly like using a built-in function or method such as Int, Rnd, or FromFile.

tip
Functions declared in standard modules are public by default. This allows them to be used in any event procedure.

Functions should have a return type.

Function Syntax

The basic syntax of a function is as follows:

```
Function FunctionName([arguments]) As Type
    function statements
    [Return value]
End Function
```

The following syntax items are important:

- *FunctionName* is the name of the function you are creating.

- As *Type* is a pair of keywords that specifies the function return type. (In Visual Basic 6, a specific type declaration was optional, but it is strongly recommended in Visual Basic .NET.)

- *arguments* is a list of optional arguments (separated by commas) to be used in the function. Each argument should also be declared as a specific type. (Visual Basic adds the ByVal keyword by default to each argument, indicating that a copy of the data is passed to the function through this argument, but that any changes to the arguments won't be returned to the calling routine.)

- *function statements* is a block of statements that accomplish the work of the function. The first statements in a function typically declare local variables that will be used in the function, and the remaining statements perform the work of the function.

- *Return* is a new statement in Visual Basic .NET—it allows you to indicate when in the function code block you want to return a value to the calling program, and what that value is. Once a Return statement is executed, the function is exited. So if there are any function statements after the Return statement, these won't be executed. (Alternatively, you can use the Visual Basic 6 syntax, and return a value to the calling routine by assigning the value to *FunctionName*.)

Brackets ([]) enclose optional syntax items. Syntax items not enclosed by brackets are required by Visual Basic.

Functions always return a value to the calling procedure in the function's name (*FunctionName*). For this reason, the last statement in a function is often an assignment statement that places the final calculation of the function in *FunctionName*. For example, the Function procedure TotalTax computes the state and city taxes for an item and then assigns the result to the TotalTax name:

TotalTax is a sample function with one argument.

```
Function TotalTax(ByVal Cost as Single) As Single
    Dim StateTax, CityTax As Single
    StateTax = Cost * 0.05   'State tax is 5%
    CityTax = Cost * 0.015   'City tax is 1.5%
    TotalTax = StateTax + CityTax
End Function
```

Alternatively, you can use the new Visual Basic .NET syntax, and return a value to the calling procedure by using the Return statement, as shown in the following function declaration:

```
Function TotalTax(ByVal Cost as Single) As Single
    Dim StateTax, CityTax As Single
    StateTax = Cost * 0.05   'State tax is 5%
    CityTax = Cost * 0.015   'City tax is 1.5%
    Return StateTax + CityTax
End Function
```

I'll use the Return syntax most often in this book, but you are free to use either mechanism for returning data from a function.

Calling a Function Procedure

To call the TotalTax function in an event procedure, you would use a statement similar to the following:

Function return values are typically assigned to variables or properties.

```
lblTaxes.Text = TotalTax(500)
```

This statement computes the total taxes required for a $500 item and then assigns the result to the Text property of the lblTaxes object. The TotalTax function can also take a variable as an argument, as shown in the following statements:

```
Dim TotalCost, SalesPrice As Single
SalesPrice = 500
TotalCost = SalesPrice + TotalTax(SalesPrice)
```

The last statement uses the TotalTax function to determine the taxes for the number in the SalesPrice variable and then adds the computed tax to SalesPrice to get the total cost of an item. See how much clearer the code is when a function is used?

Using a Function to Perform a Calculation

In the following exercise, you'll add a function to the Lucky Seven program to calculate the win rate in the game, in other words, the percentage of spins in which one or more 7s appear. To do this, you'll add a function named HitRate and a public variable named Spins to the standard module. Then you'll call the HitRate function every time the Spin button is clicked. You'll display the results in a new label you'll create on the form.

Create a win rate function

1   Display the form for the Lucky Seven program.

The user interface for the slot machine game appears.

 *Label control*

2   Use the Label control to create a new label below the Wins label. Set the following properties for the label:

Object	Property	Setting
Label5	Font	Arial, Bold Italic, 12-point
	ForeColor	Red (on Custom tab)
	Name	lblRate
	Text	"0.0%"
	TextAlign	MiddleCenter

Your form should look similar to this:

View Code button

3   In Solution Explorer, click the Module1.vb module, and then click the View Code button.

The Module1 standard module appears in the Code Editor.

4   Type the following public variable declaration below the Public Wins As Short statement:

```
Public Spins As Short
```

The standard module now includes two public variables (Wins and Spins) that will be available to all the procedures in the project. You'll use Spins as a counter to keep track of the number of spins you make.

5 Insert a blank line in the module, then type the following function declaration:

```
Function HitRate(ByVal Hits As Short, ByVal Tries As Short) As String
    Dim Percent As Single
    Percent = Hits / Tries
    Return Format(Percent, "0.0%")
End Function
```

The HitRate function goes in the Module1 standard module.

After you type the first line of the function code, Visual Basic automatically adds an End Function statement. After you type the remainder of the function's code, your screen should look identical to this:

```
Start Page | Form1.vb [Design]* | Module1.vb* | Form1.vb* |

Module1                                              HitRate

Module Module1
    Public Wins As Short
    Public Spins As Short

    Function HitRate(ByVal Hits As Short, ByVal Tries As Short) As String
        Dim Percent As Single
        Percent = Hits / Tries
        Return Format(Percent, "0.0%")
    End Function

End Module
```

The HitRate function determines the percentage of wins by dividing the Hits argument by the Tries argument and then adjusting the appearance of the result by using the Format function. The HitRate function is declared as a string because the Format function returns a string value. The Hits argument and Tries argument are placeholders for the two short integer variables that will be passed to the function during the function call. The HitRate function is general-purpose enough to be used with any integer numbers or variables, not only with Wins and Spins.

6 Display the form again, and then double-click the Spin button on the Lucky Seven form to bring up the Button1_Click event procedure.

7 Below the fourth line of the event procedure (Label3.Text = CStr(Int(Rnd() * 10))), type the following statement:

```
Spins = Spins + 1
```

This statement increments the Spins variable each time the user clicks Spin and new numbers are placed in the spin windows.

8 Scroll down in the Code Editor, and then type the following statement as the last line in the Button1_Click event procedure, between the End If and the End Sub statements:

The HitRate function call includes two variables.

```
lblRate.Text = HitRate(Wins, Spins)
```

As you type the HitRate function, notice how Visual Studio automatically displays the names and types of the arguments for the HitRate function you just built (a nice touch).

The purpose of this statement is to call the HitRate function, using the Wins and Spins variables as arguments. The result returned is a percentage in string format, and this value is assigned to the Text property of the lblRate label on the form after each spin. That's all there is to it!

9 Click the Save All button to save your project files.

Now you'll run the program.

Run the Lucky Seven program

The complete Final Track Wins program is located in the c:\vbnetsbs\chap10\final track wins folder.

1 Click the Start button to run the modified Lucky Seven program.

2 Click the Spin button 10 times.

The first five times you click Spin, the win rate stays at 100.0%. You're hitting the jackpot every time. As you continue to click, however, the win rate adjusts to 83.3%, 71.4%, 75.0% (another win), 66.7%, and 60.0% (a total of 6 for 10). After 10 spins, your screen looks like this:

The actual win rate for Lucky Seven is about 28%.

If you continue to spin, you'll notice that the win rate drops to about 28%. The HitRate function shows you that you were really pretty lucky when you started spinning, but after a while reality set in.

3 When you're finished with the program, click the End button.

The program stops and the development environment returns.

> ## tip
>
> To revise this program so that it displays a random series of spins each time you run the program, put a Randomize statement in the Form_Load event procedure. For instructions, see the section in Chapter 2 entitled "One Step Further: Adding to a Program."

Writing Sub Procedures

Sub procedures process information.

A *Sub procedure* is similar to a Function procedure, except that a Sub procedure doesn't return a value associated with its name. Sub procedures are typically used to get input from the user, display or print information, or manipulate several properties associated with a condition. Sub procedures are also used to process and return several variables during a procedure call. Like functions, Sub procedures can return one or more values to the calling program through their argument lists.

Sub Procedure Syntax

The basic syntax for a Sub procedure is

```
Sub ProcedureName([arguments])
    procedure statements
End Sub
```

The following syntax items are important:

- *ProcedureName* is the name of the Sub procedure you're creating.
- *arguments* is a list of optional arguments (separated by commas, if there's more than one) to be used in the Sub procedure. Each argument should also be declared as a specific type. (Visual Studio adds the ByVal keyword by default to each argument, indicating that a copy of the data is passed to the function through this argument, but that any changes to the arguments won't be returned to the calling routine.)
- *procedure statements* is a block of statements that accomplish the work of the procedure.

The arguments in a procedure call must match the arguments in the procedure declaration.

In the Sub procedure call, the number and type of arguments sent to the procedure must match the number and type of arguments in the Sub procedure declaration, and the entire group must be enclosed in parentheses. If variables passed to a Sub procedure are modified during the procedure, the updated variables aren't returned to the program unless the procedure defined the arguments using the ByRef keyword. By default, Sub procedures declared in a standard module are public, so they can be called by any event procedure in a project.

important

In Visual Basic .NET, all calls to a Sub procedure must include parentheses after the procedure name. A set of empty parentheses is required even if there are no arguments being passed to the procedure. This is a change from previous versions of Visual Basic, where parentheses were required only when an argument was being passed *by value* to a Sub procedure. You'll learn more about passing variables *by reference* and *by value* later in this chapter.

For example, the following Sub procedure receives a string argument representing a person's name and uses a text box to wish that person happy birthday. If this Sub procedure is declared in a standard module, it can be called from any event procedure in the program.

```
Sub BirthdayGreeting (ByVal Person As String)
    Dim Msg As String
    If Person <> "" Then
        Msg = "Happy birthday " & Person & "!"
    Else
        Msg = "Name not specified."
    End If
    MsgBox(Msg, , "Best Wishes")
End Sub
```

The BirthdayGreeting Sub procedure receives the Person string argument.

The BirthdayGreeting procedure receives the name to be greeted by using the Person argument, a string variable received by value during the procedure call. If the value of Person isn't empty, or *null*, the specified name is used to build a message string that will be displayed with a MsgBox function. If the argument is null, the procedure displays the message "Name not specified."

Calling a Sub Procedure

To call a Sub procedure in a program, you specify the name of the procedure and then list the arguments required by the Sub procedure. For example, to call the BirthdayGreeting procedure you could type the following statement:

```
BirthdayGreeting("Robert")
```

In this example, the BirthdayGreeting procedure would insert the name "Robert" into a message string and the routine would display the following message box:

The space-saving advantages of a procedure become clear when you call the procedure many times using a variable, as shown in the example below.

```
Dim NewName As String
Do
    NewName = InputBox("Enter a name for greeting.", "Birthday List")
    BirthdayGreeting(NewName)
Loop Until NewName = ""
```

Here the user is allowed to enter as many names for birthday greetings as he or she likes. The next exercise gives you a chance to practice using a Sub procedure to handle another type of input in a program.

Using a Sub Procedure to Manage Input

Sub procedures are often used to handle input in a program when information comes from two or more sources and needs to be in the same format. In the following exercise, you'll create a Sub procedure named AddName that prompts the user for input and formats the text so that it can be displayed on multiple lines in a text box. The procedure will save you programming time because you'll use it in two event procedures, each associated with a different text box. Because the procedure will be declared in a standard module, you need to type it in only one place.

Create a text box Sub procedure

1   On the File menu, click the Close Solution command.

    Visual Studio closes the current project (the Lucky Seven slot machine).

2   Create a new Visual Basic Windows Application project named **My Text Box Sub** in the c:\vbnetsbs\chap10 folder.

    The new project is created and a blank form appears in the Windows Forms Designer.

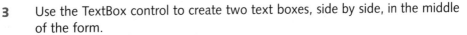
TextBox control

3   Use the TextBox control to create two text boxes, side by side, in the middle of the form.

You'll use these text boxes to hold the names of employees you'll be assigning to two departments. You get to make your own personnel decisions today.

Label control

4   Use the Label control to create two labels above the text boxes.

These labels will hold the names of the departments.

Button control

5   Use the Button control to create three buttons, a button under each text box and a separate button at the bottom of the form.

You'll use the first two buttons to add employees to their departments. You'll use the last button to quit the program.

These are typical settings for a text box used to display several lines of text.

6   Set the properties shown in the table for the objects on the form.

Because the text boxes will contain more than one line, you'll set their Multiline properties to True and their ScrollBars properties to Vertical. These settings are typically used when multiple lines are displayed in text boxes. You'll also set their TabStop properties to False and their ReadOnly properties to True so that the information can't be modified.

Object	Property	Setting
TextBox1	Multiline	True
	Name	txtSales
	ReadOnly	True
	ScrollBars	Vertical
	TabStop	False
	Text	(empty)
TextBox2	Multiline	True
	Name	txtMkt
	ReadOnly	True
	ScrollBars	Vertical
	TabStop	False
	Text	(empty)
Label1	Font	Bold
	Name	lblSales
	Text	"Sales"
Label2	Font	Bold
	Name	lblMkt
	Text	"Marketing"
Button1	Name	btnSales
	Text	"Add Name"
Button2	Name	btnMkt
	Text	"Add Name"
Button3	Name	btnQuit
	Text	"Quit"
Form1	Text	"Assign Department Teams"

7   Resize and position the objects so that your form looks similar to this:

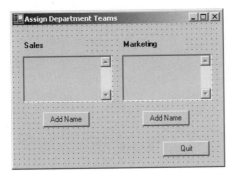

Now you'll add a standard module and create the general-purpose AddName Sub procedure.

8   On the Project menu, click the Add New Item command, select the Module template, and then click Open.

A new standard module appears in the Code Editor.

9   Type the following AddName procedure between the Module Module1 and End Module statements:

Use Chr(13) and Chr(10) to create a new line in a string.

```
Sub AddName(ByVal Team As String, ByRef ReturnString As String)
    Dim Prompt, Nm, WrapCharacter As String
    Prompt = "Enter a " & Team & " employee."
    Nm = InputBox(Prompt, "Input Box")
    WrapCharacter = Chr(13) + Chr(10)
    ReturnString = Nm & WrapCharacter
End Sub
```

This general-purpose Sub procedure uses the InputBox function to prompt the user for an employee name. It receives two arguments during the procedure call: Team, a string containing the department name; and ReturnString, an empty string variable that will contain the formatted employee name. ReturnString is declared with the ByRef keyword so that any changes made to this argument in the procedure will be passed back to the calling routine through the argument.

Before the employee name is returned, carriage return and linefeed characters are appended to the string so that each name in the text box will appear on its own line. This is a general technique that you can use in any string to create a new line.

Your Code Editor should look like this:

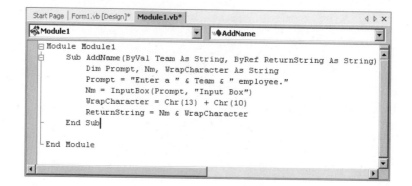

10 Display the form again, and then double-click the first Add Name button on the form (the button below the Sales text box). Type the following statements in the btnSales_Click event procedure:

```
Dim SalesPosition As String
AddName("Sales", SalesPosition)
txtSales.Text = txtSales.Text & SalesPosition
```

The call to the AddName Sub procedure includes one argument passed by value ("Sales") and one argument passed by reference (SalesPosition). The last line uses the argument passed by reference to add text to the txtSales text box. The concatenation operator (&) adds the new name to the end of the text in the text box.

11 Open the Class Name drop-down list box in the Code Editor and click the btnMkt object, then open the Method Name drop-down list box and click the Click event.

The btnMkt_Click event procedure appears in the Code Editor.

12 Type the following statements in the event procedure:

```
Dim MktPosition As String
AddName("Marketing", MktPosition)
txtMkt.Text = txtMkt.Text & MktPosition
```

This event procedure is identical to btnSales_Click, except that it sends "Marketing" to the AddName procedure and updates the txtMkt text box. The name of the local return variable (MktPosition) was renamed to make it more intuitive.

13 Open the Class Name drop-down list box and click the btnQuit object, then open the Method Name drop-down list box and click the Click event.

The btnQuit_Click event procedure appears in the Code Editor.

14 Type **End** in the btnQuit_Click event procedure.

15 Click the Save All button on the Standard toolbar.

That's it! Now you'll run the Text Box Sub program.

Run the Text Box Sub program

The complete Text Box Sub program is located in the c:\vbnetsbs\ chap10\text box sub folder.

1 Click the Start button on the Standard toolbar to run the program.

2 Click the Add Name button under the Sales text box, and then type **Maria Palermo** in the input box. (Feel free to type a different name if you want.)

Your input box should look like this:

3 Click the OK button to add the name to the Sales text box.

The name appears in the text box.

4 Click the Add Name button under the Marketing text box, type **Abraham Asante** in the Marketing input box, and then press Enter.

The name appears in the Marketing text box. Your screen should look like this:

5 Enter a few more names in each of the text boxes. This is your chance to create your own dream departments.

Each name should appear on its own line in the text boxes. The text boxes don't scroll automatically, so you won't see every name you've entered if you enter more names than can fit in a text box. You can use the scroll bars to access names that aren't visible.

6   When you've finished, click the Quit button to stop the program.

One Step Further: Passing Arguments by Value and by Reference

In the discussion of Function and Sub procedures, you learned that arguments are passed to procedures by value or by reference. Using the ByVal keyword indicates that variables should be passed to a procedure by value (the default). Any changes made to a variable passed in by value aren't passed back to the calling procedure. However, as you learned in the Text Box Sub program, using the ByRef keyword indicates that variables should be passed to a procedure by reference, meaning that any changes made to the variable in the procedure are passed back to the calling routine. Passing by reference can have significant advantages, as long as you're careful not to change a variable unintentionally in a procedure. For example, consider the following Sub procedure declaration and call:

```
Sub CostPlusInterest(ByRef Cost As Single, ByRef Total As Single)
    Cost = Cost * 1.05  'add 5% to cost...
    Total = Int(Cost)   'then make integer and return
End Sub
.
.
.
Dim Price, TotalPrice As Single
Price = 100
TotalPrice = 0
CostPlusInterest(Price, TotalPrice)
MsgBox(Price & " at 5% interest is " & TotalPrice)
```

In this example, the programmer passes two single-precision variables by reference to the CostPlusInterest procedure: Price and TotalPrice. The programmer plans to use the updated TotalPrice variable in the subsequent MsgBox call but has unfortunately forgotten that the Price variable was also updated in an intermediate step in the CostPlusInterest procedure. (Because Price was passed by reference, changes to Cost automatically result in the same changes to Price.) This produces the following erroneous result when the program is run:

Beware the pitfalls of passing variables by reference.

However, the programmer probably wanted to show the following message:

Which to Use: ByVal or ByRef?

So how should the preceding bug with the CostPlusInterest procedure be fixed? The easiest way is to declare the Cost argument using the ByVal keyword, as shown in the following program statement:

```
Sub CostPlusInterest(ByVal Cost As Single, ByRef Total As Single)
```

Declaring Cost using ByVal allows you to safely modify Cost in the CostPlusInterest procedure without sending the changes back to the calling procedure. Keeping Total declared using ByRef allows you to modify the variable that is being passed, and only those changes will be passed back to the calling procedure. In general, if you use ByRef only when it is needed, your programs will be freer of defects.

Here are some guidelines on when to use ByVal and when to use ByRef:

- Use ByVal when you don't want a procedure to modify a variable that is passed to the procedure through an argument.
- Use ByRef when you want to allow a procedure to modify a variable that is passed to the procedure.
- When in doubt, use the ByVal keyword.

Chapter 10 Quick Reference

To	Do this
Create a new module	Click the Add New Item button on the Standard toolbar, and then select the Module template. *or* Click the Add New Item command on the Project menu, and then select the Module template.
Save a module with a new name	Select the module in Solution Explorer, click the Save Module1.vb As command on the File menu, and then specify a new name.
Remove a module from a program	Select the module in Solution Explorer, and then click the Exclude From Project command on the Project menu.
Add an existing module to a project	On the Project menu, click the Add Existing Item command.
Create a public variable	Declare the variable by using the Public keyword in a standard module within the Module and End Module keywords. For example: `Public TotalSales As Integer`
Create a public function	Place the function statements between the Function and End Function keywords in a standard module. Functions are public by default. For example: ```Function HitRate(ByVal Hits As Short, ByVal _` ` Tries As Short) As String` ` Dim Percent As Single` ` Percent = Hits / Tries` ` Return Format(Percent, "0.0%")` `End Function```
Call a Function procedure	Type the function name and any necessary arguments in a program statement and assign it to a variable or property of the appropriate return type. For example: `lblRate.Text = HitRate(Wins, Spins)`

To	Do this

Create a public Sub procedure	Place the procedure statements between the Sub and End Sub keywords in a standard module. Sub procedures are public by default. For example:
	
	`Sub CostPlusInterest(ByVal Cost As Single, _`
	`  ByRef Total As Single)`
	`    Cost = Cost * 1.05`
	`    Total = Int(Cost)`
	`End Sub`

Call a Sub procedure	Type the procedure name and any necessary arguments in a program statement. For example: `CostPlusInterest(Price, TotalPrice)`
Pass an argument by value	Use the ByVal keyword in the procedure declaration. For example: `Sub GreetPerson(ByVal Name As String)`
Pass an argument by reference	Use the ByRef keyword in the procedure declaration. For example: `Sub GreetPerson(ByRef Name As String)`

11

Using Arrays and Collections to Manage Data

In this chapter you will learn how to:

- ✔ *Organize information in fixed-length and dynamic arrays.*
- ✔ *Preserve array data when you redimension arrays.*
- ✔ *Manipulate the Controls collection on a form.*
- ✔ *Use a For Each...Next loop to cycle through objects in a collection.*
- ✔ *Create your own collections for managing string data.*

Managing information in a Microsoft Visual Basic .NET application is an important task, and as your programs become more substantial, you'll need additional tools to store and process data. In this chapter, you'll learn how to organize variables and other information into useful containers called *arrays*. Arrays streamline the data management process when you have several dozen or more items to manage, and they provide a solid introduction to the database programming techniques you'll learn later in the book. You will also learn how to use groups of objects called *collections* in a Visual Basic program to manage information, and you'll learn how to process collections using the special loop For Each...Next. Considered together, arrays and collections are excellent tools for managing large amounts of information in a program.

Upgrade Notes:
What's New in Visual Basic .NET?

If you're experienced with Visual Basic 6, you'll notice some new features in Visual Basic .NET, including the following:

- Arrays in Visual Basic .NET are now always zero-based, meaning that the lowest array element is always 0. In Visual Basic 6, the Option Base statement allowed programmers to set the base of arrays to either 0 or 1. Option Base is no longer supported.

- Because arrays are now always zero-based, arrays can no longer be declared using the "To" keyword with specific lower and upper bounds. Another side effect of zero-bound arrays is that the LBound statement always returns of value of 0, because the lower bound for an array is always 0. (The UBound statement, however, continues to return the highest index in an array, which is the number of elements minus 1.)

- Arrays can now be declared and assigned data using the same program statement. For example, the syntax to declare an array named myList() and add four elements to it would be

```
Dim myList() as Integer = {5, 10, 15, 20}
```

- The ReDim statement is still valid in Visual Basic .NET, although it cannot be used to change the number of dimensions in an existing array. Also, you can't use the ReDim statement in the initial declaration.

- Visual Basic no longer has a single Collection data type. Instead, the functionality for collections is provided through the System.Collections namespace of the Microsoft .NET Framework class library. Using System.Collections, you can access several useful collection types such as Stack, Queue, Dictionary, and Hashtable.

- Visual Basic no longer supports control arrays (collections of controls that share the same name and are processed as a group), and you cannot group controls by using the Windows Clipboard as you could in Visual Basic 6. However, you can continue to store controls in an array if the array is declared in the object type.

Working with Arrays of Variables

An array is a collection of values stored under a single name.

In this section, you'll learn about *arrays*, a method for storing large amounts of information during program execution. Arrays are powerful and time-tested mechanisms for storing data in a program—the developers of BASIC, Pascal, C, and other popular programming languages incorporated arrays into the earliest versions of these products to refer to a group of values using one name, and to process those values individually or collectively.

Arrays are useful because they help you track large amounts of data in ways that would be impractical using traditional variables. For example, imagine creating a nine-inning baseball scoreboard in a program. To save the scores for each inning of the game, you might be tempted to create two groups of 9 variables (a total of 18 variables) in the program. You'd probably name them something like Inning1HomeTeam, Inning1AwayTeam, and so on, to keep them straight. Working with these variables individually would take considerable time and space in your program. Fortunately, Visual Basic lets you organize groups of similar variables into an array that has one common name and an easy-to-use index. For example, you could create a two-dimensional (2-by-9) array named Scoreboard to contain the scores for the baseball game. Let's see how this works.

Creating an Array

Before you can use an array, you must declare it.

You create, or *declare*, arrays in program code just as you declare variables. As usual, the place in which you declare the array determines where it can be used, or its scope. If an array is declared locally in a procedure, it can be used only in that procedure. If an array is declared at the top of a form, it can be used throughout the form. If an array is declared publicly in a standard module, it can be used anywhere in the project. When you declare an array, you typically include the following information in your declaration statement.

Information in an array declaration statement	Description
Array name	The name you will use to represent your array in the program. In general, array names follow the same rules as variable names. (See Chapter 5 for more information about variables.)
Data type	The type of data you will store in the array. In most cases, all the variables in an array will be of the same type. You can specify one of the fundamental data types, or, if you're not yet sure which type of data will be stored in the array or whether you will store more than one type, you can specify the Object type.

(continued)

continued

Information in an array declaration statement	Description
Number of dimensions	The number of dimensions your array will contain. Most arrays are one-dimensional (a list of values) or two-dimensional (a table of values), but you can specify additional dimensions if you're working with a complex mathematical model such as a three-dimensional shape.
Number of elements	The number of elements your array will contain. The elements in your array correspond directly to the array index. In Visual Basic .NET, the first array index is always 0 (zero).

tip

Arrays that contain a set number of elements are called *fixed-size* arrays. Arrays that contain a variable number of elements (arrays that can expand during the execution of the program) are called *dynamic* arrays.

Declaring a Fixed-Size Array

The basic syntax for a public fixed-size array is

```
Dim ArrayName(Dim1Index, Dim2Index, ...) As DataType
```

The following arguments are important:

- Dim is the keyword that declares the array. Use Public instead if you place the array in a standard module.
- *ArrayName* is the variable name of the array.
- *Dim1Index* is the upper bound of the first dimension of the array, which is the number of elements minus 1.
- *Dim2Index* is the upper bound of the second dimension of the array, which is the number of elements minus 1. (Additional dimensions can be included if separated by commas.)
- *DataType* is a keyword corresponding to the type of data that will be included in the array.

For example, to declare a one-dimensional string array named Employees that has room for 10 employee names (numbered 0 through 9), you would type the following in an event procedure:

```
Dim Employees(9) As String
```

In a standard module, the same array declaration would look like this:

```
Public Employees(9) As String
```

By default, the first element in an array has an array index of 0.

When you create the array, Visual Basic sets aside room for it in memory. The illustration below shows conceptually how the array is organized. The 10 array elements are numbered 0 through 9 rather than 1 through 10, because array indexes always start with 0. (The Option Base statement in Visual Basic 6, which allowed you to index arrays beginning with the number 1, is no longer supported.)

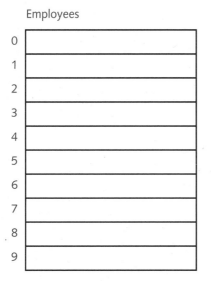

To declare a public two-dimensional array named Scoreboard that has room for two rows and nine columns of short integer data, you would type this statement in an event procedure or at the top of the form:

```
Dim Scoreboard(1, 8) As Short
```

Two-dimensional arrays require two indexes.

When you declare a two-dimensional array, Visual Basic sets aside room for it in memory. You can then use the array in your program as if it were a table of values, as shown in the following illustration. (In this case, the array elements are numbered 0 through 1 and 0 through 8.)

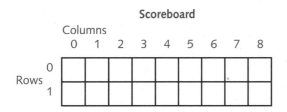

Working with Array Elements

After you've declared an array by using the Dim or Public keyword, you're ready to use the array in the program. To refer to an element of an array, you use the array name and an array index enclosed in parentheses. The index must be an integer or an expression that results in an integer. For example, the index could be a number such as 5, an integer variable such as num, or an expression such as "num – 1". (The counter variable of a For...Next loop is often used.) The following statement would assign the value "Leslie" to the element with an Index of 5 in the Employees array example in the previous section:

```
Employees(5) = "Leslie"
```

Arrays are maintained in system memory, or RAM, while the program is running.

This would produce the result shown in the following illustration in our Employees array:

Employees

0	
1	
2	
3	
4	
5	Leslie
6	
7	
8	
9	

Similarly, the following statement would assign the number 4 to row 0, column 2 (the top of the third inning) in the Scoreboard array example in the previous section:

```
Scoreboard(0, 2) = 4
```

This would produce the following result in our Scoreboard array:

Scoreboard

Columns

		0	1	2	3	4	5	6	7	8
Rows	0			4						
	1									

You can use these indexing techniques to assign or retrieve any array element.

Creating a Fixed-Size Array to Hold Temperatures

The following exercise uses a one-dimensional array named Temperatures to record the daily high temperatures for a seven-day week. The program demonstrates how you can use an array to store and process a group of related values on a form. The Temperatures array variable is declared at the top of the form, and then temperatures are assigned to the array by using an InputBox function and a For...Next loop, which you learned about in Chapter 7. The loop counter is used to reference each element in the array. The array contents are then displayed on the form by using a For...Next loop and a text box object. The average high temperature is also calculated and displayed.

The LBound and UBound Functions

To simplify working with the array, the Fixed Array program uses the UBound function to check for the upper bound, or top index value, of the array. UBound is an older BASIC and Visual Basic keyword that is still quite useful; it allows you to process arrays without referring to the declaration statements that defined exactly how many values the array would hold. The closely related LBound function, which checks the lower bounds of an array, is still valid in Visual Basic .NET, but because all Visual Basic .NET arrays now have a lower bounds of zero (0), the function simply returns a value of 0. The UBound and LBound functions have the syntax

```
LBound(ArrayName)
UBound(ArrayName)
```

where *ArrayName* is the name of an array that has been declared in the project.

11

Arrays and Collections

Use a fixed-size array

1   Start Visual Studio and create a new Visual Basic Windows Application project named **My Fixed Array** in the c:\vbnetsbs\chap11 folder.

abl

TextBox control

2   Draw a text box object on the form.

3   Set the Multiline property of the TextBox1 object to True so that you can resize the object.

4   Resize the text box object so that it fills up most of the form.

ab

Button control

5   Draw two wide button objects on the form below the text box object, oriented one beside the other.

6   Set the following properties for the form and its objects:

Object	Property	Setting
TextBox1	ScrollBars	Vertical
	Text	(empty)
Button1	Text	"Enter Temps"
Button2	Text	"Display Temps"
Form1	Text	"Fixed Array Temps"

Your form should look like this:

7   Click the View Code button in Solution Explorer to display the Code Editor.

8   Scroll to the top of the form's program code, and directly below the tag "Windows Form Designer generated code," type the following array declaration:

```
Dim Temperatures(6) As Single
```

This statement creates an array named Temperatures (of the type Single) that contains seven elements numbered 0 through 6. Because the array has been declared at the top of the form, it will be available in all of the event procedures in the form.

9 Display the form again, and then double-click the Enter Temps button (Button1).

The Button1_Click event procedure appears in the Code Editor.

10 Type the following program statements to prompt the user for temperatures and to load the input into the array:

```
Dim Prompt, Title As String
Dim i As Short
Prompt = "Enter the day's high temperature."
For i = 0 To UBound(Temperatures)
    Title = "Day " & (i + 1)
    Temperatures(i) = InputBox(Prompt, Title)
Next
```

The For...Next loop uses the short integer counter variable "i" as an array index to load temperatures into array elements 0 through 6. Rather than using the simplified For loop syntax

```
For i = 0 to 6
```

to process the array, I chose a slightly more complex syntax involving the UBound function for future flexibility. The For loop construction

```
For i = 0 To UBound(Temperatures)
```

determines the upper bounds of the array by using the UBound statement. This technique is flexible because if the array is expanded or reduced later the For loop will automatically adjust itself to the new array size.

The counter variable i is used as an array index.

To fill the array with temperatures, the event procedure uses an InputBox function, which displays the current day using the For loop counter.

11 Display the form again, and then double-click the Display Temps button (Button2).

12 Type the following statements in the Button2_Click event procedure:

```
Dim Result As String
Dim i As Short
Dim Total As Single = 0
Result = "High temperatures for the week:" & vbCrLf & vbCrLf
```

(continued)

continued

```
For i = 0 To UBound(Temperatures)
    Result = Result & "Day " & (i + 1) & vbTab & _
        Temperatures(i) & vbCrLf
    Total = Total + Temperatures(i)
Next
Result = Result & vbCrLf & _
    "Average temperature:   " & Format(Total / 7, "0.0")
TextBox1.Text = Result
```

This event procedure uses a For...Next loop to cycle through the elements in the array, and it adds each element in the array to a string variable named Result, which is declared at the top of the event procedure. I've used several literal strings, constants, and string concatenation operators (&) to pad and format the string using carriage returns (vbCrLf), tab characters (vbTab), and headings. The vbCrLf constant, used here for the first time, contains the carriage return and line feed characters and is an efficient way to create new lines. The vbTab constant is also used here for the first time to put some distance between the day and temperature values in the Result string. At the end of the event procedure, an average for the temperatures is determined, and the final string is assigned to the Text property of the text box object, as shown in this statement:

```
TextBox1.Text = Result
```

13   Click the Save All button on the Standard toolbar to save the project.

The complete Fixed Array program is located in the c:\vbnetsbs\ chap11\fixed array folder.

14   Click the Start button to run the program.

15   Click the Enter Temps button, and then enter seven different temperatures as you are prompted to by the InputBox function. (How about the temperatures during your last vacation?)

The InputBox function dialog box looks like this:

16   After you've entered the temperatures, click the Display Temps button.

Visual Basic displays each of the temperatures in the text box and prints an average at the bottom. Your screen should look similar to this:

Fixed Array Temps

High temperatures for the week:

Day 1   74
Day 2   75.5
Day 3   78
Day 4   80
Day 5   74
Day 6   68
Day 7   66.5

Average temperature: 73.7

Enter Temps   Display Temps

17 Click the Close button on the form to end the program.

Creating a Dynamic Array

As you can see, arrays are quite handy for working with lists of numbers, especially if you process them by using For...Next loops. But what if you're not sure how much array space you'll need before you run your program? For example, what if you want to let the user choose how many temperatures are entered into the Fixed Array program?

Dynamic arrays are dimensioned at runtime.

Visual Basic handles this problem efficiently with a special elastic container called a *dynamic array*. Dynamic arrays are dimensioned at runtime, either when the user specifies the size of the array or when logic you add to the program determines an array size based on specific conditions. Dimensioning a dynamic array takes several steps, because although the size of the array isn't specified until the program is running, you need to make "reservations" for the array at design time. To create a dynamic array, you follow these basic steps:

■ Specify the name and type of the array in the program at design time, omitting the number of elements in the array. For example, to create a dynamic array named Temperatures, you type

```
Dim Temperatures() as Single
```

■ Add code to determine the number of elements that should be in the array at runtime. You can prompt the user by using an InputBox function or a text box object, or you can calculate the storage needs of the program by using properties or other logic. For example, the following statements get the array size from the user and assign it to the Days short integer variable:

```
Dim Days As Short
Days = InputBox("How many days?", "Create Array")
```

■ Use the variable in a ReDim statement to dimension the array (subtract one because arrays are zero-based). For example, the following statement sets the size of the Temperatures array at runtime by using the Days variable:

```
ReDim Temperatures(Days - 1)
```

The only important qualification with ReDim is that you don't try to change the number of dimensions in an array that you have previously declared.

■ Use the UBound function to determine the upper bound in a For...Next loop, and process the array elements as necessary:

```
For i = 0 to UBound(Temperatures)
    Temperatures(i) = InputBox(Prompt, Title)
Next
```

In the following exercise, you'll use those four steps to revise the Fixed Array program so that it can process any number of temperatures by using a dynamic array.

Use a dynamic array to hold temperatures

1   Open the Code Editor to display the program code for the Fixed Array project.

2   Scroll to the top of the form's code, where you originally declared the Temperatures fixed array.

3   Remove the number 6 from the Temperatures array declaration, so that the array is now a dynamic array.

The statement should look like the following:

```
Dim Temperatures() As Single
```

4   Add the following variable declaration just below the Temperatures array declaration:

```
Dim Days As Integer
```

The integer variable Days will be used to receive input from the user and to dimension the dynamic array at runtime.

5   Scroll down in the Code Editor to display the Button1_Click event procedure, and modify the code so that it looks like the following. (The changed or added elements appear in bold text.)

```
Dim Prompt, Title As String
Dim i As Short
Prompt = "Enter the day's high temperature."
Days = InputBox("How many days?", "Create Array")
If Days > 0 Then ReDim Temperatures(Days - 1)
```

```
For i = 0 To UBound(Temperatures)
    Title = "Day " & (i + 1)
    Temperatures(i) = InputBox(Prompt, Title)
Next
```

The fourth and fifth lines prompt the user for the number of temperatures he or she wants to save, and then the input is used to dimension a dynamic array. The If...Then statement is used to verify that the number of days is greater than 0. (Dimensioning an array with a number less than 0 will generate errors.) Since index 0 of the array is used to store the temperature for the first day, the Days variable is decremented by 1 when dimensioning the array. The Days variable isn't needed to determine the upper bound of the For...Next loop—as in the previous example, the UBound function is used instead.

6   Scroll down in the Code Editor to display the Button2_Click event procedure. Modify the code so that it looks like the following routine. (The changed elements appear in bold.)

```
Dim Result As String
Dim i As Short
Dim Total As Single = 0
Result = "High temperatures:" & vbCrLf & vbCrLf
For i = 0 To UBound(Temperatures)
    Result = Result & "Day " & (i + 1) & vbTab & _
        Temperatures(i) & vbCrLf
    Total = Total + Temperatures(i)
Next
Result = Result & vbCrLf & _
    "Average temperature:   " & Format(Total / Days, "0.0")
TextBox1.Text = Result
```

The variable Days replaces the number 7 in the average temperature calculation at the bottom of the event procedure. I also edited the "High temperatures" heading that will be displayed in the text box.

On the practice files disk, I gave this project a separate name, to keep it distinct from the Fixed Array project. The complete Dynamic Array program is located in the c:\vbnetsbs\ chap11\dynamic array folder.

7   Save your changes to disk.

8   Click the Start button to run the program.

9   Click the Enter Temps button.

10   Type **5** when you are prompted for the number of days you want to record, and then click OK.

11   Enter five temperatures as you are prompted to do so.

12   When you've finished entering temperatures, click the Display Temps button.

The program displays the five temperatures on the form along with their average. Your screen should look similar to this:

```
┌─────────────────────────────────────────┐
│ ▣ Fixed Array Temps            _ □ ×     │
│ ┌─────────────────────────────────┐ ▲   │
│ │ High temperatures:              │     │
│ │                                 │     │
│ │ Day 1    73                     │     │
│ │ Day 2    77                     │     │
│ │ Day 3    75                     │     │
│ │ Day 4    70                     │     │
│ │ Day 5    68                     │     │
│ │                                 │     │
│ │ Average temperature:  72.6      │     │
│ │                                 │     │
│ │                                 │ ▼   │
│ └─────────────────────────────────┘     │
│                                          │
│     ┌──────────────┐  ┌──────────────┐  │
│     │  Enter Temps │  │ Display Temps│  │
│     └──────────────┘  └──────────────┘  │
└─────────────────────────────────────────┘
```

13   Click the Close button on the form to end the program.

Preserving Array Contents Using ReDim Preserve

In the previous exercise, you used the ReDim statement to specify the size of a dynamic array at runtime. However, there is one potential shortcoming associated with the ReDim statement that you should know about: if you redimension an array that already has data in it, all the existing data will be irretrievably lost. After the ReDim statement is executed, the contents of a dynamic array are set to their default value, such as zero or *null*. Depending on your outlook, this can be considered a useful feature for emptying the contents of arrays, or it can be an irksome feature that requires a workaround.

Fortunately, Visual Basic .NET provides the same useful feature that Visual Basic 6 provided for array redimensioning: The Preserve keyword, which you use to preserve the data in an array as you change its dimensions. The syntax for the Preserve keyword is as follows:

```
ReDim Preserve ArrayName(Dim1Elements, Dim2Elements, ...)
```

In such a redimension statement, the array must continue to have the same number of dimensions and contain the same type of data. In addition, there is a particular caveat that you can resize only the last array dimension. For example, if your array has two or more dimensions, you can change the size of only the last dimension and still preserve the contents of the array. (Single-dimension arrays automatically pass this test, so you can freely expand the size of dynamic arrays using the Preserve keyword.)

The following examples show how you can use Preserve to increase the size of the last dimension in a dynamic array without erasing any existing data contained in the array.

If you originally declared a dynamic string array named Philosophers using the following syntax:

```
Dim Philosophers() As String
```

Then redimension the array and add data to it using code similar to the following:

```
ReDim Philosophers(200)
Philosophers(200) = "Steve Harrison"
```

You can expand the size of the Philosophers array to 301 elements (0–300), and preserve the existing contents, using the following syntax:

```
ReDim Preserve Philosophers(300)
```

A more complex example involving a three-dimensional array makes use of similar syntax. Imagine that you want to make use of a three-dimensional single-precision floating point array, named myCube, in your program. You could declare the myCube array using the following syntax:

```
Dim myCube(,,) As Single
```

You could then redimension the array and add data to it using the following code:

```
ReDim myCube(25, 25, 25)
myCube(10, 1, 1) = 150.46
```

After which you could expand the size of the third dimension in the array (while preserving the array's contents) using this syntax:

```
ReDim Preserve myCube(25, 25, 50)
```

In this example, however, only the third dimension can be expanded—the first and second dimensions cannot be changed if you redimension the array using the Preserve keyword. Attempting to change the size of the first or second dimensions in this example will produce a runtime error when the ReDim Preserve statement is executed.

Experiment a little with ReDim Preserve and see how you can use it to make your own arrays flexible and robust.

You're finished working with arrays for now. In the rest of the chapter, you learn about collections.

Working with Object Collections

A collection is a group of related objects.

In previous sections, you learned about using arrays to store information during program execution. In this section, you'll learn about *collections*, a complementary method to manipulate control objects and other data in a Visual Basic program. You already know that objects on a form are stored together in the same file. But did you also know that Visual Basic considers the objects to be members of the same group? In Visual Basic terminology, the entire set of objects on a form is called the *Controls collection*. The Controls collection is created automatically when you open a new form, and when you add objects to the form, they automatically become part of the collection. In fact, Visual Basic maintains several standard collections of objects that you can use when you write your programs. In the rest of this chapter, you will learn the basic skills you need to work with any collection you encounter.

Each form has a Controls collection.

Each collection in a program has its own name so that you can reference it as a distinct unit in the program code. For example, as you just learned, the collection containing all the objects on a form is called the Controls collection. If you have more than one form in a project, you can create public variables associated with the form names and use those variables to differentiate one Controls collection from another. (You'll learn more about using public variables to store form data in Chapter 15.) You can even add controls programmatically to the Controls collection in a form.

In addition to letting you work with objects and collections in your own programs, Visual Studio lets you browse your system for other application objects and use them in your programs. We'll pick up this topic again in Chapter 13 when you learn how to use the Visual Studio Object Browser.

Referencing Objects in a Collection

You can reference the objects in a collection, or the individual members of the collection, by specifying the *index position* of the object in the group. Visual Basic stores collection objects in the reverse order of that in which they were created, so you can use an object's "birth order" to reference the object individually, or you can use a loop to step through several objects. For example, to identify the last object created on a form, you would specify the 0 (zero) index, as shown in this example:

You can reference the objects in a collection individually or in groups.

```
Controls(0).Text = "Business"
```

This statement sets the Text property of the last object on the form to "Business". (The second-to-the-last object created has an index of 1, the third-to-the-last object created has an index of 2, and so on.) Considering this logic, it is important that you don't always associate a particular object on the form with an index value—if a new object is added to the collection, the new object will take the 0 index spot, and the remaining object indexes will be incremented by 1.

The following For...Next loop displays the names of the last four controls added to a form using a message box:

```
Dim i As Integer
For i = 0 To 3
    MsgBox(Controls(i).Name)
Next i
```

Note that I've directed this loop to cycle from 0 to 3 because the last control object added to a form is in the "0" position. In the following section, you'll learn a more efficient method for writing such a loop.

Writing For Each...Next Loops

Although you can reference the members of a collection individually, the most useful way to work with objects in a collection is to process them as a group. In fact, the reason collections exist is so that you can process groups of objects efficiently. For example, you might want to display, move, sort, rename, or resize an entire collection of objects at once.

For Each...Next loops are designed to process collections.

To handle one of these tasks, you can use a special loop called For Each...Next to cycle through objects in a collection one at a time. A For Each...Next loop is similar to a For...Next loop. When a For Each...Next loop is used with the Controls collection, it looks like this:

```
Dim CtrlVar As Control
...
For Each CtrlVar In Controls
    process object
Next CtrlVar
```

The CtrlVar variable represents the current object in a For Each...Next loop.

The CtrlVar variable is declared as a Control type and represents the current object in the collection. Controls (note the "s") is the collection class I introduced earlier that represents all the control objects on the current form. The body of the loop is used to process the individual objects of the collection. For example, you might want to change the Enabled, Left, Top, Text, or Visible properties of the objects in the collection, or you might want to list the name of each object in a list box.

Experimenting with Objects in the Controls Collection

In the following exercises, you'll use program code to manipulate the objects on a form using the Controls collection. The project you create will have three button objects, and you'll create event procedures that change the Text properties of each object, move objects to the right, and give one object in the group special treatment. The program will use three For Each...Next loops to manipulate the objects each time the user clicks one of the buttons.

Use a For Each...Next loop to change Text properties

1   Click the Close Solution command on the File menu to close the current project.

2   Create a new Visual Basic Windows Application project named **My Controls Collection** in the c:\vbnetsbs\chap11 folder.

`ab`

Button control

3   Use the Button control to draw three button objects on the left side of the form, as shown here:

4   Use the Properties window to set the Name property of the third button object (Button3) to btnMoveObjects.

5   Double-click the first button object (Button1) on the form.

The Button1_Click event procedure appears in the Code Editor.

6   Type the following program statements:

```
For Each ctrl In Controls
    ctrl.Text = "Click Me!"
Next
```

This For Each...Next loop steps through the Controls collection on the form one control at a time, and sets each control's Text property to "Click Me!" The loop uses ctrl as an object variable in the loop, which you'll declare in the following step.

7   Scroll to the top of the form's program code, and directly below the tag "Windows Form Designer generated code," type the following comment and variable declaration:

```
'Declare a variable of type Control to represent form controls
Dim ctrl As Control
```

This global variable declaration creates a variable in the Control class type that will represent the current form's controls in the program. You're declaring this variable in the general declarations area of the form so that it will be valid throughout all of the form's event procedures. Now you're ready to run the program and change the Text property for each button on the form.

8   Click the Start button on the Standard toolbar to run the program.

9   Click the first button on the form (Button1).

The Button1_Click event procedure changes the Text property for each control in the Controls collection. Your form will look like this:

11

Arrays and Collections

10   Click the Close button on the form.

The program ends.

Now you're ready to try a different experiment with the Controls collection. Use the Left property to move each control in the Controls collection to the right.

Use a For Each...Next loop to move controls

Using a For Each...Next loop to adjust the Left property of each object makes the objects move as a group.

1   Display the form again, and then double-click the second button object (Button2).

Type the following program code in the Button2_Click event procedure:

```
For Each ctrl In Controls
    ctrl.Left = ctrl.Left + 25
Next
```

Each time the user clicks the second button, this For Each...Next loop steps through the objects in the Controls collection one by one and moves them 25 pixels to the right. (To move objects 25 pixels to the left, you would subtract 25 instead.) A *pixel* is a device-independent measuring unit that allows you to precisely place objects on a form.

tip

In Visual Basic 6, twips were usually used to specify measurements instead of pixels. For information about converting existing Visual Basic 6 code from twip measurements to pixel measurements, search for the topic "ScaleMode Is Not Supported" in the Visual Studio online Help.

As in the previous event procedure you typed, the ctrl variable is a "stand-in" for the current object in the collection and contains the same property settings as the object it represents. In this loop, you adjust the Left property, which determines an object's position relative to the left side of the form.

2   Click the Start button on the Standard toolbar.

The program runs, and three buttons appear on the left side of the form.

3   Click the second button several times.

Each time you click the button, the objects on the form move to the right. Your screen will look like this after five clicks:

4   Click the Close button on the form to stop the program.

Moving all the objects on a form isn't a requirement, of course. Visual Basic allows you to process collection members individually if you want to. In the next exercise, you'll learn how to keep the third button object in one place while the other two buttons move to the right.

Using the Name Property in a For Each...Next Loop

If you want to process one or more members of a collection differently than you process the others, you can use the Name property, which uniquely identifies each object on the form. You have set the Name property periodically in this book to make your program code more readable, but Name also can be used programmatically to identify specific objects in your program.

To use the Name property in this way, single out the objects that you want to give special treatment to and then note their Name properties. As you loop through the objects on the form using a For Each...Next loop, use one or more If statements to test for the important Name properties and handle those objects differently. For example, let's say you wanted to construct a For Each...Next loop that moved one object slower across the form than the other objects. You could use an If...Then statement to spot the Name property of the slower object, then move that object a shorter distance by not incrementing its Left property as much.

> **tip**
> If you plan to give several objects special treatment in a For Each...Next loop, you can use ElseIf statements with the If...Then statement, or you can use a Select Case decision structure.

In the following exercise, you'll test the Name property of the third button object (btnMoveObjects) to give that button special treatment in a For Each...Next loop. The end result will be an event procedure that moves the top two buttons right but keeps the bottom button stationary.

> **tip**
> In addition to the Name property, most objects support the Tag property. Similar to the Name property, the Tag property is a location where you can store string data about the object. The Tag property is empty by default, but you can assign information to it and test it to uniquely identify objects in your program that you want to process differently.

11

Arrays and Collections

Use the Name property to give a control in the Controls collection special treatment

1   Display the form, and then double-click the third button object.

The btnMoveObjects_Click event procedure appears in the Code Editor. Remember that you changed the Name property of this object from Button1 to btnMoveObjects in an earlier exercise.

2   Type the following program code in the event procedure:

```
For Each ctrl In Controls
    If ctrl.Name <> "btnMoveObjects" Then
        ctrl.Left = ctrl.Left + 25
    End If
Next
```

The If...Then statement checks for the Name property.

The new feature of this For Each...Next loop is the If...Then statement that checks each collection member to see if it has a Name property called btnMoveObjects. If the loop encounters this marker, it passes over the object without moving it. Note that, as in the previous examples, the ctrl variable was declared at the top of the form as a variable of the Control type with scope throughout the form.

3   Click the Save All button on the Standard toolbar.

The complete Controls Collection program is located in the c:\vbnetsbs\ chap11\controls collection folder.

4   Click the Start button.

The program runs, and the three interface objects appear on the form.

5   Click the third button object six or seven times.

As you click the button, the objects on the form move across the screen. The third button stays in the same place, however:

Giving one object in a collection special treatment can be very useful. In this case, using the Name property in the For Each...Next loop improved the readability of the program code and suggests numerous potential uses for a game or graphics program. As you use other types of collections in Visual Basic, be sure to keep the Name property in mind.

6 Click the Close button on the form to stop the program.

Creating Your Own Collections

Visual Basic allows you to create your own collections to track data in a program and manipulate it systematically. Although collections are often created to hold objects, such as user interface controls, you can also use collections to store numeric or string values while a program is running. In this way, collections nicely complement the capabilities of arrays, which you learned about at the beginning of this chapter.

New collections are declared like variables are in a program, and the location in which you declare them determines their *scope*, or the extent to which their assigned values persist. Because collections are so useful, I usually declare them at the top of a form or in a standard module. New collection declarations require the syntax

```
Dim CollectionName As New Collection()
```

where *CollectionName* is the name of your collection. If you place the collection declaration in a standard module, use the Public keyword instead of the Dim keyword. After you create a collection, you can add members to it by using the Add method, and you can examine the individual members using a For Each...Next loop.

The following exercise shows you how to create a collection to hold string data representing the Internet addresses (uniform resource locators, or URLs) you have recently used. To make a connection to the Web, the program will use the Visual Basic System.Diagnostics.Process.Start method and your default Web browser, a technique that I first introduced in Chapter 3.

Track Internet addresses using a new collection

1 Click the Close Solution command on the File menu.

The current project closes.

2 Create a new Visual Basic Windows Application project named **My URL Collection** in the c:\vbnetsbs\chap11 folder.

3 Draw a wide text box object at the top of the form, centered within the form.

TextBox control

Button control

4 Draw two wide button objects on the form below the text box object, one button below the other.

5 Set the following properties for the form and its objects:

Object	Property	Setting
TextBox1	Text	"http://www.microsoft.com/mspress"
Button1	Text	"Visit Site"
Button2	Text	"List all sites visited"
Form1	Text	"URL Collection"

6 Your form should look like this:

7 Click the View Code button in Solution Explorer to display the Code Editor.

8 Scroll to the top of the form's program code, and directly below the tag "Windows Form Designer generated code," type the following variable declaration:

```
Dim URLsVisited As New Collection()
```

This statement creates a new collection and assigns it the variable name URLsVisited. Because you are placing the declaration at the top of the form, the collection will have scope throughout all the form's event procedures.

9 Display the form again, double-click the Visit Site button, and then type the following code in the Button1_Click event procedure:

```
URLsVisited.Add(TextBox1.Text)
System.Diagnostics.Process.Start(TextBox1.Text)
```

This program code uses the Add method to fill up or "populate" the collection with members. When the user clicks the Button1 object, the program assumes that a valid Internet address has been placed in the TextBox1 object. Every time that the Button1 object is clicked, the current URL in

TextBox1 is copied to the URLsVisited collection as a string. Next, the System.Diagnostics.Process.Start method is called with URL as a parameter. Because the parameter is a URL, the Start method will attempt to open the URL using the default Web browser on the system. (If the URL is invalid or an Internet connection cannot be established, the Web browser will handle the error.)

note

The only URLs this program adds to the URLsVisited collection are those you have specified in the TextBox1 object. If you browse to additional Web sites using your Web browser, those sites won't be added to the collection. (To learn a more sophisticated way of tracking Web sites using the Internet Explorer object model, see Chapter 21.)

10   Display the form again, and then double-click the List All Sites Visited button.

11   Type the following program code using the Code Editor:

```
Dim URLName, AllURLs As String
For Each URLName In URLsVisited
    AllURLs = AllURLs & URLName & vbCrLf
Next URLName
MsgBox(AllURLs, MsgBoxStyle.Information, "Web sites visited")
```

This event procedure prints the entire collection using a For Each...Next loop and a MsgBox function. The routine declares a string variable named URLName to hold each member of the collection as it is processed, and the value is added to a string named AllURLs using the concatenation operator (&) and the vbCrLf string constant.

Finally, the AllURLs string, which represents the entire contents of the URLsVisited collection, is displayed in a message box. I added the MsgBoxStyle.Information argument in the MsgBox function to emphasize that the text being displayed is general information and not a warning. (MsgBoxStyle.Information is also a built-in Visual Basic constant.)

12   Click the Save All button to save your changes.

note

To run the URL Collection program, your computer must establish a connection to the Internet and be equipped with a Web browser, such as Microsoft Internet Explorer or Netscape Navigator.

Run the URL Collection program

1   Click the Start button to run the program.

The complete URL Collection program is located in the c:\vbnetsbs\ chap11\url collection folder.

The utility features a default Web site in the URL textbox, so it isn't necessary to type your own Internet address at first.

2   Click the Visit Site button.

Visual Basic adds the Microsoft Press Web site (http://www.microsoft.com/mspress) to the URLsVisited collection and then opens the default Web browser on your system and loads the requested Web page. Examine the content of this Web site if you are interested.

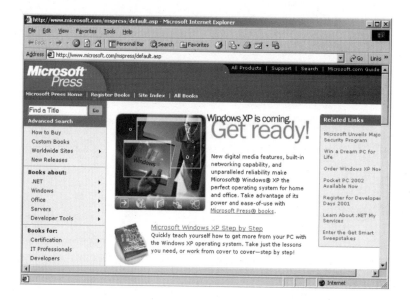

3   Click the form again (you may need to click the icon on the Windows taskbar).

4   Click the List All Sites Visited button.

Visual Basic executes the event procedure for the Button2 object. You'll see a message box that looks like this:

5   Click OK in the message box, type a different Web site in the form's text box, and then click the Visit Site button.

You might want to try visiting the Microsoft Visual Basic Web site to learn more about Visual Basic .NET (the address is http://msdn.microsoft.com/vbasic/).

6   Visit a few more Web sites using the URL Collection form, and then click the List All Sites Visited button.

Each time you click the List All Sites Visited button, the MsgBox function expands to show the growing URL history list, as shown here:

If you visit more than a few dozen Web sites, you'll need to replace the MsgBox function with a multi-line text box on the form. (Can you figure out how to write the code?)

7   When you're finished, click the Close button on the form, and then close your Web browser.

Congratulations! You've learned to use the Controls collection and create new collections, and you've learned how to process them by using a For Each...Next loop. These skills will be useful whenever you work with collections.

One Step Further: Visual Basic for Applications Collections

If you decide to write Visual Basic macros for Microsoft Office applications in the future, you'll find that collections play a big role in the object models of Microsoft Word, Microsoft Excel, Microsoft Access, Microsoft PowerPoint, and several other applications that support the Visual Basic for Applications programming language. In Microsoft Word, for example, all the open documents in the word processor are stored in the Documents collection, and each paragraph in the current document is stored in the Paragraphs collection. You can manipulate these collections with the For Each...Next loop just as you did in the preceding exercises.

For example, the following sample code comes from a Word 2002 macro that uses a For Each...Next loop to check each open document in the Documents collection for a file named MyLetter.doc. If the file is found in the collection, the macro saves the file using the Save method. If the file isn't found in the collection, the macro attempts to open the file from the My Documents folder on drive C.

```
Dim aDoc As Object
Dim docFound As Boolean
Dim docLocation As String
docFound = False
docLocation = "c:\my documents\myletter.doc"
For Each aDoc In Documents
    If InStr(1, aDoc.Name, "myletter.doc", 1) Then
        docFound = True
        aDoc.Save
        Exit For
    End If
Next aDoc
If docFound = False Then
    Documents.Open FileName:=docLocation
End If
```

tip

I've included this sample Word 2002 macro to show you how you can use collections in Visual Basic for Applications, but the source code is designed for Word, not the Visual Basic compiler. To try it, you'll need to start Word, click the Macros command on the Macro submenu of the Tools menu, create a new name for the macro, and then enter the code using Word's special macro editor. (If you're not in Word, the Documents collection won't have any meaning to the compiler.)

The macro begins by declaring three variables. The aDoc object variable will represent the current collection element in the For Each...Next loop. The Boolean variable docFound will be assigned a Boolean value of True if the document is found in the Documents collection. The string variable docLocation will contain the path of the MyLetter.doc file on disk. (This routine assumes that the MyLetter.doc file is in the My Documents folder on drive C.)

The For Each...Next loop cycles through each document in the Documents collection searching for the MyLetter file. If the file is detected by the InStr function (which detects one string in another), the file is saved. If the file isn't found, the macro attempts to open it by using the Open method of the Documents object.

Also note the Exit For statement, which I use to exit the For Each...Next loop when the MyLetter file has been found and saved. Exit For is a special program statement you can use to exit a For...Next loop or For Each...Next loop when continuing will cause unwanted results. In our example, if the MyLetter.doc file has been located in the collection, continuing the search would be fruitless. Here, the Exit For statement affords a graceful way to stop the loop as soon as its task is completed.

Chapter 11 Quick Reference

To	Do this
Create an array	Dimension the array by using the Dim keyword For example: `Dim Employees(9) As String`
Create a public array	Dimension the array by using the Public keyword in a standard module. For example: `Public Employees(9) As String`
Assign a value to an array	Specify the array name, the index of the array element, and the value. For example: `Employees(5) = "Leslie"`
Format text strings with carriage return and tab characters	Use the vbCrLf and vbTab constants within your your program code. (To add these values to strings, use the & operator.)
Create a dynamic array	Specify the name and type of the array at design time, but omit the number of elements. (If the array has multiple dimensions, insert commas between the dimensions but no numbers.) While your program is running, specify the size of the array by using the ReDim statement. For example: `ReDim Temperatures(10)`

Process the elements in an array	Write a For...Next loop that uses the loop counter variable to address each element in the array.
	For example:
	`Dim i As Short`
	`Dim Total As Single`
	`For i = 0 To UBound(Temperatures)`
	`  Total = Total + Temperatures(i)`
	`Next`

Redimension an array while preserving the data in it	Use the Preserve keyword in your ReDim statement. For example: `ReDim Preserve myCube(25, 25, 50)`

(continued)

Arrays and Collections

11

To	Do this

Process objects in a collection	Write a For Each...Next loop that addresses each member of the collection individually. For example:
	
	``vb
	Dim ctrl As Control
	For Each ctrl In Controls
	    ctrl.Text = "Click Me!"
	Next
	``

Move objects in the Controls collection from left to right across the screen	Modify the Control.Left property of each collection object in a For Each...Next loop. For example:
	
	``vb
	Dim ctrl As Control
	For Each ctrl In Controls
	    Ctrl.Left = Ctrl.Left + 25
	Next Ctrl
	``

Give special treatment to an object in a collection	Test the Name property of the objects in the collection using a For Each...Next loop. For example:
	
	``vb
	Dim ctrl As Control
	For Each ctrl In Controls
	    If ctrl.Name <> "btnMoveObjects" Then
	        ctrl.Left = ctrl.Left + 25
	    End If
	Next
	``

Create a new collection and add members to it.	Declare a variable using the New Collection syntax. Use the Add method to add members. For example:
	
	``vb
	Dim URLsVisited As New Collection()
	URLsVisited.Add(TextBox1.Text)
	``

CHAPTER

12

Exploring Text Files and String Processing

In this chapter you will learn how to:

✔ *Display a text file by using a text box object.*

✔ *Save notes in a text file.*

✔ *Use string processing techniques to sort and encrypt text files.*

Managing electronic documents is an important function in any modern business, and Visual Basic .NET provides numerous mechanisms for working with different document types and manipulating the information in them. The most basic document type is the *text file*, which is made up of non-formatted words and paragraphs, letters, numbers, and a variety of special-purpose characters and symbols. In this chapter, you'll learn how to work with information stored in text files on your system. You'll learn how to open a text file and display its contents by using a text box object, and you'll learn how to create a new text file on disk. You'll also learn more about managing strings in your programs, and you'll use methods in the .NET Framework String class to combine, sort, encrypt, and display words, lines, and entire text files.

Upgrade Notes:
What's New in Visual Basic .NET?

If you're experienced with Visual Basic 6, you'll notice some new features in Visual Basic .NET, including the following:

- In Visual Basic 6, you opened and manipulated text files using the Open, Line Input #, Print #, EOF, and Close keywords. In Visual Basic .NET, there is a new set of functions that manage text file operations. These functions are provided by the FileSystem object in the Microsoft.VisualBasic namespace, and include FileOpen, LineInput, PrintLine, and FileClose.

- In addition to the built-in Visual Basic .NET functions mentioned above, you can also use the objects in the System.IO namespace to open and manipulate files, browse drives and folders, copy and delete files, process text streams, and complete other file-management tasks. The objects in the System.IO namespace aren't a replacement for the built-in Visual Basic .NET functions listed above, but they do complement them.

- In terms of string-processing, several of the older Visual Basic text functions have been supplemented by new methods in the .NET Framework String class. For example, the new SubString method provides functionality similar to the Visual Basic Mid function, and the ToUpper method is similar to the Visual Basic UCase function. You can use either method to manipulate text strings, but the newer .NET Framework methods are recommended.

Displaying Text Files by Using a Text Box Object

The simplest way to display a text file in a program is to use a text box object. You can create text box objects in a variety of sizes. If the contents of the text file don't fit neatly in the text box, you can also add scroll bars to the text box so that the user can examine the entire file. To load the contents of a text file into a text box, you need to use four functions. These functions are described in the following table and will be demonstrated in the first exercise in this chapter. As I noted earlier, several of them replace older keywords in the Visual Basic language.

Function	Description
FileOpen	Opens a text file for input or output
LineInput	Reads a line of input from the text file
EOF	Checks for the end of the text file
FileClose	Closes the text file

Opening a Text File for Input

Text files contain recognizable numbers and characters.

A *text file* consists of one or more lines of numbers, words, or characters. Text files are distinct from *document files,* which contain formatting codes, and from *executable files,* which contain instructions for the operating system. Typical text files on your system will be identified by Microsoft Windows Explorer as "Text Documents" or will have the extension .txt, .ini, .log, or .inf. Because text files contain only ordinary, recognizable characters, you can display them easily by using text box objects.

The OpenFileDialog control on the Windows Forms tab of the Toolbox displays the Open dialog box.

You can let the user choose which text file to open in a program by using an OpenFileDialog control to prompt the user for the file's path. The OpenFileDialog control contains the Filter property, which controls which type of files are displayed, the ShowDialog method, which displays the Open dialog box, and the FileName property, which returns the path specified by the user. The OpenFileDialog control doesn't open the file; it just gets the path.

The FileOpen Function

After you get the path from the user, you open the file in the program by using the FileOpen function. The abbreviated syntax for the FileOpen function is:

```
FileOpen(filenumber, pathname, mode)
```

You can find the complete list of arguments in the Visual Basic online Help. These are the most important:

- *filenumber* is an integer from 1 through 255.
- *pathname* is a valid Microsoft Windows path.
- *mode* is a keyword indicating how the file will be used. (You'll use the OpenMode.Input and OpenMode.Output modes in this chapter.)

The file number will be associated with the file when it is opened. You then use this file number in your code whenever you need to refer to the open file. Aside from this association, there's nothing special about file numbers; Visual Basic simply uses them to keep track of the different files you open in your program.

A typical FileOpen function using an OpenFileDialog object looks like this:

```
FileOpen(1, OpenFileDialog1.FileName, OpenMode.Input)
```

Here the OpenFileDialog1.FileName property represents the path, OpenMode.Input is the mode, and 1 is the file number.

tip

Text files that are opened by using this syntax are called *sequential files*, because you must work with their contents in sequential order. By contrast, you can access the information in a database file in any order. (You'll learn more about databases in Chapter 19.)

The following exercise demonstrates how you can use an OpenFileDialog control and the FileOpen function to open a text file. The exercise also demonstrates how you can use the LineInput and EOF functions to display the contents of a text file in a text box and how you can use the FileClose function to close a file.

tip

For more information about using controls on the Windows Forms tab of the Toolbox to create standard dialog boxes, see Chapter 3.

Run the Text Browser program

1 Start Visual Studio and open the Text Browser project in the c:\vbnetsbs\chap12\text browser folder.

   The project opens in the development environment.

2 If the project's form isn't visible, display it now.

   The Text Browser form appears, as shown on the next page.

   The form contains a large text box object that has scroll bars. It also contains a main menu object (with Open, Close, and Exit commands), a file open dialog object, and a label providing operating instructions. I also created the property settings shown in the table on the next page. (Note especially the text box settings.)

Object	Property	Setting
txtNote	Enabled	False
	Multiline	True
	Name	txtNote
	ScrollBars	Both
	Text	(empty)
mnuOpenItem	Name	mnuOpenItem
mnuCloseItem	Enabled	False
	Name	mnuCloseItem
lblNote	Text	"Load a text file with the Open command."
	Name	lblNote
Form1	Text	"Text Browser"

3   Click the Start button on the Standard toolbar.

The Text Browser program runs.

4   On the Text Browser File menu, click the Open command.

The Open dialog box appears.

5   Open the c:\vbnetsbs\chap12\text browser folder.

The contents of the Text Browser folder are shown on the following page.

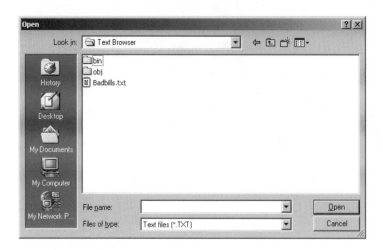

6   Double-click the filename Badbills.txt.

Badbills, a text file containing an article written in 1951 about the dangers of counterfeit money, appears in the text box:

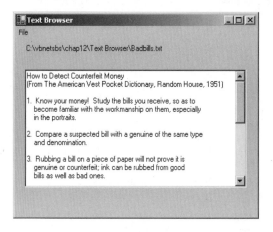

7   Use the scroll bars to view the entire document. Memorize number 5.

8   When you've finished, click the Close command on the File menu to close the file, and then click the Exit command to quit the program.

The program stops, and the development environment returns.

Now you'll take a look at two important event procedures in the program.

Examine the Text Browser program code

1   On the Text Browser form File menu, double-click the Open command.

The mnuOpenItem_Click event procedure appears in the Code Editor.

2   Resize the Code Editor to see more of the program code, if necessary.

The mnuOpenItem_Click event procedure contains the following program code:

A partial listing of the Text Browser program.

```
Dim AllText, LineOfText As String
OpenFileDialog1.Filter = "Text files (*.TXT)|*.TXT"
OpenFileDialog1.ShowDialog() 'display Open dialog box
If OpenFileDialog1.FileName <> "" Then
    Try 'open file and trap any errors using handler
        FileOpen(1, OpenFileDialog1.FileName, OpenMode.Input)
        Do Until EOF(1) 'read lines from file
            LineOfText = LineInput(1)
            'add each line to the AllText variable
            AllText = AllText & LineOfText & vbCrLf
        Loop
        lblNote.Text = OpenFileDialog1.FileName   'update label
        txtNote.Text = AllText 'display file
        txtNote.Select(1, 0)    'remove text selection
        txtNote.Enabled = True 'allow text cursor
        mnuCloseItem.Enabled = True   'enable Close command
        mnuOpenItem.Enabled = False   'disable Open command
    Catch
        MsgBox("Error opening file.")
    Finally
        FileClose(1) 'close file
    End Try
End If
```

This event procedure performs the following actions:

■   Declares variables and assigns a value to the Filter property of the open file dialog object.

■   Prompts the user for a path by using the OpenFileDialog1 object.

■   Traps errors using a Try…Catch code block.

- Opens the specified file for input using the FileOpen function.
- Uses the LineInput function to copy one line at a time from the file into a string named AllText.
- Copies lines until the end of the file is reached (EOF) or until there is no more room in the string. The AllText string has room for a very large file, but if an error occurs during the copying process, the Catch clause will display the error.
- Displays the AllText string in the text box, removes any selection, and enables the scroll bars and text cursor.
- Updates the File menu commands and closes the file using the FileClose function.

Take a moment to see how the statements in the mnuOpenItem_Click event procedure work—especially the FileOpen, LineInput, EOF, and FileClose functions. For more information about these statements and functions, highlight the keyword you're interested in and press F1 to see a discussion of it in the Visual Basic online Help. The error handler in the procedure displays a message and aborts the loading process if an error occurs.

3 Display the mnuCloseItem_Click event procedure, which is executed when the Close menu command is clicked.

The mnuCloseItem_Click event procedure looks like this:

```
txtNote.Text = ""                  'clear text box
lblNote.Text = "Load a text file with the Open command."
mnuCloseItem.Enabled = False   'disable Close command
mnuOpenItem.Enabled = True      'enable Open command
```

The procedure clears the text box, updates the lblNote label, disables the Close command, and enables the Open command.

Now you can use this simple program as a template for more advanced utilities that process text files. In the next section, you'll learn how to type your own text into a text box and how to save the text in the text box to a file on disk.

Using the StreamReader Class to Open Text Files

In addition to the Visual Basic commands that open and display text files, the new StreamReader class in the .NET Framework library allows you to open and display text files in your programs. In this book, I'll use both the built-in Visual Basic functions and the StreamReader class to work with text files.

To use the StreamReader class, you add the following Imports statement to the top of your code, which provides access to the StreamReader class:

```
Imports System.IO
```

Then, if your program contains a text box object, you can display a text file inside the text box by using the following program code. (The text file opened in this example is Readme.txt, and the code assumes an object named TextBox1 has been created on your form.)

```
Dim StreamToDisplay As StreamReader
StreamToDisplay = New StreamReader("c:\vbnetsbs\chap14\readme.txt")
TextBox1.Text = StreamToDisplay.ReadToEnd
StreamToDisplay.Close()
TextBox1.Select(0, 0)
```

StreamReader is a .NET Framework alternative to opening a text file using the Visual Basic FileOpen function. In this StreamReader example, I declare a variable named StreamToDisplay of the type StreamReader to hold the contents of the text file, and then I specify a valid path for the file I want to open. Next I read the contents of the text file into the StreamToDisplay variable using the ReadToEnd method, which retrieves all the text in the file from the current location (the beginning of the text file) to the end of the text file and assigns it to the Text property of the text box object. The final statements close the text file and use the Select method to remove the selection in the text box.

You'll use this StreamReader syntax in Chapter 15 as an alternative to using the built-in Visual Basic file functions.

Text Files and Strings

12

Creating a New Text File on Disk

To create a new text file on disk by using Visual Basic, you'll use many of the functions and keywords you used in the last example. Creating new files on disk and saving data to them will be useful if you plan to generate custom reports or logs, save important calculations or values, or create a special-purpose word processor or text editor. Here's an overview of the steps you'll need to follow in the program:

You use the keyword OpenMode. Output in the FileOpen function when you want to create a new file on disk.

1   Get input from the user or perform mathematical calculations, or do both.

2   Assign the results of your processing to one or more variables. For example, you could assign the contents of a text box to a string variable named InputForFile.

3   Prompt the user for a path by using a SaveFileDialog control. You use the ShowDialog method to display the dialog box.

4   Use the path received in the dialog box to open the file for output.

The PrintLine function sends output to the specified file.

5   Use the PrintLine function to save one or more values to the open file.

6   Close the file when you've finished using the FileClose function.

The following exercise demonstrates how you can use TextBox and SaveFileDialog controls to create a simple note-taking utility. The program uses the FileOpen function to open a file, the PrintLine function to store string data in it, and the FileClose function to close the file. You can use this tool to take notes at home or at work and then to stamp them with the current date.

Run the Quick Note program

1   Click the Close Solution command on the File menu.

2   Open the Quick Note project in the c:\vbnetsbs\chap12\quick note folder.

The project opens in the development environment.

3   If the project's form isn't visible, display it now.

The Quick Note form appears, as shown in the following illustration. It looks similar to the Text Browser form. However, I replaced the OpenFileDialog control with the SaveFileDialog control on the form. The File menu also contains different commands, including Save As, Insert Date, and Exit.

I set the following properties in the project:

Object	Property	Setting
txtNote	Multiline	True
	Name	txtNote
	ScrollBars	Both
	Text	(empty)
lblNote	Text	"Type your note and then save it to disk."
Form1	Text	"Quick Note"

4   Click the Start button on the toolbar.

5   Type the following text, or some text of your own, in the text box:

How to Detect Counterfeit Coins

1. **Drop coins on a hard surface. Genuine coins have a bell-like ring; most counterfeit coins sound dull.**

2. **Feel all coins. Most counterfeit coins feel greasy.**

3. **Cut edges of questionable coins. Genuine coins are not easily cut.**

When you've finished, your screen should look similar to the illustration on the following page.

12

Text Files and Strings

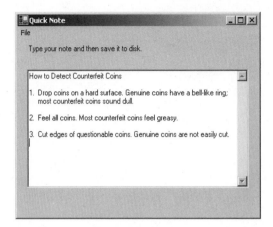

tip

To paste text from the Windows Clipboard into the text box, press Ctrl+V or Shift+Ins. To copy text from the text box to the Windows Clipboard, select the text and then press Ctrl+C.

Now try using the commands on the File menu.

6 On the File menu, click the Insert Date command.

The current date appears as the first line in the text box:

The Insert Date command provides a handy way to include the current date in a file. This is useful if you're creating a diary or a log book.

7 On the File menu, click the Save As command.

8 In the Save As dialog box, open the c:\vbnetsbs\chap12\quick note folder if it isn't already open. Then type **Badcoins.txt** in the File Name text box, and click Save.

The text of your document is saved in the new text file Badcoins.txt.

9 On the File menu, click the Exit command.

The program stops, and the development environment returns.

Now you'll take a look at the event procedures in the program.

Examine the Quick Note program code

1 On the Quick Note form File menu, double-click the Insert Date command.

The mnuInsertDateItem_Click event procedure appears in the Code Editor. You'll see the following program code:

```
txtNote.Text = DateString & vbCrLf & txtNote.Text
txtNote.Select(1, 0)  'remove selection
```

The DateString property retrieves the current date.

This event procedure adds the current date to the text box by linking together, or concatenating, the current date (generated by the DateString property), a carriage return (added by the vbCrLf constant), and the Text property. You could use a similar technique to add the current time or any other information to the text in the text box.

2 Take a moment to see how the concatenation statements work, and then examine the mnuSaveAsItem_Click event procedure in the Code Editor.

You'll see the following program code:

```
SaveFileDialog1.Filter = "Text files (*.txt)|*.txt"
SaveFileDialog1.ShowDialog()
If SaveFileDialog1.FileName <> "" Then
    FileOpen(1, SaveFileDialog1.FileName, OpenMode.Output)
    PrintLine(1, txtNote.Text)  'copy text to disk
    FileClose(1)
End If
```

12

Text Files and Strings

This block of statements uses a save file dialog object to display a Save As dialog box, checks to see whether the user selected a file, opens the file for output as file number 1, writes the value in the txtNote.Text property to disk by using the PrintLine function, and then closes the text file. Note especially the statement

The PrintLine function takes a file number as its first argument.

```
PrintLine(1, txtNote.Text)  'copy text to disk
```

which assigns the entire contents of the text box to the open file. PrintLine is similar to the older Visual Basic Print and Print # statements; it directs output to the specified file rather than to the screen or the printer. The important thing to note here is that the entire file is stored in the txtNote.Text property.

3   Review the FileOpen, PrintLine, and FileClose functions, and then close the program using the Close Solution command on the File menu.

You've finished with the Quick Note program.

Processing Text Strings with Program Code

As you learned in the preceding exercises, you can quickly open, edit, and save text files to disk with the TextBox control and a handful of well-chosen program statements. Visual Basic also provides a number of powerful statements and functions specifically designed for processing the textual elements in your programs. In this section, you'll learn how to extract useful information from a text string, copy a list of strings into an array, and sort a list of strings.

An extremely useful skill to develop when working with textual elements is the ability to sort a list of strings. The basic concepts in sorting are simple. You draw up a list of items to sort and then compare the items one by one until the list is sorted in ascending or descending alphabetical order. In Visual Basic, you compare one item to another using the same relational operators that you use to compare numeric values. The tricky part (which sometimes provokes long-winded discussion among computer scientists) is the specific sorting algorithm you use to compare elements in a list. We won't get into the advantages and disadvantages of different sorting algorithms in this chapter. (The bone of contention is usually speed, which makes a difference only when several thousand items are sorted.) Instead, we'll explore how the basic string comparisons are made in a sort. Along the way, you'll learn the skills necessary to sort your own text boxes, list boxes, files, and databases.

Processing Strings Using Methods and Keywords

The most common task you have accomplished so far with strings is concatenating them by using the concatenation operator (&). For example, the following program statement concatenates three literal string expressions and assigns the result "Bring on the circus!" to the string variable Slogan:

```
Dim Slogan As String
Slogan = "Bring" & " on the " & "circus!"
```

You can also concatenate and manipulate strings using methods in the String class of the .NET Framework library. For example, the String.Concat method allows equivalent string concatenation using this syntax:

```
Dim Slogan As String
Slogan = String.Concat("Bring", " on the ", "circus!")
```

Accordingly, Visual Basic .NET features two methods for string concatenation and many other string-processing tasks—you can use operators and functions from earlier versions of Visual Basic (Mid, UCase, LCase, and so on), or you can use newer methods from the .NET Framework (Substring, ToUpper, ToLower, etc.). There is no real "penalty" for either string-processing technique. In the rest of this chapter, I'll introduce several useful string-processing functions from the .NET Framework String class, but I'll occasionally use the older string-processing functions, too. You can use either string-processing method or a combination of both.

The following table lists several of the .NET Framework methods that appear in subsequent exercises, and their close equivalents in the Visual Basic .NET programming language. The fourth column in the table provides sample code for the methods in the String class of the .NET Framework.

.NET Framework Method	Visual Basic Function	Description	.NET Framework Example

ToUpper	UCase	Changes letters in a string to uppercase	```Dim Name, NewName As String```
			```Name = "Kim"```
			```NewName = Name.ToUpper```
			```'NewName = "KIM"```

ToLower	LCase	Changes letters in a string to lowercase	```Dim Name, NewName As String```
			```Name = "Kim"```
			```NewName = Name.ToLower```
			```'NewName = "kim"```

(continued)

continued

.NET Framework Method	Visual Basic Function	Description	.NET Framework Example

Length	Len	Determines the number of characters in a string	```Dim River As String```
			```Dim Size As Short```
			```River = "Mississippi"```
			```Size = River.Length```
			```'Size = 11```

Substring	Mid	Returns a fixed number of characters in a string from a given starting point. (Note: The first element in a string has an index of 0.)	```Dim Cols, Middle As String```
			```Cols = "First Second Third"```
			```Middle = Cols.SubString(6, 6)```
			```'Middle = "Second"```

IndexOf	InStr	Finds the starting point of one string within a larger string	```Dim Name As String```
			```Dim Start As Short```
			```Name = "Abraham"```
			```Start = Name.IndexOf("h")```
			```'Start = 4```

Trim	Trim	Remove leading and following spaces from a string	```Dim Spacey, Trimmed As String```
			```Spacey = " Hello "```
			```Trimmed = Spacey.Trim```
			```'Trimmed = "Hello"```

Remove		Remove characters from the middle of a string	```Dim RawStr, CleanStr As String```
			```RawStr = "Hello333 there!"```
			```CleanStr = RawStr.Remove(5, 3)```
			```'CleanStr = "Hello there!"```

Insert		Add characters to the middle of a string	```Dim Oldstr, Newstr As String```
			```Oldstr = "Hi Felix"```
			```Newstr = Oldstr.Insert(3, "there ")```
			```'Newstr = "Hi there Felix"```

StrComp		Compares strings and disregards case differences	```Dim str1 As String = "Soccer"```
			```Dim str2 As String = "SOCCER"```
			```Dim Match As Short```
			```Match = StrComp(str1, _```
			``` str2, CompareMethod.Text)```
			```'Match = 0 [strings match]```

Sorting Text

Before Visual Basic can compare one character to another in a sort, it must convert each character into a number by using a translation table called the *ASCII character set* (also called the ANSI character set). ASCII is an acronym standing for American Standard Code for Information Interchange. Most of the basic symbols that you can display on your computer have different ASCII codes. These codes include the basic set of "typewriter" characters (codes 32 through 127) and special "control" characters, such as tab, linefeed, and carriage return (codes 0 through 31). For example, the lowercase letter "a" corresponds to the ASCII code 97, and the uppercase letter "A" corresponds to the ASCII code 65. This fact explains why Visual Basic treats these two characters quite differently when sorting or performing other comparisons.

To see a table of the codes in the ASCII character set, search for "ASCII character codes" in the Visual Basic online Help.

In the 1980s, IBM extended ASCII with codes 128-255 that contained accented characters, Greek characters, graphic characters, and miscellaneous symbols. ASCII and these additional characters are typically known as the *IBM extended character set.*

The ASCII character set is still the most important numeric code for beginning programmers to learn, but it isn't the only character set. As the market for computers and application software has become more global in nature, a more comprehensive standard for character representation called Unicode has emerged, which contains room for up to 65,536 symbols—plenty of space to represent the traditional symbols in the ASCII character set and numerous international symbols as well. (As of this writing, about 45,000 characters are defined.) A standards body maintains the Unicode character set and adds symbols to it periodically. Windows NT, Windows 2000, Windows XP, and Visual Basic .NET have been specifically designed to manage ASCII and Unicode character sets. (For more information about the relationship between Unicode, ASCII, and Visual Basic .NET data types, see Chapter 5.)

In the following sections, you'll learn more about using the ASCII character set to process strings in your programs. As your applications become more sophisticated and you start planning for the global distribution of your software, you'll need to learn more about Unicode and other international settings.

Working with ASCII Codes

To determine the ASCII code of a particular letter, you can use the Visual Basic Asc function. For example, the following program statement assigns the number 122 (the ASCII code for the lowercase letter "z") to the AscCode short integer variable:

```
Dim AscCode As Short
AscCode = Asc("z")
```

12

Text Files and Strings

Conversely, you can convert an ASCII code to a letter with the Chr function. For example, this program statement assigns the letter "z" to the letter character variable:

```
Dim letter As Char
letter = Chr(122)
```

The same result could also be achieved if you used the AscCode variable, declared above:

```
letter = Chr(AscCode)
```

How can you compare one text string or ASCII code with another? You simply use one of the six relational operators Visual Basic supplies for working with textual and numeric elements. These relational operators are shown in the following table:

Operator	Meaning
<>	Not equal
=	Equal
<	Less than
>	Greater than
<=	Less than or equal to
>=	Greater than or equal to

A character is "greater than" another character if its ASCII code is higher. For example, the ASCII value of the letter "B" is greater than the ASCII value of the letter "A", so the expression

```
"A" < "B"
```

is true, and the expression

```
"A" > "B"
```

is false.

When comparing two strings that each contain more than one character, Visual Basic begins by comparing the first character in the first string to the first character in the second string and then proceeds through the strings character by character until it finds a difference. For example, the strings Mike and Michael are the same up to the third characters ("k" and "c"). Because the ASCII value of "k" is greater than that of "c", the expression

```
"Mike" > "Michael"
```

is true.

If no differences are found between the strings, they are equal. If two strings are equal through several characters but one of the strings continues and the other one ends, the longer string is greater than the shorter string. For example, the expression

```
"AAAAA" > "AAA"
```

is true.

Sorting Strings in a Text Box

The following exercise demonstrates how you can use relational operators and several string methods and functions to sort lines of text in a text box. The program is a revision of the Quick Note utility and features an Open command that allows you to open an existing file and a Close command that closes the file. There is also a Sort Text command on the File menu you use to sort the text currently displayed in the text box.

Because the entire contents of a text box are stored in one string, the program must first break that long string into smaller individual strings. These strings can then be sorted by using the ShellSort Sub procedure, a sorting routine based on an algorithm created by Donald Shell in 1959. To simplify these tasks, I created a standard module that defines a dynamic string array to hold each of the lines in the text box. I also placed the ShellSort Sub procedure in the standard module so that I could call it from any event procedure in the project. (For more about standard modules, see Chapter 10.)

One interesting part of this program is the routine that determines the number of lines in the text box object. No existing Visual Basic function computes this value automatically. I wanted the program to be able to sort a text box of any size line by line. To accomplish this, I created the code that follows. It uses the Substring method to examine one letter at a time in the text box object and then uses the Chr function to search for the carriage return character (which is ASCII code 13) at the end of each line. (Note in particular how the Substring method is used as part of the Text property of the txtNote object—the String class automatically provides this method, and many others, for any properties or variables that are declared in the String type.)

```
Dim ln, curline, letter As String
Dim i, charsInFile, lineCount As Short

'determine number of lines in text box object (txtNote)
lineCount = 0 'this variable holds total number of lines
charsInFile = txtNote.Text.Length 'get total characters
For i = 0 To charsInFile - 1 'move one char at a time
    letter = txtNote.Text.Substring(i, 1) 'get letter
    If letter = Chr(13) Then 'if carriage ret found
        lineCount += 1 'go to next line (add to count)
        i += 1 'skip linefeed char (always follows cr)
    End If
Next i
```

The total number of lines in the text box is assigned to the lineCount short integer variable. I use this value a little later to dimension a dynamic array in the program to hold each individual text string. The resulting array of strings then gets passed to the ShellSort Sub procedure for sorting, and ShellSort returns the string array in alphabetical order. Once the string array is sorted, I can simply copy it back to the text box by using a For loop.

Run the Sort Text program

1   Open the Sort Text project located in the c:\vbnetsbs\chap12\sort text folder.

2   Click the Start button to run the program.

3   Type the following text, or some text of your own, in the text box:

   Zebra
   Gorilla
   Moon
   Banana
   Apple
   Turtle

   Be sure to press Enter after you type "Turtle", or a last line of your own, so that Visual Basic will calculate the number of lines correctly.

4   On the File menu, click the Sort Text command.

The text you typed is sorted and redisplayed in the text box as follows:

5   On the File menu, click the Open command and open the file abc.txt in the c:\vbnetsbs\chap12 folder.

The abc.txt file contains 36 lines of text. Each line begins with either a letter or a number (1–10).

6   On the File menu, click the Sort Text command to sort the contents of the abc.txt file.

The Sort Text program sorts the file in ascending order and displays the sorted list of lines in the text box.

7 Scroll through the file to see the results of the alphabetical sort.

Notice that although the alphabetical portion of the sort ran perfectly, the sort did produce a strange result for one of the numeric entries—the line beginning with the number 10 appears second in the list rather than tenth. What's happening here is that Visual Basic is reading the 1 and the 0 in the number 10 as two independent characters, not as a number. Because we're comparing the ASCII codes of these strings from left to right, the program produces a purely alphabetical sort. If you want to sort numbers with this program, you'll need to store the numbers in numeric variables and compare them as numbers instead of strings.

Examine the Sort Text program code

1 On the Sort Text program File menu, click the Exit command to stop the program.

2 Open the Code Editor, and display the code for the mnuSortTextItem_Click event procedure.

We've already discussed the first routine in this event procedure, which counts the number of lines in the text box by using the Substring method to search for carriage return codes. The remainder of the event procedure dimensions a string array, copies each line of text into the array, calls a procedure to sort the array, and displays the reordered list in the text box.

The entire mnuSortTextItem_Click event procedure looks like this:

```
Dim ln, curline, letter As String
Dim i, charsInFile, lineCount As Short

'determine number of lines in text box object (txtNote)
lineCount = 0 'this variable holds total number of lines
```

```
charsInFile = txtNote.Text.Length 'get total characters
For i = 0 To charsInFile - 1 'move one char at a time
    letter = txtNote.Text.Substring(i, 1) 'get letter
    If letter = Chr(13) Then 'if carriage ret found
        lineCount += 1 'go to next line (add to count)
        i += 1 'skip linefeed char (always follows cr)
    End If
Next i

'build an array to hold the text in the text box
ReDim strArray(lineCount) 'create array of proper size
curline = 1
ln = "" 'use ln to build lines one character at a time
For i = 0 To charsInFile - 1 'loop through text again
    letter = txtNote.Text.Substring(i, 1) 'get letter
    If letter = Chr(13) Then 'if carriage return found
        curline = curline + 1 'increment line count
        i += 1 'skip linefeed char
        ln = "" 'clear line and go to next
    Else
        ln = ln & letter 'add letter to line
        strArray(curline) = ln 'and put in array
    End If
Next i

'sort array
ShellSort(strArray, lineCount)

'then display sorted array in text box
txtNote.Text = ""
curline = 1
For i = 1 To lineCount
    txtNote.Text = txtNote.Text & _
      strArray(curline) & vbCrLf
    curline += 1
Next i
txtNote.Select(1, 0)    'remove text selection
```

The array strArray was declared in a standard module (Module1.vb) that is also part of this program. By using the ReDim statement, I am dimensioning strArray as a dynamic array with the lineCount variable. This statement creates an array that has the same number of elements as the text box has lines of text (a requirement for the ShellSort Sub procedure). Using a For loop and the In variable, I scan through the text box again, looking for carriage return characters and copying each complete line found to strArray. After the array is full of text, I call the ShellSort procedure I created previously in the Module1.vb standard module.

3   Display the code for the Module1.vb standard module in the Code Editor.

This module declares the public array variable strArray, then defines the content of the ShellSort procedure. The ShellSort procedure uses the <= relational operator to compare array elements and swap any that are out of order. The procedure looks like this:

```
Sub ShellSort(ByRef sort() As String, ByVal numOfElements As Short)
    Dim temp As String
    Dim i, j, span As Short
    'The ShellSort procedure sorts the elements of sort()
    'array in descending order and returns it to the calling
    'procedure.

    span = numOfElements \ 2
    Do While span > 0
        For i = span To numOfElements - 1
            j = i - span + 1
            For j = (i - span + 1) To 1 Step -span
                If sort(j) <= sort(j + span) Then Exit For
                'swap array elements that are out of order
                temp = sort(j)
                sort(j) = sort(j + span)
                sort(j + span) = temp
            Next j
        Next i
        span = span \ 2
    Loop
End Sub
```

The method of the sort is to continually divide the main list of elements into sublists that are smaller by half. The sort then compares the tops and the bottoms of the sublists to see whether the elements are out of order. If the top and bottom are out of order, they are exchanged. The end result is an array named sort() that is sorted alphabetically in descending order. To change the direction of the sort, simply reverse the relational operator (change <= to >=).

Let's move on to another variation of the Quick Note program that tackles basic encryption string processing.

Protecting Text with Encryption

Now that you've had some experience with ASCII codes, you can begin to write simple encryption routines that shift the ASCII codes in your documents and "scramble" the text to hide it from intruding eyes. This process, known as *encryption*, mathematically alters the characters in a file, making them unreadable to the casual observer. Of course, to use encryption successfully you also need to be able to reverse the process—otherwise, you'll simply be "trashing" your files rather than protecting them. And you'll want to create an encryption scheme that can't be easily recognized—a complicated process that is only begun by the sample programs in this chapter.

The following exercises show you how to encrypt and decrypt text strings safely. You'll run the Encrypt Text program now to see a simple encryption scheme in action.

Encrypt text by changing ASCII codes

1 Close the Sort Text solution and open the Encrypt Text project located in the c:\vbnetsbs\chap12\encrypt text folder.

2 Click the Start button to run the program.

3 Type the following text, or some text of your own, in the text box:

   Here at last, my friend, you have the little book long since expected and promised, a little book on vast matters, namely, "On my own ignorance and that of many others."

   Francesco Petrarca, c. 1368

4 On the File menu, click the Save Encrypted File As command and save the file in the c:\vbnetsbs\chap12 folder with the name **padua.txt**.

   As you save the text file, the program scrambles the ASCII code and displays the results in the text box shown below.

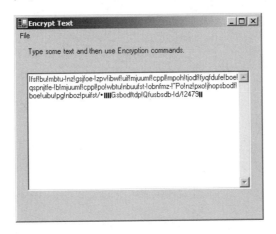

If you open this file in Microsoft Word or another text editor, you'll see the same result—the characters in the file have been encrypted to prevent unauthorized reading.

5   To restore the file to its original form, choose the Open Encrypted File command on the File menu, and open the padua.txt file in the c:\vbnetsbs\chap12 folder.

The file appears again in its original form, as shown here:

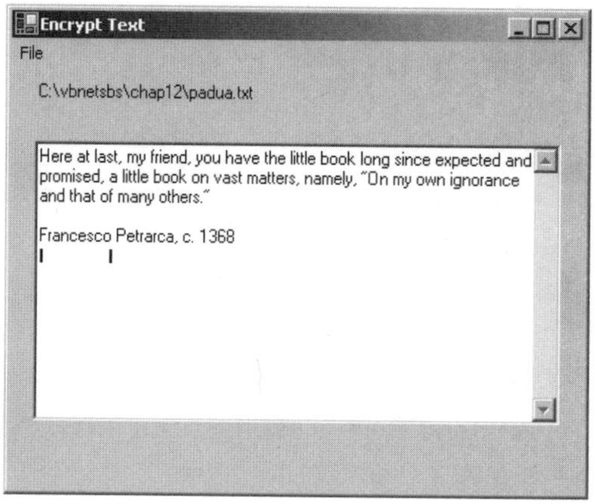

You may see one or two additional characters or symbols at the bottom of the text box window, depending on the number of carriage return and/or line feed characters you placed at the end of the document.

6   On the File menu, click the Exit command to end the program.

Examine the Encrypt program code

1   Open the mnuSaveAsItem_Click event procedure in the Code Editor to see the program code that produces the encryption you observed when you ran the program.

Although the effect you saw might have looked mysterious, it was a very straightforward encryption scheme. Using the Asc and Chr functions and a For loop, I simply added one number to the ASCII code for each character in the text box, and then saved the encrypted string to the specified text file.

The entire event procedure is listed here—in particular, note the items formatted with bold:

```
Dim Encrypt As String = ""
Dim letter As Char
Dim i, charsInFile As Short
```

```
SaveFileDialog1.Filter = "Text files (*.txt)|*.txt"
SaveFileDialog1.ShowDialog()
If SaveFileDialog1.FileName <> "" Then
    'save text with encryption scheme (ASCII code + 1)
    charsInFile = txtNote.Text.Length
    For i = 0 To charsInFile - 1
        letter = txtNote.Text.Substring(i, 1)
        'determine ASCII code and add one to it
        Encrypt = Encrypt & Chr(Asc(letter) + 1)
    Next
    FileOpen(1, SaveFileDialog1.FileName, OpenMode.Output)
    PrintLine(1, Encrypt) 'copy text to disk
    FileClose(1)
    txtNote.Text = Encrypt
    txtNote.Select(1, 0)    'remove text selection
    mnuCloseItem.Enabled = True
End If
```

Note especially the statement

```
Encrypt = Encrypt & Chr(Asc(letter) + 1)
```

which determines the ASCII code of the current letter, adds 1 to it, converts the ASCII code back to a letter, and adds it to the Encrypt string.

2   Now display the mnuOpenItem_Click event procedure in the Code Editor to see how the program reverses the encryption.

This program code is nearly identical to that of the Save Encrypted File As command, but rather than adding 1 to the ASCII code for each letter, it subtracts 1. Here is the complete mnuOpenItem_Click event procedure, with important statements in bold:

```
Dim AllText, LineOfText As String
Dim i, charsInFile As Short
Dim letter As Char
Dim Decrypt As String = ""

OpenFileDialog1.Filter = "Text files (*.TXT)|*.TXT"
OpenFileDialog1.ShowDialog() 'display Open dialog box
If OpenFileDialog1.FileName <> "" Then
    Try 'open file and trap any errors using handler
        FileOpen(1, OpenFileDialog1.FileName, OpenMode.Input)
```

(continued)

12

Text Files and Strings

```
        Do Until EOF(1) 'read lines from file
            LineOfText = LineInput(1)
            'add each line to the AllText variable
            AllText = AllText & LineOfText & vbCrLf
        Loop

        'now, decrypt string by subtracting one from ASCII code
        charsInFile = AllText.Length 'get length of string
        For i = 0 To charsInFile - 1 'loop once for each char
            letter = AllText.Substring(i, 1) 'get character
            Decrypt = Decrypt & Chr(Asc(letter) - 1) 'subtract 1
        Next i 'and build new string
        txtNote.Text = Decrypt 'then display converted string
        lblNote.Text = OpenFileDialog1.FileName
        txtNote.Select(1, 0)    'remove text selection
        txtNote.Enabled = True 'allow text cursor
        mnuCloseItem.Enabled = True   'enable Close command
        mnuOpenItem.Enabled = False   'disable Open command
    Catch
        MsgBox("Error opening file. It might be too big.")
    Finally
        FileClose(1) 'close file
    End Try
End If
```

This type of simple encryption may be all you need to conceal the information in your text files. However, files encrypted in this way can easily be decoded. By searching for possible equivalents of common characters such as the space character, determining the ASCII shift required to restore the common character, and running the conversion for the entire text file, a person experienced in encryption could readily decipher the file's content. Also, this sort of encryption doesn't prevent a malicious user from physically tampering with the file—for example, simply by deleting it if it is unprotected on your system or by modifying it in significant ways. But if you just want to hide information quickly, this simple encryption scheme should do the trick.

One Step Further: Using the Xor Operator

The encryption scheme demonstrated above is quite "safe" for text files, because it only shifts the ASCII character code value up by one. However, you'll want to be careful about shifting ASCII codes more than a few characters if you store the result as text in a text file. Keep in mind that dramatic shifts in ASCII codes (such as adding 500 to each character code) won't produce actual ASCII characters that can be decrypted later. For example, adding 500 to the ASCII code for the letter "A" (65) would give a result of 565. This value could not be translated into a character by the Chr function and would generate an error.

A safe way around this problem is to convert the letters in your file to numbers when you encrypt the file so that you can reverse the encryption no matter how large (or small) the numbers get. If you followed this line of thought, you could then apply mathematical functions—multiplication, logarithms, and so on—to the numbers as long as you knew how to reverse the results.

One of the best tools for encrypting numeric values is already built into Visual Basic. This tool is the *Xor operator,* which performs the "exclusive or" operation, a function carried out on the bits that make up the number itself. The Xor operator can be observed by a using a simple MsgBox function. For example, the program statement

```
MsgBox(Asc("A") Xor 50)
```

would display a numeric result of 115 in a message box when it is executed by the Visual Basic compiler. Likewise, the program statement

```
MsgBox(115 Xor 50)
```

would display a result of 65 in a message box, the ASCII code for the letter A (our original value). In other words, the Xor operator produces a result that can be reversed—if the original Xor code is used again on the result of the first operation. This interesting behavior of the Xor function is used in many popular encryption algorithms. It can make your secret files much more difficult to decode.

Run the Xor Encryption program now to see how the Xor operator works in the note-taking utility you've been building.

Encrypt text with the Xor operator

1.   Close the Encrypt Text solution, and then open the Xor Encryption project in the c:\vbnetsbs\chap12\xor encryption folder.

2.   Click the Start button to run the program.

3.   Type the following text (or some of your own) for the encrypted text file:

Rothair's Edict (Lombard Italy, c. 643)

296. On Stealing Grapes. He who takes more than three grapes from another man's vine shall pay six soldi as compensation. He who takes less than three shall bear no guilt.

4   On the File menu, click the Save Encrypted File As command, and save the file in the c:\vbnetsbs\chap12 folder with the name **oldlaws.txt**.

The program prompts you for a secret encryption code (a number) that will be used to encrypt the file and decrypt it later. (Take note—you'll need to remember this code to decode the file.)

5   Type **500**, or another numeric code, and then press Enter.

Visual Basic encrypts the text by using the Xor operator and stores it on disk as a series of numbers. You won't see any change on your screen, but rest assured that the program created an encrypted file on disk. (You can verify this with a word processor or a text editor.)

6   Click the Close command on the program's File menu to clear the text in the text box.

Now you'll restore the encrypted file.

7   On the File menu, click the Open Encrypted File command.

8   Open the c:\vbnetsbs\chap12 folder, and then double-click the oldlaws.txt file.

9   Type **500** in the encryption code dialog box when it appears, and click OK. (If you specified a different encryption code, enter that instead.)

The program opens the file and restores the text by using the Xor operator and the encryption code you specified.

10   On the File menu, click the Exit command to end the program.

Examining the Encryption Code

The Xor operator is used in both the mnuSaveAsItem_Click and the mnuOpenItem_Click event procedures. By now, these generic menu processing routines will be fairly familiar to you. The mnuSaveAsItem_Click event procedure consists of these program statements (important lines in bold):

```
Dim letter As Char
Dim strCode As String
Dim i, charsInFile, Code As Short

SaveFileDialog1.Filter = "Text files (*.txt)|*.txt"
SaveFileDialog1.ShowDialog()
If SaveFileDialog1.FileName <> "" Then
    strCode = InputBox("Enter Encryption Code")
    If strCode = "" Then Exit Sub 'if cancel clicked
    'save text with encryption scheme
    Code = CShort(strCode)
    charsInFile = txtNote.Text.Length
    FileOpen(1, SaveFileDialog1.FileName, OpenMode.Output)
    For i = 0 To charsInFile - 1
        letter = txtNote.Text.Substring(i, 1)
        'convert to number w/ Asc, then use Xor to encrypt
        Print(1, Asc(letter) Xor Code) 'and save in file
    Next
    FileClose(1)
    mnuCloseItem.Enabled = True
End If
```

In the Print function, used here for the first time, the Xor operator is used to convert each letter in the text box to a numeric code, which is then saved to disk one number at time. (So far in this chapter I've used the PrintLine function, which copies an entire line to a file, but in this case it is more useful to copy the numbers one at a time.)

The final result of this encryption is no longer textual, but numeric—guaranteed to bewilder even the nosiest snooper. For example, the following illustration shows the encrypted file produced by the preceding encryption routine, displayed in Windows Notepad. (I've enabled Word Wrap so that you can see all of the codes.)

The mnuOpenItem_Click event procedure contains the following program statements. (Again, pay particular attention to the lines formatted with bold type.)

```
Dim ch As Char
Dim strCode As String
Dim Code, Number As Short
Dim Decrypt As String = ""

OpenFileDialog1.Filter = "Text files (*.TXT)|*.TXT"
OpenFileDialog1.ShowDialog() 'display Open dialog box
If OpenFileDialog1.FileName <> "" Then
    Try 'open file and trap any errors using handler
        strCode = InputBox("Enter Encryption Code")
        If strCode = "" Then Exit Sub 'if cancel clicked
        Code = CShort(strCode)
        FileOpen(1, OpenFileDialog1.FileName, OpenMode.Input)
        Do Until EOF(1) 'read lines from file
            Input(1, Number) 'read encrypted numbers
            ch = Chr(Number Xor Code) 'convert with Xor
            Decrypt = Decrypt & ch 'and build string
        Loop
```

```
            txtNote.Text = Decrypt 'then display converted string
            lblNote.Text = OpenFileDialog1.FileName
            txtNote.Select(1, 0)    'remove text selection
            txtNote.Enabled = True 'allow text cursor
            mnuCloseItem.Enabled = True   'enable Close command
            mnuOpenItem.Enabled = False   'disable Open command
        Catch
            MsgBox("Error opening file.")
        Finally
            FileClose(1) 'close file
        End Try
    End If
```

When the user clicks the Open Encrypted File command, this event procedure opens the encrypted file, prompts the user for an encryption code, and displays the translated file in the text box object. The Input function, introduced here for the first time, reads one number at a time from the encrypted file and stores it in the Number short integer variable. (Input is closely related to LineInput, but the Input function just reads one character from a file, not an entire line.) The Number variable is then combined with the Code variable using the Xor operator, and the result is converted to a character using the Chr function. These characters (stored in the ch variable of type Char) are then concatenated with the Decrypt string variable, which eventually contains the entire decrypted text file:

```
ch = Chr(Number Xor Code) 'convert with Xor
Decrypt = Decrypt & ch 'and build string
```

Encryption techniques like this are useful, and they can also be very instructional. Because encryption relies so much on string processing techniques, it is a good way to practice a fundamental and important Visual Basic programming skill. Just be sure not to lose your encryption key!

Chapter 12 Quick Reference

To	Do this
Open a text file	Use the FileOpen function. For example: ```FileOpen(1, OpenFileDialog1.FileName, _` ` OpenMode.Input)```
Get a line of input from a text file	Use the LineInput function. For example: ```Dim LineOfText As String` `LineOfText = LineInput(1)```
Check for the end of a file	Use the EOF function. For example: ```Dim LineOfText, AllText As String` `Do Until EOF(1)` ` LineOfText = LineInput(1)` ` AllText = AllText & LineOfText & _` ` vbCrLf` `Loop```
Close an open file	Use the FileClose function. For example: ```FileClose(1)```
Display a text file	Use the LineInput function to copy text from an open file to a string variable, and then assign the string variable to a text box object. For example: ```Dim AllText, LineOfText As String` `Do Until EOF(1) 'read lines from file` ` LineOfText = LineInput(1)` ` AllText = AllText & LineOfText & _` ` vbCrLf` `Loop` `txtNote.Text = AllText 'display file```
Display an Open dialog box	Add an OpenFileDialog control to your form, and then use the ShowDialog method of the open file dialog object. For example: ```OpenFileDialog1.ShowDialog()```
Create a new text file	Use the FileOpen function. For example: ```FileOpen(1, SaveFileDialog1.FileName _` ` OpenMode.Output)```
Display a Save As dialog box	Add a SaveFileDialog control to your form, and then use the ShowDialog method of the save file dialog object object. For example: ```SaveFileDialog1.ShowDialog()```
Save text to a file	Use the Print or PrintLine functions. For example: ```PrintLine(1, txtNote.Text)```

To	Do this
Convert text characters to ASCII codes	Use the Asc function. For example: ``` Dim Code As Short Code = Asc("A") 'Code equals 65 ```
Convert ASCII codes to text characters	Use the Chr function. For example: ``` Dim Letter As Char Letter = Chr(65) 'Letter equals "A" ```
Extract characters from the middle of a string	Use the Substring method or the Mid function. For example: ``` Dim Cols, Middle As String Cols = "First Second Third" Middle = Cols.SubString(6, 6) 'Middle = "Second" ```

Encrypt text	Use the Xor operator and a user-defined encryption code. For example, this code block uses Xor and a user code to encrypt the text in the txtNote text box and to save it in the encrypt.txt file as a series of numbers:
	``
	strCode = InputBox("Enter Encryption Code")
	Code = CShort(strCode)
	charsInFile = txtNote.Text.Length
	FileOpen(1, SaveFileDialog1.FileName, _
	  OpenMode.Output)
	For i = 0 To charsInFile - 1
	    letter = txtNote.Text.Substring(i, 1)
	    Print(1, Asc(letter) Xor Code)
	Next
	FileClose(1)
	``

Decrypt text	Request the code the user chose to encrypt the text, and use Xor to decrypt the text. For example, this code block uses Xor and a user code to reverse the encryption created in the preceding example:
	``
	strCode = InputBox("Enter Encryption Code")
	Code = CShort(strCode)
	FileOpen(1, OpenFileDialog1.FileName, _
	  OpenMode.Input)
	Do Until EOF(1)
	    Input(1, Number)
	    ch = Chr(Number Xor Code)
	    Decrypt = Decrypt & ch
	Loop
	txtNote.Text = Decrypt
	``

12

Text Files and Strings

13

Automating Microsoft Office Applications and Managing Processes

In this chapter you will learn how to:

✔ *Use the Object Browser to examine objects.*

✔ *Use Microsoft Excel to compute mortgage payments.*

✔ *Manipulate an Excel worksheet from Visual Basic .NET.*

✔ *Start and stop Windows applications using the Process component.*

Automating Applications

In this chapter, you'll learn how to control Microsoft Office XP applications from Visual Basic .NET. You'll use the Visual Studio Object Browser to examine the exposed objects in Windows-based programs, and you'll learn how to incorporate the functionality of Office applications on your system into your Visual Basic programs. In particular, you'll use Microsoft Excel 2002 to create two Automation solutions—you'll build a mortgage payment calculator that uses Excel's Pmt function, and you'll open a worksheet object in Excel and perform several worksheet-manipulation commands. Finally, you'll learn how to start and stop Windows applications from within a Visual Basic program by using the Process component and the Start and CloseMainWindow methods. You experimented with the Start method briefly in Chapters 3 and 11.

Upgrade Notes: What's New in Visual Basic .NET?

If you're experienced with Visual Basic 6, you'll notice some new features in Visual Basic .NET, including the following:

- In Visual Basic 6, you could use the OLE Container control to add application objects to your Visual Basic forms. The OLE Container control is no longer included in the Toolbox.

- Visual Basic 6 featured ActiveX controls that were based on Component Object Model (COM) technology. In Visual Basic .NET, controls are no longer designed to COM specifications. However, you can still use COM components and applications in Visual Basic .NET programs by adding a reference to the components on the COM tab of the Add Reference dialog box. When you select a COM component, Visual Studio automatically generates a "wrapper" with the necessary types and classes for you.

- Microsoft Office XP applications and components (which continue to conform to COM specifications) can still be controlled in Visual Basic .NET applications through Automation, a popular method for accessing the objects of another application. However, in Visual Basic .NET, application objects should not be assigned at runtime, but rather should be assigned at compile time. (In other words, early binding is preferred to late binding when Automation is used.)

- In Visual Basic 6, programmers often used the Shell function to start Windows applications from within a program. In Visual Basic .NET, the task of starting and stopping applications is more easily handled by the Process component on the Components tab of the Toolbox.

Programming Application Objects by Using Automation

Automation is a technology based on the Component Object Model (COM) interoperability standard, an important guideline for designing applications and components that can be used together—even without an understanding of how the underlying components work. The goal of Automation is to use one application's features from within another application. Windows-based applications that fully support Automation make available, or *expose,* their application features as a collection of objects with associated properties and methods. The Windows-based applications that expose their objects are called *object*, or *server*, applications, and the programs that use the objects are called *controlling*, or *client*, applications. Although Visual Studio .NET controls are no longer designed in accordance with COM specifications, you can still use COM components in Visual Basic .NET programs if you follow a few simple guidelines.

Currently, the following Microsoft applications can be used as either object or controlling applications:

- Microsoft Visual Studio .NET, Microsoft Visual Basic 6
- Microsoft Word 2002, Microsoft Word 2000, Microsoft Word 97
- Microsoft Excel 2002, Microsoft Excel 2000, Microsoft Excel 97, Microsoft Excel 95, Microsoft Excel 5.0
- Microsoft PowerPoint 2002, Microsoft PowerPoint 2000, Microsoft PowerPoint 97
- Microsoft Project 2000, Microsoft Project 97, Microsoft Project 95
- Microsoft Outlook 2002, Microsoft Outlook 2000, Microsoft Outlook 97/98

tip

Microsoft is currently licensing the Visual Basic for Applications programming language, so you'll find other non-Microsoft applications for Windows that support Automation and Visual Basic programming techniques.

Using Automation in Visual Basic

In Visual Basic .NET, you can create both object and controlling applications that support Automation. Creating an application that supports Automation is beyond the scope of this chapter. However, creating controlling applications that use the features of Automation is a straightforward process in all editions of Visual Basic.

> **tip**
>
> The applications in Microsoft Office XP (Excel 2002, Word 2002, Access 2002, PowerPoint 2002, and Outlook 2002) are all capable of exposing their functionality through Automation. Because the features and objects provided by each of these applications are unique, you'll need to review the product documentation or online Help for each program before you move beyond the examples I show you here. If you have Microsoft Office installed on your system now, you can use the Visual Basic Object Browser to explore the available objects, properties, and methods.

In the next few sections, you will learn how to write Visual Basic programs that work with Excel 2002. As you work through the exercises, note that the objects, properties, and methods exposed by an application typically correspond to the menu commands and dialog box options provided by the application. You can use these basic skills to automate the objects in Word, Outlook, PowerPoint, and the other applications and components that support COM standards.

The Visual Studio Object Browser

The Visual Studio Object Browser is a viewing utility that has two uses:

- It can display the objects, properties, and methods used by the program you're working on in the Visual Studio development environment.

- It can display the objects, properties, and methods available to you from applications that support Automation installed on your system.

The Object Browser lets you view objects on your system.

In the following exercise, you'll use the Object Browser to view the Automation objects that Excel 2002 exposes.

Use the Object Browser to view Excel objects

1   Start Visual Studio and create a new Visual Basic Windows Application project named **My Excel Automation** in the c:\vbnetsbs\chap13 folder.

A new project appears in the development environment.

2   On the Project menu, click the Add Reference command.

The Add Reference dialog box lets you add object library references to your project.

The Add Reference dialog box appears, as shown here:

The Add Reference dialog box contains three tabs representing the available objects on your system: .NET, COM, and Projects. The .NET tab contains objects that conform to the .NET specifications, including Crystal Reports components, objects exposed by the Visual Studio .NET development environment, and various system objects. The COM tab contains Component Object Model applications and components, including Microsoft Office application objects. The Projects tab contains objects exposed by your own Visual Basic projects that you can incorporate. Adding references to your project won't make your compiled program any bigger. However, the more references you have, the longer it will take Visual Basic to load and compile the program. Therefore, Visual Basic adds references to Automation object libraries only if you ask it to.

3 Click the COM tab in the Add Reference dialog box.

A list box displays the COM components recorded in your computer's system registry. This list will vary from computer to computer.

4 Scroll down the alphabetical list and click the reference entitled Microsoft Excel 10.0 Object Library.

The list is usually quite long, and you'll need to scroll considerably to get through it—especially when you encounter the catalog of Microsoft object libraries.

tip
The illustrations show the Excel 10.0 Object Library included in Excel 2002 (in other words, Office XP). If you don't have a version of Excel, use the Object Browser to examine other application objects on your system.

5   After you click the Microsoft Excel 10.0 Object Library, click the Select button. Your screen should look like this:

6   Click OK to close the dialog box and add the reference to your project. You may see the following dialog box at this point:

Because COM components are no longer native to the Visual Studio development environment, Visual Studio requires either that a *primary interoperability assembly* reference be included with the project, or that a local "wrapper" containing the same class declarations be generated within the project by Visual Studio. Most COM applications and components, including the tools in the Microsoft Office XP suite, will require a "wrapper" for any new library references you make.

7 If you see the primary interoperability assembly dialog box, click Yes to allow Visual Studio to create the needed class "wrapper" automatically for you.

The types associated with the "wrapper" are added to the project in Solution Explorer. Now you're ready to use the Object Browser.

8 On the View menu, click the Other Windows submenu, and then click the Object Browser command. (The keyboard shortcut to display the Object Browser is F2.)

The Object Browser appears, as shown here:

Browse   Back   Find Symbol

```
Start Page | Form1.vb [Design] | Object Browser |                              ◁ ▷ ✕
Browse: Selected Components              ▾ Customize...  ⌕↕ ▾ ⁺⁄ ▾  ⌖ ⌕ ⌖⌖
Objects                                   Empty
⊞ 🔲 Excel Automation
⊞ ↦◻ Interop.Excel
⊞ ↦◻ Interop.Microsoft.Office.Core
⊞ ↦◻ Interop.VBIDE
⊞ ↦◻ Microsoft Visual Basic .NET Runtime
⊞ ↦◻ mscorlib
⊞ ↦◻ stdole
⊞ ↦◻ System
⊞ ↦◻ System.Data
⊞ ↦◻ System.Drawing
⊞ ↦◻ System.Windows.Forms
⊞ ↦◻ System.Xml



Project Excel Automation
```

The Object Browser lists references and components in a tree hierarchy; the object hierarchy is shown in the left pane of the Object Browser, and individual members are shown in the right pane. At the bottom of the Object Browser is a pane that contains syntax information for the selected object when it is available.

The Object Browser also offers a few useful tools for locating the information you want to find. The Browse drop-down list box lets you display the individual object libraries and components in your project. There is also a Find Symbol button that you can use to search for individual objects, properties, methods, and events in the occasionally vast object library listings. A Back button allows you to review earlier object listings.

9 Click the plus sign (+) next to the Interop.Excel object library and then click the plus sign (+) next to Excel.

A list of the Automation objects exposed by Excel fills the Objects pane.

10   If necessary, scroll down the list in the Objects pane, and then click the Application object.

A list of the methods, properties, and events associated with the Application object appears in the Members pane. These are some of the properties, methods, and events Excel provides for manipulating information in worksheets.

11   Scroll down in the Members pane, and click the Quit method.

Your screen will look like this:

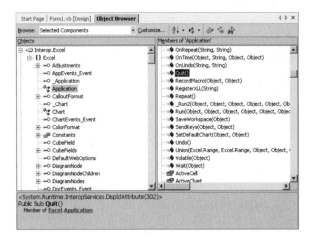

The syntax for the Quit method appears at the bottom of the Object Browser. This method closes the Excel application when you are done using it. It is a standard feature of most Office Automation sessions. The method syntax shows you the basic arguments for the method (none in this case), and the parent objects for the method (Excel.Application).

12   Continue to examine the Excel object library, and the other object libraries associated with your Visual Basic application, if you like.

13   When you're finished, close the Object Browser.

You've finished exploring objects for the time being. Now it's time to put a few Excel Automation commands to work.

Automating Excel from Visual Basic

To use Excel commands in a Visual Basic program, you need to complete the following programming steps. Because these steps apply to other applications, you can use these guidelines to incorporate into your own programs the functionality of most applications that support Automation.

Step 1 Add references to the necessary object libraries to your project by using the Visual Studio Add Reference command.

Step 2 Write your Visual Basic program. In the event procedure in which you plan to use Automation, use the Dim statement to declare the Automation object type. Then use the CType and CreateObject functions to create an instance of that object:

```
Dim xlApp As Excel.Application
xlApp = CType(CreateObject("Excel.Application"), Excel.Application)
```

In Visual Basic 6, you were allowed to create a variable of type Object for the application and then assign it a specific application type at runtime. This variable assignment technique, called *late binding*, isn't recommended in Visual Basic .NET code. Variables that hold Automation objects should be assigned a type at design time, so that they are bound to the data during compilation (so-called *early binding*), as I have demonstrated here. The CType function is the mechanism that returns the specific application type to the application variable at compilation.

Step 3 Use the methods and properties of the Automation object in the event procedure, consulting the Object Browser schematics or the application documentation for the proper syntax. The following sample code uses the Excel WorksheetFunction.Pmt method:

```
Dim LoanPayment As Single
LoanPayment = xlApp.WorksheetFunction.Pmt _
   (txtInterest.Text / 12, txtMonths.Text, txtPrincipal.Text)
MsgBox("The monthly payment is " & _
   Format(Abs(LoanPayment), "$#.##"), , "Mortgage")
```

Step 4 When you've finished using the application, issue a specific command to quit the application (unless you want to keep it running). For example:

```
xlApp.Quit()
```

This Quit command is the same method you just learned about using in the Visual Studio Object Browser.

In the following exercise you'll create a Visual Basic application that uses the Excel Pmt method to compute loan payments for a home mortgage. The arguments for Pmt will be drawn from three text box objects on your form. The program will be built entirely in Visual Basic, using the functionality of Excel through Automation.

> ## tip
> The following steps require that you have Excel 2002 installed on your system. You may be able to adapt this program code if you have a different version of Excel, but in my experience this is a non-trivial process. For this reason, I don't recommend Automation for programs that will be widely distributed—especially among users with different versions of Office.

Build a mortgage payment calculator

1   Display the form in the development environment, if it isn't visible.

A

Label control

2   At the top of the form, use the Label control to draw a large label object for your program's title.

3   Below the label, use the TextBox control to draw three text box objects on the right side of the form.

TextBox control

The text box objects will allow you to enter arguments for the Pmt function.

4   Using the Label control, draw a label object next to each of the text box objects.

The labels you've created will identify the Pmt function arguments, to help you type them in the right place.

5   Use the Button control to draw a button object at the bottom of the form.

Button control

6   Set the following properties for the objects on your form:

Object	Property	Setting
Label1	Font	Microsoft Sans Serif, Bold, 11 point
	Text	"Calculate Payments Using Excel"
	TextAlign	MiddleCenter
TextBox1	Name	txtInterest
	Text	(empty)
TextBox2	Name	txtMonths
	Text	(empty)
TextBox3	Name	txtPrincipal
	Text	(empty)
Label2	Text	Interest
Label3	Text	Months
Label4	Text	Principal
Button1	Name	btnCalculate
	Text	Calculate
Form1	Text	Mortgage

Your form should look like this:

7   Double-click the Calculate button to display the btnCalculate_Click event procedure in the Code Editor.

8   Type the following program code to issue Excel commands via Automation and calculate the home mortgage payment:

```
Dim xlApp As Excel.Application
Dim LoanPayment As Single
xlApp = CType(CreateObject("Excel.Application"), Excel.Application)
LoanPayment = xlApp.WorksheetFunction.Pmt _
  (txtInterest.Text / 12, txtMonths.Text, txtPrincipal.Text)
MsgBox("The monthly payment is " & _
  Format(Abs(LoanPayment), "$#.##"), , "Mortgage")
xlApp.Quit()
```

This event procedure declares a variable named xlApp of the Excel.Application type, which is valid in the project now that you have made a reference to the Microsoft Excel 10.0 object library.

tip

If you see the type Excel.Application with a jagged blue underline in the Code Editor, it is probably because you forgot to add the reference, or simply started typing this code without working through the Object Browser exercise. Go back and make the library reference now using the Add Reference command on the Project menu.

The routine then assigns a type to the xlApp variable using the CreateObject and CType functions, and puts the variable to work by calling the Excel WorksheetFunction.Pmt method. The three arguments for the Pmt method are drawn from the three text box objects on the form. Because the Pmt function returns a negative number for payments, I have used the Abs (absolute value) function from the .NET Framework System.Math class to display the number as a positive floating point value. (In Excel, loan payments are typically displayed as negative numbers, or debits, but on a Visual Basic form, payments usually look best as positive values.) Note that if one of the required arguments for the Pmt function is missing, the event procedure will produce a runtime error message. (Can you see how this shortcoming might be fixed using a decision structure or error handler?)

Finally, the routine displays the mortgage payment using a message box, and closes the Excel application using the Quit method. In this example, the Excel application is never displayed, so the user won't even know it has been loaded.

9 Scroll to the top of the form's code in the Code Editor, and then type the following program statement:

```
Imports System.Math
```

This declaration will incorporate the System.Math class library in the project, and provide access to the Abs function you specified. (After you make this reference, the Abs method will no longer have a jagged blue underline—a visual clue that an object, method, or property is currently undefined.)

You'll run the program now to see how Excel Automation works.

Run the Excel Automation program

The complete Excel Automation program is located in the c:\vbnetsbs\ chap13\excel automation folder.

1 Click the Start button on the Standard toolbar.

The mortgage payment calculator appears.

2 Type **0.09** in the Interest text box.

3 Type **360** in the Months text box.

4 Type **150000** in the Principal text box.

Your form should look like this:

5   Click the Calculate button.

The program uses Excel to calculate the mortgage payment for a $150,000 loan at 9% interest over 360 months (30 years). As shown in the following illustration, a message box displays the result of $1206.93. (Remember that if this were a home mortgage payment, this amount would represent principal and interest only—not taxes, insurance, or other items that are typically included!)

> **Mortgage**   ✕
>
> The monthly payment is $1206.93
>
> OK

6   Click the OK button in the message box, and then make a few more mortgage payment calculations using different values.

7   When you're finished, click the Close button on the form's title bar.

Now let's try an Excel Automation exercise that makes more detailed use of a visible Excel worksheet.

Manipulate Excel worksheets

1   Click the Close Solution command on the File menu, and then create a new Visual Basic Windows Application project named **My Excel Sheet Tasks** in the c:\vbnetsbs\chap13 folder.

In this exercise, you'll issue Excel Automation commands that insert numbers and labels in worksheet cells, apply character formatting, insert a Sum function, and save the worksheet to disk. Using these basic skills, you can generate extensive Excel worksheets from within your Visual Basic applications.

2   On the Project menu, click the Add Reference command.

The Add Reference dialog box appears.

3   Click the COM tab, click the Microsoft Excel 10.0 Object Library in the component list, click the Select button, and click OK. If you see the primary interoperability assembly dialog box, click Yes.

Button control

4   Using the Button control, add a large button object to the form.

5   Use the Properties window to set the Text property of the button object to **Create Worksheet**, and then set the Text property of the form to **Excel Worksheet Builder**.

These are the only properties you'll set for this demonstration program— most of the work will be accomplished in Microsoft Excel.

6   Double-click the Create Worksheet button to open the Button1_Click event procedure in the Code Editor.

7   Type the following program statements:

```
' Declare Excel object variables and create types
Dim xlApp As Excel.Application
Dim xlBook As Excel.Workbook
Dim xlSheet As Excel.Worksheet
xlApp = CType(CreateObject("Excel.Application"), Excel.Application)
xlBook = CType(xlApp.Workbooks.Add, Excel.Workbook)
xlSheet = CType(xlBook.Worksheets(1), Excel.Worksheet)

' Insert data
xlSheet.Cells(1, 2) = 5000
xlSheet.Cells(2, 2) = 75
xlSheet.Cells(3, 1) = "Total"
' Insert a Sum formula in cell B3
xlSheet.Range("B3").Formula = "=Sum(R1C2:R2C2)"
' Format cell B3 with bold
xlSheet.Range("B3").Font.Bold = True
' Display the sheet
xlSheet.Application.Visible = True
' Save the sheet to c:\vbnetsbs\chap13 folder
xlSheet.SaveAs("C:\vbnetsbs\chap13\myexcelsheet.xls")
' Leave Excel running and sheet open
```

The program code for this event procedure is a little longer than the last Excel Automation sample—it could be much longer still if you choose to add numerous values and formatting options to the worksheet. Of particular interest are the first three variable declarations and CreateObject statements. Because I'm actually manipulating an Excel worksheet, not just running Excel commands, I need to create three Excel variables and assign them the proper types from the Microsoft Excel 10.0 object library. The first variable declaration references the Excel.Application type, the second variable declaration references the Excel.Workbook type (which relies on Excel.Application), and the third variable declaration references the Excel.Worksheet type (which relies on Excel.Workbook). Take note of these important variable and type declarations for your future work with Excel.

The remainder of the event procedure loads values into Excel cells. (Note the difference between how numeric and string values are entered.) A formula is then entered in cell B3 that uses a Sum function to total cells B1 and B2, and the result is formatted with Bold type. At this point, the event procedure displays the active worksheet, and the worksheet is saved to disk in the c:\vbnetsbs\chap13 folder. (If the file already exists, a dialog box will appear asking you if you want to overwrite the file, which you may do.) At this point the event procedure ends, and the Excel application remains open and visible, inviting the user to complete additional Excel tasks. (Note that the Visual Basic program, too, continues running.) We could also have closed the program using the Quit method, as we did in the first Excel Automation sample.

8   Click the Save All button on the Standard toolbar to save the project and its reference to disk.

Run the Excel Sheet Tasks program

The complete Excel Sheet Tasks program is located in the c:\vbnetsbs\ chap13\excel sheet tasks folder.

1   Click the Start button on the Standard toolbar.

The simple form for your project appears, as shown here:

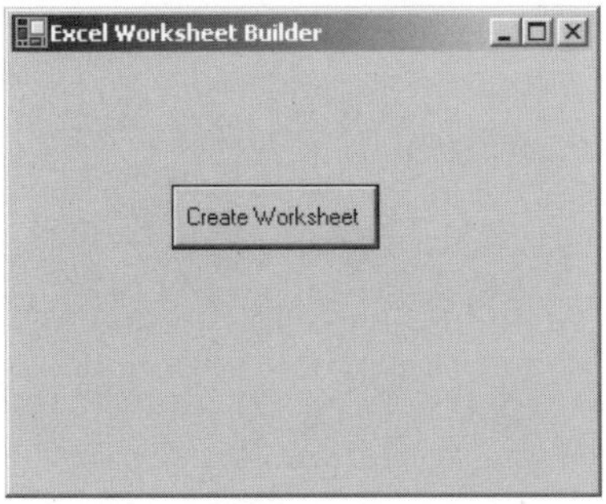

2   Click the Create Worksheet button.

Visual Basic starts Excel and quickly performs the Automation tasks you requested. After the Visible property is set to True, an Excel worksheet appears on your screen, as shown here:

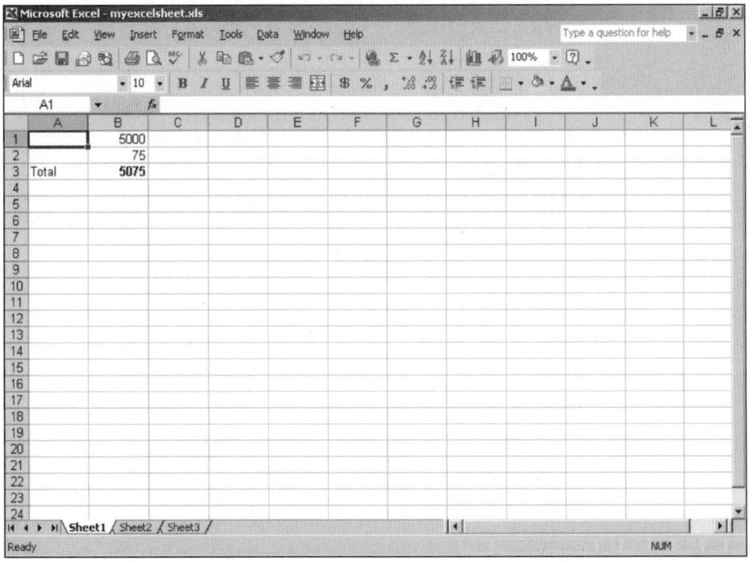

Note the position and content of the cells in columns A and B—the Automation commands have completed their work, and the Sum function produced the correct result in cell B3 (5000 + 75 = 5075). The current filename also appears on the Excel title bar (myexcelsheet.xls).

3   Continue to manipulate the Excel worksheet if you like, and then close the application. Note that the program you have written will work whether the Excel application is open or not.

4   Click the Close button on your Visual Basic program to stop it, too.

That's it! You've learned the essential skills to automate the Excel application. The Object Browser will teach you more about the details of the application objects if you choose to explore Automation on your own.

One Step Further: Starting and Stopping Windows Applications Using the Process Component

In Chapters 3 and 11, you used the Process.Start method to start the default Internet browser on your system and view a Web page. The Process.Start method can be used to start any Windows application on your system that is registered in the system registry. You don't need to specify a path when you use the Process.Start method as long as the application or file extension you specify is recognized by the system, and the Process.Start method doesn't rely on Automation to do its work. For example, the following Process.Start command starts the Notepad application:

```
System.Diagnostics.Process.Start("notepad.exe")
```

The only problem with the technique I have demonstrated so far is that once the Notepad application is running, there is no easy way to control it—Visual Basic has started the Windows application, but it can't stop it. The solution to this shortcoming is to use one of the new Visual Studio features more closely associated with Windows process control. In particular, you can start your applications or *processes* by using the Process component on the Components tab of the Visual Studio Toolbox. In the following exercise, you'll learn how to use the Process component to start and stop a Notepad application from within a Visual Basic program. You can use this basic technique to start and stop any Windows application program.

Control Notepad process execution

1   Click the Close Solution command on the File menu, and then create a new Visual Basic Windows Application project named **My Start App** in the c:\vbnetsbs\chap13 folder.

Button control

2   Display the project's form, and then add two button objects to the form using the Button control.

3   Set the Text property for the Button1 object to **Start Notepad**, and set the Text property for the Button2 object to **Stop Notepad**. Set the form's Text property to **Process Start Examples**.

Now you'll add a Process component to the project, an invisible component that Visual Basic will use to keep track of the Notepad application as it runs.

4   Click the Components tab in the Visual Studio Toolbox.

The tab looks like this:

Toolbox	📌 ✕
Data	
Components	▲
▸ Pointer	
📊 FileSystemWatcher	
🗒 EventLog	
🗂 DirectoryEntry	
🔍 DirectorySearcher	
🗳 MessageQueue	
📈 PerformanceCounter	
🖳 Process ———————— Process component	
📇 ServiceController	
⏲ Timer	
📄 ReportDocument	

So far you've only used the Windows Forms tab of the Toolbox, but the Components tab also is very useful. It contains .NET components that monitor events within the operating system and within the Visual Studio development environment.

5   Double-click the Process component on the Components tab of the Toolbox.

The Process component is added to the component tray below the form, just like other non-visible Toolbox controls. This component has no visible user interface; it just represents an application that is launched by your project.

6   Click the Process1 object, and then use the Properties window to set the object's Name property to **noteProcess**.

7   In the Properties window, click the plus sign (+) next to the StartInfo category to open it, and then set the FileName property to **notepad.exe**.

You'll use the object name noteProcess in your program code when you want to start, stop, or monitor the Notepad application. The FileName property sets the application name to notepad.exe, which the system registry can find if the Notepad application has been installed correctly. (Change this name if you want to run another application, such as winword.exe or excel.exe.)

Automating Applications

13

> **tip**
> To pass command-line arguments to the application you are starting, set the Arguments property in the StartInfo category.

Your form now looks like this:

noteProcess object

8   Double-click the Start Notepad button on the form, and then type the following program statement in the Code Editor:

```
noteProcess.Start()
```

Because you have already specified the application name using the Process component, you don't need to specify it again here. The noteProcess object name carries the required information.

9   Display the form again, and then double-click the Stop Notepad button.

10 Type the following program statement in the Code Editor:

```
noteProcess.CloseMainWindow()
```

The CloseMainWindow method is the equivalent to clicking the Close button on Notepad's title bar. If the user has an unsaved file in the application, he or she will be prompted to save the file before the application closes. (Alternatively, you could close the application using the Kill method, but that technique would not allow the changes to be saved.)

11 Scroll to the top of the form's program code, and then type the following class references:

```
Imports System.Threading
Imports System.Diagnostics
```

These System classes are useful when you manipulate processes in your program code, although they are not required if you only use the Start and CloseMainWindow methods as I do here. (I'm including them to identify the Framework classes you may want to investigate further down the road.)

*The complete
Start App
program is
located in the
c:\vbnetsbs\
chap13\start
app folder.*

12 Click the Save All button on the toolbar, and then run the program.

The following form appears:

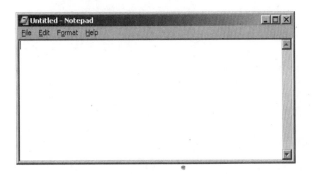

13 Click the Start Notepad button.

Your program starts the Notepad process and the Notepad application opens in a window:

14 Display the form again, and then click the Stop Notepad button.

Visual Basic uses the CloseMainWindow method to quit the Notepad application.

Continue to start and stop Notepad as much as you like—your Visual Basic program can now track the application processes you start because it has assigned them to the noteProcess object. By using the Visual Basic online Help, you can learn more about processes and the other techniques you can employ to make even greater use of them.

15   When you're finished, click the Close button on the form to close the program.

Chapter 13 Quick Reference

To	Do this
Add a reference in your project to a component or application that supports Automation	On the Project menu, click the Add Reference command. Click the COM tab, click the object library you want, click the Select button, and then click OK.
View objects that are available for use in your project	On the View menu, click the Other Windows submenu, and then click the Object Browser command. Select the objects you want to examine using the hierarchical tree structure in the Objects pane.

Create an Automation object in a program	Use the Dim statement and the CType and CreateObject functions. For example:
	`Dim xlApp As Excel.Application`
	`xlApp = CType(CreateObject _`
	`   ("Excel.Application"), Excel.Application)`

Access application features by using Automation	Create an Automation object, and then reference the methods or properties of the object. For example: `xlApp.Quit()`

Start and stop applications from within Visual Basic	Add a Process component to your form by double-clicking the Process item on the Components tab of the Toolbox. Set the Name and Filename properties for the process object, and then use the following program statements in your program code to start and stop the process, respectively:
	`Objectname.Start()`
	`Objectname.CloseMainWindow()`

14

Deploying Visual Basic .NET Applications

In this chapter you will learn how to:

✔ *Add a deployment project to your solution.*

✔ *Run the Setup Wizard to create a setup program for your application.*

✔ *Customize your setup program using properties and build settings.*

✔ *Test installing and uninstalling your application.*

When your Visual Basic .NET application is finished, you may want to distribute the application to other computer users in your workgroup, share it with friends on the Internet, or sell it to paying customers. Visual Studio .NET helps you to distribute your Visual Basic applications by providing several options for *deployment*—in other words, installing the application on one or more computer systems. In this chapter, you'll learn how to deploy Visual Basic applications by adding a deployment project to your solution, and you'll run the Setup Wizard to create the installation files that you need. In addition, you'll learn how to customize your installation by using property settings and adjusting the deployment options in your build configuration.

Building a deployment project is a complex process, and you'll find that each edition of Visual Basic .NET offers a slightly different assortment of installation options. For example, Visual Basic .NET Standard doesn't include the Setup Wizard to automate a typical deployment. Visual Studio .NET Professional and advanced editions contain additional installation templates, plus the ability to deploy solutions on the Web and create cabinet files. Notice that as you work through this chapter, you may see a few settings or options that aren't available in your edition of Visual Basic.

Upgrade Notes:
What's New in Visual Basic .NET?

If you're experienced with Visual Basic 6, you'll notice some new features in Visual Basic .NET, including the following:

- In Visual Basic 6, you deployed applications using the Package and Deployment Wizard. In Visual Studio .NET, you deploy applications by adding a deployment project to the solution you want to distribute and configuring the deployment project for the type of installation that you want to perform.

- Visual Basic 6 applications typically relied on COM (Component Object Model) components, and over time we have realized that COM components can be problematic to install, register, and uninstall. Visual Studio addresses this problem by installing the .NET Framework class libraries on client computers (if necessary), packing applications in assemblies, and eliminating most COM dynamic link libraries (DLLs).

- Visual Basic .NET applications can now be installed without interacting with the computer's system registry (the so-called XCOPY installation), but in practice I recommend that you install and uninstall Visual Basic .NET applications by using the Visual Studio deployment tools and the Windows Installer.

Planning a Deployment

In the early days of personal computer programming, creating an application that could be installed successfully on another computer was often as simple as compiling an .exe file for your project and copying it to a floppy disk. As application programs have become more sophisticated, however, the number of files needed for a typical installation has grown from a handful of files to several hundred or more. Although the Microsoft Windows operating system has helped to reduce the overall scope of application development (Windows provides common application services like printing, Clipboard functionality, memory management, and user interface support), Windows applications have historically required sophisticated setup programs to copy the correct dynamic link libraries (DLLs) and support files to the host computer and to register the application appropriately with the operating system.

At one time or another, most computer users have experienced the "dark side" of installing Windows programs—an application is "successfully" installed but it won't run, or the new program creates a DLL conflict with another program that was running fine until the new one came along. An equally irritating problem is the newly installed program that can't be uninstalled, either because the uninstall program no longer works, or because the uninstall process leaves DLLs, registry entries, and other support files scattered throughout the file system. These shortcomings—known as "DLL Hell" by some of the more tortured users and developers—is a major limitation of COM (Component Object Model) components and traditional setup programs, including (potentially) those created by the Visual Basic 6 programming system.

Visual Studio .NET was designed, in part, to address the installation shortcomings of Visual Basic and Visual C++ applications, especially those that rely on COM components. In Visual Studio .NET, it is possible to simplify the installation process because Visual Studio applications rely on .NET Framework class libraries for much of their functionality, instead of COM components and numerous function calls to the Windows API (application programming interface). In addition, Visual Studio applications are compiled as *assemblies*, a deployment unit consisting of one or more files necessary for the program to run.

Assemblies contain four elements: Microsoft intermediate language (MSIL) code, metadata, a manifest, and supporting files and resources. *MSIL code* is your program code compiled into a language that the common language runtime understands. *Metadata* is information about the types, methods, and other elements defined and referenced in your code. A *manifest* includes name and version information, a list of files in the assembly, security information, and other information about the assembly. The following illustration shows a diagram of a single file assembly we will look at in this chapter:

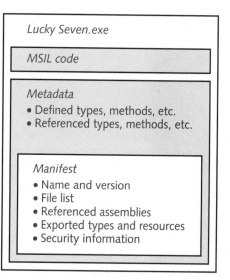

Assemblies are so comprehensive and self-describing that Visual Studio .NET applications don't need to be formally registered with the operating system to run. This means that a Visual Basic .NET application can be installed by simply copying the assembly for an application to a new computer that has the .NET Framework installed—a process called XCOPY installation, after the MS-DOS XCOPY command that copies a complete directory (folder) structure from one location to another. In practice, however, it isn't practical to deploy Visual Basic .NET applications using a simply copy procedure such as XCOPY (via the command prompt) or Windows Explorer. For commercial applications, an installation program with a graphical user interface is usually preferred, and it is often desirable to register the program with the operating system so that it can be uninstalled later using Add/Remove Programs in Control Panel.

To manage the installation process, Visual Studio .NET allows developers to add a *deployment project* to their solutions, which automatically creates a setup program for the application. This deployment project can be customized to allow for different methods of installation, such as CDs and Web servers. Best of all, you can add a deployment project to your solution at any time during the development process—at the beginning, when you are just defining your solution, at the end, when you are ready to distribute your solution, or in the middle, when you are having difficulty with some code and want to do something else for a few hours.

Different Ways to Deploy an Application

As you think about distributing your solution, consider the different methods that you can use to deploy your application. You can:

- Install the application on your own computer and register it in the Windows system registry
- Create an installation program that allows your application to be installed from a local network or from the Internet
- Deploy your application using one or more CDs
- Deploy your application using cabinet files (.cab), a technique that can be used to download files using a Web browser

In Visual Studio, you can quickly create a deployment project by running the Setup Wizard. You can customize the deployment project by setting various properties. If you deploy using CDs, your computer will need a writable CD-ROM drive, often called a CD burner, and you will need to copy the deployment files to the CDs.

The .NET Framework is required on each system that runs Visual Basic .NET applications. The .NET Framework is available as a single redistributable file (Dotnetfx.exe) on the Visual Studio .NET Windows Component Update CD. The .NET Framework will also be available as a download from the Microsoft Web site. Dotnetfx.exe is quite large (more than 20 MB), and when installed the .NET Framework is approximately 30 MB. However, Microsoft has committed to distributing the .NET Framework along with its future operating systems and application programs. If the target computer already has the .NET Framework installed, you could just copy the application and any required files to the computer and the application should run properly. However, to create a complete setup program, the deployment files must include the .NET Framework redistributable.

> ## note
>
> Deployment using floppy disks wasn't supported when this chapter was written. Some of the deployment files that Visual Studio creates are too large to fit on floppy disks. It is possible to partition a large Windows installer file into smaller cabinet files, but some of the supporting files are still too large. If you are interested in deploying to floppy disks, you should create a test deployment project to verify that the deployment files will fit on 1.4 MB floppy disks.

14

Deploying Applications

Creating a Deployment Project

Now let's get some practice creating an actual deployment project and setup program for a Visual Basic application you have created in this book. The setup program you create will be designed for deployment on your own system, and you'll have the application and its Readme file install in the c:\program files\ microsoft press\lucky seven folder. The setup program will add an application shortcut to the user's Programs list on the Start menu. In addition, the setup program will register the Lucky Seven application in the Windows system registry, and you'll see how this application can be uninstalled at the end of the chapter by using Add/Remove Programs in Control Panel. This deployment can also be copied to a CD-ROM and used for CD installation.

important

The following steps use the Setup Wizard in the Setup and Deployment Projects folder of the New Project dialog box. If your edition of Visual Basic .NET doesn't include the Setup Wizard, you won't be able to perform these steps. You can, however, use the Setup Project template instead to create a deployment project manually. Skip to the section "Create a deployment project using the Setup Project template" later in this chapter for the important steps you need to follow if you don't have the Setup Wizard.

Create a deployment project using the Setup Wizard

1   Start Visual Studio and open the Lucky Seven project in the c:\vbnetsbs\chap14\lucky seven folder.

   The Lucky Seven solution is identical to the Track Wins program you created in Chapter 10. It is a slot machine game that displays a bitmap if the number 7 appears one or more times on the form when you click the Spin button.

2   On the File menu, click New, and then click Project.

   Visual Studio opens the New Project dialog box.

   Now you'll add a deployment project to the solution that will automatically create a setup program for this application. Although most of the solutions you have created in this book have contained only one project, solutions that include a setup program have a minimum of two projects. (As you'll see, you use Solution Explorer to manage these projects.)

3   Click the Setup and Deployment Projects folder.

This option presents four templates and a wizard that you can use to create the deployment project. The New Project dialog box will look like this:

The four templates are designed to configure many of the settings in the deployment project for you. The Cab Project template configures the deployment project to create one or more cabinet files for the project (you determine the size of the files); choose this option if you want to have users download the solution from the Internet (recommended for older browsers that can't accommodate a full Web setup). The Merge Module Project template is designed to create a general-purpose deployment project that can be used for several different Visual Basic applications (it creates a .msm file that can be merged into other solutions). The Setup Project template creates a setup program that uses the Windows Installer for installation. The Web Setup Project creates a setup program that uses the Windows Installer and a Web server for installation over the Internet.

Perhaps the most useful item in the Templates pane of the New Project dialog box is the Setup Wizard, which is a wizard that builds a deployment project based on how you answer several questions about installation media, Web preferences, and so on. You can use the Setup Wizard to create a cabinet project, a merge module project, a Windows Installer project, or a Windows Installer project for the Web.

Deploying Applications   14

> **tip**
> If you click the More button in the New Project dialog box, you can also specify a separate name and folder for the solution you are creating. This isn't required, but it is a useful way to isolate the deployment files that you are creating.

4 Click the Setup Wizard icon.

5 Type **Lucky** in the Name text box and specify **c:\vbnetsbs\chap14** in the Location text box.

6 Click the Add To Solution option button, and then click OK.

The Add To Solution option button is important here—if you don't click it, Visual Studio will close the Lucky Seven solution before it opens the deployment project, and you'll miss the benefits of combining the application with the setup files.

When you click OK, Visual Studio starts the Setup Wizard, which you'll complete in the following exercise.

Run the Setup Wizard

1 Read the first dialog box displayed by the Setup Wizard.

Your screen will look like this:

The purpose of the Setup Wizard is to customize the new deployment project and create an installation program for your solution. The Setup Wizard cannot control every installation feature, but it configures a basic deployment project that can be used in a variety of different contexts.

2 Click Next to display the Choose A Project Type dialog box.

Your screen will look like this:

The Choose A Project Type dialog box lets you control how your solution will be distributed. The options map closely to the deployment templates you saw earlier in the New Project dialog box. In this exercise, you'll accept the default deployment type—Create a Setup for a Windows Application.

3 Click Next to display the Choose Project Outputs To Include dialog box.

You use this dialog box to identify the files that you want to include on the systems that will run your application. The Primary Output option is usually mandatory—by selecting it you include the .exe file for your project or .dll if you are creating a dynamic-link library. The other options allow you to include information that might be useful in internationally deployed applications (Localized Resources) and programs that might require further debugging (Debug Symbols) or development work (Content Files/Source Files).

4   Click the Primary Output option.

Your screen will look like this:

5   Click Next to display the Choose Files To Include dialog box.

In this dialog box, you pick additional files that you want to include with your deployment project, such as a Readme.txt file, troubleshooting tips, marketing information, and so on.

6   Click the Add button to add a Readme.txt file to this solution.

I created a simple Readme.txt file in the c:\vbnetsbs\chap14 folder with which you can practice.

7   Browse to the c:\vbnetsbs\chap14 folder, select the Readme.txt file, and then click Open.

Your screen will look like this:

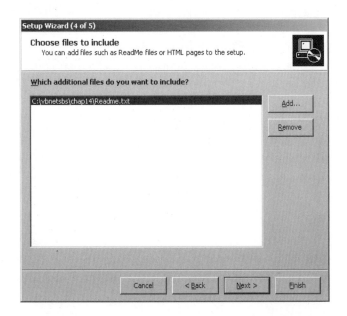

8   Click the Next button to display the Create Project dialog box.

A summary of your deployment selections is listed, as shown here:

If you want to change any selections you have made, click the Back button and make your adjustments, and then click Next until this dialog box is visible again.

9   Click Finish to create the deployment project for the Lucky Seven application.

Visual Studio adds a deployment project named Lucky to the solution, and it appears as another component in Solution Explorer. The File System Editor also appears as shown here:

File System Editor

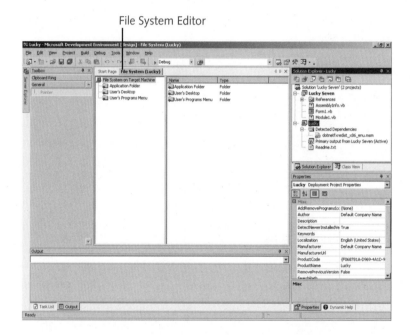

You use the File System Editor to add project output, files, and other items to a deployment project and determine where they will be placed on the computer receiving the installation. The File System Editor displays a standard set of folders that correspond to the standard folder structure on the setup computer. You can customize this folder list and add special folders if you want. You can also create application shortcuts using the File System Editor.

Take a moment to examine the contents of the Lucky deployment project in Solution Explorer. You'll see the .NET Framework dependency in the Detected Dependencies folder, a placeholder for the .exe file (called Primary Output), and the Readme.txt file you included.

Lucky deployment project

tip

Although the .NET Framework is listed as a dependency, you can't include it within the installation files. If you try to include the .NET Framework by changing the Exclude property for the dependency to False, an error will be displayed when you build the solution. Earlier betas of Visual Studio .NET did allow you to include the .NET Framework. This change was made because including the .NET Framework within the installation files doesn't allow the .NET Framework to be separately updated when fixes and new versions are released. Future versions of Visual Studio and the .NET Framework might permit different installation options.

10   Skip to the "Customizing Your Deployment Options" section later in this chapter.

The following section describes how to create the Lucky deployment project without using the Setup Wizard. Because you have already created the deployment project, you can skip to the "Customizing Your Deployment Options" section to learn how to customize your deployment project.

Create a deployment project using the Setup Project template

1   Start Visual Studio and open the Lucky Seven project in the c:\vbnetsbs\chap14\lucky seven folder.

2   On the File menu, click New, and then click Project.

Visual Studio opens the New Project dialog box.

Now you'll add a deployment project to the solution that will automatically create a setup program for this application.

3   Click the Setup and Deployment Projects folder.

This option presents the Setup Project template, which can be used to create a Windows Installer setup program. The New Project dialog box will look like this:

4   Click the Setup Project icon.

5   Type **Lucky** in the Name text box and specify **c:\vbnetsbs\chap14** in the Location text box.

6   Click the Add To Solution option button, and then click OK to create the deployment project for the Lucky Seven application.

Visual Studio adds a deployment project named Lucky to the solution, and it appears as another component in Solution Explorer. The File System Editor also appears, which lets you add project output, files, and other items to a deployment project and determine where they will be placed on the computer receiving the installation.

Now you'll need to add the Lucky Seven.exe file (called Primary Output) to the Lucky deployment project.

7   Make sure the Lucky deployment project is selected in Solution Explorer.

8   On the Project menu, click Add, and then click Project Output.

The Add Project Output Group dialog box appears as shown here:

You use this dialog box to identify the files that you want to include on the systems that will run your application. The Primary Output option is usually mandatory—by selecting it you include the .exe file for your project or .dll if you are creating a dynamic-link library.

9   Click the Primary Output item, and then click OK.

A Primary Output component is added to the Lucky project in Solution Explorer. Also, the .NET Framework dependency is added to the Detected Dependencies folder in Solution Explorer.

10   With the Lucky project still selected in Solution Explorer, click the Project menu, click Add, and then click File to display the Add Files dialog box.

In this dialog box, you pick additional files that you want to include with your deployment project, such as a Readme.txt file, troubleshooting tips, marketing information, and so on.

I created a simple Readme.txt file in the c:\vbnetsbs\chap14 folder with which you can practice.

11   Browse to the c:\vbnetsbs\chap14 folder, select the Readme.txt file, and
then click Open.

The Readme.txt file is added to the Lucky project in Solution Explorer. Solution Explorer, along with the open File System Editor, is shown here:

File System Editor

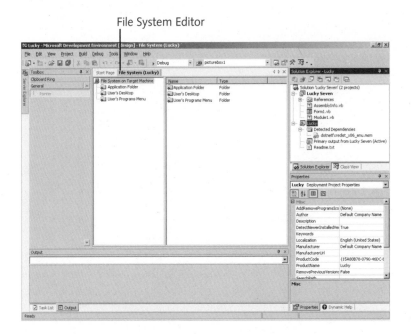

You'll now learn how to customize your deployment project.

Customizing Your Deployment Options

Your deployment project is basically ready to go now—the next time that you
build your solution, the necessary setup program will be generated in the
c:\vbnetsbs\chap14\lucky folder and stored in an .msi (Windows Installer) file,
which you can use to deploy your application. However, there are still a few
customization options that you might want to set to fine-tune your program
deployment. In this section, I'll discuss how you use the Configuration Manager
to modify your build settings, how to create a shortcut to your application, and
how you can change useful property settings such as the company name and
version information your setup program displays.

Configure build settings

1 Click the Configuration Manager command on the Build menu.

You'll see this dialog box:

The Configuration Manager dialog box shows the current build mode for the projects in your solution. The Lucky Seven project and the Lucky deployment project are probably set to debug build, meaning that the compiler will generate files containing additional information for debugging and testing. When you are preparing your final projects for distribution, it is important to use the Configuration Manager dialog box to set all projects for release build.

2 Click the Active Solution Configuration drop-down list box, and then select Release.

3 Click the Configuration option for the Lucky project, and then click Release.

4 Click the Configuration option for the Lucky Seven project, and then click Release.

The Configuration Manager now shows that both projects are set for release builds. Later if you need to switch back to a debug build, you should be able to just select Debug in the Active Solution Configuration drop-down list box.

5 Add check marks to the Build check boxes for both the Lucky project and the Lucky Seven project.

Deploying Applications

14

> **tip**
> If you remove the check mark from the Build check box in Configuration Manager, Visual Studio won't compile that project when the Build Solution command on the Build menu or the Start command on the Debug menu is selected. While you won't want to remove the check mark for your final builds, removing the check mark can be useful as you work on a solution because building the deployment project can be very time-consuming, and it isn't necessary if you are just working on the application project.

6   Click the Close button.

Next you'll use the File System Editor to create a shortcut to the Lucky Seven application so that users can easily start it.

Create an application shortcut

1   Select the Application Folder in the left pane of the File System Editor.

> **tip**
> If the File System Editor isn't visible, you can open it by first selecting the Lucky deployment project in Solution Explorer. Next click the View menu, click Editor, and then click File System.

2   In the right pane, right-click Primary Output From Lucky Seven, and then select Create Shortcut To Primary Output From Lucky Seven.

A shortcut icon appears with its name selected so that it can be renamed.

3   Rename the shortcut to **Lucky Seven,** and then press Enter.

4   Drag the Lucky Seven shortcut into the User's Programs Menu folder in the left pane.

The contents of the User's Programs Menu folder will look like this:

When this application is installed, a shortcut will be added to the user's Programs menu, which can be accessed from the Start button on the Windows taskbar.

Now set the company name and version information for your setup program.

Set company name and version information

1   Select the Lucky deployment project in Solution Explorer.

2   Open the Properties window and enlarge it so that it is big enough to show several of the deployment project properties and settings.

The Lucky deployment project properties fill the Properties window because Lucky is the project that is currently selected in Solution Explorer. The properties aren't related to visible objects in the project but rather are optional settings related to how the application is installed on a new computer. The Author and Manufacturer properties are usually set to the name of the company producing the software, and this value is also used to construct the default path for your program on disk (for an example of this pattern, see the c:\program files folder). Once the application is installed, the Author property is also displayed in the Contact field of the Support Info dialog box, which you can access for individual applications through Add/Remove Programs in Control Panel.

The Title property contains the name of the setup program, and the Version property allows you to specify version information for your setup program. A few properties, such as Product Code and Package Code, contain unique alphanumeric codes generated by Visual Studio that you can use to identify individual releases of your setup program. (Note that these property settings apply to the setup program and not the Lucky Seven application.)

3   Change the Author and Manufacturer properties to **Microsoft Press** using the Properties window.

4   Change the Version property to **1.5.0** using the Properties window.

When you change the Version property and press Enter, Visual Studio displays a dialog box asking you if you want to generate new ProductCode and PackageCode numbers.

5   Click Yes to create new code numbers.

6   Spend a few moments examining the remaining property settings, and then return the Properties window to its normal size.

Now you'll open the Property Pages dialog box to see where the media-related property settings are located.

Set deployment property pages

1   Select the Lucky deployment project in Solution Explorer.

2   Click the Properties command on the Project menu.

The Property Pages dialog box opens for the Lucky deployment project, as shown here:

This dialog box gives you an opportunity to rethink a few of the decisions you made in the Setup Wizard (if you used the Setup Wizard), and to customize a few additional settings that weren't available in the wizard. I'll walk you through several of the settings in this dialog box now.

The Output File Name setting controls the name of the file your installation files are packaged into. This is usually one large file with an extension of .msi (Windows Installer) and a few supporting files, such as Setup.ini and Setup.exe. These supporting files are added based on additional deployment project options that will be discussed. The user installing your program can launch the .msi file directly or through a Setup.exe program. When they do so, the installation process copies the .exe application file and any associated files to the default folder for the application.

3   Click the Package Files drop-down list box.

This list box contains three options: As Loose Uncompressed Files, In Setup File, and In Cabinet File(s). In Setup File is currently selected because that is the option you selected when you ran the Setup Wizard earlier; this option creates one large .msi file in the specified folder. The As Loose Uncompressed Files option will create uncompressed files in the same folder as the .msi file. The In Cabinet File(s) option creates one or more .cab files to hold the application and places them in the same folder as the .msi file.

4   Select the In Cabinet File(s) option.

When you select this option, the CAB Size options become available. If you click the Custom option button, you can specify the maximum size of each cabinet file in the Custom text box.

5   Click the Package Files drop-down list box again, and then select In Setup File.

In this exercise, you'll create a single installation file that contains all the support files you need.

6   Click the Bootstrapper drop-down list box.

The Bootstrapper list box determines whether a bootstrapping program will be included in the setup program you are creating. A bootstrapping program includes the files needed to install Microsoft Windows Installer 2.0 on the target computer if it isn't already installed. This version of the installer is the default version included with Visual Studio .NET and Microsoft Windows XP, but if your users don't have one of these products, it is a good idea to include the bootstrapping programs along with your application. In the list box, you can choose a Windows-based or Web-based bootstrapping program. If you select Web Bootstrapper, the Web Bootstrapper Settings dialog box appears, where you can specify the Web location for the bootstrapping files.

7   Click the Windows Installer Bootstrapper option.

8   Now click the Compression drop-down list box.

The options in this list describe how your files will be packaged in the setup program. Optimized For Size is the most common option for developers who are trying to squeeze their installations into cabinet files. Optimized For Speed is the best choice if you have plenty of media space (in other words, a CD-ROM) but you want things to move along as fast as possible.

9   Click the Optimized For Size option.

You'll try to minimize the size of your single installation file because the file will remain on your own system during the installation tests.

The final option in the Property Pages dialog box relates to the inclusion of an Authenticode Signature in your project. An Authenticode Signature is a digital document (an .spc file) that identifies you as the manufacturer of this software product. Such a file verifies that you are a "reputable" software vendor and are trustworthy to the extent that you can be located down the road if problems occur with your application. Although the creation and use of Authenticode Signatures is beyond the scope of this book (I won't enable it), this is an option you should investigate if you are planning a commercial release of your Visual Basic application. It allows your program to register as a "trusted source" in the end user's operating system.

10 Click OK to save your changes in the Property Pages dialog box.

Visual Studio records your selections and is ready to compile the projects.

Building a Deployment Project and Testing Setup

When you're finished adding and customizing your deployment project, you're ready to build the solution and test the setup program. Here are the steps you should follow:

1   **Build the solution using the Build Solution command on the Build menu.** This command will compile the entire solution, including the final version of the application and the deployment project you have included in the solution.

2   **Run the setup program to install the application.** Test the setup program and the installation process. In this exercise, you'll launch the setup program by double-clicking the Setup.exe file you build.

3   **Test the installation and examine the installed files.** Verify that the installed application works and that the expected files (such as Readme.txt) were installed in the proper folder.

The following exercises demonstrate this process for the Lucky Seven application and the Lucky deployment project.

Build the project

1   Click Build Solution on the Build menu.

Visual Studio compiles both the Lucky Seven and the Lucky projects, and creates an .msi file in the c:\vbnetsbs\chap14\lucky\release folder. The build process takes longer than normal because Visual Studio must package files required to deploy your application.

During longer compilations, a progress bar and a repeating compilation pattern is displayed on the Visual Studio status bar, indicating that the build process is under way. Staring at this box can be soothing.

If the compilation finishes with no errors, the words "Build Succeeded" appear on the left side of the status bar.

2   Click the Start button on the taskbar, click Programs, click Accessories, and then click Windows Explorer.

You'll use Windows Explorer to locate and identify the files that were created during the build process.

3   Browse to the c:\vbnetsbs\chap14\lucky\release folder, and then click the Lucky.msi file once to select it.

You'll see the following list of files:

When you specify a release build in the Configuration Manager, Visual Studio places the compiled files in a Release folder. You specified this particular location and name for the files in the Lucky Property Pages dialog box. In this case, Visual Studio created two Windows Installer files (Instmsia.exe and Instmsiw.exe), a setup file (Setup.exe), an installation package for the Windows Installer (Lucky.msi), and a configuration settings file (Setup.ini).

Because you selected the Lucky.msi file, Windows Explorer displays the file type, author, and file size information for the file in the status bar. The Microsoft Press author name reflects a setting you made using the Properties window earlier in this chapter. Lucky.msi contains the LuckySeven.exe file, the Readme.txt file, and setup program information.

tip

To create an actual installation CD for your application, you would copy the entire contents of the Release folder to a writable CD-ROM at this point. If the target computers don't include the .NET Framework, you should also copy the .NET Framework redistributable file (Dotnetfx.exe), which the user will have to install separately. You need a CD-RW drive to do this; check your computer documentation to see whether you have this capability, which is called "burning a CD" in industry slang.

Run the Setup program

1   Double-click the Setup.exe file in the c:\vbnetsbs\chap14\lucky\release folder to run the setup program for your application.

The Setup.exe program starts the Windows Installer program and gives users who don't have a copy of Windows Installer on their system a chance to install it, which might require a reboot. After a moment, a dialog box entitled Welcome To The Lucky Setup Wizard appears, as shown here:

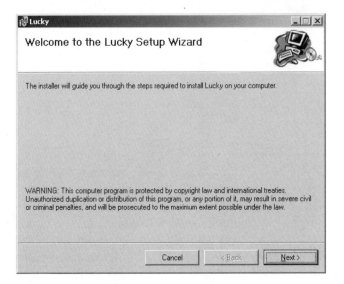

2   Click the Next button to continue the installation.

You'll see the Select Installation Folder dialog box, which prompts you for a folder location and allows you to set additional installation options:

Notice that the default installation folder proposed is c:\program files\ microsoft press\lucky. The "Microsoft Press" label matches the Author and Manufacturer property settings you made earlier in this chapter using the Properties window. The Everyone and Just Me option buttons have to do with underlying security settings in the Windows operating system.

3 Click the Everyone option button, and then click Next.

The setup program asks you to confirm your installation settings by clicking the Next button. If you're not sure, click Back to return to one or more dialog boxes to verify your selections, and then click Next until this dialog box is visible again.

4 Click Next to start the installation.

The setup program begins copying the necessary files to the folder location you specified. The program also registers the Lucky Seven application using the system registry so that you can uninstall it later if you want to.

5 Click Close when the installation is complete.

You did it! You created a working setup program that installs your application in a very professional manner.

tip

If you attempt to install this application on another computer, you must make sure that the target computer meets the minimum system requirements. Applications created with Visual Studio .NET require Windows 98 or later with Internet Explorer 5.01 or later, Windows NT 4.0 Service Pack 6a or later with Internet Explorer 5.01 or later. Windows 95 isn't supported. The target computer also requires the .NET Framework.

Run the Lucky Seven application

1 Click the Start button on the Windows taskbar, click Programs, and then click Lucky Seven.

Recall that this is the shortcut that you created using the File System Editor.

Windows starts the program. The installation works!

tip

You can also start the Lucky Seven program by browsing to the c:\program files\microsoft press\lucky folder using Windows Explorer and then double-clicking the Lucky Seven.exe program.

2   Click the Spin button several times to play the game and verify that every-thing is running properly.

After 25 spins, your screen will look like this:

3   When you're finished, click the End button.

You've tested both the setup process and the final application—everything seems to be working fine!

One Step Further: Examining Setup Files and Uninstalling

As one final experiment with your installation, use Windows Explorer to examine the content of the c:\program files\microsoft press\lucky folder, and then uninstall the Lucky Seven test application. It's always a good idea to see exactly what your deployment project installed, and how Add/Remove Programs in Control Panel can be used to uninstall the program files. Complete the following exercises.

Check final installation files

1   Open Windows Explorer and browse to the c:\program files\microsoft press\lucky folder.

This folder contains the Lucky Seven.exe program file and the Readme.txt file you included when you configured deployment project properties.

2   Click the View menu in Windows Explorer, and then click Details.

Windows Explorer displays a more detailed file listing, which allows you to see the file sizes and attributes associated with each file. Windows Explorer will look like this:

From the detailed file listing, you can see that the Lucky Seven.exe application file itself takes up only about 48 KB of disk space. However, a significant amount of disk space will be required for the .NET Framework. The .NET Framework files will take up approximately 30 MB of disk space or more and are primarily installed in the Windows\Microsoft.NET folder. Notice that these file sizes may vary from system to system, and among different builds of the Visual Studio development suite and the .NET Framework libraries, so your exact file sizes may be different.

3 Double-click the Readme.txt file.

The simple Readme.txt file I created for the Lucky Seven program appears in the Notepad application, as shown here:

Deploying Applications **14**

Recall that you incorporated the Readme.txt file in your deployment project earlier in this chapter. When you create your own applications, be sure to create a simple Readme.txt file that contains basic usage information, instructions for uninstalling the program, and how to contact the company for help or more information.

4   Review the file, and then close the Notepad application.

Now you'll practice uninstalling the Lucky Seven program and its support files.

Uninstall the test application

1   Click the Start button on the Windows taskbar, click Settings, and then click Control Panel.

Windows displays the Control Panel folder, containing tools for defining basic system settings and preferences.

2   Double-click Add/Remove Programs.

Add/Remove Programs allows you to install new applications or uninstall unwanted applications using the application settings in the system registry. Because you installed the Lucky Seven application using a setup program and the Windows Installer, Lucky is now included in the list of installed programs.

3   Locate the Lucky application in the list of installed programs.

Your screen will look like this:

4   Click the Support Information link in the Lucky application listing.

The following dialog box appears, which contains publisher, version, and contact information. You added this information by setting properties for the deployment project earlier in the chapter.

5   Click Close to close the Support Info dialog box.

6   Click the Remove button in the Lucky application listing to uninstall the program.

7   Click Yes when you are asked to verify your decision to uninstall.

Add/Remove Programs starts the Windows Installer, which manages the uninstall process. After a few moments, the registry entries, .exe file, Readme file, shortcut, and supporting files for the Lucky Seven application are removed from the system. The Lucky listing is also removed from the list of installed programs.

8   Click Close to close Add/Remove Programs, and then close the Control Panel folder.

You're done working with deployment projects in this chapter. You now have the skills to install and uninstall Visual Basic projects safely. In future chapters, you'll learn more about creating applications that are powerful, interesting, and worth deploying to friends and co-workers.

Deploying Applications   14

Chapter 14 Quick Reference

To	Do this
Create a setup program for your Visual Basic application	Open the Visual Basic solution that you want to create a setup program for, and then add a deployment project to it by clicking New Project on the File menu. Click the Setup and Deployment Project folder, and then click a setup template or the Setup Wizard. Specify the deployment project name and location, select the Add To Solution option, and then click OK.
Automatically create an installation program for your project	Select the Setup Wizard in the Setup and Deployment Projects folder, and then specify settings in the wizard.
Adjust how the compiler will build your application	Click the Configuration Manager command on the Build menu. Specify a release build if you are preparing final installation files.
Customize deployment options	Select the deployment project in Solution Explorer, and then set its properties using the Properties window and the Properties command on the Project menu.
Create an application shortcut	In the File System Editor, right-click the Primary Output icon and select the Shortcut To Primary Output option. Give the shortcut a name and drag the shortcut into the User's Programs Menu folder.
Compile an application and its setup files	Click the Build Solution command on the Build menu.
Run a setup program	The mechanism for launching a setup program depends on the type of setup files you create. To run a Windows application setup that uses the Windows Installer, double-click the Setup.exe file or the .msi (Windows Installer) file.
Uninstall a Visual Basic application	Visual Basic applications installed using the Windows Installer should be uninstalled using Add/Remove Programs in Control Panel.

PART 4

Advanced User Interface Design

15

Managing Windows Forms

In this chapter you will learn how to:

✔ *Add new forms to a program.*

✔ *Change the position of a form on the Windows desktop.*

✔ *Add controls to a form at runtime.*

✔ *Change the alignment of objects within a form.*

✔ *Specify the startup object.*

In Part 3, you learned how to construct sophisticated Visual Basic .NET programs that used modules, arrays, collections, text files, and Microsoft Office applications to manage data and perform useful work. In Part 4, you'll focus again on the user interface and you'll learn how to add multi-form projects, animation effects, visual inheritance, and printing support to your Visual Basic applications.

In this chapter, you'll learn how to add additional forms to an application to handle input, output, or special messages. You'll also learn how to use the DesktopBounds property to size and position a form, how to add Toolbox controls to a form at runtime, how to change the alignment of objects within a form, and how to specify the form or procedure that runs when a program is started.

Upgrade Notes:
What's New in Visual Basic .NET?

If you're experienced with Visual Basic 6, you'll notice some new features in Visual Basic .NET, including the following:

- In Visual Basic .NET, you cannot set the properties of a second form in the project without having an instance variable of the form that you want to manipulate.

- In Visual Basic 6, you could set a form's runtime position on the Windows desktop using the graphical Form Layout window. There is no Form Layout window in Visual Basic .NET, but you can use a new form property named DesktopBounds to set the size and location of a form at runtime.

- In Visual Basic 6, you could add new controls to a form at runtime using program code, and in Visual Basic .NET you have a similar capability. The syntax changes for adding controls at runtime will be discussed in this chapter.

- The new Anchor property for objects on a form specifies which sides should remain at a constant from the edges of the form when the form is resized. The new Dock property forces an object to remain attached to one edge of the form when the form is resized. The Anchor and Dock properties allow you to create forms where the objects are sized accordingly as the form is resized.

- In Visual Basic 6, you could create MDI (multiple document interface) projects by creating an MDI parent form using the Add MDI Form command on the Project menu. In Visual Basic .NET, MDI parent forms are just regular forms that have their IsMdi-Container properties set to True. MDI child forms are regular forms that have their MdiParent properties set to the name of a parent form.

Adding New Forms to a Program

Each new form has a unique name and its own set of objects, properties, methods, and event procedures.

Each program you have written so far has used only one form for input and output. In many cases, one form will be sufficient for communicating with the user. But if you need to exchange more information with the user, Visual Basic lets you add additional forms to your program. Each new form is considered an object that inherits its capabilities from the System.Windows.Forms.Form class. The first form in a program is named Form1.vb. Subsequent forms are named Form2.vb, Form3.vb, and so on. (You can change the default name for forms in the Add New Item dialog box, or by using Solution Explorer.) The following table lists several practical uses for additional forms in your programs.

Form or forms	Description
Introductory form	A form that displays a welcome message, artwork, or copyright information when the program starts
Program instructions	A form that displays information and tips about how the program works
Dialog boxes	Custom dialog boxes that accept input and display output in the program
Document contents	A form that displays the contents of one or more files and artwork used in the program

How Forms Are Used

Visual Basic gives you significant flexibility when using forms. You can make all of the forms in a program visible at the same time, or you can load and unload forms as the program needs them. If you display more than one form at once, you can allow the user to switch between the forms or you can control the order in which the forms are used. A form that must be addressed when it is displayed on the screen is called a dialog box. Dialog boxes (called *modal* forms in Visual Basic 6) retain the focus until the user clicks OK, clicks Cancel, or otherwise dispatches it. To display an existing form as a dialog box in Visual Basic .NET, you open it using the ShowDialog method.

If you want to display a form that the user can switch away from, use the Show method instead of the ShowDialog method. In Visual Basic 6, forms that could lose the application focus were called *nonmodal* or *modeless* forms, and you may still hear these terms being used. Most applications for Microsoft Windows use regular, nonmodal forms when displaying information because they give the user more flexibility, so this style is the default when you create a new form in Visual Studio. Because forms are simply members of the System.Windows.Forms.Form class, you can also create and display forms using program code.

For information about how the default form is defined in a Visual Basic application, examine the code in the Windows Form Designer generated code section at the top of each new form—you have learned enough about program code at this point to understand some of this form code.

Working with Multiple Forms

The following exercises demonstrate how you can use a second form to display Help information for the Lucky Seven program that you worked with in the previous chapter. You'll add a second form using the Add Windows Form command on the Project menu, and you'll display the form in your program code using the ShowDialog method. The second form will display the Readme.txt file that you used to display usage and Help information in Chapter 14.

Add a second form

1   Start Visual Studio, and then open the Lucky Seven project in the c:\vbnetsbs\chap15\lucky seven folder.

    The Lucky Seven project is the same slot machine game that you worked with in the previous chapter, except that it doesn't include the deployment project you created.

2   Display the primary form (Form1.vb) in the Windows Forms Designer, if it isn't already visible.

3   Click the Add Windows Form command on the Project menu to add a second form to the project.

    You'll see this dialog box:

You use the Add New Item dialog box to add forms, classes, modules, and other components to your Visual Basic project. Although you selected the Add Windows Form command, forms aren't the only components listed here (the Windows Forms template is selected by default, however). The Add New Item dialog box is flexible enough so that you can pick other project components if you change your mind.

4　Type **HelpInfo.vb** in the Name text box, and then click Open.

A second form named HelpInfo.vb is added to the Lucky Seven project, and the form appears in Solution Explorer, as shown here:

tip

You can rename or delete form files using Solution Explorer. To rename a file, right-click the file and then click the Rename command. To remove a file from your project, right-click the file and then click the Exclude From Project command. To remove a file from your project and permanently delete it from your computer, select the file and press Delete.

Now you'll add some controls to the HelpInfo.vb form.

Label control

5　Use the Label control to draw a long label at the top of the HelpInfo.vb form. Make the label the width of the form, so it has room for a long line of text.

6　Use the TextBox control to create a text box object.

TextBox control

7　Set the Multiline property for the text box object to True, so that you can resize the object easily.

8　Resize the text box object so that it covers most of the form.

9　Use the Button control to create a button at the bottom of the form.

Button control

10　Set the properties shown on the following page for the objects on the HelpInfo.vb form.

Managing Forms

15

Object	Property	Setting
Label1	Text	"Operating Instructions for Lucky Seven Slot Machine"
TextBox1	Scrollbars	Vertical
	Text	(empty)
Button1	Text	"OK"
Form1	Text	"Help"

The HelpInfo.vb form looks like this:

Now you'll enter a line of program code for the HelpInfo.vb form's Button1_Click event procedure.

11 Double-click the OK button to display the Button1_Click event procedure in the Code Editor.

12 Type the following program statement:

```
Me.DialogResult = DialogResult.OK
```

The HelpInfo.vb form acts as a dialog box in this project because it will be opened in a Form1 event procedure with the ShowDialog method. After the user has read the Help information displayed by the dialog box, the OK button closes the form by setting the DialogResult property of the current form (Me) to DialogResult.OK, a Visual Basic constant that indicates the dialog box has been closed and should return a value of "OK" to the calling procedure. A more sophisticated dialog box might allow for other values to be returned by parallel button event procedures, such as DialogResult.Cancel, DialogResult.No, DialogResult.Yes, and DialogResult.Abort. When the DialogResult property is set, however, the form is automatically closed.

13 Scroll to the top of the program code in the Code Editor. Type the following Imports statement:

```
Imports System.IO
```

This statement incorporates the class library containing the StreamReader class into the project. The StreamReader class isn't specifically related to defining or using additional forms—I'm just using it as a quick way to add textual information to the new form I'm using.

14 Display the HelpInfo.vb form again, and then double-click the form background.

The HelpInfo_Load event procedure appears in the Code Editor. This is the event procedure that runs when the form is first loaded into memory and displayed on the screen.

15 Type the following program statements:

```
Dim StreamToDisplay As StreamReader
StreamToDisplay = New StreamReader("c:\vbnetsbs\chap14\readme.txt")
TextBox1.Text = StreamToDisplay.ReadToEnd
StreamToDisplay.Close()
TextBox1.Select(0, 0)
```

Rather than type the contents of the Help file into the Text property of the text box object (which would take a long time), I've used the StreamReader class to open, read, and display the Readme.txt file from Chapter 14 in the text box object. If you worked through Chapter 14, you'll remember the Readme.txt file as a product support document with usage information about the Lucky Seven program. It contains operating instructions, uninstall information, and general contact information.

The Stream-Reader class provides one way to access information in a text file.

The StreamReader class was introduced in Chapter 12, but you haven't seen it used in an actual code sample yet. StreamReader is a .NET Framework alternative to opening a text file using the Visual Basic FileOpen function. To use StreamReader you include the System.IO class library at the top of the code for your form. Next declare a variable of the type StreamReader to hold the contents of the text file (StreamToDisplay), and open the text file using a specific path. Finally, you read the contents of the text file into the StreamToDisplay variable using the ReadToEnd method, which reads all the text in the file from the current location (the beginning of the text file) to the end of the text file, and assigns it to the Text property of the text box object. The StreamReader.Close statement closes the text file, and the Select method removes the selection from the text in the text box object.

You're finished with the HelpInfo.vb form. Now add a button object and some code to the first form.

Display the second form using an event procedure

View Designer button

1   Click Form1.vb in Solution Explorer, and then click the View Designer button.

The Lucky Seven form appears in the development environment. Now you'll add a Help button to the lower right corner of the form.

Button control

2   Use the Button control to draw a small button object in the lower right corner of the form.

3   Use the Properties window to set the button object's Text property to **Help**. Your form should look like this:

4   Double-click the Help button to display the Button3_Click event procedure in the Code Editor.

5   Type the following program statements:

```
Dim frmHelpDialog As New HelpInfo()
frmHelpDialog.ShowDialog()
```

These two program statements demonstrate how to declare and display a second form in your program code. Unlike Visual Basic 6, which allowed you to simply reference a second form in code by using its name (a technique called *implicit instantiation*), Visual Basic .NET requires that you specifically declare a variable of the form's type before you use a second form. You created the class named HelpInfo when you added the HelpInfo.vb form to your project; now you are using it to declare a variable named frmHelpDialog using the Dim statement.

The second program statement uses the frmHelpDialog variable to open the HelpInfo.vb form as a dialog box using the ShowDialog method. Alternatively, you could have used the Show method to open the form, but then Visual Basic would not consider HelpInfo.vb to be a dialog box; the form would be a non-modal form that the user could switch away from and return to as needed. In addition, the DialogResult property in the HelpInfo.vb form's Button1_Click event procedure wouldn't close the HelpInfo form—the program statement

```
Me.Close
```

would be required instead. Keep the differences between modal and non-modal forms in mind as you build your own projects. There are differences between each type of form, and you'll find that each style provides a benefit to the user.

Now you'll run the program to see how a multiple form application works.

Run the program

The completed project is named Multiple Forms and is located in the c:\vbnetsbs\ chap15\multiple forms folder.

1 Click the Start button on the Standard toolbar.

The opening Lucky Seven form appears.

2 Click the Spin button 7 or 8 times to play the game a little.

Your screen will look like this:

Using the DialogResult Property in the Calling Form

Although I didn't demonstrate it in the Multiple Forms sample program, you can use the DialogResult property that you assigned in the dialog box to great effect in a Visual Basic program. As I mentioned, a more sophisticated dialog box might have offered additional buttons to the user—Cancel, Yes, No, Abort, and so on. Each dialog box button could have been associated with a different type of action in the main program. And in each of the dialog box's button event procedures, you could have assigned the DialogResult property for the form that corresponded to the button name, such as the following program statement:

```
Me.DialogResult = DialogResult.Cancel    'user clicked Cancel button
```

In the calling event procedure, in other words, in the Button3_Click event procedure of Form1, you can write additional program code to detect which button the user clicks in a dialog box. This information is passed back to the calling procedure through the DialogResult property, which is stored in the variable name you used to declare and instantiate the second form. For example, the following code in Form1 could be used to check whether the user clicked OK, Cancel, or another button in the dialog box. (The first two lines aren't new, but show the variable name you need to use.)

```
Dim frmHelpDialog As New HelpInfo()
frmHelpDialog.ShowDialog()

If frmHelpDialog.DialogResult = DialogResult.OK Then
    MsgBox("The user clicked OK")
ElseIf frmHelpDialog.DialogResult = DialogResult.Cancel Then
    MsgBox("The user clicked Cancel")
Else
    MsgBox("Another button was clicked")
End If
```

By using creative event procedures that declare, open, and process dialog box choices, you can add any number of forms to your programs, and you can create a user interface that looks professional and feels flexible and user friendly.

3   Click the Help button on the first form.

Visual Basic opens the second form in the project, HelpInfo.vb, and displays the Readme.txt file in the text box object. The form looks like this:

4   Use the vertical scroll bar to view the entire Readme file.

5   Click the OK button to close the HelpInfo.vb form.

The form closes and the first form becomes active again.

6   Click the Spin button a few more times, and then click the Help button again.

The HelpInfo.vb form appears again and is fully functional. Notice that you cannot activate the first form while the second form is active. This behavior is the case because the second form is a dialog box or modal form—you must address the dialog box before you can continue with the program.

7   Click the OK button, and then click the End button on the first form.

The program stops and the development environment returns.

Positioning Forms on the Windows Desktop

You have learned how to add forms to your Visual Basic project and how to open and close forms using program code. But which tool or setting determines the placement of forms on the Windows desktop when your program runs? As you may have noticed, the placement of forms on the screen at runtime is different from the placement of forms at design time within the Visual Studio development environment. In this section, you'll learn how to position your forms just where you want them at runtime, so that the user sees just what you want them to see.

In Visual Basic 6, the placement of forms at runtime was controlled by a graphical tool called the Form Layout window. You dragged a tiny form icon within the Form Layout window to the place where you wanted the final form to appear at runtime, and Visual Basic recorded the screen coordinates you specified. In Visual Basic .NET, there is no Form Layout window, but you can still position your forms precisely on the Windows desktop. The tool you use isn't a graphical layout window, but a new property named DesktopBounds that is maintained for each form in your project. DesktopBounds can be read or set at runtime only, and it takes the dimensions of a rectangle as an argument—in other words, two point pairs that specify the coordinates of the upper left corner of the window and the lower right corner of the window. The coordinate points are expressed in pixels, and the distances to the upper left and lower right corners are measured from the upper left corner of the screen. (You'll learn more about the Visual Basic coordinate system in the next chapter.) Because the DesktopBounds property takes a rectangle structure as an argument, it allows you to set both the *size* and the *location* of the form on the Windows desktop.

In addition to the DesktopBounds property, there is a simpler mechanism for setting the location of a form that you can set at design time, although it has fewer capabilities. This mechanism is the StartPosition property, which positions a form on the Windows desktop using one of the following property settings: Manual, CenterScreen, WindowsDefaultLocation, WindowsDefaultBounds, or CenterParent. The default setting for the StartPosition property is Windows-DefaultLocation. If you accept this setting, Visual Basic will let Windows position the form on the desktop where it chooses—usually the upper left corner of the screen.

If you set StartPosition to Manual, you can manually set the location of the form using the Location property, where the first number (x) is the distance from the left edge of the screen and the second number (y) is the distance from the top border of the screen. (You'll learn more about the Location property in the next chapter.) If you set StartPosition to CenterScreen, the form will appear in the middle of the Windows desktop. (This is my preferred StartPosition setting.) If you set StartPosition to WindowsDefaultBounds, the form will be resized to fit the standard window size for a Windows application, and then the form will be opened in the default location for a new Windows form. If you set StartPosition to CenterParent, the form will be centered within the bounds of the parent form. This final setting is especially useful in so-called MDI (multiple document interface) applications in which parent and child windows have a special relationship.

The following exercises demonstrate how you can set the StartPosition and DesktopBounds properties to position a Visual Basic form. You can use either technique to locate your forms on the Windows desktop at runtime.

Use the StartPosition property to position the form

1   Click the Close Solution command on the File menu, and then create a new Visual Basic Windows Application project named **My Desktop Bounds** in the c:\vbnetsbs\chap15 folder.

2   If the project's form isn't visible, display it now.

3   Click the form to display its properties in the Properties window.

4   Set the StartPosition property to CenterScreen.

Changing the StartPosition property to CenterScreen directs Visual Basic to display the form in the center of the Windows desktop when you run the program.

5   Click the Start button to run the application.

Visual Basic loads the form and displays it in the middle of the screen, as shown here:

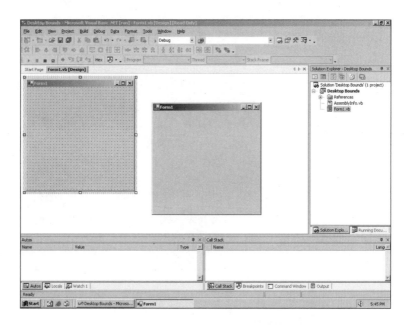

6   Click the Close button on the form to stop the program.

The development environment returns.

7   Set the StartPosition property to Manual.

The Manual property directs Visual Basic to position the form based on the values in the Location property.

8   Set the Location property to **100, 50**.

The Location property specifies the position of the upper left corner of the form.

9   Click the Start button to run the application.

Visual Basic loads the form, and then displays it on the Windows desktop 100 pixels from the left and 50 pixels from the top:

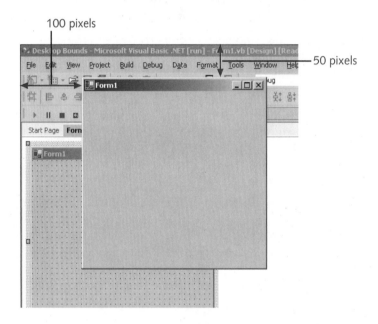

10   Click the Close button on the form to close the program.

You've experimented with a few basic StartPosition settings for positioning a form. Now you'll use the DesktopBounds property to size and position a second form window while the program is running. You'll also learn how to create a new form at runtime without using the Add Windows Form command on the Project menu.

Set the DesktopBounds property

Button control

1   Use the Button control to add a button object to the form, and then change the Text property of the button object to **Create Form**.

2   Double-click the Create Form button to display the Button1_Click event procedure in the Code Editor.

3 Type the following program code:

```
'Create a second form named form2
Dim form2 As New Form()

'Define the Text property and border style of the form
form2.Text = "My New Form"
form2.FormBorderStyle = FormBorderStyle.FixedDialog

'Specify that the position of the form will be set manually
form2.StartPosition = FormStartPosition.Manual

'Declare a Rectangle structure to hold the form dimensions
'Upper left corner of form (200, 100)
'Width and height of form (300, 250)
Dim Form2Rect As New Rectangle(200, 100, 300, 250)

'Set the bounds of the form using the Rectangle object
form2.DesktopBounds = Form2Rect

'Display the form as a modal dialog box
form2.ShowDialog()
```

When the user clicks the Create Form button, this event procedure creates a new form with the title "My New Form" and a fixed border style. To create a new form using program code, you use the Dim statement and specify a variable name for the form and the Form class, which is automatically included in projects as part of the System.Windows.Forms namespace. You can then set properties such as Text, FormBorderStyle, StartPosition, and DesktopBounds. The StartPosition property is set to FormStartPosition.Manual to indicate that the position will be set manually. The DesktopBounds property sizes and positions the form and requires an argument of type Rectangle. The Rectangle type is a structure that defines a rectangular region and is automatically included in Visual Basic projects. Using the Dim statement, the Form2Rect variable is declared of type Rectangle and initialized with the form position and size values. At the bottom of the event procedure, the new form is opened as a dialog box using the ShowDialog method.

The complete Desktop Bounds program is located in the c:\vbnetsbs\ chap15\desktop bounds folder.

4 Click the Start button to run the program.

Visual Basic displays the first form on the desktop.

5 Click the Create Form button.

Managing Forms

15

Visual Basic displays the My New Form dialog box with the size and position you specified in the program code:

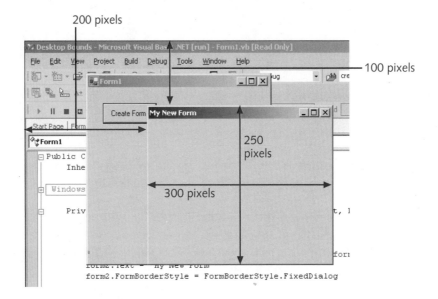

Notice that you can't resize the second form. This is because the FormBorderStyle was set to FixedDialog.

6   Close the second form, and then close the first form.

Your program stops running and the development environment returns.

Minimizing, Maximizing, and Restoring Windows

In addition to establishing the size and location of a Visual Basic form, you can minimize a form on the Windows taskbar, maximize a form so that it takes up the entire screen, or restore a form to its normal shape. These settings can be changed at design time, or at runtime based on current program conditions.

To allow a form to be both minimized and maximized, first verify that the form's minimize and maximize boxes are available. Using the Properties window or program code, specify the following settings:

```
MaximizeBox = True
MinimizeBox = True
```

Then, in program code or using the Properties window, set the WindowState property for the form to Minimized, Maximized, or Normal. (In code you need to add the FormWindowState constant, as shown below.) For example, the following program statement minimizes a form and places it on the Windows taskbar:

```
WindowState = FormWindowState.Minimized
```

If you want to control the maximum or minimum size a form can be, set the MaximumSize or MinimumSize properties at design time using the Properties window. To set the MaximumSize or MinimumSize in code, you will need to use a Size structure similar to the Rectangle structure used in the previous exercise:

```
Dim FormSize As New Size(400, 300)
MaximumSize = FormSize
```

Adding Controls to a Form at Runtime

Throughout this book, you have added objects to forms using the Toolbox and the Windows Forms Designer. However, you can also create Visual Basic objects on forms at runtime, either to save you development time, or to respond to a current need in the program. For example, you might want to generate a simple dialog box containing objects to process input.

Creating objects is very simple, because the fundamental classes that define controls in the Toolbox are available to all programs. Objects are declared and instantiated using the Dim and New keywords. The following program statement shows how this process works when a new button object named button1 is created on a form:

```
Dim button1 as New Button()
```

After you create an object at runtime, you also can use code to customize it with property settings. In particular, it is useful to specify a name and location for the object, because you didn't specify them manually using the Windows Forms Designer. For example, the following program statements configure the Text and Location properties for the new button1 object:

```
button1.Text = "Click Me"
button1.Location = New Point(20, 25)
```

Finally, your code must add a new object to the Controls collection of the form where it will be created, so that it becomes visible and is active in the program:

```
form2.Controls.Add(button1)
```

You can use this process to add any control in the Toolbox to a Visual Basic form. The class name you use to declare and instantiate the control is a variation of the name that appears in the Name property for each control.

The following exercise demonstrates how you can add a Label control and a Button control to a new form at runtime. The new form will act as a dialog box that displays the current date.

Create new Label and Button controls

1   Click the Close Solution command on the File menu, and then create a new Visual Basic Windows Application project named **My Add Controls** in the c:\vbnetsbs\chap15 folder.

2   Display the form (Form1.vb), and then open the Properties window.

ab

Button control

3   Use the Button control to add a button object to the form, and then change the Text property of the button object to **Display Date**.

4   Double-click the Display Date button to display the Button1_Click event procedure in the Code Editor.

5   Type the following program code:

```
'Declare new form and control objects
Dim form2 As New Form()
Dim lblDate As New Label()
Dim btnCancel As New Button()

'Set label properties
lblDate.Text = "Current date is: " & DateString
lblDate.Size = New Size(150, 50)
lblDate.Location = New Point(80, 50)

'Set button properties
btnCancel.Text = "Cancel"
btnCancel.Location = New Point(110, 100)

'Set form properties
form2.Text = "Current Date"
form2.CancelButton = btnCancel
form2.StartPosition = FormStartPosition.CenterScreen

'Add new objects to Controls collection
form2.Controls.Add(lblDate)
form2.Controls.Add(btnCancel)

'Display form as a dialog box
form2.ShowDialog()
```

This event procedure displays a new form on the screen containing a label object and a button object. The label object contains the current date as recorded in your computer's system clock (returned through DateString), and the Text property of the button object is set to "Cancel". As I mentioned earlier, you add controls to a form by declaring a variable to hold the control, setting object properties, and adding the objects to the Controls collection. In this exercise I also demonstrate the Size and CancelButton properties for the first time. The Size property requires a Size structure. The New keyword is used to immediately create the Size structure. The CancelButton property allows the user to close the dialog box by pressing Esc or clicking the Cancel button (both actions are considered equivalent).

The complete Add Controls program is located in the c:\vbnetsbs\ chap15\add controls folder.

6 Click the Start button to run the program.

Visual Basic displays the first form on the desktop.

7 Click the Display Date button.

Visual Basic displays the second form on the desktop, and this form contains the label object and the button object that you defined using program code. The label object contains the current date.

8 Click the Cancel button to close the new form.

9 Click the Display Date button again.

The new form appears as it did the first time.

10 Press Esc to close the form.

Because you set the CancelButton property to the btnCancel object, both actions (clicking Cancel and pressing Esc) produce the same result.

11 Click the Close button on the form to end the program.

The program stops and the development environment returns.

Organizing Controls on a Form

When you add controls to a form programmatically, it takes a bit of trial and error to position the new objects so that they are aligned properly and look nice. After all, you don't have the Windows Forms Designer to help you—just the (x, y) coordinates of the Location and Size properties, which are clumsy values to work with unless you have a knack for two-dimensional thinking or have the time to run the program repeatedly to verify the placement of your objects.

Fortunately, Visual Basic .NET contains several new property settings that allow you to organize objects on the form at runtime. These include the Anchor property, which forces an object on the form to remain at a constant distance from the specified edges of the form, and the Dock property, which forces an object to remain attached to one edge of the form. You can use the Anchor and Dock properties at design time, but I find that they are also very useful when used to programmatically align objects at runtime. The following exercise shows you how these properties work.

Anchor and Dock objects at runtime

1 Click the Close Solution command on the File menu, and then create a new Visual Basic Windows Application project named **My Anchor and Dock** in the c:\vbnetsbs\chap15 folder.

2 Display the form.

3 Click the PictureBox control, and then add a picture box object in the top middle of the form.

PictureBox control

4 Use the TextBox control to create a text box object.

TextBox control

5 Set the Multiline property for the text box object to True so that you can resize the object appropriately.

6 Resize the text box object so that it covers most of the bottom half of the form.

7 Click the Button control and add a button object to the lower right corner of the form.

Button control

8 Set the following properties for the form and the objects on it:

Object	Property	Setting
PictureBox1	Image	"c:\vbnetsbs\chap16\sun.ico"
	SizeMode	StretchImage
Button1	Text	"Align Now"
Form1	Text	"Anchor and Dock Samples"

Your form should look similar to this:

9 Double-click the Align Now button to open the Button1_Click event procedure in the Code Editor.

10 Type the following program code:

```
PictureBox1.Dock = DockStyle.Top
TextBox1.Anchor = AnchorStyles.Bottom Or _
    AnchorStyles.Left Or AnchorStyles.Right Or _
    AnchorStyles.Top
Button1.Anchor = AnchorStyles.Bottom Or _
    AnchorStyles.Right
```

When this event procedure is executed, the Dock property of the Picture-Box1 object is used to dock the picture box to the top of the form. This forces the top edge of the picture box object to touch and adhere to the top edge of the form—much like Visual Studio's own docking feature works in the development environment. The only surprising behavior here is that the picture box object is also resized so that its sides adhere to the left and right edges of the form. You'll see this behavior in the following steps.

Next, the Anchor property for the TextBox1 and the Button1 objects is used. The Anchor property will maintain the current distance from the specified edges of the form, even if the form is resized. Note that the Anchor property maintains the object's current distance from the specified edges—it doesn't attach the object to the specified edges, unless it is already there. In this example, I specify that the TextBox1 object should be anchored to all four edges of the form (bottom, left, right, and top). I use the Or operator to combine my edge selections. For the Button1 object, I anchor to the bottom and right edges of the form.

The complete Anchor and Dock program is located in the c:\vbnetsbs\ chap15\anchor and dock folder.

11 Click the Start button to run the program.

The form appears, just as you designed it.

12 Move the mouse pointer to the lower right corner of the form until it changes into a Resize pointer, and then enlarge the size of the form.

Notice that the size and position of the objects on the form do not change.

13 Resize the form back to its original size.

14 Click the Align Now button on the form.

The picture box object is now docked to the top edge of the form. The picture box is also resized so that its sides adhere to the left and right edges of the form, as shown here:

Notice that the Sun icon in the picture box is now distorted, which is a result of the docking process.

15 Enlarge the size of the form again.

As you resize the form, the picture box and the text box objects are also resized. Since the text box is anchored on all four sides, the distance between the edges of the form and the text box remains constant. During the resizing activity, it also becomes apparent that the button object is being repositioned. Although the distance between the button object and the top and left edges of the form changes, the distance to the bottom and right edges remains constant.

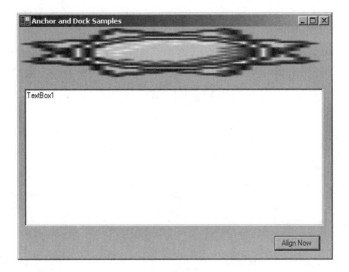

16   Experiment with the Anchor and Dock properties for a while. When you're finished, click the Close button on the form to end the program.

You now have the skills necessary to add new forms to a project, position them on the Windows desktop, populate them with new controls, and align the controls using program code. You've gained a number of useful skills for working with forms in a Visual Basic program.

One Step Further: Specifying the Startup Object

If your project contains more than one form, which form is loaded and displayed first when you run the application? Although Visual Basic normally loads the first form that you created in a project (Form1.vb), you can actually change the form that Visual Basic loads first by adjusting a setting in the project's Property Pages dialog box. Alternatively, you can direct Visual Basic to execute a procedure named Sub Main first, which can declare public variables and load one or more forms after specific tests have been made. By modifying which form or procedure is run first, you can create a truly custom and adaptable user interface for your program.

The following exercise shows you how to change the first form, or *startup form*, that is displayed by Visual Basic when you run a program. You'll also learn how to set the startup object to a Sub Main procedure in your project.

Switch from Form1 to Form2

1   Click the Close Solution command on the File menu, and then create a new Visual Basic Windows Application project named **My Startup Form** in the c:\vbnetsbs\chap15 folder.

2   Display Form1.vb, if it isn't already visible.

3   Click the Add Windows Form command on the Project menu.

You'll add a new form to the project to demonstrate how switching the startup form works.

4   Click Open to add the second form (Form2.vb) to Solution Explorer.

5   Click the My Startup Form project icon in Solution Explorer, and then click Properties on the Project menu.

The Startup Form Property Pages dialog box appears, as shown here:

The Property Pages dialog box lets you adjust property settings that apply to the entire project. In this case, you'll use the Startup Object drop-down list box to specify a new startup form.

6   Click the Startup Object drop-down list box, and then click Form2.

Visual Basic changes the startup form in your project from Form1 to Form2. When the program runs, Form2 will be displayed, and Form1 will only appear if it is opened using the Show or ShowDialog method.

7   Click OK to close the Property Pages dialog box.

8   Click the Start button on the toolbar.

The program runs in the development environment, and Form2 appears.

9   Click the Close button on the form to end the program.

Now you'll add a Sub Main procedure to the project in a module, and you'll set the startup object to Sub Main so that execution begins in the standard module.

Start program execution with Sub Main

1   Click the Add New Item command on the Project menu, click the Module template, and then click Open to add the Module1.vb module to Solution Explorer.

2   If Module1 doesn't open in the Code Editor, select Module1.vb in Solution Explorer and then click the View Code button.

3   Type the following code between the Module and End Module program statements:

```
Public MyForm1 As New Form1()
Public MyForm2 As New Form2()
Public Sub Main()
    MsgBox("This is Sub Main")
    'place additional program code here
    MyForm1.ShowDialog()
End Sub
```

When you add a Sub Main procedure to your project, you must add it to a standard module. The Sub Main procedure must be declared as Public, and it doesn't accept any arguments (except in a console application, described shortly). Note that in addition to defining the Sub Main procedure, which displays a message box and then opens Form1 as a dialog box, I also declared two Public variables to represent Form1 and Form2 in the project. The New keyword is used to create instances of the Form1 and Form2 objects. In Visual Basic 6, form objects were automatically available in modules and it wasn't necessary to create new instances.

4   Click the My Startup Form project icon in Solution Explorer, and then click Properties on the Project menu.

The Startup Form Property Pages dialog box appears.

5   Click the Startup Object drop-down list box, and then click Sub Main.

Visual Basic changes the startup object in your project from Form2 to Sub Main. When the program runs, the Sub Main procedure will be executed first, and then the Form1 window will be displayed.

6   Click OK to close the Property Pages dialog box.

7   Click the Start button on the toolbar.

The program runs in the development environment, and the Sub Main procedure is executed. You'll see this message box:

15

Managing Forms

8   Click OK in the message box.

The Sub Main procedure closes the message box and displays Form1 as a new dialog box in the program.

9   Click the Close button on the form to end the program.

Although this demonstration exercise was fairly simple, you can see that Visual Basic is quite flexible in how you start your programs. You can specify a different startup form to begin your application, or you can add a Sub Main procedure to your project so that execution begins directly in program code.

tip

If you want to write a Visual Basic application that displays no graphical user interface at all, consider writing a *console application*, a new project type in Visual Studio .NET that processes input and output using a command line console (a character-based window also known as the command prompt). For more information about writing console applications, search for "Building Console Applications" in the Visual Basic online Help.

Chapter 15 Quick Reference

To	Do this
Add new forms to a program	Click the down arrow to the right of the Add New Item button on the Standard toolbar, and then click Add Windows Form. *or* On the Project menu, click Add Windows Form, and then click Open.
Create and modify a new form using program code	Create the form using the Dim and New keywords and the Form class, and then set any necessary properties. For example: `Dim form2 As New Form()` `form2.Text = "My New Form"`
Display a form on the screen	Use the Show or ShowDialog method. For example: `form2.ShowDialog()`

To	Do this
Position a startup form on the Windows desktop	Set the StartPosition property to one of the available options such as CenterScreen or CenterParent.

Size and position a startup form on the Windows desktop using code	Set the StartPosition to Manual, declare a Rectangle structure that defines the form's size and position, and then use the DesktopBounds property to size and position the form on the desktop. For example:
	``vb
	form2.StartPosition = FormStartPosition.Manual
	Dim Form2Rect As New Rectangle _
	  (200, 100, 300, 250)
	form2.DesktopBounds = Form2Rect
	``

Minimize, Maximize, or Restore a form at runtime	Set the MaximizeBox and MinimizeBox properties for the form to True in design mode, to allow for maximize and minimize operations. In the program code, set the form's WindowState property to Form-WindowState.Minimized, FormWindowState-.Maximized, or FormWindowState.Normal when you want to change the window state of the form.

Add controls to a form at runtime	Create a control of the desired type, set its properties, and then add it to the form's Controls collection. For example:
	``vb
	Dim button1 as New Button()
	button1.Text = "Click Me"
	button1.Location = New Point(20, 25)
	form2.Controls.Add(button1)
	``

Anchor an object a set distance from the specified edges of the form	Set the Anchor property of the object and specify the edges you want to remain a constant distance from. Use the Or operator when specifying multiple edges. For example:
	``vb
	Button1.Anchor = AnchorStyles.Bottom Or _
	  AnchorStyles.Right
	``

Dock an object to one of the form's edges	Set the Dock property of the object and specify the edge you want the object to be attached to. For example:
	``vb
	PictureBox1.Dock = DockStyle.Top
	``

Specify the startup object in a project	Click the project icon in Solution Explorer, and then click Properties on the Project menu. Specify the startup object in the Startup Object drop-down list box (choose either a form in the project or the Sub Main procedure).

15

Managing Forms

16

Adding Graphics and Animation Effects

In this chapter you will learn how to:

- ✔ *Use the System.Drawing namespace to add graphics to your forms.*
- ✔ *Create animation effects on your forms.*
- ✔ *Expand or shrink objects on your form at runtime.*
- ✔ *Change the transparency of a form.*

For many developers, adding artwork and special effects to an application is the most exciting—and addictive—part of programming. Fortunately, creating impressive and useful graphical effects with Microsoft Visual Basic .NET is both satisfying and easy. In this chapter, you'll learn how to add interesting "bells and whistles" to your programs. You'll learn how to create compelling artwork on a form, create simple animation effects using PictureBox and Timer controls, and expand or contract controls at runtime using the Height and Width properties. When you've finished, you'll have many of the skills you need to create the ultimate user interface.

Upgrade Notes:
What's New in Visual Basic .NET?

If you're experienced with Visual Basic 6, you'll notice some new features in Visual Basic .NET, including the following:

■ In Visual Basic 6, you used the Line and Shape controls to create simple lines, rectangles, and circles on your forms. In Visual Basic .NET, no drawing controls are provided in the Toolbox. Instead, you are encouraged to use the GDI+ graphics services directly through the System.Drawing namespace.

■ The Visual Basic 6 keywords Circle, Line, and PSet have been replaced by two methods—DrawEllipse and DrawLine—and the Point structure in the System.Drawing.Graphics class.

■ The default coordinate system in Visual Basic is now pixels rather than twips.

■ In Visual Basic 6, many controls could be relocated or "animated" on the form by rapidly calling the control's Move method. Visual Basic .NET controls don't have a Move method, but they can still be relocated quickly if you update the control's Left, Top, or Location property, or if you use the SetBounds method.

■ Visual Basic .NET controls continue to support drag-and-drop effects, but they handle them in a different way. For example, although Visual Basic .NET continues support for the DragDrop event, the DragIcon and DragMode properties are no longer available.

■ Visual Studio .NET can work with more image formats than Visual Basic 6. In particular, the System.Drawing.Imaging namespace contains functions to work with the following image formats: BMP, EMF, EXIF, GIF, Icon, JPEG, MemoryBMP, PNG, TIFF, and WMF.

Adding Artwork Using the System.Drawing Namespace

You've already learned how to add bitmaps, icons, and Windows metafiles to a form by creating picture box objects. Adding ready-made artwork to your programs is easy in Visual Basic, and you've had practice doing it in almost every chapter. Now you'll learn how to create original artwork on your forms by using the GDI+ functions in the System.Drawing namespace, a new API (application programming interface) for creating graphics. The images you create can add color, shape, and texture to your forms, and they are powerful and easy to use.

Using a Form's Coordinate System

The first thing to learn about creating graphics is the layout of the form's pre-defined coordinate system. In Visual Basic, each form has its own coordinate system. The coordinate system's starting point, or *origin,* is the upper left corner of a form. The default coordinate system is made up of rows and columns of device-independent picture elements, or *pixels,* which represent the smallest points that you can locate, or *address,* on a Visual Basic form.

The Visual Basic coordinate system is a grid of rows and columns on the form.

In the Visual Basic coordinate system, rows of pixels are aligned to the x-axis (horizontal axis) and columns of pixels are aligned to the y-axis (vertical axis). You define locations in the coordinate system by identifying the intersection of a row and column with the notation (x, y). The (x, y) coordinates of the upper left corner of a form are always $(0, 0)$. The following illustration shows how the location for a picture box object on the form is described in the Visual Basic coordinate system:

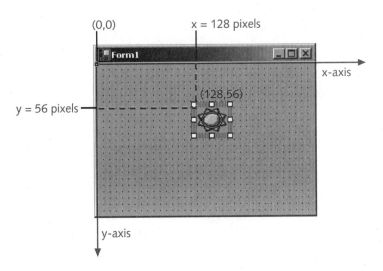

Visual Basic works along with your computer's video display driver software to determine how pixels are displayed on the form, and how shapes such as lines, rectangles, curves, and circles are displayed. Occasionally, more than one pixel is turned on to display a particular shape, such as the line drawing shown in the following illustration. The logic to handle this type of rendering isn't your responsibility—it is handled by your display adapter and the drawing routines in the GDI+ graphics library. This illustration shows a zoomed-in view of the distortion or jagged edges you sometimes see in Visual Basic and Windows applications:

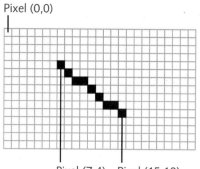

The System.Drawing.Graphics Class

The System.Drawing namespace includes numerous classes for creating artwork in your programs. In this section, you'll learn a little about the System.Drawing.Graphics class, which provides methods and properties for drawing shapes on your forms. You can learn about the other classes by referring to the Visual Basic .NET online Help.

Whether you're creating simple shapes or building complex drawings, it is important to be able to render many of the standard geometric shapes in your programs. The following table lists several of the fundamental drawing shapes and the method you use in the System.Drawing.Graphics class to create them.

Shape	Method	Description
Line	DrawLine	Simple line with two points
Rectangle	DrawRectangle	Rectangle or square with four points
Arc	DrawArc	Curved line with two points (a portion of an ellipse)
Circle/Ellipse	DrawEllipse	Elliptical shape that is "bounded" by a rectangle

Shape	Method	Description
Polygon	DrawPolygon	Complex shape with a variable number of points and sides (stored in an array)
Curve	DrawCurve	A curved line that passes through a variable number of points (stored in an array). Also called a cardinal spline.
Bézier splines	DrawBezier	A curve drawn using four points (points two and three are "control" points)

In addition to the methods listed above, which create empty or "non-filled" shapes, there are several methods that draw shapes which are automatically filled with color. These methods usually have a "Fill" prefix, such as FillRectangle, FillEllipse, and FillPolygon.

When you use a graphics method in the System.Drawing.Graphics class, you need to create a Graphics object in your code to represent the class, and either a Pen or Brush object to indicate the attributes of the shape you want to draw, such as line width and fill color. The Pen object is passed as one of the arguments to the methods that aren't filled with color. The Brush object is passed as an argument when a fill color is desired. For example, the following call to the DrawLine method uses a Pen object and four integer values to draw a line that starts at pixel (20, 30) and ends at pixel (100, 80). The Graphics object is declared using the name GraphicsFun and the Pen object is declared using the name PenColor.

```
Dim GraphicsFun As System.Drawing.Graphics
Dim PenColor As New System.Drawing.Pen(System.Drawing.Color.Red)
GraphicsFun = Me.CreateGraphics
GraphicsFun.DrawLine(PenColor, 20, 30, 100, 80)
```

The syntax for the DrawLine method is important, but also note the three lines above it, which are required to use a method in the System.Drawing.Graphics class. You must create variables to represent both the Graphics and Pen objects, and the Graphics variable needs to be instantiated using the CreateGraphics method for the Windows Form. Note that the System.Drawing.Graphics namespace is included in your project automatically—you don't need to include an Imports statement in your code to declare the necessary class.

Using the Form's Paint Event

If you test the previous DrawLine method in a program, you'll notice that the line you created only lasts or *persists* on the form as long as nothing else covers it up. If a dialog box appears on the form momentarily and covers the line, when the dialog box disappears the line will no longer be visible. The line will also disappear if you minimize the form window and then maximize it again. To address this shortcoming, you need to place your graphics code in the form's Paint event procedure, so that each time the form is refreshed, the graphics will be repainted, too.

In the following exercise, you'll create three shapes on a form using the form's Paint event procedure. The shapes you draw will continue to persist even if the form is covered or minimized.

Create line, rectangle, and ellipse shapes

1   Start Visual Studio and create a new Visual Basic Windows Application project named **My Draw Shapes** in the c:\vbnetsbs\chap16 folder.

2   Resize the form so that it is longer and wider than the default form size.

You'll need a little extra space to create the graphics shapes. You won't be using any Toolbox controls, however. You'll create the shapes by placing program code in the form's Form1_Paint event procedure.

3   Set the Text property of Form1 to **Draw Shapes**.

4   Click the View Code button in Solution Explorer to display the Code Editor.

5   In the Class Name drop-down list box, click Base Class Events.

Base Class Events is the list of events in your project associated with the Form1 object.

6   In the Method Name drop-down list box, click the Paint event.

7   The Form1_Paint event procedure appears in the Code Editor.

This is the place where you type program code that should be executed when Visual Basic refreshes the form.

8   Type the following program code:

```
'Prepare GraphicsFun variable for graphics calls
Dim GraphicsFun As System.Drawing.Graphics
GraphicsFun = Me.CreateGraphics

'Use a red pen color to draw a line and an ellipse
Dim PenColor As New System.Drawing.Pen(System.Drawing.Color.Red)
GraphicsFun.DrawLine(PenColor, 20, 30, 100, 80)
GraphicsFun.DrawEllipse(PenColor, 10, 120, 200, 160)

'Use a green brush color to create a filled rectangle
Dim BrushColor As New SolidBrush(Color.Green)
GraphicsFun.FillRectangle(BrushColor, 150, 10, 250, 100)
```

Graphics and Animation

This sample event procedure draws three graphic shapes on your form—a red line, a red ellipse, and a green filled rectangle. To enable graphics programming, the routine declares a variable named GraphicsFun in the code, and uses the CreateGraphics method to activate or instantiate the variable. The PenColor variable of type System.Drawing.Pen is used to set the drawing color in the line and ellipse, and the BrushColor variable of type SolidBrush is used to set the fill color in the rectangle. These examples are obviously just the tip of the graphics library iceberg—there are many more shapes, colors, and variations that you could create by using the methods in the System.Drawing.Graphics class.

The complete Draw Shapes program is located in the c:\vbnetsbs\ chap16\draw shapes folder.

9 Click the Start button to run the program.

Visual Basic loads the form and executes the form's Paint event. Your form will look like this:

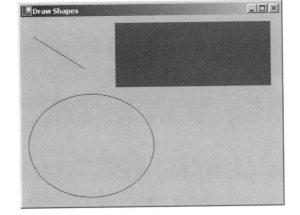

10 Minimize the form, and then restore it again.

The form's Paint event is executed again and the graphics shapes are refreshed on the form.

11 Click the Close button to end the program.

Now you're ready to move on to some simple animation effects.

Adding Animation to Your Programs

Animation makes objects "come alive" in a program.

Displaying bitmaps and drawing shapes adds visual interest to a program, but for programmers, the king of graphical effects has always been animation. *Animation* is the simulation of movement produced by rapidly displaying a series of related images on the screen. Real animation involves moving objects programmatically, and it often involves changing the size or shape of the images along the way.

In this section, you'll learn how to add simple animation to your programs. You'll learn how to update a picture box's Top and Left properties, control the rate of animation using a timer object, and sense the edge of your form's window.

Moving Objects on the Form

In Visual Basic 6, a special method named Move allowed you to move objects in the coordinate system. The Move method is no longer supported by Visual Basic .NET controls; however, you can use the following method and properties instead:

Keyword	Description
Left	This property can be used to move an object horizontally (left or right)
Top	This property can be used to move an object vertically (up or down)
Location	This property can be used to move an object to the specified location
SetBounds	This method sets the boundaries of an object to the specified location and size

The following sections discuss how you can use the Left, Top, and Location properties to move objects. For additional information about the SetBounds method, search for the SetBounds keyword in the Visual Basic online Help.

The Left and Top properties allow you to move an object. To move an object sideways in a horizontal direction, use the Left property. Left takes the syntax

```
object.Left = horizontal
```

where *object* is the name of the object on the form that you want to move, and *horizontal* is the new horizontal or x-axis coordinate of the left edge of the object, measured in pixels. For example, the following program statement moves a picture box object to a location 300 pixels to the right of the left window edge:

```
PictureBox1.Left = 300
```

To move a relative distance to the left or right, you would add or subtract pixels from the current Left property setting. For example, to move an object 50 pixels to the right, you would add 50 to the Left property, as follows:

```
PictureBox1.Left = PictureBox1.Left + 50
```

In a similar way, you can change the vertical location of an object on a form by setting the Top property. The syntax for the Top property is

```
object.Top = vertical
```

where *object* is the name of the object on the form that you want to move, and *vertical* is the new vertical or y-axis coordinate of the top edge of the object, measured in pixels. For example, the following program statement moves a picture box object to a location 150 pixels below the window's title bar:

```
PictureBox1.Top = 150
```

Relative movements up or down are easily made by adding or subtracting pixels from the current Top property setting. For example, to move 30 pixels in a downward direction, you would add 30 to the current Top property, as follows:

```
PictureBox1.Top = PictureBox1.Top + 30
```

The Location Property

To move an object in both vertical and horizontal directions, it is easy enough to use a combination of the Left and Top property settings. For example, to relocate a picture box object to the (*x*, *y*) coordinates (300, 200), you would enter the following program code:

```
PictureBox1.Left = 300
PictureBox1.Top = 200
```

However, the designers of Visual Basic .NET don't recommend using two program statements to relocate an object if you plan to make numerous object movements in a program (for example, if you plan to move an object hundreds or thousands of times during an elaborate animation effect). Instead, Microsoft recommends using the Location property with the syntax

```
object.Location = New Point(horizontal, vertical)
```

where *object* is the name of the object, *horizontal* is the horizontal x-axis coordinate, *vertical* is the vertical y-axis coordinate, and Point is a structure identifying the pixel location for the upper left corner of the object. For example, the following program statement moves a picture box object to an (*x*, *y*) coordinate of (300, 200):

```
PictureBox1.Location = New Point(300, 200)
```

To perform a relative movement using the Location property, the Location.X and Location.Y properties are needed. For example, the program statement

```
PictureBox1.Location = New Point(PictureBox1.Location.X - 50, _
   PictureBox1.Location.Y - 40)
```

moves the picture box object 50 pixels left and 40 pixels up on the form. Although this construction seems a bit unwieldy, it is the recommended way to relocate objects in relative movements on your form at runtime.

Creating Animation Using a Timer Object

A timer object sets the pace of movement in a program.

The trick to creating animation in a program is placing one or more Location property updates in a timer event procedure so that at set intervals the timer will cause one or more objects to drift across the screen. In Chapter 7, you learned to use a timer object to update a simple clock utility every second so that it displayed the correct time. When you create animation, you set the Interval property of the timer to a much faster rate—1/5 second (200 milliseconds), 1/10 second (100 milliseconds), or less. The exact rate you choose depends on how fast you want the animation to run.

Another trick is to use the Top and Left properties and the size of the form to "sense" the edges of the form. Using these values in an event procedure will let you stop the animation (disable the timer) when an object reaches the edge of the form. Using the Top property, the Left property, form size properties, and an If...Then or Select Case decision structure, you can make an object appear to bounce off one or more edges of the form.

You can create animation by using the Location property.

The following exercise demonstrates how you can animate a picture box containing a Sun icon (Sun.ico) by using the Location property and a timer object. In this exercise, you'll use the Top property to detect the top of the form, and you'll use the Size.Height property to detect the bottom edge of the form. The Sun icon will move back and forth between these extremes each time you click a button.

Animate a Sun icon on your form

1   Click the Close Solution command on the File menu, and then create a new Visual Basic Windows Application project named **My Moving Icon** in the c:\vbnetsbs\chap16 folder.

2   Using the Button control, draw two button objects in the lower left corner of the form.

Button control

3   Using the PictureBox control, draw a small rectangular picture box object in the lower right corner of the form. This is the object that you will animate in the program.

PictureBox control

4   Double-click the Timer control on the Windows Forms tab of the Toolbox to add it to the component tray below the form.

Timer control

The timer object will be the mechanism that controls the pace of the animation. Recall that the timer object itself isn't visible on the form, so it is shown below the form in the component tray reserved for non-visible objects.

5   Set the following properties for the button, picture box, timer, and form objects:

Object	Property	Setting
Button1	Text	Move Up
Button2	Text	Move Down
PictureBox1	Image	"c:\vbnetsbs\chap16\sun.ico"
	SizeMode	StretchImage
Timer1	Enabled	False
	Interval	75
Form1	Text	Basic Animation

After you set these properties, your form will look similar to this:

6 Double-click the Move Up button to edit its event procedure.

The Button1_Click event procedure appears in the Code Editor.

7 Type the following program code:

```
GoingUp = True
Timer1.Enabled = True
```

This simple event procedure sets the GoingUp variable to True and enables the timer object. The actual program code to move the picture box object and sense the correct direction is stored in the Timer1_Tick event procedure.

8 Scroll to the top of the form's program code, and below "Windows Form Designer generated code" type the following variable declaration:

```
Dim GoingUp As Boolean   'GoingUp stores current direction
```

This variable declaration makes the GoingUp variable available to all the event procedures in the form. I've used a Boolean variable because there are only two possible directions for movement in this program—up and down.

9   Display the form again, double-click the Move Down button, and then enter the following program code in the Button2_Click event procedure:

```
GoingUp = False
Timer1.Enabled = True
```

This routine is very similar to the Button1_Click event procedure, except that it changes the direction from up to down.

10   Display the form again, double-click the Timer1 object, and then enter the following program code in the Timer1_Tick event procedure:

```
If GoingUp = True Then
    'move picture box toward the top
    If PictureBox1.Top > 10 Then
        PictureBox1.Location = New Point _
            (PictureBox1.Location.X - 10, _
            PictureBox1.Location.Y - 10)
    End If
Else
    'move picture box toward the bottom
    If PictureBox1.Top < (Me.Size.Height - 75) Then
        PictureBox1.Location = New Point _
            (PictureBox1.Location.X + 10, _
            PictureBox1.Location.Y + 10)
    End If
End If
```

As long as the timer is enabled, this If...Then decision structure is executed every 75 milliseconds. The first line in the procedure checks whether the GoingUp Boolean variable is set to True, indicating the icon is moving toward the top of the form. If it is, the procedure moves the picture box object to a relative position 10 pixels closer to the left edge of the form, and 10 pixels closer to the top edge of the form.

If the GoingUp variable is currently False, the decision structure moves the icon down instead. In this case, the picture box object moves until the edge of the form is detected. The height of the form can be determined by using the Me.Size.Height property. (I subtract 75 from the form height so that the icon is still displayed on the form.) The Me object in this example represents the form (Form1).

As you'll see when you run the program, this movement gives the icon animation a steady drifting quality. To make the icon move faster, you would decrease the Interval setting for the timer object. To make the icon move slowly, change the Interval setting to a larger number.

Run the Moving Icon program

The complete Moving Icon program is located in the c:\vbnetsbs\ chap16\moving icon folder.

1   Click the Start button to run the program.

The Moving Icon program runs in the development environment.

2   Click the Move Up button.

The picture box object moves up the form on a diagonal path, as shown here:

The animation stops when the button reaches the top of the form.

After a few moments, the button comes to rest at the upper edge of the form.

3   Click the Move Down button.

The picture box moves back down again to the lower right corner of the screen.

4   Click both buttons again several times and ponder the animation effects.

Note that you don't need to wait for one animation effect to end before you click the next button—the Timer1_Tick event procedure uses the GoingUp variable immediately to manage your direction requests, so it doesn't matter if it hasn't finished going one direction or not. Consider this effect for a moment, and imagine how you could use a similar type of logic to build your own Visual Basic video games—you could increase or decrease the animation rates according to specific conditions or "collisions" on screen, and you could also force the animated objects to move in different directions.

5   When you're finished running the program, click the Close button on the form to stop the demonstration.

Expanding and Shrinking Objects While a Program Is Running

The Height and Width properties let you expand and shrink an object.

In addition to maintaining a Top property and a Left property, Visual Basic maintains a Height property and a Width property for most objects on a form. You can use these properties in clever ways to expand and shrink objects while a program is running. The following exercise shows you how to do it.

Expand a picture box at runtime

1   On the File menu, click the Close Solution command.

2   Create a new Visual Basic Windows Application project named **My Zoom In** in the c:\vbnetsbs\chap16 folder.

PictureBox control

3   Display the form, click the PictureBox control in the Toolbox, and then draw a small picture box object near the upper left corner of the form.

4   Set the following properties for the picture box and the form. When you set the properties for the picture box, note the current values in the Height and Width properties within the Size property. (You can set these at design time, too.)

Object	Property	Setting
PictureBox1	Image	"c:\vbnetsbs\chap16\earth.ico"
	SizeMode	StretchImage
Form1	Text	"Approaching Earth"

5   Double-click the PictureBox1 object on the form.

The PictureBox1_Click event procedure appears in the Code Editor.

6   Type the following program code in the PictureBox1_Click event procedure:

```
PictureBox1.Height = PictureBox1.Height + 15
PictureBox1.Width = PictureBox1.Width + 15
```

Increasing the Height and the Width properties of the Earth icon makes the Earth icon grow larger.

These two lines increase the height and width of the Earth icon by 15 pixels each time the user clicks the picture box. If you let your imagination run a little, watching the effect makes you feel like you're approaching Earth in a spaceship.

The complete Zoom In program is located in the c:\vbnetsbs\chap16\zoom in folder.

7   Click the Start button to run the program.

The Earth icon appears alone on the form, as shown here:

8   Click the Earth icon several times to expand it on the screen.

After 10 or 11 clicks, your screen should look similar to this:

9   When you get close enough to establish a standard orbit, click the Close button to quit the program.

The program stops, and the programming environment returns.

One Step Further: Changing Form Transparency

Interested in one last special effect? With GDI+ you can do things that were difficult or even impossible in earlier versions of Visual Basic. For example, you can make a form partially transparent so that you can see through it. Let's say you were designing a photo-display program that included a separate form that had various options to manipulate the photos. You could make the option form partially transparent so that the user could see any photos beneath it, while still having access to the options.

The following exercise shows you how to change the transparency of a form. This is accomplished by changing the value of the Opacity property.

Set the Opacity property

1   On the File menu, click the Close Solution command.

2   Create a new Visual Basic Windows Application project named **My Transparent Form** in the c:\vbnetsbs\chap16 folder.

3   Display the form, click the Button control in the Toolbox, and then draw two buttons on the form.

Button control

4   Set the following properties for the two buttons and the form.

Object	Property	Setting
Button1	Text	"Set Opacity"
Button2	Text	"Restore"
Form1	Text	"Transparent Form"

5   Double-click the Set Opacity button on the form.

6   Type the following program code in the Button1_Click event procedure:

```
Me.Opacity = 0.75
```

Opacity is specified as a percentage, so it has a range of 0 to 1. This line sets the Opacity of Form1 (Me) to 75 percent.

16

Graphics and Animation

7 Display the form again, double-click the Restore button, and then enter the following program code in the Button2_Click event procedure:

```
Me.Opacity = 1
```

This line restores the opacity to 100 percent.

The complete Transparent Form program is located in the c:\vbnetsbs\ chap16\ transparent form folder.

8 Click the Start button to run the program.

9 Click the Set Opacity button.

Notice how you can see through the form, as shown here:

10 Click the Restore button.

The transparency effect is removed.

11 When you are done testing the transparency effect, click the Close button to quit the program.

The program stops, and the programming environment returns.

Chapter 16 Quick Reference

To	Do this
Create lines or shapes on a form	Use methods in the System.Drawing.Graphics namespace. For example, the following program statements draw an ellipse on the form: ```\nDim GraphicsFun As System.Drawing.Graphics\nGraphicsFun = Me.CreateGraphics\nDim PenColor As New System.Drawing.Pen _\n (System.Drawing.Color.Red)\nGraphicsFun.DrawEllipse(PenColor, 10, _\n 120, 200, 160)\n```
Create lines or shapes that persist on the form during window redraws	Place the graphics methods in the Paint event procedure for the form.
Move an object on a form	Relocate the object by using the Location property, the New keyword, and the Point structure. For example: ```\nPictureBox1.Location = New Point(300, 200)\n```
Animate an object	Change the Left, Top, or Location properties for an object in a timer event procedure. Animation speed is controlled by the timer's Interval property.
Expand or shrink an object at runtime	Change the object's Height property or Width property.
Change the transparency of a form	Change the Opacity property.

17

Inheriting Forms and Creating Base Classes

In this chapter you will learn how to:

✔ *Use the Inheritance Picker to incorporate existing forms in your projects.*

✔ *Create your own base classes with custom properties and methods.*

✔ *Derive new classes from base classes using the Inherits statement.*

A popular buzzword among software developers today is *object-oriented programming* (OOP). Visual Basic 4 added several object-oriented programming features to the Visual Basic language, but according to experts, Visual Basic still lagged behind the "true" OOP languages, such as Microsoft Visual C++, because it lacked *inheritance*, a mechanism that allows one class to acquire the pre-existing interface and behavior characteristics from another class. At long last, Visual Basic .NET *does* support inheritance, which means that you can build one form in the development environment and pass its characteristics and functionality on to other forms. In addition, you can build your own classes and inherit properties, methods, and events from them as well. In this chapter, you'll experiment with both types of inheritance. You'll learn how to integrate existing forms into your projects by using a new Visual Studio .NET tool called the Inheritance Picker, and you'll learn how to create your own classes and derive new ones from them using the Inherits statement. With these skills you'll be able to utilize many of the forms and coding routines you have already developed, making Visual Basic programming a faster and more flexible endeavor.

Upgrade Notes: What's New in Visual Basic .NET?

If you're experienced with Visual Basic 6, you'll notice some new features in Visual Basic .NET, including the following:

- The ability to inherit forms in the Visual Studio development environment using the Inheritance Picker tool.

- Classes are now defined between the Public Class and End Class keywords.

- Several user-defined classes can now be stored in a single source file. (In Visual Basic 6, each new class had to be stored in its own file.)

- Properties are added to classes using a new syntax in Visual Studio .NET, and the Property Get, Property Let, and Property Set syntax is no longer supported.

- The Inherits keyword allows a new derived class to inherit the interface and behaviors of an existing class.

Inheriting a Form Using the Inheritance Picker

In object-oriented programming syntax, inheritance means having one class receive the objects, properties, methods, and other attributes of another class. As I mentioned in Chapter 15, Visual Basic goes through this process routinely when it creates a new form in the development environment. The first form in a project (Form1) relies on the System.Windows.Forms.Form class for its definition and default values. In fact, this class is identified at the top of each form with the Inherits keyword each time a new form is created using the Add Windows Form command on the Project menu:

```
Inherits System.Windows.Forms.Form
```

Although you haven't realized it, you have been using inheritance all along to define the Windows Forms that you have been using to build Visual Basic applications.

Although existing forms can be inherited using program code as well, the designers of Visual Studio .NET considered the task to be so important that they designed a special tool in the development environment to facilitate the process. This tool is called the Inheritance Picker, and it is accessed through the Add Inherited Form command on the Project menu. In the following exercise, you'll use the Inheritance Picker to create a second copy of a dialog box in a project.

Inherit a simple dialog box

1   Start Visual Studio, and create a new Visual Basic Windows Application project named **My Form Inheritance** in the c:\vbnetsbs\chap17 folder.

ab|

Button control

2   Display the form in the project, and use the Button control to add two button objects at the bottom of the form, positioned side by side.

3   Change the Text properties of the Button1 and Button2 buttons to **OK** and **Cancel** respectively.

4   Double-click the OK button to display the Button1_Click event procedure in the Code Editor.

5   Type the following program statement:

```
MsgBox("You clicked OK")
```

6   Display the form again, double-click the Cancel button, and then type the following program statement in the Button2_Click event procedure:

```
MsgBox("You clicked Cancel")
```

7   Display the form again and set the Text property of the form to **Dialog Box**.

You now have a simple form that can be used as the basis of a dialog box in a program. With some customization, you could use this basic form to process several tasks—you just need to add the controls that are specific to your individual application.

Now you'll practice inheriting the form. The first step in this process is building (compiling) the project, because you can only inherit from forms that are compiled into .EXE or .DLL files. Each time that the base form is recompiled, changes made to the base form are passed to the derived (inherited) form.

8   Click the Build Solution command on the Build menu.

Visual Basic compiles your project and creates an .EXE file.

9   Click the Add Inherited Form command on the Project menu.

You'll see this dialog box:

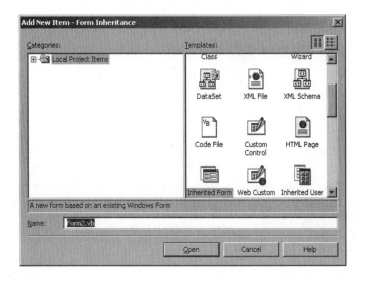

As usual, Visual Studio lists all the possible templates you could include in your projects, not just those related to inheritance. But because Inherited Form is the default selection in the Templates pane, you don't need to make any adjustments.

The Name text box at the bottom of the dialog box lets you assign a name to your inherited form; this is the name that will appear in Solution Explorer and in the filename of the form on disk.

10   Click Open to accept the default settings for the new, inherited form.

Visual Studio displays the Inheritance Picker dialog box, as shown here:

This dialog box lists all the inheritable forms in the current project. If you want to browse for other compiled forms, click the Browse button and locate the .DLL file on your hard disk. (If you want to inherit a form that isn't a component in the current project, the form must be compiled as a .DLL file.)

11 Click Form1 in the Inheritance Picker dialog box, and then click OK.

Visual Studio creates the Form2.vb entry in Solution Explorer and displays the inherited form in the Windows Forms Designer. Notice that the form looks identical to the Form1 window you created earlier, except that the two buttons contain tiny icons, which indicate that the objects come from an inherited source.

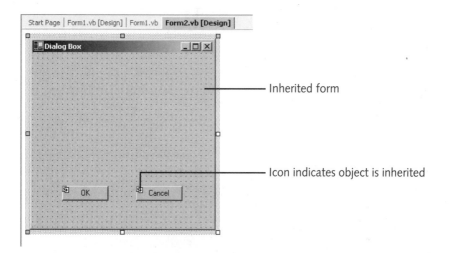

It can be difficult to tell an inherited form from a base form (the tiny inheritance icons aren't that obvious), so be sure that you use Solution Explorer and the development environment window tabs to distinguish between the forms.

Now add a few new elements to the inherited form.

Customize the inherited form

1 Use the Button control to add a third button object to Form2 (the inherited form).

2 Set the Text property for the button object to **Click Me!**

3 Double-click the Click Me! button.

4 In the Button3_Click event procedure, type the following program statement:

```
MsgBox("This is the inherited form!")
```

5   Display Form2 again, and then try double-clicking the OK and Cancel buttons on the form.

You can't display or edit the event procedures for these inherited objects without taking additional steps that are beyond the scope of this chapter. However, you can add new objects to the form to customize it.

6   Enlarge the form.

You can also change other characteristics of the form, such as its size and location. Notice that if you use the Properties window to customize a form, the Object drop-down list box displays the form that the current form derives from.

Now set the startup object to Form2.

7   Click the My Form Inheritance project icon in Solution Explorer, and then click the Properties command on the Project menu.

The Property Pages dialog box appears.

8   Click the Startup Object drop-down list box, click Form2, and then click OK.

Now run the new project.

9   Click the Start button.

The inherited form opens, as shown here:

10   Click the OK button.

The inherited form runs the event procedure it inherited from Form1, and it displays the following message box:

11   Click OK, and then click the Click Me! button.

Form2 displays the inherited form message.

The inherited form has been customized to include a new object, as well as the two inherited button objects. Congratulations! You've taken your first steps with inheritance by using the Inheritance Picker dialog box.

12   Click OK to close the message box, and then click Close on the form to end the program.

The program stops and the development environment returns.

Creating Your Own Base Classes

The Inheritance Picker tool managed the inheritance process in the last exercise by creating a new class in your project named Form2. To build the Form2 class, the Inheritance Picker established a link between the Form1 class in the My Form Inheritance project and the new form. Here's what the new Form2 class looks like in the Code Editor:

```
Public Class Form2
    Inherits My_Form_Inheritance.Form1
    ⋮
    Private Sub Button3_Click(ByVal sender As System.Object, _
      ByVal e As System.EventArgs) Handles Button3.Click
        MsgBox("This is the inherited form!")
    End Sub
End Class
```

In addition to the Inherits statement at the top of the form's code, the Button3_Click event procedure that you added is also a member of the new class. But recall for a moment that the Form1 class relied itself on the System.Windows.Forms.Form class for its fundamental behavior and characteristics. So the last exercise demonstrates that one derived class (Form2) can inherit its functionality from a second derived class (Form1), which in turn inherited its core functionality from an original base class (Form), which is a member of the System.Windows.Forms namespace in the .NET Framework library.

Recognizing that classes are such a fundamental building block in Visual Basic .NET programs, one might very well ask how new classes are created, and how these new classes might be inherited down the road by subsequently derived classes. To ponder these possibilities, I will devote the remainder of this chapter to discussing the new syntax for creating classes in Visual Basic .NET, and introducing how these user-defined classes might be inherited later by still more classes. Along the way, you'll learn how very useful creating your own classes can be.

Nerd Alert

There is a potential danger for terminology overload when discussing class creation and inheritance. A number of very smart computer scientists have been thinking about these object-oriented programming concepts for several years, and there are numerous terms and definitions in use for the concepts that I plan to cover. However, if you stick with me you'll find that creating classes and inheriting them is quite simple in Visual Basic .NET and that you can accomplish a lot of useful work by adding just a few lines of program code to your projects. Let's get started.

Adding a New Class to Your Project

A user-defined class allows you to define your own objects in a program—objects that have properties, methods, and events, just like the objects that Toolbox controls create on Windows Forms. To add a new class to your project, you click the Add Class command on the Project menu, and then you define the class using program code and a few new Visual Basic keywords.

In the following exercise, you'll create a program that prompts a new employee for first name, last name, and date of birth. You'll store this information in the properties of a new class named Person, and you'll create a method in the class to compute the current age of the new employee. This project will teach you how to create your own classes and also how to use the classes in the event procedures of your program.

Build the Person Class project

A

Label control

1   Click the Close Solution command on the File menu, and then create a new Visual Basic Windows Application project named **My Person Class** in the c:\vbnetsbs\chap17 folder.

2   Use the Label control to add a long label object to the top of Form1.

[abl]

Textbox control

3   Use the TextBox control to draw two wide text box objects below the label object.

[📅]

DateTimePicker control

4   Use the DateTimePicker control to draw a date time picker object below the text box objects.

You last used the DateTimePicker control to enter dates in Chapter 3. For a review of its basic methods and properties, see Chapter 3.

Button control

5 Use the Button control to draw a button object below the date time picker object.

6 Set the following properties for the objects on the form:

Object	Property	Setting
Label1	Text	"Enter employee first name, last name, and date of birth."
TextBox1	Text	"First name"
TextBox2	Text	"Last name"
Button1	Text	"Display Record"
Form1	Text	"Person Class"

7 Your form should look like this:

This is the basic user interface for a form that defines a new employee record in a business. (The form isn't connected to a database, so only one record can be stored at a time.) Now you'll add a class to the project to store the information in the record.

8 Click the Add Class command on the Project menu.

Visual Studio displays the Add New Item dialog box, as shown on the following page.

17

Creating Base Classes

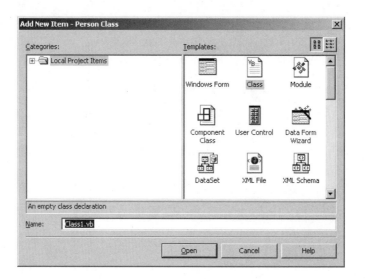

The Add New Item dialog box gives you the opportunity to name your class. As you assign a name, notice that you can store more than one class in a new class module, so you may want to specify a name that is somewhat general.

9   Type **Person.vb** in the Name text box, and then click Open.

Visual Studio opens a blank class module in the Code Editor and lists a file named Person.vb in Solution Explorer for your project.

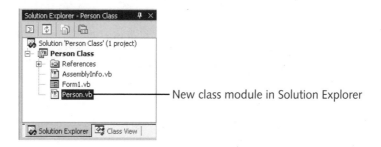

New class module in Solution Explorer

Now you'll type the definition of your class in the class module and learn a few new Visual Basic keywords. You'll follow three steps: declare class variables, create properties, and create methods.

Declare class variables

1   Below the Public Class Person program statement, type the following variable declarations:

```
Private Name1 As String
Private Name2 As String
```

Here you declare two variables that will be used exclusively within the class module to store the values for two string property settings. I have declared the variables using the Private keyword because by convention Visual Basic programmers keep their internal class variables private—in other words, not available for inspection outside the class module itself.

Create properties

1   Below the variable declarations, type the following program statement and press Enter:

```
Public Property FirstName() As String
```

This statement creates a property in your class named FirstName, which is of type String. When you pressed Enter, Visual Studio immediately supplied a code structure for the remaining elements in the property declaration. The required elements are a Get block, which determines what the programmers sees when they check the FirstName property, a Set block, which determines what happens when the FirstName property is set or changed, and an End Property statement, which marks the end of the property procedure.

> **note**
>
> In Visual Basic 6, property procedures contained Property Get, Property Let, and Property Set code blocks. This syntax is no longer supported.

2   Fill out the property procedure structure so that it looks like the code that follows. (The elements you type are formatted in bold type.)

```
Public Property FirstName() As String
    Get
        Return Name1
    End Get
    Set(ByVal Value As String)
        Name1 = Value
    End Set
End Property
```

The Return keyword specifies that the Name1 String variable will be returned when the FirstName property is referenced. The Set block assigns a string value to the Name1 variable when the property is set. Notice here especially the Value variable, which is used in property procedures to stand for the value that is assigned to the class when a property is set. Although this syntax might look strange, trust me for now—this is how property settings are created in controls, although more sophisticated properties would add additional program logic here to test values or make computations.

3   Below the End Property statement, type a second property procedure for the LastName property in your class. It should look like the code that follows. (The bold lines are the ones you type.)

```
Public Property LastName() As String
    Get
        Return Name2
    End Get
    Set(ByVal Value As String)
        Name2 = Value
    End Set
End Property
```

This property procedure is similar to the first one, except that it uses the second string variable (Name2) that you declared at the top of the class.

You're finished defining the two properties in your class. Now let's move on to a method named Age that will determine the new employee's current age based on his or her birth date.

Create a method

1   Below the LastName property procedure, type the following function definition:

```
Public Function Age(ByVal Birthday As Date) As Integer
    Return Int(Now.Subtract(Birthday).Days / 365.25)
End Function
```

To create a method in the class that performs a specific action, add a function or a Sub procedure to your class. Although many methods don't require arguments to accomplish their work, the Age method I'm defining requires a Birthday argument of type Date to complete its calculation. The method uses the Subtract method to subtract the new employee's birth date from the current system time, and it returns the value expressed in days divided by 365.25—the approximate length in days of a single year. The Int function converts this value to an integer, and this number is returned to the calling procedure via the Return statement—just like a normal function. (For more information about function definitions, see Chapter 10.)

Your class definition is finished! Now return to Form1 and use the new class in an event procedure.

tip

Although it wasn't done for this example, it is wise to add some type-checking logic to the class modules in actual projects so that properties or methods that are improperly used don't trigger runtime errors that halt the program.

Create an object based on the new class

1   Click the Form1.vb icon in Solution Explorer, and then click the View Designer button.

The Form1 user interface appears.

2   Double-click the Display Record button to open the Button1_Click event procedure in the Code Editor.

3   Type the following program statements:

```
Dim Employee As New Person()
Dim DOB As Date

Employee.FirstName = TextBox1.Text
Employee.LastName = TextBox2.Text
DOB = DateTimePicker1.Value.Date

MsgBox(Employee.FirstName & " " & Employee.LastName _
    & " is " & Employee.Age(DOB) & " years old.")
```

This routine stores the values entered by the user into an object named Employee that is declared as type Person. The New keyword indicates that you want to immediately create a new instance of the Employee object. You have declared variables often in this book—now you get to declare one based on a class you created yourself! The routine then declares a Date variable named DOB to store the date entered by the user, and the FirstName and LastName properties of the Employee object are set to the first and last names returned by the two text box objects on the form. The value returned by the date and time picker object is stored in the DOB variable, and the final program statement displays a message box containing the FirstName and LastName properties, plus the age of the new employee as determined by the Age method, which returns an integer value when the DOB variable is passed to it. Once you define a class in a class module, it is a simple matter to use it in an event procedure, as this routine demonstrates.

17

Creating Base Classes

The complete Person Class program is located in the c:\vbnetsbs\ chap17\person class folder.

4   Click the Start button to run the program.

The user interface appears in the development environment, ready for your input.

5   Type your first name in the First Name text box and your last name in the Last Name text box.

6   Click the drop-down list arrow in the date time picker object, and scroll to your birth date. (Mine is March 1, 1963.)

> **tip**
> You can scroll faster into the past by clicking the year field when the date time picker dialog box is open. Tiny scroll arrows appear, and you can move one year at a time backward or forward. You can also move quickly to the month you want by clicking the month field and then clicking the month in a popup menu.

Your form will look like this:

7   Click the Display Record button.

Your program stores the first name and last name values in property settings and uses the Age method to calculate the new employee's current age. A message box displays the result:

8 Click OK to close the message box, and then experiment with a few different date values, clicking Display Record each time you change the birth date field.

9 When you're finishing experimenting with your new class, click the Close button on the form.

The development environment returns.

One Step Further: Inheriting a Base Class

As promised at the beginning of the chapter, I have one more trick to show you regarding user-defined classes and inheritance. Just as it is possible to inherit form classes, you can also inherit regular classes that you have defined yourself using the Add Class command and a class module. The mechanism for inheriting a base (parent) class is to use the Inherits statement to include the previously defined class in a new class. You can then add additional properties or methods to the derived (child) class to distinguish it from the base class.

In the following exercise, you'll modify the My Person Class project by adding a second user-defined class to the Person class module. This new class, called Teacher, will inherit the FirstName property, the LastName property, and the Age method from the Person class and will add an additional property named Grade to record the grade in which the new teacher teaches.

Use the Inherits keyword

1 Click the Person.vb class in Solution Explorer, and then click the View Code button.

2 Scroll to the bottom of the Code Editor so that the insertion point is below the End Class statement.

As I mentioned earlier, you can include more than one class in a class module, as long as each class is delimited by Public Class and End Class statements. You'll create a class named Teacher in this class module, and you'll use the Inherits keyword to incorporate the method and properties you defined in the Person class.

3 Type the following class definition in the Code Editor. (Type the statements formatted in bold below—the remaining statements will be added automatically by Visual Studio.)

```
Public Class Teacher
    Inherits Person
    Private Level As Short
```

(continued)

```
      Public Property Grade() As Short
          Get
              Return Level
          End Get
          Set(ByVal Value As Short)
              Level = Value
          End Set
      End Property
  End Class
```

The Inherits statement links the Person class to this new class, incorporating all of its variables, properties, and methods. If the Person class was located in a separate module or project, you could identify its location by using a namespace designation, just like you identify classes when you use the Imports statement at the top of a program that uses classes in the .NET Framework class libraries. Basically, I have defined the Teacher class as a special type of Person class—in addition to a FirstName and LastName property, the Teacher class has a Grade property that records the level of student the teachers teaches.

Now you'll use the new class in the Button1_Click event procedure.

4   Display the Button1_Click event procedure in Form1.

Rather than create a new variable to hold the Teacher class, I'll just use the Employee variable as it is—the only difference will be that I can now set a Grade property for the new employee.

5   Modify the Button1_Click event procedure as follows (the lines you need to change are formatted in bold type):

```
Dim Employee As New Teacher()
Dim DOB As Date

Employee.FirstName = TextBox1.Text
Employee.LastName = TextBox2.Text
DOB = DateTimePicker1.Value.Date
Employee.Grade = InputBox("What grade do you teach?")

MsgBox(Employee.FirstName & " " & Employee.LastName _
```

```
& " teaches grade " & Employee.Grade)
```

In this example, I've removed the current age calculation (the Age method isn't used), but I only did this to keep information to a minimum in the message box. When you define properties and methods in a class, you aren't required to use them in the program code.

The complete Class Inheritance program is located in the c:\vbnetsbs\ chap17\class inheritance folder.

6 Click the Start button to run the program.

The new employee form appears on the screen.

7 Type your first name in the First Name text box and your last name in the Last Name text box.

8 Click the date time picker object, and scroll to your birth date.

9 Click the Display Record button.

Your program stores the first name and last name values in property settings and then displays the following input box, which prompts the new teacher for the grade they teach:

10 Type **3**, and then click OK to close the input box.

The application stores the number 3 in the new Grade property and uses the FirstName, LastName, and Grade properties to display the new employee information in a confirming message box. You'll see this message:

11 Experiment with a few more values if you like, and then click the Close button on the form.

The program stops and the development environment returns. You're finished working with classes and inheritance in this chapter. Nice job!

Further Experiments with Object-Oriented Programming

If you've enjoyed this foray into object-oriented programming, more fun awaits you in Visual Basic .NET—the first version of Visual Basic that can truly be called an object-oriented programming language. In particular, you may wish to add events to your class definitions, create default property values, and experiment with a new polymorphic feature called *method overloading*. These and other OOP features can be explored by using the Visual Basic online Help or by perusing an advanced book on Visual Basic .NET programming. (See Appendix B: Where To Go For More Information for a reading list.)

Chapter 17 Quick Reference

To	Do this
Inherit an existing form's interface and functionality	Click the Add Inherited Form command on the Project menu, specify a name for the inherited form, and then click Open. Use the Inheritance Picker to select the form you want to inherit, and then click OK. (Note: To be eligible for inheritance, base forms must be compiled as .EXE or .DLL files. If you want to inherit a form that isn't a component in the current project, the form must be compiled as a .DLL file.)
Customize an inherited form	Add Toolbox controls to the form and set property settings. Note that you won't be able to set the properties of inherited objects on the form, however. These objects can be identified by small icons and will be inactive.
Create your own base classes	Click the Add Class command on the Project menu, specify the class name, and then click Open. Define the class in a class module using program code.
Declare variables in a class	Use the Private keyword to make class variables hidden when others examine your class. For example: `Private Name1 As String`

To	Do this

Create a new property in the class	Define a Public property procedure in the class. For example:
	
	``
	Public Property FirstName() As String
	    Get
	        Return Name1
	    End Get
	    Set(ByVal Value As String)
	        Name1 = Value
	    End Set
	End Property
	``

Create a new method in the class	Define a Sub or function procedure in the class. For example:
	
	``
	Public Function Age(ByVal Birthday As Date) _
	  As Integer
	    Return Int(Now.Subtract(Birthday).Days _
	      / 365.25)
	End Function
	``

Declare an object variable to use the class	Use the Dim and New keywords, a variable name, and the user-defined class in a program statement. For example: ``` Dim Employee As New Person() ```
Set properties for an object variable	Use the regular syntax for setting object properties. For example: ``` Employee.FirstName = TextBox1.Text ```

Inherit a base class in a new class	Create a new class, and use the Inherits keyword to incorporate the base class's class definitions. For example:
	
	``
	Public Class Teacher
	    Inherits Person
	    Private Level As Short
	
	    Public Property Grade() As Short
	        Get
	            Return Level
	        End Get
	        Set(ByVal Value As Short)
	            Level = Value
	        End Set
	    End Property
	End Class
	``

17

Creating Base Classes

18

Working with Printers

In this chapter you will learn how to:

✔ *Print graphics from a Visual Basic program.*

✔ *Print text from a Visual Basic program.*

✔ *Print multi-page documents.*

✔ *Use the Print, Page Setup, and Print Preview dialog boxes.*

In the following sections, you'll complete your survey of advanced user interface components by learning how to add printer support to your Windows Forms applications. Visual Basic .NET supports printing by offering the PrintDocument class and its many objects, methods, and properties that facilitate printing. In this chapter, you'll learn how to print graphics and text from Visual Basic programs, manage multi-page printing tasks, and add printing dialog boxes to your user interface.

For my money, this chapter is one of the best in the book, with lots of practical code that you can immediately incorporate into real-world programming projects. Printing support doesn't come automatically in Visual Basic .NET, but the routines in this chapter will help you print longer text documents and display helpful dialog boxes such as Page Setup, Print, and Print Preview.

Upgrade Notes:
What's New in Visual Basic .NET?

If you're experienced with Visual Basic 6, you'll notice some new features in Visual Basic .NET, including the following:

- In Visual Basic 6, printing was accomplished using the methods and properties of the Printer object. For example, the Printer.Print method sent a string of text to the default printer. In Visual Basic .NET, printing is accomplished using the new PrintDocument class, which provides more functionality than the older method, but is also more complex.

- In Visual Basic 6, you had access to one predefined dialog box for printing services—the Print dialog provided by the CommonDialog ActiveX control. In Visual Basic .NET, you have access to several predefined dialog box controls for printing, including PrintDialog, PrintPreviewDialog, and PageSetupDialog.

- To implement multipage printing in Visual Basic .NET, you must create a PrintPage event handler that prints each page of your document one at a time. Although managing this printing process can be somewhat involved, it is simplified by functionality provided by the System.Drawing.Printing namespace.

Using the PrintDocument Class

Most Windows applications allow users to print documents after they create them, and by now you may be wondering just how printing works in Visual Basic programs. This is one area where Visual Basic .NET has improved considerably over Visual Basic 6, although the added functionality comes at a little cost. It isn't trivial to produce printed output from Visual Basic .NET programs, and the technique you use depends on the type and amount of printed output you want to generate. In all cases, however, the fundamental mechanism that regulates printing in Visual Basic .NET is the PrintDocument class, which you can create in a project by adding the PrintDocument control to a form or can define programmatically using a few lines of Visual Basic code.

The PrintDocument class provides several useful objects for printing text and graphics, including the PrinterSettings object, which contains the default print settings for a printer; the PageSettings object, which contains print settings for a particular page; and the PrintPageEventArgs object, which contains event information about the page that is about to be printed. The PrintDocument class is located in the System.Drawing.Printing namespace. If you add a PrintDocument control to your form, some of the objects in the PrintDocument class are automatically incorporated into your project, but you still need to add the following Imports statement to the top of your form:

```
Imports System.Drawing.Printing
```

This defines PrintPageEventArgs and other important values.

To learn how to use the PrintDocument class in a program, complete the following exercise, which teaches you how to add a PrintDocument control to your project and use it to print a graphics file on your system.

Use the PrintDocument control

1   Start Visual Studio and create a new Visual Basic Windows Application project named **My Print Graphics** in the c:\vbnetsbs\chap18 folder.

      A blank form appears in the Visual Studio development environment.

Label control

2   Use the Label control to draw a label object near the top of the form. Make the label wide enough to display one line of instructions for the user.

TextBox control

3   Use the TextBox control to draw a text box object below the label object.

      The text box object will be used to type the name of the artwork file that you want to open. A single-line text box will be sufficient.

Button control

4   Use the Button control to draw a button object below the text box.

      This button object will print the graphics file. Now add a PrintDocument control to your form.

PrintDocument control

5   Scroll down on the Windows Forms tab of the Toolbox until you see the PrintDocument control, and then double-click it.

      Like the Timer control, the PrintDocument control is invisible at runtime, so it is placed in the component tray beneath the form when you create it. Your project now has access to the PrintDocument class and its useful printing objects.

6   Set the following properties for the objects on your form:

Object	Property	Setting
Label1	Text	"Type the name of a graphic file to print."
TextBox1	Text	"c:\vbnetsbs\chap16\sun.ico"
Button1	Text	"Print Graphic"
Form1	Text	"Print Graphics"

Working with Printers   18

Your form will look like this:

Print document object

Now add the program code necessary to print a graphic file (bitmap, icon, metafile, JPEG file, etc.).

7   Double-click the Print Graphic button.

The Button1_Click event procedure appears in the Code Editor.

8   Scroll to the very top of the form's code, and then type the following program statement:

```
Imports System.Drawing.Printing
```

This Imports statement declares the System.Drawing.Printing namespace, which is needed to define the PrintPageEventArgs object in the PrintGraphic procedure. The PrintGraphic procedure will be added in a later step. (The other PrintDocument objects will receive their definitions from the PrintDocument control.)

9   Now scroll back down to the Button1_Click event procedure, and then enter the following program code:

```
' Print using an error handler to catch problems
Try
    AddHandler PrintDocument1.PrintPage, AddressOf Me.PrintGraphic
    PrintDocument1.Print()    'print graphic
```

```
Catch ex As Exception  'catch printing exception
    MessageBox.Show("Sorry--there is a problem printing", _
        ex.ToString())
End Try
```

This code uses the AddHandler statement, which specifies that the Print-Graphic event handler should be called when the PrintPage event of the PrintDocument1 object fires. You have seen *error handlers* in previous chapters—an *event handler* is a closely related mechanism that handles system events which aren't technically errors but which also represent crucial actions in the lifecycle of an object. In this case, the event handler being specified is related to printing services, and the request comes with specific information about the page to be printed, the current printer settings, and other attributes of the PrintDocument class. Technically, the AddressOf operator is used to identify the PrintGraphic event handler by determining its internal address and storing it. The AddressOf operator implicitly creates an object known as a *delegate* that forwards calls to the appropriate event handler when an event occurs.

The third line of the previous code uses the Print method of the Print-Document1 object to send a print request to the PrintGraphic event procedure, a routine that you'll create in the next step. This print request is located inside a Try code block to catch any printing problems that might occur during the printing activity. Note that I'm using a slightly different syntax in the Catch block than what I introduced in Chapter 9. Here the ex variable is being declared of type Exception to get a detailed message about any errors that occur. Using the Exception type is another way to get at the underlying error condition that created the problem.

10   Scroll above the Button1_Click event procedure in the Code Editor to the general declaration space below the label, "Windows Form Designer generated code." Type the following Sub procedure declaration:

```
'Sub for printing graphic
Private Sub PrintGraphic(ByVal sender As Object, _
    ByVal ev As PrintPageEventArgs)
      ' Create the graphic using DrawImage
      ev.Graphics.DrawImage(Image.FromFile(TextBox1.Text), _
        ev.Graphics.VisibleClipBounds)
      ' Specify that this is the last page to print
      ev.HasMorePages = False
End Sub
```

This is the routine that handles the printing event generated by the Print-Document1.Print method. I've declared the Sub procedure within the form's code, but you could also declare the Sub as a general-purpose procedure in a standard module. Note the ev variable in the argument list for the Print-Graphic procedure—this is the crucial carrier of information about the current print page, and it is declared of type PrintPageEventArgs, an object in the System.Drawing.Printing namespace.

To actually print the graphic, the procedure uses the Graphics.DrawImage method associated with the current print page, and this method loads a graphics file using the filename stored in the Text property of the TextBox1 object. (By default, I set this property to c:\vbnetsbs\chap16\sun.ico—the Sun icon you used in Chapter 16—but you can change this value at runtime and print any artwork files that you like.) Finally, I set the ev.HasMorePages property to False so that Visual Basic understands the print job doesn't have multiple pages.

11 Click the Save All button on the toolbar to save your changes.

Now you're ready to run the program. Before you do so, you may want to locate a few graphics files on your system that you can print. (Just jot down the paths for now and type them in.)

Run the Print Graphics program

The complete Print Graphics program is located in the c:\vbnetsbs\ chap18\print graphics folder.

1 Click the Start button on the toolbar.

Your program runs in the development environment. You'll see this form:

2 Turn on your printer and verify that it is online and has paper.

3 If you installed your sample files in the default c:\vbnetsbs folder, click the Print Graphic button now to print the Sun.ico icon graphic.

If you didn't use the default sample file location, or if you want to print a different artwork file, modify the text box path accordingly, then click the Print Graphic button.

The DrawImage method will expand the graphic to the maximum size your printer can produce on one page and then send it to the printer. (This "expansion feature" gives you a closer look at the image.) If you want to modify the location or size of your output, search the Visual Basic online Help for the Graphics.DrawImage topic, and then study the different argument variations available to you and modify your program code.

If you look very closely, you'll see the following dialog box appear when Visual Basic sends your print job to the printer:

This status box is also a product of the PrintDocument class, and it provides users with a professional-looking print interface, including the page number for each printed page.

4   Type additional paths if you like, and then click the Print Graphic button for more printouts.

5   When you're finished experimenting with the program, click the Close button on the form.

The program stops. Not bad for your first attempt at printing from a Visual Basic program!

Printing Text from a Text Box Object

You've had a quick introduction to the PrintDocument control and printing graphics. Now try using a similar technique to print the contents of a text box on a Visual Basic form. In the following exercise, you'll build a project that prints text using the PrintDocument class, but this time you'll define the class using program code without adding the PrintDocument control to your form. In addition, you'll use the Graphics.DrawString method to send the entire contents of a text box object to the default printer.

> **note**
>
> The following program is designed to print one page or less of text. To print multiple pages, you need to add additional program code, which will be explored later in the chapter.

Working with Printers   18

Use the Graphics.DrawString method to print text

1 Click the Close Solution command on the File menu, and then create a new Visual Basic Windows Application project named **My Print Text** in the c:\vbnetsbs\chap18 folder.

A blank form appears.

Label control

2 Use the Label control to draw a label object near the top of the form.

This label will also display a line of instructions for the user.

3 Use the TextBox control to draw a text box object below the label object.

The text box object will contain the text you want to print.

TextBox control

4 Set the Multiline property of the text box object to True, and then expand the text box so that it is large enough to enter several lines of text.

5 Use the Button control to draw a button object below the text box.

This button object will print the text file.

Button control

6 Set the following properties for the objects on your form:

Object	Property	Setting
Label1	Text	"Type some text in this text box object, then click Print Text."
TextBox1	ScrollBars	Vertical
	Text	(empty)
Button1	Text	"Print Text"
Form1	Text	"Print Text"

Your form will look like this:

Now add the program code necessary to print the contents of the text box.

7 Double-click the Print Text button.

The Button1_Click event procedure appears in the Code Editor.

8 Scroll to the very top of the form's code, and then type the following Imports declaration:

```
Imports System.Drawing.Printing
```

This defines the System.Drawing.Printing namespace, which is needed to define the PrintDocument class and its necessary objects.

9 Now scroll back down to the Button1_Click event procedure, and then enter the following program code:

```
' Print using an error handler to catch problems
Try
    ' Declare PrintDoc variable of type PrintDocument
    Dim PrintDoc As New PrintDocument()
    AddHandler PrintDoc.PrintPage, AddressOf Me.PrintText
    PrintDoc.Print()    'print text
Catch ex As Exception  'catch printing exception
    MessageBox.Show("Sorry--there is a problem printing", _
        ex.ToString())
End Try
```

The lines that are new or changed from the Print Graphics program are highlighted with bold formatting. Rather than add a PrintDocument control to your form, this time you simply created the PrintDocument programmatically using the Dim keyword and the PrintDocument type, which is defined in your program when you define the System.Drawing.Printing namespace. From this point on, the PrintDoc variable represents the PrintDocument object, and it is used to declare the error handler and to print the text document. Note that for clarity, I also renamed the Sub procedure that will handle the print event PrintText (rather than PrintGraphic).

10 Scroll above the Button1_Click event procedure in the Code Editor to the general declaration area. Type the following Sub procedure declaration:

```
'Sub for printing text
Private Sub PrintText(ByVal sender As Object, _
  ByVal ev As PrintPageEventArgs)
    'Use DrawString to create text in a Graphics object
    ev.Graphics.DrawString(TextBox1.Text, New Font("Arial", _
        11, FontStyle.Regular), Brushes.Black, 120, 120)
    ' Specify that this is the last page to print
    ev.HasMorePages = False
End Sub
```

Working with Printers 18

This is the routine that handles the printing event generated by the Print-Doc.Print method. The changes from the PrintGraphic procedure in the last exercise are also formatted with bold type. As you can see, when you print text you need to use a new method. Rather than Graphics.DrawImage, which renders a graphics image, you must use Graphics.DrawString, which prints a text string. I've specified the text in the Text property of the text box object to print, and some basic font formatting (Arial, 11 point, regular style, black color) and an (x, y) coordinate on the page of (120, 120). This will give the printed output a default look that is similar to the text box on the screen. Like last time, I also set the ev.HasMorePages property to False to indicate that the print job doesn't have multiple pages.

11   Click the Save All button on the toolbar to save your changes.

Now run the program to see how a text box object prints.

Run the Print Text program

The complete Print Text program is located in the c:\vbnetsbs\ chap18\print text folder.

1   Click the Start button on the toolbar.

Your program runs in the development environment.

2   Verify that your printer is on.

3   Type some sample text in the text box. If you type multiple lines, be sure to include a carriage return at the end of each line.

Wrapping isn't supported in this demonstration program—very long lines will potentially extend past the right margin. Your form should look like this:

4   Click the Print Text button.

The program displays a printing dialog box and prints the contents of your text box.

5   Modify the text box and try additional printouts, if you like.

6   When you're finished, click the Close button on the form.

   The program stops. Now you know how to print both text and graphics from a program.

Printing Multipage Text Files

The printing techniques that you have just learned are useful for simple text documents, but they have a few important limitations. First, the method I used doesn't allow for long lines—in other words, text that extends beyond the right margin. Unlike the text box object, the PrintDocument object doesn't automatically "wrap" lines when they reach the edge of the paper. If you have files that don't contain carriage returns at the end of lines, you'll need to write the code that handles these long lines.

The second limitation is that the Print Text program can't print more than one page of text. Indeed, it doesn't even understand what a page of text *is*—the printing procedure simply sends the text to the default printer. If the text block is too long to fit on a single page, the additional text won't be printed. To handle multipage printouts, you need to create a virtual page of text called the PrintPage, and then add text to it until the page is full. When the page is full, it will be sent to the printer, and this process continues until there is no more text to print. At this point, the print job ends.

If fixing these two limitations sounds complicated, don't despair yet—there are a few handy mechanisms that help you create virtual text pages in Visual Basic and help you print text files with long lines and several pages of text. The first mechanism is the PrintPage event, which occurs when a page is printed. Print-Page receives an argument of the type PrintPageEventArgs, which provides you with the dimensions and characteristics of the current printer page. Another mechanism is the Graphics.MeasureString method. The MeasureString method can be used to determine how many characters and lines can fit in a rectangular area of the page. Using these mechanisms and others, it is relatively straightforward to construct procedures that process multipage print jobs.

Complete the following steps to build a program named Print File that opens text files of any length and prints them. The Print File program also demonstrates how to use the RichTextBox, PrintDialog, and OpenFileDialog controls. The RichTextBox control is a more robust version of the TextBox control you just used to display text. The PrintDialog control displays a standard Print dialog box so that you can specify various print settings. The OpenFileDialog control lets you select a text file for printing. (You used OpenFileDialog in Chapter 4.)

Manage print requests with
RichTextBox, OpenFileDialog, and PrintDialog controls

1   Click the Close Solution command on the File menu, and then create a new Visual Basic Windows Application project named **My Print File** in the c:\vbnetsbs\chap18 folder.

A blank form appears.

Button control

2   Use the Button control in the Toolbox to draw two buttons in the upper left corner of the form.

This program has a simple user interface, but the printing techniques you'll learn are easily adaptable to much more complex solutions.

RichTextBox control

3   Click the RichTextBox control in the Toolbox, and then draw a rich text box object that covers the bottom half of the form.

OpenFileDialog control

4   Double-click the OpenFileDialog control to add an open file dialog object to the component tray below your form.

You'll use the open file dialog object to browse for text files on your system.

PrintDocument control

5   Double-click the PrintDocument control to add a print document object to the component tray.

You'll use the print document object to support printing in your application.

PrintDialog control

6   Double-click the PrintDialog control to add a print dialog object to the component tray.

You'll use the print dialog object to open a Print dialog box in your program.

7   Now set the following properties for the objects on your form:

Object	Property	Setting
Button1	Name	btnOpen
	Text	"Open"
Button2	Name	btnPrint
	Enabled	False
	Text	"Print"
RichTextBox1	Text	(empty)
Form1	Text	"Print File"

Your form will look like this:

Now add the program code necessary to open the text file and print it.

8   Double-click the Open button.

The btnOpen_Click event procedure appears in the Code Editor.

9   Scroll to the top of the form and enter the following code:

```
Imports System.IO  'for FileStream class
Imports System.Drawing.Printing
```

These library definitions make available the FileStream class and the classes for printing.

10   Move the cursor below the "Windows Form Designer generated code" tag, and then enter the following variable declarations:

```
Private PrintPageSettings As New PageSettings()
Private StringToPrint As String
Private PrintFont As New Font("Arial", 10)
```

These statements define important information about the pages that will be printed.

11   Scroll to the btnOpen_Click event procedure, and then type the following program code:

```
Dim FilePath As String
'Display Open dialog box and select text file
OpenFileDialog1.Filter = "Text files (*.txt)|*.txt"
OpenFileDialog1.ShowDialog()
'If Cancel button not selected, load FilePath variable
If OpenFileDialog1.FileName <> "" Then
    FilePath = OpenFileDialog1.FileName
    Try
        'Read text file and load into RichTextBox1
        Dim MyFileStream As New FileStream(FilePath, FileMode.Open)
        RichTextBox1.LoadFile(MyFileStream, _
          RichTextBoxStreamType.PlainText)
        MyFileStream.Close()
        'Initialize string to print
        StringToPrint = RichTextBox1.Text
        'Enable Print button
        btnPrint.Enabled = True
    Catch ex As Exception
        'display error messages if they appear
        MessageBox.Show(ex.Message)
    End Try
End If
```

When the user clicks the Print button, this event procedure displays an Open dialog box using a filter that displays only text files. When the user selects a file, the filename is assigned to a public string variable named FilePath, which is declared at the top of the event procedure. The procedure then uses a Try...Catch error handler to load the text file into the RichText-Box1 object. To facilitate the loading process, I've used the FileStream class and the Open file mode, which places the complete contents of the text file into the MyFileStream variable. Finally, the event procedure enables the Print button (btnPrint) so that the user can print the file. In short—this routine opens the file and enables the print button on the form but doesn't do any printing itself.

Now you'll add the necessary program code to display the Print dialog box and print the file using logic that monitors the dimensions of the current text page.

Add code for the btnPrint and PrintDocument1 objects

1   Display the form again, and then double-click the Print button (btnPrint) to display its event procedure in the Code Editor.

2 Type the following program code:

```
Try
    'Specify current page settings
    PrintDocument1.DefaultPageSettings = PrintPageSettings
    'Specify document for print dialog box and show
    StringToPrint = RichTextBox1.Text
    PrintDialog1.Document = PrintDocument1
    Dim result As DialogResult = PrintDialog1.ShowDialog()
    'If click OK, print document to printer
    If result = DialogResult.OK Then
        PrintDocument1.Print()
    End If
Catch ex As Exception
    'Display error message
    MessageBox.Show(ex.Message)
End Try
```

This event procedure sets the default print settings for the document and assigns the contents of the RichTextBox1 object to the StringToPrint string variable (defined at the top of the form) in case the user changes the text in the rich text box. It then opens the Print dialog box and allows the user to adjust any print settings he or she would like (printer, number of copies, the print to file option, and so on). If the user clicks the OK button, the event procedure sends this print job to the printer by issuing the following statement:

```
PrintDocument1.Print()
```

3 Display the form again, and then double-click the PrintDocument1 object in the component tray.

Visual Studio adds the PrintPage event procedure for the PrintDocument1 object.

4 Type the following program code in the PrintDocument1_PrintPage event procedure:

```
Dim numChars As Integer
Dim numLines As Integer
Dim stringForPage As String
Dim strFormat As New StringFormat()
'Based on page setup, define drawable rectangle on page
Dim rectDraw As New RectangleF( _
    e.MarginBounds.Left, e.MarginBounds.Top, _
    e.MarginBounds.Width, e.MarginBounds.Height)
```

```vb
'Define area to determine how much text can fit on a page
'Make height one line shorter to ensure text doesn't clip
Dim sizeMeasure As New SizeF(e.MarginBounds.Width, _
   e.MarginBounds.Height - PrintFont.GetHeight(e.Graphics))

'When drawing long strings, break between words
strFormat.Trimming = StringTrimming.Word
'Compute how many chars and lines can fit based on sizeMeasure
e.Graphics.MeasureString(StringToPrint, PrintFont, _
   sizeMeasure, strFormat, numChars, numLines)
'Compute string that will fit on a page
stringForPage = StringToPrint.Substring(0, numChars)
'Print string on current page
e.Graphics.DrawString(stringForPage, PrintFont, _
   Brushes.Black, rectDraw, strFormat)
'If there is more text, indicate there are more pages
If numChars < StringToPrint.Length Then
    'Subtract text from string that has been printed
    StringToPrint = StringToPrint.Substring(numChars)
    e.HasMorePages = True
Else
    e.HasMorePages = False
    'All text has been printed, so restore string
    StringToPrint = RichTextBox1.Text
End If
```

This event procedure handles the actual printing of the text document, and it does so by carefully defining a printing area (or printing rectangle) based on the settings in the Page Setup dialog box. Any text that fits within this area can be printed normally; text that is outside this area needs to be wrapped to the following lines, or pages, as you would expect from a normal Windows application.

The printing area is defined by the rectDraw variable, which is based on the RectangleF class. The strFormat variable and the Trimming method are used to trim strings that extend beyond the edge of the right margin. The actual text strings are printed by the DrawString method, which you have already used in this chapter. The e.HasMorePages property is used to specify whether there are additional pages to be printed. If no additional pages remain, the HasMorePage property is set to False and the contents of the StringToPrint variable are restored to the contents of the RichTextBox1 object.

5   Click the Save All button on the toolbar to save your changes.

That's a lot of typing! But now you're ready to run the program and see how printing text files on multiple pages works.

Run the Print File program

The complete Print File program is located in the c:\vbnetsbs\ chap18\print file folder.

1   Click the Start button on the toolbar.

Your program runs in the development environment. Notice that the Print button is currently disabled because you haven't selected a file yet.

2   Click the Open button.

The program displays an Open dialog box.

3   Browse to the c:\vbnetsbs\chap18 folder, and then click the longfile.txt file.

Your Open dialog box will look like this:

4   Click Open to select the file.

Your program loads the text file into the rich text box object on the form, and then enables the Print button. This file is long and has a few lines that wrap so that you can test the wide margin and multipage printing options. Your form will look like this:

5   Verify that your printer is on, and then click the Print button.

6   Visual Basic displays the Print dialog box, as shown in the following illustration:

Many of the options in the Print dialog box are active, and you can experiment with them as you would a regular Windows application.

7   Click OK to print the document.

Your program submits the four-page print job to the printer. After a moment, your printer starts printing the document. As in previous exercises, a dialog box automatically appears to give you some indication of how many pages your printed document will be.

8   Click the Close button on the form to stop the program.

The program stops. You've just created a set of very versatile printing routines!

One Step Further: Adding Print Preview and Page Setup Dialog Boxes

The Print File application is ready to handle several printing tasks, but its interface isn't as visual as a commercial Windows application. You can make your program more flexible and interesting by adding a few extra dialog box options to supplement the Print dialog box you just experimented with in the previous exercise. The following additional printing controls are available on the Windows Forms tab of the Toolbox, and they work much like the familiar PrintDialog and OpenFileDialog controls you've used in this book:

■ PrintPreviewDialog, a control that displays a custom Print Preview dialog box

■ PageSetupDialog, a control that displays a custom Page Setup dialog box

Like other dialog boxes, these printing controls can be added using the Toolbox, or they can be created programmatically.

In the following exercise, you'll add print preview and page setup dialog boxes to the Print File program you've been working with. In the completed practice files, I've named this project Print Dialogs so that you can keep the code straight between the projects, but you can just add the dialog box features directly to the Print File project if you want.

Add PrintPreviewDialog and PageSetupDialog controls

1 Open the Print File project now from the c:\vbnetsbs\chap18\print file folder if you didn't complete the last exercise.

The Print File project is the starting point for this project.

Button control

2 Display the form, and then use the Button control to add two additional buttons to the top of the form.

PrintPreview-Dialog control

3 Double-click the PrintPreviewDialog control on the Windows Forms tab of the Toolbox.

A print preview dialog object is added to the component tray.

4 Double-click the PageSetupDialog control on the Windows Forms tab of the Toolbox.

PageSetup-Dialog control

A page setup dialog object is added to the component tray. If the objects in the component tray obscure one another, you can drag them to a better (more visible) location or you can right-click the component tray and select Line Up Icons.

5 Set the following properties for the button objects on the form:

Object	Property	Setting
Button1	Name	btnSetup
	Enabled	False
	Text	"Page Setup"
Button2	Name	btnPreview
	Enabled	False
	Text	"Print Preview"

Your form will look like this:

6 Double-click the Page Setup button (btnSetup) to display the btnSetup_Click event procedure in the Code Editor.

7 Type the following program code:

```
Try
    'Load page settings and display page setup dialog box
    PageSetupDialog1.PageSettings = PrintPageSettings
    PageSetupDialog1.ShowDialog()
Catch ex As Exception
    'Display error message
    MessageBox.Show(ex.Message)
End Try
```

The code for creating a Page Setup dialog box in this program is quite simple because the PrintPageSettings variable has already been defined at the top of the form. This variable holds the current page definition information, and when it is assigned to the PageSettings property of the PageSetupDialog1 object, the ShowDialog method automatically loads a dialog box that allows the user to modify what the program has selected as the default page orientation, margins, and so on. The Try...Catch error handler simply handles any errors that might occur when the ShowDialog method is used.

8   Display the form again, and then double-click the Print Preview button (btnPreview) to display the btnPreview_Click event procedure.

9   Type the following program code:

```
Try
    'Specify current page settings
    PrintDocument1.DefaultPageSettings = PrintPageSettings
    'Specify document for print preview dialog box and show
    StringToPrint = RichTextBox1.Text
    PrintPreviewDialog1.Document = PrintDocument1
    PrintPreviewDialog1.ShowDialog()
Catch ex As Exception
    'Display error message
    MessageBox.Show(ex.Message)
End Try
```

In a similar way, the btnPreview_Click event procedure assigns the Print-PageSettings variable to the DefaultPageSettings property of the Print-Document1 object, and then it copies the text in the rich text box object to the StringToPrint variable and opens the Print Preview dialog box. Print Preview automatically uses the page settings data to display a visual representation of the document as it will be printed—you don't need to display this information manually.

Now you'll make a slight modification to the program code in the btnOpen_Click event procedure.

10   Scroll up to the btnOpen_Click event procedure in the Code Editor.

This is the procedure that displays the Open dialog box, opens a text file, and enables the printing buttons. Because you just added two new printing buttons, you have to add program code to enable the Page Setup and Print Preview buttons.

11   Scroll to the bottom of the event procedure, just before the final Catch code block, and locate the following program statement:

```
btnPrint.Enabled = True
```

12   Below that statement, add the following lines of code:

```
btnSetup.Enabled = True
btnPreview.Enabled = True
```

Now your program will enable the print buttons when there is a document available to print.

13   Click the Save All button on the toolbar to save your changes.

Test the Page Setup and Print Preview features

*The complete
Print Dialogs
program is
located in the
c:\vbnetsbs\
chap18\print
dialogs folder.*

1   Click the Start button on the toolbar.

The program opens and only the first button object is enabled.

2   Click the Open button, and then open the longfile.txt file in the c:\vbnetsbs\chap18 folder.

The remaining three button objects are now enabled, as shown here:

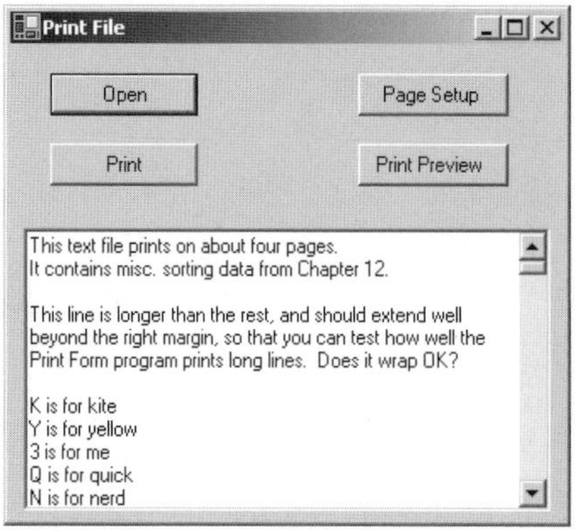

3   Click the Page Setup button.

Your program displays the Page Setup dialog box, as shown here:

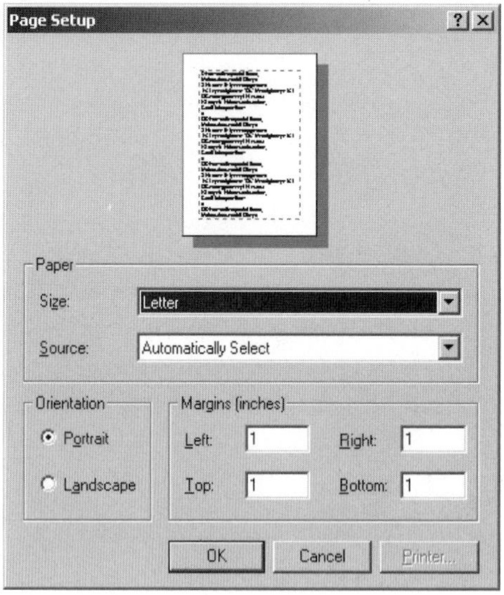

Page Setup has numerous useful options, including the ability to change the paper size and source, the orientation of the printing (Portrait or Landscape), and the page margins (Left, Right, Top, and Bottom).

4 Change the Left margin to 2, and then click OK.

The left margin will now be 2 inches.

5 Click the Print Preview button.

Your program displays the Print Preview dialog box, as shown in the following illustration:

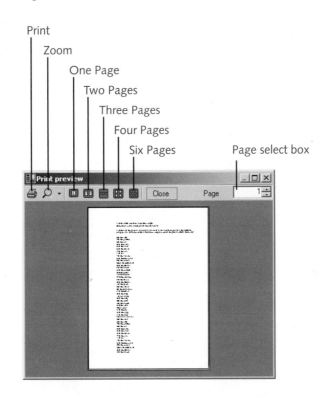

The Print Preview dialog box has several recognizable buttons and preview features, especially if you've used the Print Preview command in Microsoft Word or Microsoft Excel. The Zoom, One Page, Two Pages, Three Pages, Four Pages, Six Pages, and Page Select Box controls all work automatically in the dialog box. No program code is required to make them operate.

6 Click the Four Pages button to see your document four pages at a time.

7 Click the Maximize button on the Print Preview title bar to see the window full size.

8   Click the arrow to the right of the Zoom button and click 150 percent. Your screen will look like this:

9   Click the One Page button, and then click the Up arrow in the Page Select box to view pages 2–4.

As you can see, this Print Preview window is quite impressive—and you incorporated it into your program with just a few lines of code!

10   Click the Close button to close the Print Preview dialog box, and then click the Close button to close the program.

You're done working with printers for now.

Chapter 18 Quick Reference

To	Do this
Incorporate the Print-Document class in your projects and prepare for printing	Add the following Imports statement to the top of your form: `Imports System.Drawing.Printing`

Create a printing event handler	Use the AddHandler statement and the AddressOf operator. For example:
	`AddHandler PrintDocument1.PrintPage, _`
	`    AddressOf Me.PrintGraphic`

To	Do this
Create a Print-Document object in your project	Double-click the PrintDocument control on the Windows Forms tab of the Toolbox, or include the following variable declaration in your program code: `Dim PrintDoc As New PrintDocument()`

Print graphics from a printing event handler	Use the Graphics.DrawImage method. For example:
	`ev.Graphics.DrawImage(Image.FromFile _`
	`    (TextBox1.Text), ev.Graphics.VisibleClipBounds)`

Print text from a printing event handler	Use the Graphics.DrawString method in an event handler. For example:
	`ev.Graphics.DrawString(TextBox1.Text, _`
	`    New Font("Arial", 11, FontStyle.Regular), _`
	`    Brushes.Black, 120, 120)`

Call a printing event handler	Use the Print method of an object of type Print-Document. For example: `PrintDoc.Print()`
Print multipage text documents	Write a handler for the PrintPage event, which receives an argument of the type PrintPageEventArgs. Compute the rectangular area on the page for the text, use the MeasureString method to determine how much text will fit on the current page, and use the DrawString method to print the text on the page. If additional pages are needed, set the HasMorePages property to True. When all text has been printed, set HasMorePages to False.

Open a text file using the FileStream class and load into a RichTextBox object	Create a variable of type FileStream, specifying the path and file mode, load stream into a RichTextBox, and then close the stream. For example:
	`Imports System.IO  'at the top of the form`
	`...`
	`Dim MyFileStream As New FileStream( _`
	`    FilePath, FileMode.Open)`
	`RichTextBox1.LoadFile(MyFileStream, _`
	`    RichTextBoxStreamType.PlainText)`
	`MyFileStream.Close()`

Display printing dialog boxes in your programs	Use the PrintDialog, PrintPreviewDialog, and PageSetupDialog controls on the Windows Forms tab of the Toolbox.

PART 5

Database Programming

19

Getting Started with ADO.NET

In this chapter you will learn how to:

✔ *Use Server Explorer to establish a connection to a database.*

✔ *Create a data adapter that extracts specific database information.*

✔ *Create a dataset to represent one or more database tables in your program.*

✔ *Use TextBox, Label, and Button controls to display database information and navigation controls on a Windows Form.*

In Part 5, you'll learn how to work with information stored in databases. You'll learn about ADO.NET, Microsoft's newest paradigm for working with database information, and you'll learn how to display, modify, and search for database information using a combination of program code and Windows Forms controls. Microsoft Visual Basic. NET was specifically designed to create custom interfaces, or *front ends,* for existing databases, so if you'd like to customize or dress up data that you've already created with another application, such as Microsoft Access, you can get started immediately.

In this chapter, you'll take your first steps with ADO.NET database programming. You'll use the Server Explorer window to establish a connection to an Access database on your system, you'll configure the connection using the Data Link Properties dialog box, you'll use a data adapter to select the data table that you want to use, and you'll create a dataset based on the table that will represent a portion of the database in your program. After you have completed these preliminary steps, you'll use the TextBox, Label, and Button controls to display database information on a Windows Form.

Upgrade Notes:
What's New in Visual Basic .NET?

If you're experienced with Visual Basic 6, you'll notice some new features in Visual Basic .NET, including the following:

■ The Remote Data Objects (RDO) and ActiveX Data Objects (ADO) data access models have been replaced by the ADO.NET data access model. ADO.NET offers a wider range of data access possibilities than its predecessors and is based on a recent Microsoft data access technology known as ADO+.

■ ADO.NET is the standard data model for all programs in Microsoft Visual Studio .NET, including Microsoft Visual Basic .NET, Microsoft Visual C++ .NET, and Microsoft Visual C# .NET.

■ The familiar Data control and ADO Data control are no longer available in Visual Basic .NET. To display data on a form, you typically create a data adapter and a dataset and then add controls to your form that can display the data and allow users to navigate from one record to the next.

■ In Visual Basic 6, database information was represented in a program by the recordset object. In Visual Basic .NET, database information is represented by the dataset object, a disconnected image of the database table you are accessing.

■ The internal data format of ADO.NET is XML, making it easier to use existing XML data sources, and to use ADO.NET in programs designed for the Web.

Database Programming with ADO.NET

A *database* is an organized collection of information stored in a file. You can create powerful databases by using a variety of database products, including Microsoft Access, Microsoft FoxPro, Btrieve, Paradox, Oracle, and Microsoft SQL Server. You can also store and transmit database information using XML (Extensible Markup Language), a file format designed for exchanging structured data over the Internet and in other settings.

Creating and maintaining databases has become an essential task for all major corporations, government institutions, non-profit agencies, and most small businesses. Rich data resources—be they customer addresses, manufacturing inventories, account balances, employee records, donor lists, or order histories—have become the lifeblood of the business world.

Microsoft Visual Basic .NET isn't designed for creating new databases, but for displaying, analyzing, and manipulating the information in existing databases. Although previous versions of Visual Basic have also provided this capability, Visual Basic .NET offers a new data model called ADO.NET that provides access to an even greater number of database formats. In particular, ADO.NET has been designed for Internet use, meaning that it uses the same method for accessing local, client-server, and Internet-based data sources. As a testimony to Microsoft's goal of making ADO.NET a great technology for manipulating databases over the Internet, Microsoft has made XML, a standard defined by the World Wide Web Consortium, the internal data format of ADO.NET. Using XML in this way makes ADO.NET easier to use with existing Internet data sources, and it makes it easier for software vendors to write data adapters or "providers" that convert third-party database formats to be compatible with ADO.NET.

Visual Basic .NET and ADO.NET can read from and write to a variety of database formats, including XML.

Database Terminology

When working with databases and ADO.NET, it's important to understand some basic database terminology. *Fields* are the categories of information stored in a database. Typical fields in a customer database might include customer names, addresses, phone numbers, and comments. All the information about a particular customer or business is called a *record*. When databases are created, information is entered in tables of fields and records. Records correspond to rows in a table and fields correspond to columns.

Field (column)

Record (row)

In ADO.NET, various objects are used to retrieve and modify information in a database. The illustration on the following page shows an overview of the approach that will be covered in more detail in this chapter.

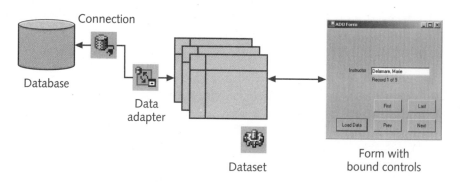

Database   Connection   Data adapter   Dataset   Form with bound controls

First a *connection* is made, which specifies connection information about the database. Next a *data adapter* is created, which manages retrieving data from the database and posting data changes. Then a *dataset* is created, which is a representation of one or more database tables you plan to work with in your program. (You don't manipulate the actual data, but a copy of it.) Information in the dataset can then be bound to controls on a form.

Working with an Access database

In the following sections, you'll learn how to use the ADO.NET data access technology in Visual Basic .NET. You'll get started by using Server Explorer to establish a connection to a database named Students.mdb that I created in Microsoft Access. Students.mdb contains various tables of academic information that would be useful for a teacher who is tracking student coursework or a school administrator who is scheduling rooms, assigning classes, or building a time schedule. You'll learn how to create a dataset based on a table of information in the Students database, and you'll display this information on a Windows Form. When you've finished, you'll be able to put these skills to work in your own database projects.

tip

Although the sample in this chapter uses a Microsoft Access database, you don't have to have Microsoft Access installed. Visual Studio and ADO.NET include the necessary support to understand the Access file format, as well as other formats.

Establish a connection to a database

1   Start Visual Studio .NET and create a new Visual Basic Windows Application project named **My ADO Form** in the c:\vbnetsbs\chap19 folder.

A new project appears in the development environment.

2   On the View menu, click the Server Explorer command.

The Server Explorer window appears in the development environment, as shown here:

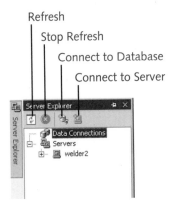

Refresh

Stop Refresh

Connect to Database

Connect to Server

---

tip

Depending on your configuration and edition of Visual Studio, the Connect To Server button and the Servers node might not be displayed. These options aren't required to complete the steps in this chapter.

Server Explorer is a graphical tool that lets you establish connections to local, client-server, or Internet-based data sources. Using Server Explorer, you can view the structure of database tables and learn more about the attributes of tables, fields, and records in a database. You can also log on to network servers and explore the databases and system services that they offer. Finally, you can drag database components or *nodes* from Server Explorer and drop them onto Visual Studio .NET designers, such as the Windows Forms Designer. This process creates new data components that are preconfigured to reference the database item you selected.

3   Click the Connect To Database button in Server Explorer.

Connect to Database button

Before you can manipulate the information in a database, you need to establish a connection to it. The Connect To Database button begins that process by opening the Data Link Properties dialog box, which lets you specify information about the database format, the database location and password (if necessary), and other information.

> **tip**
> You can also open the Data Link Properties dialog box by clicking the Connect To Database command on the Tools menu.

4   Click the Provider tab in the dialog box.

A *provider* (or *managed provider*) is an underlying database component that knows how to connect to a database and extract data from it. The two most popular types of providers offered by Visual Studio .NET are OLE DB and SQL, but there are also third-party providers available for many of the most popular database formats. In this example, you'll use the Microsoft Jet 4.0 OLE DB provider, a component designed to connect to Microsoft Access databases.

5   Click Microsoft Jet 4.0 OLE DB Provider on the Provider tab.

Your screen will look like this:

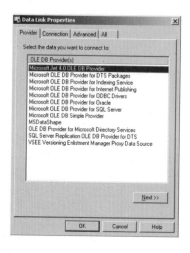

6   Click the Next button to display the Connection tab of the Data Link Properties dialog box.

Because you selected a Jet OLE DB format, the internal format of Microsoft Access, the Connection tab has been configured to receive information about the name, location, and log on information of an Access database.

7   Click the ellipsis button next to the Select Or Enter A Database Name field, select the Students.mdb database in the c:\vbnetsbs\chap19 folder, and then click Open.

Your screen will look like this:

tip

You can specify your own database if you like, but you will need to modify the steps in this chapter accordingly to fit your database's structure.

8   Click the Test Connection button on the Connection tab.

Visual Studio attempts to establish a database connection with the Students.mdb database. If the message "Test Connection Succeeded" appears in a message box, you know the provider is working properly and that your database is structured in a recognizable format. If Visual Studio detects a problem at this point, verify that you are using an appropriate provider and that you selected a database file, and then try the connection again.

9   Click OK in the Test Connection Succeeded message box to continue, and then click OK in the Data Link Properties dialog box.

Visual Studio completes your connection and adds a node representing your database to Server Explorer.

10   Open the Data Connections node, the ACCESS node, and finally the Tables node in Server Explorer.

To open nodes in Server Explorer, click the plus signs (+), which function as toggle switches. The structure of the Students database appears in Server Explorer, as shown on the following page.

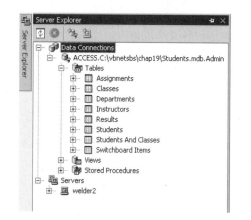

Server Explorer provides this great advantage: It lets you see how a database is organized graphically so that you can immediately make use of its tables, fields, and other objects.

Creating a Data Adapter

Now that you have an active database connection, you need to create a *data adapter* to extract specific information from the database for your program to use. A data adapter defines the specific information you will use and serves as a foundation for the dataset object, which is the representation of the data you want to use in your program. Creating a data adapter is a required step when using a dataset because some databases are highly structured and have many tables to choose from—much more than you might want to make use of in a single program. You might think of a data adapter as a kind of filter for the data.

Visual Studio provides several mechanisms for creating data adapters in a program. The easiest way is to simply drag a graphical table icon from Server Explorer to the Windows Forms Designer. (This procedure creates a data adapter object in the component tray directly below the form.) However, the following exercise shows you how to create a data adapter using a second method—a tool called the Data Adapter Configuration wizard. This tool is easy to use (you launch the wizard by dragging the OleDbDataAdapter control from the Data tab of the Toolbox onto a form), and it gives you the opportunity to fine-tune your data selection by writing a SQL SELECT statement. Give this second method a try now.

Use the OleDbDataAdapter control

1   Open the Toolbox, and click the Data tab.

The Data tab contains controls that help you access data in your programs. If you're familiar with Visual Basic 6, you'll see that the familiar Data and

19

ADO Data controls are no longer provided. Instead, you access data by adding a data adapter object and a dataset object to your program's component tray.

tip

The OleDbConnection and SqlConnection controls can also be used to establish a connection between your program and a data source on a local computer, network server, or Internet resource. However, you already created a database connection using Server Explorer in this chapter, so using the OleDbConnection control isn't necessary now.

OleDbData-Adapter control

2   Drag the OleDbDataAdapter control from the Data tab of the Toolbox to the form.

The OleDbDataAdapter control is designed to handle connections to Access/Jet databases and many other popular database formats. When you drag the control to your form, Visual Studio starts the Data Adapter Configuration Wizard.

3   Read the opening statement about data adapters, and then click Next.

The second wizard dialog box appears, prompting you for the name of a valid data adapter. Your screen should look like this:

Data Adapter Configuration Wizard	☒
Choose Your Data Connection The data adapter will execute queries using this connection to load and update data.	

Choose from the list of data connections currently in Server Explorer or add a new connection if the one you want is not listed.

Which data connection should the data adapter use?

ACCESS.C:\vbnetsbs\chap19\Students.mdb.Admin ▾	New Connection...

	Cancel	< Back	Next >	Finish

Since you already created a data connection to an Access database using Server Explorer, the connection appears in the drop-down list box. (If you hadn't created the connection, or wanted to create a new one, you could do so now by clicking the New Connection button.)

4   Click Next to continue configuring the data adapter.

You'll see the following dialog box asking you how the data adapters should access data in the database:

The first option, Use SQL Statements, gives you the opportunity to create a SQL SELECT statement that will fine-tune, or *filter*, the data you plan to use. For Visual Basic users who are familiar with database programming, writing Access queries, or using SQL Server, creating a SQL SELECT statement is relatively straight-forward. If you're not familiar with this syntax, however, you can use the Query Builder tool to visually generate an appropriate SELECT statement. (We'll use the Query Builder in the following steps.)

5   Click Next to accept the Use SQL Statements option.

You'll see the following dialog box, which prompts you for a valid SQL SELECT statement:

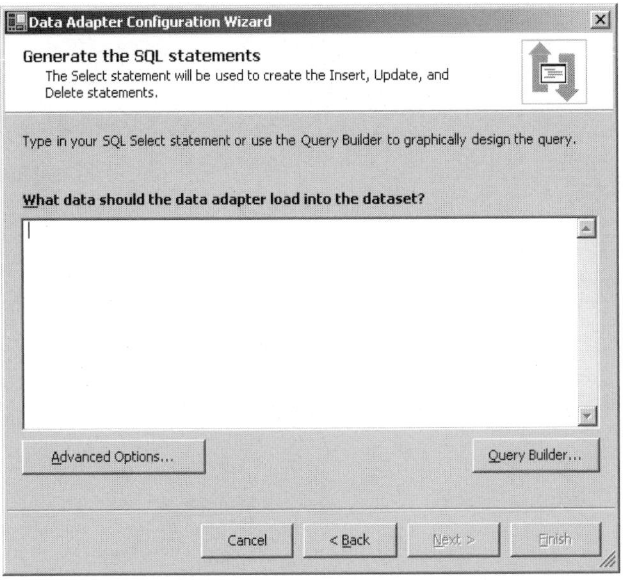

6 Click the Query Builder button to build your SELECT statement graphically. The Add Table dialog box appears, as shown here:

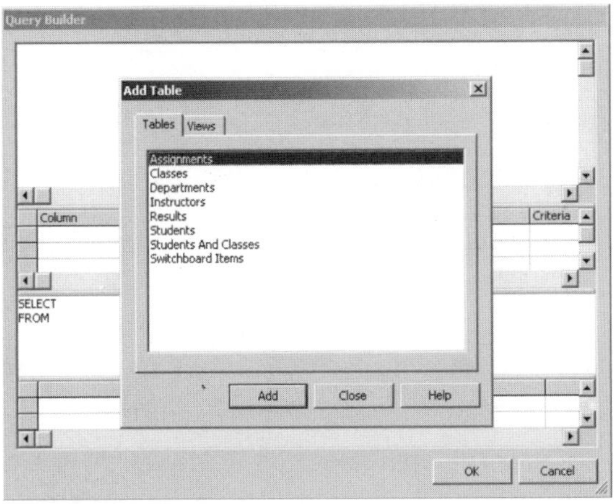

To build your SELECT statement, you need to pick one or more tables provided by the Students.mdb database.

7   Click Instructors, click Add, and then click Close.

Visual Studio displays the graphical Query Builder tool, which now contains a representation of the Instructors table.

8   In the Instructors table, click the check box next to the Instructor field.

The Query Builder creates a SELECT statement that extracts the Instructor field from the Instructors table, as shown here:

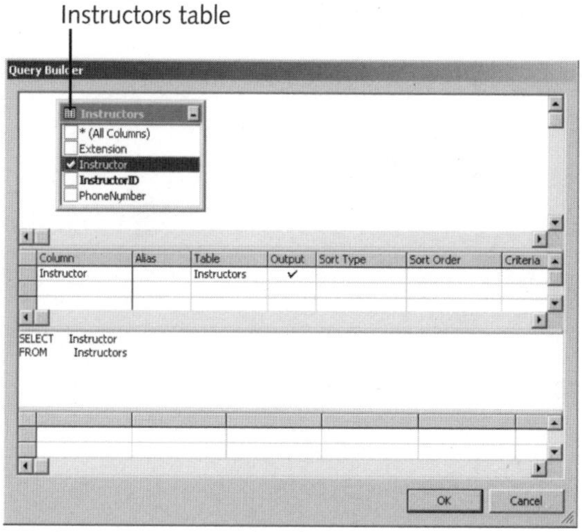

Instructors table

In this example, you're just extracting one field from one table, but you could easily create a SQL SELECT statement that extracted multiple fields from more than one table.

9   Click OK to complete the SELECT statement.

The Generate The SQL Statements dialog box reappears with your new SELECT statement. (You might remember this simple syntax—you can use it to write your own SELECT statements without using the Query Builder in the future.)

10 Click the Finish button.

Visual Studio adds the completed data adapter to the component tray beneath your form. Visual Studio also adds a representation of the OleDbConnection object to the component tray. Each object is identified by a unique number because you can have more than one data connection or data adapter in a project. Your screen looks like this:

OleDbConnection1 object

OleDbDataAdapter1 object

Working with Datasets

The next step in ADO.NET database programming is creating an object that represents the data you want to use in your program. As I mentioned above, this object is called the dataset, and it is a representation of the data provided by the data connection object and extracted by the data adapter object. A dataset can contain information from one or more database tables, and the contents can also be the result of a SQL SELECT statement, like the one you just used to extract data from the Students.mdb database. Unlike recordsets, the mechanisms for accessing data in previous versions of Visual Basic, datasets only *represent* the data in a database—when you modify a dataset, you don't actually modify the underlying database tables until you issue a command that writes your changes back to the original database.

In the following exercise, you'll create a dataset that represents the Instructor field of the Instructors table in the Students.mdb database. As you'll see, creating a dataset is easy once you have a properly configured data adapter to build on.

Create a dataset to hold Instructor data

1   Click the form to make sure that it is active.

    If the form doesn't have the focus, the command you need to create a dataset isn't available on the Data menu.

2   Click the Generate Dataset command on the Data menu.

    The Generate Dataset dialog box appears.

3   In the New box, set the name of the new dataset to **DsInstructors**.

4   Verify that the Add This Dataset To The Designer check box is selected so that Visual Studio will add the new dataset to the component tray.

Your dialog box will look like this:

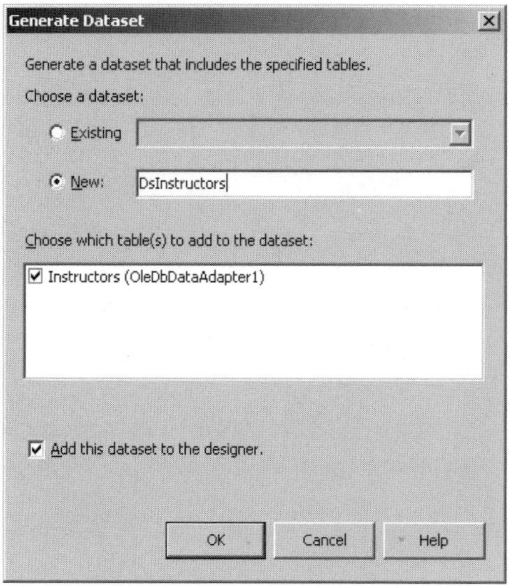

5   Click OK to create a dataset for the Instructor field and add it to your project.

The dataset appears in the component tray, as shown here:

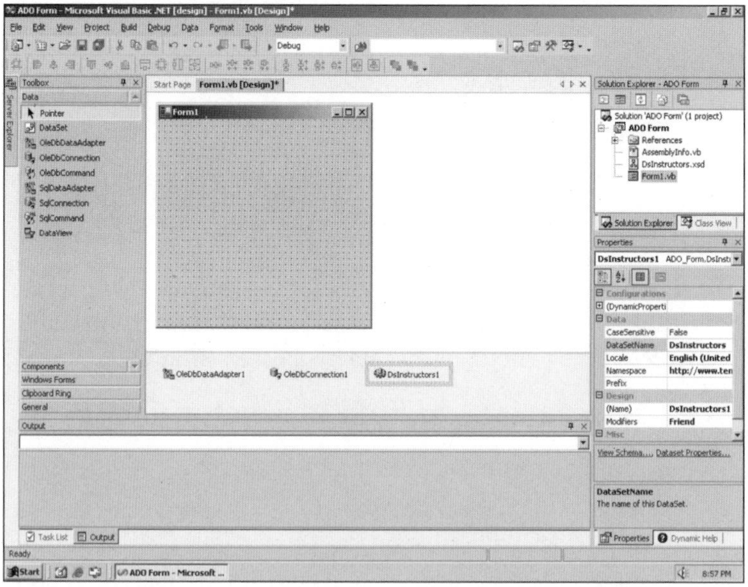

Visual Studio also adds a file named DsInstructors.xsd to Solution Explorer, which represents the database *schema* you just added to your project. This schema is an XML file that describes the tables, fields, data types, and other elements in the dataset. Typed datasets have a schema (.xsd) file associated with them, but un-typed datasets don't. Typed datasets with schema files are advantageous because they enable the statement completion feature of the Visual Studio Code Editor and they give you specific information about the fields and tables you are using.

Now that you've created a dataset, you're ready to display the records from the Instructors table on your form using bound controls.

Using Bound Controls to Display Database Information on a Form

After several steps and procedures, you're finally ready to display some database information on your form. This is the exciting part—but how do you actually do it? Rather than re-creating an Access database table on your form, Visual Basic allows you to display only the fields and records that you want to—you can present an entire grid of database information for your users or only the specific fields that you want them to see. In addition, you can supply a navigation mechanism so that users can browse through all the records in a database, or you can display only specific records. Finally, of course, you can allow your users to modify or even delete information in the underlying database, or you can limit their activities to simply viewing database records. In short, Visual Basic allows you to create a database viewer, or *front end*, that presents only the information and data access features that you want your users to have.

Although I haven't discussed it, most of the controls on the Windows Forms tab of the Toolbox have the built-in ability to display database information on a form. In Visual Basic terminology, these controls are typically called *bound controls*. A control is said to be bound to a data source when its DataBindings properties are set to valid fields (or columns) in a dataset. After the connection has been established, you can display database information by using methods and properties in the ADO.NET object model. A few of the controls on the Windows Forms tab of the Toolbox that can display database information include TextBox, ComboBox, ListBox, CheckBox, RadioButton, DataGrid, and PictureBox.

tip
For specific information about using the DataGrid control to display database information, see Chapter 20.

ADO.NET Datasets

19

The following exercise shows how you can add a text box object to your form to display information from the Instructors table of the Students.mdb database.

Use a TextBox object to display data

|abl|

TextBox control

1   Use the TextBox control to draw a text box object in the middle of the form.

Make the text box object wide enough to display the first and last name of a hypothetical instructor from the Students.mdb database.

A

Label control

2   Use the Label control to draw a label object to the left of the text box object.

|ab|

Button control

3   Use the Button control to draw one button object in the lower left corner of the form.

4   Set the following property settings for the objects on the form:

Object	Property	Setting
TextBox1	Name	txtInstructor
	Text	(empty)
Label1	Name	lblInstructor
	Text	"Instructor"
	TextAlign	MiddleRight
Button1	Name	btnLoad
	Text	"Load Data"
Form1	Text	"ADO Form"

Your form should look like this:

Now you'll bind the Instructor field to the text box object (txtInstructor).

5 Click the text box object on the form, and then open the Properties window.

I recommend that you undock and widen the Properties window so that you have plenty of room to see the structure of the Instructors table in the database.

6 Open the DataBindings category, click the Text property, and then click the drop-down arrow.

The Properties window displays a list of data sources that you can bind to the text box. If you've completed the previous exercises, you'll see a dataset object named DsInstructors1 in the drop-down list box.

7 Click the plus sign (+) to expand the DsInstructors1 dataset, and then expand the Instructors table beneath it.

You'll see the following database structure in the Properties window:

As you may recall, Instructors is the name of a table in the Students.mdb database, and Instructor is a field within the table containing the names of teachers that work at a hypothetical college.

8 Click the Instructor field to select it as the field that will be displayed in the txtInstructor text box. Be sure to click the "Instructor" text and not the icon, otherwise the Instructor field won't be selected.

The dataset, table, and field names appear in the Text property setting of the Properties window. Now you're ready to write the program code that loads data into the dataset and displays it in the text box object.

9   Restore the Properties window, double-click the Load Data button, and then type the following program code in the btnLoad_Click event procedure of the Code Editor:

```
DsInstructors1.Clear()
OleDbDataAdapter1.Fill(DsInstructors1)
```

You must manually fill the data adapter with data using the Fill method, which subsequently loads, or *populates*, the bound text box object on your form with information from the dataset you defined earlier. Although this may feel like an extra step, it is accomplished easily with two lines of program code. In this context, the Clear method is necessary so that records returned by subsequent queries to the database aren't appended to the dataset. Using ADO.NET does sometime require additional steps that weren't needed in ADO and Visual Basic.

tip

For demonstration purposes, I've placed these two lines into a button event procedure, but you could just as easily place them in the Form1_Load event procedure so that the text box object is populated when the opening form is displayed.

10   Click the Start button to run the ADO Form program.

The ADO Form program runs in the development environment. Note that there is currently no instructor name in the text box.

11   Click the Load Data button.

After a moment, the name "Delamare, Marie" appears in the text box, as shown in the following illustration. This is the first instructor name in the Students database.

12   Click the Close button on the form to stop the program.

You've successfully displayed an instructor name from the Students database. Now it's time to add some more sophisticated features to your database front end.

Creating Navigation Controls

Right now, the ADO Form program displays the first instructor name in the Students.mdb database. But how do you browse through the list of instructor names, and how do you make jumps to the first record or the last record in the database? ADO.NET keeps track of information about the current record and the total number of records by using an object named the CurrencyManager. There is a CurrencyManager object for each dataset, and each Windows Form has a BindingContext object that keeps track of all the CurrencyManager objects on the form.

In the following exercise, you'll create button objects named First, Last, Prev, and Next in the ADO Form program that provide basic database navigation features for the user. After you create these buttons on your form, you'll add program code to each button's Click event procedure that displays a different database record using the BindingContext object, the DsInstructors1 dataset, and the Instructors table. You can also customize this program code to fit your own needs by substituting my dataset and table names with parameters from your own database structure.

Add First, Last, Prev, and Next buttons

`ab`

Button control

1   Display the ADO Form user interface, and then use the Button control to create four button objects on your form.

Add two button objects in the middle of the form and two at the bottom of the form.

2   Set the following properties for the button objects:

Object	Property	Setting
Button1	Name	btnFirst
	Text	"First"
Button2	Name	btnLast
	Text	"Last"
Button3	Name	btnPrev
	Text	"Prev"
Button4	Name	btnNext
	Text	"Next"

Your form should look like this:

Now you'll add the program code that enables the navigation functionality of the buttons.

3   Double-click the First button.

The btnFirst_Click event procedure appears in the Code Editor.

4   Type the following program code:

```
Me.BindingContext(DsInstructors1, "Instructors").Position = 0
```

This is the syntax for using the BindingContext object to display the first record in the DsInstructors1 dataset of the Instructors table. The program statement sets the Position property to 0, which changes the current record in the dataset to the first record. (Like arrays and collections, datasets start their numbering at the 0 position.) Also note the use of the Me object, which specifically identifies the BindingContext object for the current form.

5   Display the form, and then double-click the Last button.

The btnLast_Click event procedure appears in the Code Editor.

6   Type the following program code:

```
Me.BindingContext(DsInstructors1, "Instructors").Position = _
   Me.BindingContext(DsInstructors1, "Instructors").Count - 1
```

This long statement (broken into two lines) causes the last record in the dataset to be displayed on the form. It is a variation of the BindingContext statement used above, but rather than setting the Position property to 0, this statement sets the current record to the value held in the Count property minus 1. Count is the total number of records in the dataset. One is subtracted because the dataset is zero-based.

7   Display the form, and then double-click the Prev button.

The btnPrev_Click event procedure appears in the Code Editor.

8   Type the following program code:

```
Me.BindingContext(DsInstructors1, "Instructors").Position -= 1
```

This statement displays the previous record in the dataset by subtracting 1 from the current record. Although this statement won't have meaning if the current record is already 0, it won't create a syntax error—ADO.NET won't let the current record be a number less than zero. Note the use of the -= syntax in this statement to decrement the Position property. This is the math shortcut syntax I first introduced for decrementing variables in Chapter 5.

9   Display the form, and then double-click the Next button.

The btnNext_Click event procedure appears in the Code Editor.

10   Type the following program code:

```
Me.BindingContext(DsInstructors1, "Instructors").Position += 1
```

This statement increments the Position property to display the next record in the dataset. See that I used the math shortcut operator += here as well to update the Position property using a minimum of program code.

Now you'll run the updated program and test the navigation buttons you just configured.

11   Click the Start button on the Standard toolbar.

The program runs in the development environment.

12   Click the Load Data button to populate the text box on the form with the first instructor name in the dataset.

13   Click the Next button to display the next database record.

Your form will look like this:

The Next button displays the next instructor name

14   Click the Prev button to display the first record again.

15   Click the Next button several times to browse through several instructor names in the list.

16   Click the First button to display the first record in the dataset.

17   Click the Last button to display the last record in the dataset.

Notice that the program doesn't produce an error if you display the Last record and then click Next. In addition, the program doesn't produce an error if you display the First record and then click Prev. This error handling is built into the BindingContext object.

18   Click the Close button on the form to stop the program.

One Step Further: Displaying the Current Record Position

In addition to providing basic navigation tools on your form, you might want to provide some indication of the current record number on the form, along with the total number of records in the dataset. You can accomplish this by creating a label object on the form to display the current position. The current position count is held in the Position property of the BindingContext object, as you have already learned. If you want to update the current position when each of the navigation buttons is used, you should create a procedure at the top of the form's program code to determine the current position and display it on the form.

In the following exercise, you'll create a Sub procedure named Count that declares two variables to track the total number of records and the current record, and then displays this information using the Text property of a new label named lblCount.

Create a Count procedure to display current record statistics

Label control

1   Display the form, and then use the Label control to draw a wide label object directly below the text box object.

2   Set the Name property of the label object to **lblCount**.

3   Set the Text property of the label object to **Record 0 of 0**.

4   Click the View Code button in Solution Explorer to display the Code Editor.

5   Scroll to the top of the Code Editor, and place the cursor below the tag, "Windows Form Designer generated code."

By placing procedures in the Form class, the procedure can be accessed from anywhere within the form.

6   Type the following program code for the Count Sub procedure. (Note that Visual Basic adds the End Sub statement automatically).

```
Private Sub Count()
    Dim Records, Current As Integer
    Records = Me.BindingContext( _
        DsInstructors1, "Instructors").Count
    Current = Me.BindingContext( _
        DsInstructors1, "Instructors").Position + 1
    lblCount.Text = "Record " & Current.ToString & " of " & _
        Records.ToString
End Sub
```

The Count procedure assigns the value of the Count property to the Records Integer variable, and it assigns the value of the Position property plus one to the Current Integer variable. 1 is added to the Position property because the list of records is zero-based (like arrays and collections)—an interesting detail for programmers, but not something that the user should see. Finally, the Records and Current variables are converted to strings and copied to the Text property of the lblCount object along with some formatting information so that the label will appear in the following format: *Record x of y*, where *x* is the value of the Current variable, and *y* is the value of the Records variable.

Now you need to add a call to the Count procedure to each of the five button event procedures in the ADO Form program. This is important because each button performs a navigation activity, so the label needs to be updated appropriately each time that the Position property changes.

7   Scroll down to the btnFirst_Click event procedure, add a blank line to the procedure at the bottom, and type the following procedure call:

```
Count()
```

Your event procedure should now look like this (although the first line doesn't need to be broken):

```
Private Sub btnFirst_Click(ByVal sender As System.Object, _
    ByVal e As System.EventArgs) Handles btnFirst.Click
    Me.BindingContext(DsInstructors1, "Instructors").Position = 0
    Count()
End Sub
```

8   Repeat this step by adding a call to the Count procedure in each of the following event procedures in your program: btnLast_Click, btnPrev_Click, btnNext_Click, and btnLoad_Click.

That's it! Now you're ready to run the program and see how the current record statistics work.

The complete ADO Form program is located in the c:\vbnetsbs\chap19\ado form folder.

9   Click the Start button to run the program.

10   Click the Load Data button.

The form is populated with data, and the first instructor name appears. In addition, the text "Record 1 of 9" appears below the text box in the new label you created. Your form should look like this:

11   Click the Next button several times to see the current record statistics change as you scroll through the instructor records in the dataset.

12   Click the Prev, First, and Last buttons to verify that the Count procedure works for those navigation buttons too.

13   Click the Close button on the program's title bar to stop the ADO Form application.

That's it! You've written your first database front end with Visual Basic and ADO.NET. Although you used a Microsoft Access database in this example, you'll find that the basic data access techniques are very similar for other types of database information, including SQL Server databases and databases stored at remote locations such as network servers or the Internet. The reason for this similarity is the distributed architecture of ADO.NET, which uses a similar mechanism for establishing connections, configuring data adapters, and creating datasets based on diverse data resources.

Although it takes several steps to establish the basic connections and settings in an ADO.NET session, the advantage of this upfront work is that manipulating database information on a form is a very uniform process. This is the case even when the data you're using has come from a very remote setting or is the result of combining different database tables or data formats. In the next chapter, you'll continue working with database information by exploring how to use the DataGrid control to work with several database records at once.

Data Access in a Web Forms Environment

The data access techniques discussed in this chapter were designed for use in a Windows Forms environment—the fundamental Visual Studio designer you have used to build most of the programs in this book. However, you can also use ADO.NET programming techniques in a Web Forms environment, which allows you to share data resources over the Internet and write database front ends that are accessible through a Web browser such as Internet Explorer. The major differences between the Windows Forms environment and the Web Forms environment are covered in Chapter 22. For additional information about writing database applications in a Web Forms environment, see "Introduction to Data Access in Web Forms Pages" in the Visual Basic online Help.

Chapter 19 Quick Reference

To	Do this
Establish a connection to a database	Click the Server Explorer command on the View menu, click the Connect To Database button, and identify the database that you want to access using the Data Link Properties dialog box.
Create a data adapter	Click the Data tab in the Toolbox, drag the OleDbDataAdapter control or SqlDataAdapter control to the form, and then specify the database information that you want to use in the Data Adapter Configuration wizard.
Create a dataset	Click the Generate Dataset command on the Data menu, specify a name for the dataset, and then verify that the Add This Dataset To The Designer check box is selected.

(continued)

To	Do this
Binding a Windows Forms control to an active dataset	Add a suitable control to the form, open the Properties window, and then set one of the control's DataBinding properties to a valid field (column) in the dataset. (One of the most useful DataBinding properties is Text.)
Fill a dataset with data and populate any bound control on a Windows Form	Place the following program statement in the event procedure that should populate the form's controls. (Substitute the adapter and dataset names with your own.) `OleDbDataAdapter1.Fill(DsInstructors1)`

Add navigation controls to a Windows Form	Create button objects on the form and add statements that update the Position property of the BindingContext object in each button's Click event procedure. For example, the following program statement displays the next record in a dataset named DsInstructors1 and in a table named Instructors:
	`Me.BindingContext(DsInstructors1, _`
	`    "Instructors").Position += 1`

20

Data Presentation Using the DataGrid Control

In this chapter you will learn how to:

✔ *Create a data grid object on a Windows Form and use it to display database records.*

✔ *Sort database records by column.*

✔ *Change the format and color of cells in a data grid.*

✔ *Permit changes in data grid cells and write updates to the underlying database.*

In Chapter 19, you learned how to use ADO.NET database programming techniques to establish a connection to a Microsoft Access database and display fields from the database on a Windows Form. You also learned how to add navigation buttons such as First, Last, Prev, and Next to the form to provide a mechanism for browsing through the records of the database. In this chapter, you'll continue working with the database programming features of Visual Basic .NET and the useful classes and objects in ADO.NET. In particular, you'll learn how to use the DataGrid control, which allows you to present several fields and records of a database at once.

Upgrade Notes: What's New in Visual Basic .NET?

If you're experienced with Visual Basic 6, you'll notice some new features in Visual Basic .NET, including the following:

■ In Visual Basic 6, there were several grid controls that you could use to display database information on a form, including FlexGrid, Hierarchical FlexGrid, and DataGrid. In Visual Basic .NET, the DataGrid control is the only spreadsheet-style control that is provided to display database records.

■ The DataGrid control included with Visual Basic .NET is quite different from the DataGrid control included with Visual Basic 6. One important improvement is that the Visual Basic .NET DataGrid control doesn't require data-specific commands because all the data access functionality is handled by the underlying data adapter and dataset objects. However, many of the familiar properties and methods have changed in the new DataGrid control. For a list of these updates, see the Visual Basic .NET online Help topic entitled "DataGrid Control Changes in Visual Basic .NET."

Using DataGrid to Display Database Records

The DataGrid control presents information by establishing a grid of *rows* and *columns* on a form to display data as you might see in a program such as Microsoft Excel or Microsoft Access. A DataGrid control can be used to display any type of tabular data: text, numbers, dates, or the contents of an array. In this chapter, however, you'll focus on DataGrid's ability to display the fields and records of the Students.mdb database, a file of structured student information you started working with in Chapter 19. You'll start by filling a simple data grid object with text from the database, and then you'll set a few formatting options. Next you'll move on to sorting records in the data grid object and learning how to write changes in the data grid back to the underlying database.

The DataGrid control is connected, or *bound*, to database information through the DataGrid's DataSource and DataMember properties. These properties will contain useful information only after your program has established a connection to a valid data source by using a data adapter and a dataset object. (The tools and processes involved in this connection were described in detail in Chapter 19;

if you are uncertain how to establish this connection, read the section entitled "Database Programming with ADO.NET" in that chapter.) Once a data grid object is bound to a valid data source, you can populate the object by using the Fill method of the data adapter object. The syntax for the Fill method looks like this:

```
OleDbDataAdapter1.Fill(DsInstructors1)
```

The following exercises demonstrate how you can display the Instructors table of the Students.mdb database using a data grid object.

Establish a connection to the Instructors table

1   Start Visual Studio .NET and create a new Visual Basic Windows Application project named **My DataGrid Sample** in the c:\vbnetsbs\chap20 folder.

A new project appears in the development environment.

2   On the View menu, click the Server Explorer command.

The Server Explorer window opens in the development environment. If you just completed the exercises in Chapter 19, there will be a current connection to an Access database named Students.mdb in Server Explorer under the Data Connections node. If there is a red "x" on the connection, it means that the connection isn't current, but if you click the ACCESS node, it should reestablish itself.

> **note**
> If you see a valid connection to the Students.mdb database now, don't complete steps 3–7 below. I have only included steps 3–7 for readers who didn't complete the exercises in Chapter 19, or for those who completed the exercises some time ago and don't see a valid database connection now. If you see a valid database connection, continue working at step 8.

Connect To Database button

3   Click the Connect To Database button in Server Explorer.

As you learned in Chapter 19, the Connect To Database button helps you establish a connection to a database in your program.

4   Click the Provider tab in the Data Link Properties dialog box, and then click the entry Microsoft Jet 4.0 OLE DB Provider.

5   Click the Next button to display the Connection tab of the Data Link Properties dialog box.

In this tab, you'll specify the name and location of the Access database that you plan to use—Students.mdb.

6   Click the ellipsis button next to the Select Or Enter A Database Name field, select the Students.mdb database in the c:\vbnetsbs\chap19 folder, and click Open.

7   Click OK in the Data Link Properties dialog box.

Visual Studio completes your connection and adds a node representing your database to Server Explorer.

8   Expand the Data Connections node, the ACCESS node, and then the Tables node in Server Explorer by clicking the plus signs (+).

The structure of the Students database appears in Server Explorer, as shown here:

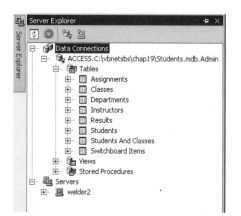

Now you'll create a data adapter for the Instructors table in the database.

9   Open the Toolbox, click the Data tab, and then drag the OleDbDataAdapter control to the form.

*OleDbData-
Adapter control*

When you drag the control to your form, Visual Studio starts the Data Adapter Configuration wizard.

10   Click the Next button to accept the opening screen.

11   Make sure your data connection to Students.mdb is selected in the Choose Your Data Connection dialog box, and then click Next.

12   Make sure the Use SQL Statements option is selected in the Choose A Query Type dialog box, and then click Next.

You'll see a dialog box prompting you for a valid SQL SELECT statement.

13   Type the following SELECT statement in the text box:

```
SELECT
     Extension,
     Instructor,
     InstructorID,
     PhoneNumber
FROM
     Instructors
```

This statement will retrieve the Extension, Instructor, InstructorID, and PhoneNumber fields from the Instructors table of the Students.mdb database and load them into your data adapter.

Your dialog box will look like this:

14   Click the Next button to view the wizard results.

The wizard should have successfully created the appropriate SQL statements (SELECT, INSERT, UPDATE, and DELETE) and table mappings. If there are any errors, click the Back button and verify that your SQL statement is correct.

15   Click the Finish button to add the completed data adapter and connection objects to the component tray beneath your form.

Now you'll create a dataset object to represent the Instructors table in your program.

16   Click the form to make sure that it is active, and then click the Generate Dataset command on the Data menu.

The Generate Dataset dialog box appears.

17   In the New box, set the name of the new dataset to **DsInstructors**.

Verify that the Add This Dataset To The Designer check box is selected so that Visual Studio will add the new dataset to the component tray.

18   Click OK to create a dataset for the Instructors table and add it to your project.

The dataset appears in the component tray with the connection and data adapter objects, as shown here:

Start Page   **Form1.vb [Design]***

Form1

OleDbDataAdapter1   OleDbConnection1   DsInstructors1

Now that you've established a connection to the Instructors table, you're ready to display the records using a DataGrid control.

Create a data grid object

1   Resize the form so that it is large enough to display four columns and about ten rows of data.

DataGrid control

2   Click the Windows Forms tab in the Toolbox, and then click the DataGrid control.

3   Create a large data grid object on the form with the DataGrid control.

4   Add a button control below the data grid.

Button control

Your form should look like this:

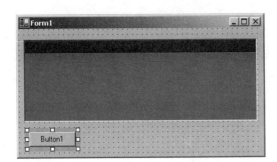

5   Click the data grid on the form, and then open the Properties window.

6   Set the Anchor property to all four sides as shown here:

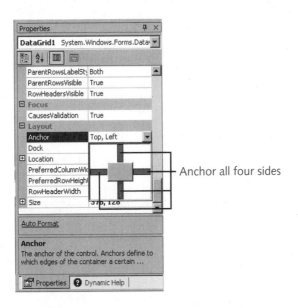

Anchor all four sides

Now you'll use the DataSource and DataMember properties to bind the data grid object to the DsInstructors1 dataset.

7   Display the DataSource property options in the Properties window.

The DataSource property contains the name of the dataset you are displaying in the data grid. Remember that there can be more than one active dataset in a program, so you may have more than one selection here.

8   Click the DsInstructors1 dataset (not the DsInstructors1.Instructors entry).

The Properties window looks like the illustration on the following page as you pick the DsInstructors1 dataset.

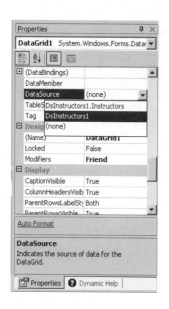

Now you'll use the DataMember property to specify the sublist (in this case, the table) that you want to display in the data grid.

9 Click the DataMember property, and then click the Instructors entry.

As soon as you specify the DataMember property, a grid appears in the data grid object containing the fields you specified in the Instructors table. The fields appear as columns in the grid, and a row is reserved for the first record in the dataset. When you run your program and populate the data grid with data, the specific records in the Students.mdb database will also be added to this grid.

10 Click the form and set its Text property to **DataGrid Sample**.

11 Click Button1 on the form, set its Anchor property to Bottom, Left, set its Name property to **btnLoad**, and then set its Text property to **Load**.

Your form should look like this:

	Extension	Instructor	InstructorID	PhoneNumbe
*				

Load

Now you'll add the program code necessary to populate the data grid. You'll add the Fill method to the btnLoad_Click event procedure.

12 Double-click the Load button to display the btnLoad_Click event procedure.

13 Type the following program statements:

```
DsInstructors1.Clear()
OleDbDataAdapter1.Fill(DsInstructors1)
```

The Clear method makes sure that no records are present in the dataset from previous queries—it clears the dataset out and prepares it for new data. The Fill method fills the dataset with data from the DsInstructors1 dataset—data from the Instructors table of the Students.mdb database.

14 Click the Save All button on the toolbar to save your changes.

You're ready to run the program.

15 Click the Start button on the Standard toolbar.

16 Click the Load button.

The data grid object is populated with data from the dataset. Your screen will look like this:

Each row in the grid represents a record of data from the Instructors table in the database. The SELECT statement that we used included all the fields (columns) in the Instructors table, but could have easily limited the number of fields so that the entire table isn't currently visible or included in the dataset. Notice that the fields are organized in the order you placed them in your SELECT statement—you can change this order by placing the fields in the SELECT statement in a different sequence. Also note that scroll bars appear so that you can view any records that aren't immediately visible. This is a handy ease-of-use feature that comes automatically with the DataGrid control.

17 Scroll down the list of records to view all the database information, which represents instructor data for a college or university.

18   Resize the form to see more of the instructor data.

Because you set the Anchor property for the data grid and the button, their size and position adjust accordingly.

Note that you can widen the columns of the data grid (to see their entire contents) by dragging the column cell borders to the right. The following illustration shows what the data grid looks like after the Instructor column has been widened:

You can also take advantage of an automatic sorting feature of the DataGrid control when it is filled with data.

19   Click the Instructor column heading.

The data grid is sorted alphabetically by instructor name. (Bein, Martin is now first.) When database records are sorted, a sorting column, or *key*, is required—you establish this key by clicking on the column heading that you want to use for the sort.

The DataGrid provides visual identification for the current sort key—a tiny arrow to the right of the column header. If the arrow is pointed up, the sort order is an alphabetical A–Z list. However, you can click the column heading again and reverse the sort order, making it an alphabetical Z–A list. The arrow acts like a toggle, so you can switch back and forth between sorting directions.

tip

Sorting is only allowed in the DataGrid control if the AllowSorting property is set to True, its default setting. If you don't want to allow sorting, set this property to False at design time.

20 Click the Instructor column several times to see how the sort order can be switched back and forth.

21 Click other column headings such as InstructorID and PhoneNumber to sort the database by those keys.

22 When you're finished experimenting with the scrolling, resizing, and sorting features of the DataGrid control, click the Close button on the form to stop the program.

The program closes, and the development environment returns.

Formatting DataGrid Cells

You can control the look and orientation of several DataGrid characteristics with property settings at design time, to customize the appearance of your dataset on the form. For example, you can change the default width of cells in the grid, add or remove column headers, change the grid or header background colors, and change the color of the gridlines. The following exercise steps you through some of these useful property settings.

Set data grid properties at design time

1 Display the form and click the data grid object, and then open the Properties window.

2 Set the PreferredColumnWidth property to 110.

A setting of 110 (measured in pixels) will provide enough room for the data in the fields in the Instructors table.

3 Set the ColumnHeadersVisible property to False.

This property setting will remove the field names from the table. This is useful if the field names in your database don't clearly identify their contents, or if the field names contain abbreviations or words that you want to hide from your users.

4 Click the BackColor property, click the drop-down arrow, click the Custom tab, and then select the light yellow color for the cells of the data grid.

The BackColor property controls the color that appears in the background of the data grid cells. If you change this setting it will usually produce an alternating effect (white and the color you select) from row to row in the data grid. (Note: the color that appears around the edges of the cell grid is controlled by the BackgroundColor property.) Remember that the default font color is black, so pick a background color that will look good with black if you change this setting. (Don't get carried away with distracting colors if you change the property from its default value.)

tip
To change the background color used for the header cells, modify the HeaderBackColor property.

5   Click the GridLineColor property, click the drop-down arrow, click the Custom tab, and then click Blue.

This property setting sets the color of the gridlines in the data grid. If you change the background color of the cells, you might also want to modify the gridline color.

Now run the program to see the effect of your formatting changes.

6   Click the Start button.

7   Click the Load button.

After a few moments, the data grid appears with information from the Instructors table.

8   Resize the form to accommodate the wider columns.

Your screen will look like this:

Custom column width

Alternating yellow background

Blue gridlines

Notice that the column headers are missing now but that the cells are wider and contain more room for text. Notice also the alternating yellow and white row pattern and the blue gridlines (not discernible in this book, alas, but on the screen).

9   Click the Close button on the form to stop the program.

Scan the Properties window for additional property settings and customizations—there are several possibilities if you look closely at the list of formatting options.

One Step Further: Updating the Original Database

As I mentioned earlier, the dataset object in your program is only a representation of the data in your original database. This is also true of the information stored in the data grid on your form—if the user makes a change to this data, it isn't written back to the original database unless you specifically direct the data adapter object in your program to make the change. The designers of ADO.NET and Visual Studio created this relationship to protect the original database and to allow you to manipulate data freely in your programs—whether you planned to save the changes or not.

In the following exercise, you'll examine the DataGrid ReadOnly property, which enables or disables changes in the data grid. You'll also learn how to use the Update method, which writes changes back to your original database on disk if you need this feature.

Enable updates to the database

1   Click the data grid object on the form, and then open the Properties window.

2   Scroll to the ReadOnly property and examine its property setting.

If the ReadOnly property is set to False, the user is free to make changes to the information in data grid cells. You should keep this default setting if you want to allow your users to modify the information in the data grid, so that it can be written back to the original database your program is connected to. If you want to disable editing, you would set the ReadOnly property to True.

Keep the default setting of False in this case—you want to test updating the underlying Students.mdb database.

Button control

3   Use the Button control to draw a button object near the bottom of the form.

4   Set the Anchor property of the button object to Bottom, Left, set the Name property to **btnUpdate**, and set the Text property to **Update**.

This is the button the user will click when he or she makes a change and wants to pass it to the underlying database.

5   Double-click the Update button, and then type the program code on the following page in the btnUpdate_Click event procedure.

The DataGrid Control

20

```
Try
    OleDbDataAdapter1.Update(DsInstructors1)
Catch ex As Exception
    MsgBox(ex.ToString)
End Try
```

This program statement uses the Update method of the OleDbDataAdapter1 object to write any changes that have been made in the DsInstructors1 dataset. When you make a change to the data grid, the data grid object automatically updates the dataset to which the data grid is bound. However, you need to take the further step of updating the data adapter in the program if you want to write the change all the way back to the underlying database.

The complete DataGrid Sample program is located in the c:\vbnetsbs\ chap20\datagrid sample folder.

6 Click the Start button to test your addition to the DataGrid Sample program.

7 Click the Load button.

The data grid appears with data from the Instructors table of the Students.mdb database.

8 Resize the form and change the contents of one of the data grid cells by selecting the existing value with the mouse, pressing Delete, and then typing a new value.

As you make the change, a tiny pencil icon appears in the left row header, indicating a change is being made. Your screen will look like this:

— A modified cell in the data grid

When you click a different cell in the grid, the change is written to the DsInstructors1 dataset.

9 Click the Update button.

Visual Basic uses the Update method of the program's data adapter object to write the changed dataset to the underlying database. The Students.mdb database is now permanently changed.

10   Click in a cell of the last row, which has a star icon in the left row header.

11   Modify the cells that have "(null)" values.

A new row appears in the grid.

12   Click the Update button.

A new row is permanently inserted in the Instructors table of the Students.mdb database.

A new row in the data grid

13   Click the left row header of the row you just inserted to select the entire row, and then press the Delete key.

The row is deleted.

14   Click the Load button.

The deleted row reappears. Why is this? Didn't you just delete the row? The row was deleted from the DsInstructors1 dataset, but the row still exists in the Students.mdb database. To permanently delete a row, you'll need to click the Update button to update the underlying database.

15   Make a few additional changes if you like, and then close the program when you are finished.

Congratulations! You've learned to display several fields and records using the DataGrid control, and you've learned how to customize the data grid with property settings and how to write updates in the grid back to the original database. If you want to learn more about ADO.NET programming, consult one of the books or resources I have listed in Appendix B.

Chapter 20 Quick Reference

To	Do this
Create a data grid object on a form	Click the Windows Forms tab in the Toolbox, and then drag the DataGrid control from the Toolbox to your form. Resize the data grid object and set its Anchor property so that it is resized when the form is resized.
Bind a data grid to an active dataset in the program	Set the data grid's DataSource property to the dataset that you want to use, and then set the data grid's DataMember property to the sublist within the dataset that you want to access.
Populate a data grid with data from the dataset	Use the following program statements in an event procedure (change the name of the data adapter and dataset to match your particular application): `DsInstructors1.Clear()` `OleDbDataAdapter1.Fill(DsInstructors1)`
Sort the records in a data grid at runtime	Click the data grid column header that you want to sort by. Visual Basic will sort the data grid alphabetically based on the column you select.
Reverse the direction of a sort	Click the data grid column header a second time to reverse the direction of the sort (from A–Z to Z–A).
Prohibit sorting in a data grid	Set the data grid's AllowSorting property to False.
Change the default width of data grid cells	Set the data grid's PreferredColumnWidth property.
Change the background color of the cells in a data grid	Set the data grid's BackColor property.
Prohibit changes in a data grid	Set the data grid's ReadOnly property to True.
Write changes made in the data grid back to the underlying database	Use the data adapter's Update method in an event procedure that is executed when the user wants to write the changes back to the underlying database. For example, the following program statement writes changes made to the DsInstructors1 dataset back to the database: `OleDbDataAdapter1.Update(DsInstructors1)`

PART 6

Internet Programming

21

Displaying HTML Documents Using Internet Explorer

In this chapter you will learn how to:

✔ *Investigate the Microsoft Internet Explorer object model.*

✔ *View HTML documents from within your application.*

✔ *Use Internet Explorer events.*

In Chapter 3, you used the LinkLabel control to display a Web site address on a form, and on several occasions you've used the System.Diagnostics.Process.Start method in code to open the default Internet browser on your system. In Part 6, you will focus again on connecting your Visual Basic .NET programs to the Internet. You'll learn to use the methods, properties, and events of the Internet Explorer application in a program, and you'll learn how to create Visual Basic .NET Web applications using the controls on the Web Forms tab of the Toolbox. As you'll see, many Web programming techniques work hand-in-hand with the programming skills you have learned in Parts 1 through 5.

In this chapter, you'll learn how to display HTML documents in your applications using the Internet Explorer object, a programmable component with properties, methods, and events that are available on every computer that maintains an installed copy of the Internet Explorer software. As you investigate the Internet Explorer object model, you'll learn how to add the Internet Explorer object to your Visual Basic projects and how to use Internet Explorer methods, properties, and events to display HTML documents. The advantage of using Internet Explorer directly is that you can display complex HTML documents and Web pages without writing the browser software yourself.

Upgrade Notes:
What's New in Visual Basic .NET?

If you're experienced with Visual Basic 6, you'll notice some new features in Visual Basic .NET, including the following:

■ The version of Internet Explorer that was shipped with the first release of Visual Basic 6 was Internet Explorer version 4. Internet Explorer version 6 is included with the initial release of Visual Basic .NET. Both versions are largely compatible, so if you wrote Visual Basic 6 programs that used earlier versions of Internet Explorer, you should have little trouble compiling them under Visual Basic .NET and the new version of Internet Explorer.

■ To use Internet Explorer features in a Visual Basic .NET program, you need to add a reference to the Microsoft Internet Controls object library (SHDocVw) using the Add Reference command on the Project menu. Because the Microsoft Internet Controls object library is based on COM specifications, Visual Studio will create a "wrapper" for the library containing the necessary types and classes for the component.

Getting Started with
the Internet Explorer Object

Microsoft Internet Explorer is a general-purpose browser application that displays HTML documents located on the Internet or on your hard disk. Microsoft designed Internet Explorer so that you could use it as an individual application (started from the Windows Start menu) or as a component object in a program of your own creation. Accordingly, Internet Explorer exposes its features as a collection of properties, methods, and events in a recognizable object model that you can put to work in your programs. You can investigate the Internet Explorer object model by using the Visual Studio Object Browser.

The *Internet Explorer object* isn't a Toolbox control included in Microsoft Visual Basic .NET. Instead, it is a COM library that resides on all systems that have an installed copy of Internet Explorer (in other words, on all systems in which Internet Explorer is recorded and active in the system registry). Because Microsoft uses Internet Explorer to display Help files in many of its applications, you'll find the Internet Explorer object library on most systems that contain Microsoft software.

important

The version of Internet Explorer described in this chapter is version 6 (the version shipped with Visual Basic .NET). Core properties, methods, and events in the Internet Explorer object haven't changed significantly between versions. However, be sure to check which version of Internet Explorer you are using before you start this chapter. (Use the About command on the Internet Explorer Help menu.) If you have a version other than version 6, use the Object Browser to verify that it contains the properties, methods, and events that you plan to use. Like the object libraries in Microsoft Office applications, the Internet Explorer object model is updated from time to time. Undoubtedly, future versions will be a little different (and richer in terms of features).

Adding the Microsoft Internet Controls Reference to Your Application

The first step in using the Internet Explorer object is adding a COM reference to the object library in your application. You accomplish this by using the Add Reference command on the Visual Basic Project menu, as shown in the following exercise. Practice adding a reference now, if you like, or simply note the steps for later use. (The program I use in this chapter already includes this reference, but you should practice adding it now if you want to investigate the object model later in this section.)

Include the Internet Explorer object in your project

1   Start Visual Studio and create a new Visual Basic Windows Application project named **My Explorer Objects** in the c:\vbnetsbs\chap21 folder.

    The new project is created and a blank form appears in the Windows Forms Designer.

2   On the Project menu, click the Add Reference command.

3   Click the COM tab in the Add Reference dialog box.

4   Scroll to the Microsoft Internet Controls reference, click Microsoft Internet Controls in the dialog box, and then click Select.

    Your dialog box will look similar to the illustration on the following page.

5   Click OK to add the reference to your project.

You may see the following dialog box at this point:

Because COM components are no longer native to the Visual Studio development environment, Visual Studio requires that either a primary interoperability assembly reference be located for the project or a local "wrapper" containing the same class declarations be generated within the project by Visual Studio. As you learned in Chapter 13, many COM applications and components, including Internet Explorer, will require a "wrapper" for any new library references you make.

6   If you see the primary interoperability assembly dialog box, click Yes to allow Visual Studio to create the needed class "wrapper" automatically for you.

Visual Basic adds the Internet Explorer object library to your project, and the types associated with the "wrapper" are added to the project in Solution Explorer.

Investigating the Internet Explorer Object Model

Before you use the Internet Explorer object in a program, take a moment to examine its properties, methods, and events with the Visual Studio Object Browser. The Internet Explorer object is stored in a class named InternetExplorer, which is a member of the SHDocVw library—the Microsoft Internet Controls reference you just added to your project. Within the InternetExplorer class are the properties, methods, and events that you can use to display HTML documents in your programs. As you learned in Chapter 13, the Object Browser is your best source of information for an object library that isn't shipped with Visual Basic. The Internet Explorer object library is a good case in point.

Use the Object Browser

1   On the View menu, click the Other Windows submenu, and then click the Object Browser command. (The keyboard shortcut to display the Object Browser is F2.)

    As you learned in Chapter 13, the Object Browser lists references and components in a tree hierarchy. The object hierarchy is shown in the left pane of the Object Browser, and individual members are shown in the right pane. At the bottom of the Object Browser is a pane that contains syntax information for the selected object when it is available.

2   Click the plus sign (+) next to the Interop.SHDocVw object, and then click the plus sign next to SHDocVw.

    A list of the objects exposed by the Microsoft Internet Controls library fills the Objects pane, as shown here:

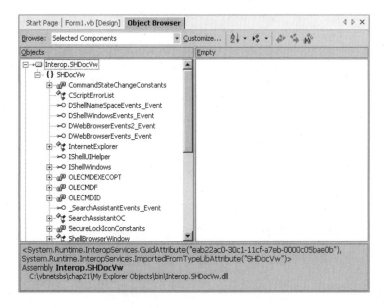

3   Scroll down the alphabetical list of objects, and then click the first object named Internet Explorer.

A list of the methods and properties associated with the Internet Explorer object appears in the Members pane. These are some of the commands Internet Explorer exposes for manipulating Internet Explorer.

4   Scroll down in the Members pane, and then click the Navigate method.

Your screen will look like this:

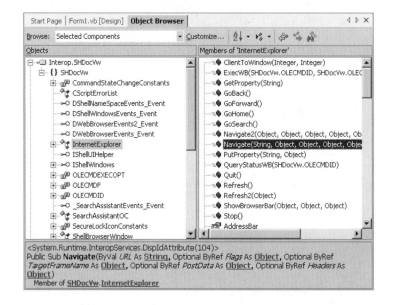

The Navigate method opens the URL specified in the parameter list, which can be either an Internet address or an HTML document somewhere on your system. The *Flags* argument specifies whether to add this URL to the Internet Explorer's history list or disk cache. The *TargetFrameName*, *PostData*, and *Headers* arguments describe how the HTML document should be opened and identified in the browser window. (The *Flags*, *TargetFrameName*, *PostData*, and *Headers* arguments are all optional.) Although it may appear complex, the Navigate method is easy to use. In many cases, it's all you'll need to view an HTML document from within your application.

Navigate opens a URL.

5   Scroll down in the Members pane and click the LocationURL property.

The LocationURL property contains the path of the HTML document that is currently open in the Internet Explorer browser. If you want to keep track of each Web site a user visits in a computing session, you can copy the string in the LocationURL property to a text box or combo box after each successful connection to a Web page.

6   Take a moment to explore other properties and methods that look interesting with the Object Browser.

7   When you're finished exploring the object model, click the Close button to quit the Object Browser.

8   Click the Save All button on the toolbar to save your changes.

You're finished working with the My Explorer Objects project.

Displaying HTML Documents

Displaying HTML documents with the Internet Explorer object requires just a few lines of program code in a Visual Basic application. First you declare a variable in your application that represents the Internet Explorer type. You use the New keyword to create an instance of the Internet Explorer object. Then you display the Internet Explorer application by setting the Visible property of the object to True. Next you load an HTML document into Internet Explorer by issuing the Navigate method with a valid URL or local path as an argument. Here's what the process looks like in program code:

```
Dim Explorer As SHDocVw.InternetExplorer
Explorer = New SHDocVw.InternetExplorer()
Explorer.Visible = True
Explorer.Navigate("http://www.microsoft.com")
```

In this example, I created a variable named Explorer to represent the InternetExplorer class in the shdocvw.dll object library. If you want to use this variable in every event procedure in your form, you could declare it as a public variable using the Public keyword in a standard module or in the general declarations section of your form.

To see how the Internet Explorer object works in a program, you'll run the Show HTML demonstration that I created for this chapter. Show HTML uses a combo box to present a list of favorite Web sites to the user, and it uses Internet Explorer's Navigate method to display whichever HTML document the user selects.

Run the Show HTML program

1   Click the Close Solution command on the File menu.

2   Open the Show HTML project in the c:\vbnetsbs\chap21\show html folder.

3   Click the Start button on the Standard toolbar to run the program.

Your form will look like the illustration on the following page.

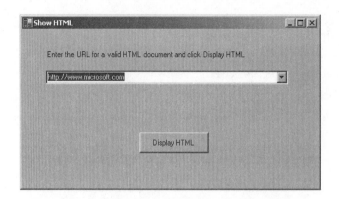

4   Click the down arrow in the combo box on the form to display a list of favorite Web sites for Visual Basic programmers.

You'll see the following list of URLs:

As you've probably noticed in your Internet browser, a combo box can be a handy control for presenting URLs to the user. In my Web applications, I usually try to display four or five URLs for users to choose from when they start their Web applications, and they can add their own favorites when they visit additional sites. The Internet addresses I've included here will connect you to a few sites that I think are of general interest to Visual Basic programmers. Feel free to use them, but note that one or two of the URLs might not be valid a year or two from now. (These things change rapidly.)

The following table lists the Web sites I present in the program:

Internet address	Description
http://www.microsoft.com	Microsoft Corporation home page
http://www.microsoft.com/mspress	Microsoft Press home page (with links for Visual Basic books)
http://msdn.microsoft.com/vbasic	Microsoft Visual Basic Programming home page
http://www.devx.com	General resources for computer programming and Visual Studio .NET

5 Click the Microsoft Visual Basic Programming home page (http://msdn.microsoft.com/vbasic) in the combo box.

6 Click the Display HTML button.

Visual Basic opens Internet Explorer and loads the Microsoft Visual Basic URL into the browser. If you're not on line, Internet Explorer prompts you for your Internet service provider (ISP) member ID and password with a sign-in dialog box and connects you to the Internet. (If you connect to the Internet through a corporate network, you might have a different logon process.) After a moment, you'll see the Microsoft Visual Basic home page, which will look similar to the following illustration. (Your HTML document will contain more recent information.)

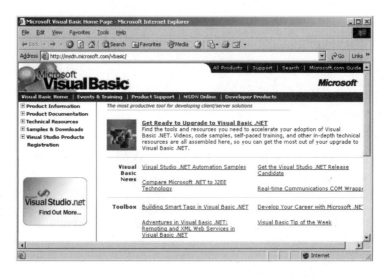

7 Maximize the Internet Explorer window if it isn't already full-size, and then click one or two links of interest to you.

The Microsoft Visual Basic Programming home page is an excellent resource for late-breaking news about programming tools, tips, conferences, books, and other information about Visual Basic.

21

Internet Explorer

8 After you have finished reviewing the page, close the Internet Explorer window. If you are asked whether you want to disconnect from the Internet, click No to remain connected.

9 Display the Show HTML form again.

The Show HTML program is still running, although it may have settled beneath a few other open applications by this point.

10 Place the cursor in the combo box on the Show HTML form, remove the current URL, and enter a URL of your own choosing. Then click Display HTML to open it.

In addition to entering URLs, you can also enter file paths in the combo box to display HTML documents stored on your hard disk.

11 After you've displayed three or four HTML documents, click the Close button on the Show HTML program's title bar, and then close any open Internet Explorer windows.

Now you'll take a look at the program code in the Show HTML application that utilizes the Internet Explorer object.

Examine the Internet Explorer code in Show HTML

1 View the code for Form1 in the Code Editor and scroll to the top where general variable declarations are defined.

You'll see the following program code:

```
Public Explorer As SHDocVw.InternetExplorer
```

Explorer is a public variable. The Show HTML program begins by declaring a public variable named Explorer that will facilitate the program's connection to the Internet Explorer object. The variable type is associated with the InternetExplorer class in the shdocvw.dll file, which must be included in your project by using the Add Reference command on the Project menu. (I made this reference for you in this project.)

2 Display the Button1_Click event procedure in the Code Editor.

You'll see the following program code:

```
Private Sub Button1_Click(ByVal sender As System.Object, _
  ByVal e As System.EventArgs) Handles Button1.Click
    Explorer = New SHDocVw.InternetExplorer()
    Explorer.Visible = True
    Explorer.Navigate(ComboBox1.Text)
End Sub
```

The Button1_Click event procedure runs when the user clicks the Display HTML button on the form and attempts to navigate to the URL or HTML document currently specified in the combo box. The event procedure begins by assigning a new Internet Explorer object to the Explorer public variable. Next, the procedure makes the Internet Explorer window visible and opens a document in the browser that corresponds to the user's selection in the combo box (a value currently held in the combo box object's Text property) by using the Navigate method. At this point, the Show HTML application has completed its part of the navigation and the user's attention is shifted to the open Internet Explorer window, which manages the connection to the Internet (if necessary) and allows the user to view the selected Web site and click any existing hyperlinks on the page.

3   Display the Form1_Load event procedure in the Code Editor.

You'll see the following program code:

```
Private Sub Form1_Load(ByVal sender As System.Object, _
   ByVal e As System.EventArgs) Handles MyBase.Load
      'Add a few useful Web sites to the combo box at startup
      ComboBox1.Items.Add("http://www.microsoft.com")
      ComboBox1.Items.Add("http://www.microsoft.com/mspress")
      ComboBox1.Items.Add("http://msdn.microsoft.com/vbasic")
      ComboBox1.Items.Add("http://www.devx.com")
End Sub
```

When the Show HTML program loads, the user is presented with a list of several "favorite" Web sites automatically. These URLs are presented in a combo box that I configured initially in the Form1_Load event procedure by using the Add method. Feel free to add your own favorite URLs to this list by including additional Add statements—the combo box object includes scroll bars when necessary and can accommodate many entries.

One Step Further:
Responding to Internet Explorer Events

In this chapter, you've used the Visible property and the Navigate method of the Internet Explorer object to display HTML documents. You can also take greater control of your browsing activities by responding to events that occur in the Internet Explorer object. As you may recall from previous chapters, each Visual Basic control has the ability to track status activities, or *events,* in the regular course of its operation. These events can include anything from a simple mouse movement in the PictureBox control (the MouseMove event) to notification that a key has been pressed in the TextBox control (the KeyPress event). The Internet Explorer object also produces events that you can respond to programmatically with event procedures. These include NavigateComplete2, DownloadBegin, DownloadComplete, TitleChange, DocumentComplete, and OnQuit.

If you want to use Internet Explorer events in your program, you first need to modify the statement in your program code that declares the Internet Explorer variable. Events produced by COM components aren't automatically listed in the Method Name drop-down list box of the Code Editor. However, you can include these events by using the WithEvents keyword when you make your variable declaration. In the Show HTML program developed in this chapter, you edit the variable declaration section of your form as follows:

WithEvents adds events to the Code Editor

```
Public WithEvents Explorer As SHDocVw.InternetExplorer
```

After you use the WithEvents keyword, the Explorer variable appears automatically in the Class Name drop-down list box in the Code Editor. When you select the Explorer object, its events appear in the Method Name drop-down list box. You can then select each event that you want to control and build an event procedure for it. You'll see how this works in a revision to the Show HTML program.

In the following exercise you'll write an event procedure that adds the URL for the current Web site in Internet Explorer to the combo box object in the Show HTML program.

Use the NavigateComplete2 event

The Show HTML program is located in the c:\vbnetsbs\ chap21\show html folder.

1   If the Show HTML project isn't open, load it into the Visual Studio development environment.

2   Display the variable declarations section of the program in the Code Editor (the area just below the tag "Windows Form Designer generated code").

3   Add the WithEvents keyword to the Internet Explorer variable declaration after the Public keyword.

    Your object declaration should look like this:

```
Public WithEvents Explorer As SHDocVw.InternetExplorer
```

4   Move your cursor to another line so that Visual Studio can recognize the WithEvents change.

5   Click the Class Name drop-down list box in the Code Editor, and then click the Explorer object.

6   Click the Method Name drop-down list box in the Code Editor, and then click the NavigateComplete2 event.

    The Explorer_NavigateComplete2 event procedure and its parameters appear in the Code Editor.

7   Type the following statement in the Explorer_NavigateComplete2 event procedure:

```
ComboBox1.Items.Add(Explorer.LocationURL)
```

Your procedure should now look like this:

```
Private Sub Explorer_NavigateComplete2(ByVal pDisp As Object, _
   ByRef URL As Object) Handles Explorer.NavigateComplete2
      ComboBox1.Items.Add(Explorer.LocationURL)
End Sub
```

The NavigateComplete2 event occurs when the Internet Explorer object has successfully loaded the specified document into the browser—an invalid Web page or URL won't trigger the event. As a result, watching for the NavigateComplete2 event is a useful way to keep track of the Web documents you've recently loaded. If you use the LocationURL property of the Explorer object, you can build your own history list of HTML documents. In this example, I've simply added the visited URL to the combo box on the form, so you can easily revisit the site with a mere mouse click. However, you also could store this information permanently by writing the URL to a file or a database.

8   Click the Save All button on the toolbar to save your changes.

9   Click the Start button on the Standard toolbar to run the program.

10   Click one of the Web sites listed in the combo box, and then click the Display HTML button.

11   After the connection is established, click some of the hyperlinks on the site to jump to a few new URLs.

12   Click the Show HTML program icon on the taskbar, and then click the combo box again.

The new sites you visited are added to the Show HTML combo box, as shown here:

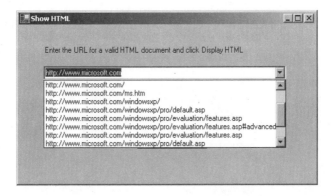

Experiment with the NavigateComplete2 event by visiting a few more Web sites and seeing how they are added to the combo box.

13   When you're finished, close the Internet Explorer windows you have open. Then click the Close button on the Show HTML application's title bar.

You're finished working with the Internet Explorer object in this chapter. Nice job!

Chapter 21 Quick Reference

To	Do this
Add a COM reference to the Internet Explorer object library to your program	On the Project menu, click the Add Reference command, click the COM tab, click the Microsoft Internet Controls entry, click the Select button, and then click OK.
Investigate the Internet Explorer object model	Press F2 to open the Object Browser, click the plus sign (+) next to the Interop.SHDocVw object, and then click the plus sign next to SHDocVw. Scroll down the list of objects, and then click the object named Internet Explorer. Click individual members of the Internet Explorer object in the Members pane to learn more about them.

Start Internet Explorer in your program	Declare a variable of the SHDocVw.InternetExplorer type, create a new instance using the New keyword, and set its Visible property to True. For example:
	`Dim Explorer As SHDocVw.InternetExplorer`
	`Explorer = New SHDocVw.InternetExplorer`
	`Explorer.Visible = True`

Display a Web site with the Internet Explorer object	Use the Navigate method. For example: `Explorer.Navigate("http://www.microsoft.com/")`

Access the events of an external object (such as Internet Explorer)	Declare your object by using the WithEvents keyword. For example:
	`Public WithEvents Explorer As _`
	`  SHDocVw.InternetExplorer`

Using Web Forms to Build Interactive Web Applications

In this chapter you will learn how to:

✔ *Create a new Web application.*

✔ *Use the Web Forms Designer.*

✔ *Add text and formatting effects to a Web Forms page.*

✔ *Use Web Forms controls to make Web applications interactive.*

✔ *Create an HTML page.*

✔ *Use the HyperLink control to link one page to another within a Web application.*

In Chapter 21, you learned the fundamental concepts of HTML and how to display HTML pages in a Visual Basic .NET application using Microsoft Internet Explorer. In this chapter, you'll learn how to build your own Web applications using the Web Forms Designer that is supplied with Microsoft Visual Basic .NET. *Web Forms* is a new programming model for Internet user interfaces based on ASP.NET, the Visual Studio .NET Framework component designed to provide state-of-the-art Internet functionality. Web Forms is a replacement for WebClasses and the DHTML Page Designer in Visual Basic 6, and it is distinct from the Windows Forms components that you have used for most of the projects in this book. Although a complete description of Web Forms and ASP.NET isn't possible here, there is enough in common between Web Forms and Windows Forms to allow you some useful experimentation right away— even if you have little or no experience in Internet programming and HTML page design. Invest a few hours in this chapter and see if Web Forms is for you!

Upgrade Notes:
What's New in Visual Basic .NET?

If you're experienced with Visual Basic 6, you'll notice some new features in Visual Basic .NET, including the following:

- A new Internet programming model called Web Forms, which is part of ASP.NET. Web Forms and the Web Forms Designer are a replacement for the Visual Basic 6 WebClasses and DHTML Page Designer, which are no longer supported in Visual Basic .NET.

- Although the Web Forms Designer is distinct from the Windows Forms Designer, both user-interface tools offer similar controls and support drag-and-drop programming techniques. Because the Web Forms Designer is part of Visual Studio .NET, it is available to Visual Basic .NET and Visual C# .NET.

- Web Forms applications are designed to be displayed by Web browsers, such as Internet Explorer. The controls on Web Forms are visible in the client's Web browser (in other words, on the end-user's computer), but the functionality for the controls resides on the Web server that hosts the actual Web application.

- Although many of the Web Forms controls have the same names as the Windows Forms controls, the controls aren't identical. For example, Web Forms controls have an ID property, rather than a Name property.

Inside ASP.NET

The Web Forms Designer helps you create Web applications.

ASP.NET is Microsoft's latest Web development platform. Although ASP.NET has some similarities with the previous version, named ASP (Active Server Pages), ASP.NET has been completely redesigned based on the .NET Framework. Web Forms is the design component of ASP.NET that allows you to create and manage Internet user interfaces, commonly called Web pages, or (in a more comprehensive sense) Web applications. Using Web Forms, you can create a Web application that displays a user interface, processes data, and provides many of the commands and features that a standard application for Windows might offer. However, the Web application you create runs in a Web browser such as Internet Explorer or Netscape Navigator, and it is stored on one or more *Web servers*, which display the correct Web pages and handle most of the computing tasks required by your Web application. This distributed strategy allows your Web applications to potentially run anywhere on the Internet while residing physically in one manageable location on the Web server where rich data resources may also be stored.

To create a Web application in Visual Basic .NET, you create a new ASP.NET Web Application project in the Visual Studio development environment, and then use the Web Forms Designer to build one or more Web Forms that will collectively represent your program. Each Web Form consists of two pieces—a Web Forms page and a code-behind file. The Web Forms page contains HTML and controls to create the user interface. The code-behind file is a code module that contains program code that "stands behind" the Web Forms page. This division is conceptually much like Windows Forms you have been creating in Visual Basic—there is a user interface component and a code module component. The code for both of these components may be stored in a single .aspx file, but typically the Web Forms page code is stored in an .aspx file and the code-behind is stored in an .aspx.vb file. The following illustration shows a conceptual view of how an ASP.NET Web application is displayed in a Web browser:

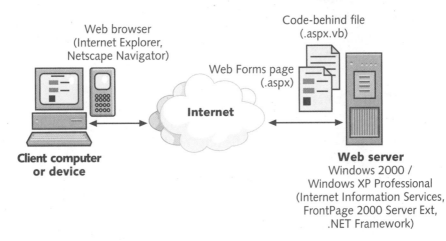

In addition to Web Forms, Web applications can contain code modules (.vb files), HTML pages (.htm files), configuration information (a Web.config file), global Web application information (a Global.asax file), and other components. You can use the Web Forms Designer and Solution Explorer to switch back and forth between these components quickly and efficiently.

Web Forms vs. Windows Forms

What are the important differences between Web Forms and Windows Forms? To begin with, Web Forms offers a slightly different programming paradigm than Windows Forms. While Windows Forms uses a Windows application window as the primary user interface for a program, Web Forms presents information to the user via one or more Web pages with supporting program code. These pages are viewed through a Web browser, and they can be created using the Web Forms Designer.

Like a Windows Form, a Web Form can include text, graphic images, buttons, list boxes, and other objects that are used to provide information, process input, or display output. However, the basic set of controls you use to create a Web Forms page isn't the same as the set Visual Studio offers on the Windows Forms tab of the Toolbox. Instead, ASP.NET Web applications must use controls on either the HTML tab or the Web Forms tab of the Toolbox. Each of the HTML and Web Forms controls has its own unique methods, properties, and events, and although there are many similarities between these controls and Windows Forms controls, there are also several important differences.

Web Forms controls are *server controls*, meaning they run and can be programmed on the Web server. Server controls can be identified on a Web Form by the small green icon that appears in the upper left corner of the control at design time. HTML controls are client controls by default, meaning they run only within the end user's browser. HTML controls can be configured as server controls by right-clicking the controls in the Web Forms Designer and selecting Run As Server Control or by setting their Runat attribute to Server. For now, however, you simply need to know that you can use HTML controls, Windows Forms controls, or a combination of both in your Web application projects.

HTML Controls

The HTML controls are a set of older user interface controls that are supported by most Web browsers and conform closely to the early HTML standards developed for managing user interface elements on a typical Web page. They include Button, Text Field, and Checkbox—useful base controls for managing information on a Web page that can be represented entirely with HTML code. Indeed, you may recognize these controls if you have coded in HTML before or if you have had some experience with the Visual Basic 6 DHTML Page Designer. However, although they are easy to use and have the advantage of being a "common denominator" for most Web browsers, they are limited by the fact that they have no ability to maintain their own state unless they are configured as server controls. (In other words, the data that they contain will be lost between views of a Web page.) The following illustration shows the HTML controls offered on the HTML tab of the Toolbox in Visual Studio:

HTML controls

Toolbox
Data
Web Forms
Components
HTML
➤ Pointer
A Label
Button
Reset Button
Submit Button
Text Field
Text Area
File Field
Password Field
Checkbox
Radio Button
Hidden
Table
Flow Layout Panel
Grid Layout Panel
Image
Listbox
Dropdown
Horizontal Rule
Clipboard Ring
General

Web Forms Controls

Web Forms controls are the newest addition to Visual Studio .NET and offer more features and capabilities than HTML controls. Web Forms controls are more capable than HTML controls and function in many ways like the Windows Forms controls. Indeed, many of the Web Forms controls have the same names as the Windows Forms controls and offer many of the same properties, methods, and events. Not only are simple controls such as Button, TextBox, and Label provided, but also more sophisticated controls such as DataGrid, Calendar, and RequiredFieldValidator. The following illustration shows some of the Web Forms controls on the Web Forms tab of the Toolbox:

Web Forms controls

Toolbox
Data
Web Forms
➤ Pointer
A Label
TextBox
Button
LinkButton
ImageButton
A HyperLink
DropDownList
ListBox
DataGrid
DataList
Repeater
CheckBox
CheckBoxList
RadioButtonList
RadioButton
Image
Panel
PlaceHolder
Components
HTML
Clipboard Ring
General

Web Browser Support

You might be wondering, "Do these exciting new controls mean that all the users of my application will need to be using the latest, most up-to-date version of a specific Web browser? What if such an upgrade is not possible for our Web customers?"

Visual Studio .NET Web applications don't require the latest browser—Visual Studio .NET includes a targetSchema property for the DOCUMENT object that allows you to target a specific Web browser and versions. The targetSchema options are Internet Explorer 3.02 / Navigator 3.0, Internet Explorer 5.0, and Navigator 4.0. The default is Internet Explorer 5.0. The value of the targetSchema property affects the HTML code that Visual Studio generates and the features available in Visual Studio. For example, if the targetSchema property is set to Internet Explorer 3.02 / Navigator 3.0 and the pageLayout property is set to GridLayout, HTML tables are used for positioning objects instead of cascading style sheets (CSS).

The targetSchema property won't be discussed any further, but I will use the pageLayout property later in this chapter. If you are interested in learning more about targetSchema, search the Visual Studio online Help for the topic "targetSchema".

Getting Started with a Web Application

The best way to learn about ASP.NET and Web applications is to get some hands-on practice. In the exercises in this chapter, you'll create a simple Web application. This application is a car loan calculator that determines monthly payments and displays a second Web page containing Help text. You'll begin by verifying that Visual Studio is properly configured for ASP.NET programming, and then you'll create a new Web application project. Next you'll use the Web Forms Designer to create a Web Forms page with text and links on it, and you'll add controls to the Web Forms page by using controls on the Web Forms tab of the Toolbox.

Installing the Software for ASP.NET Programming

Before you write your first ASP.NET Web application, you need to verify that you have the necessary support files on your system. ASP.NET Web applications rely on a Web server running Windows 2000 or Windows XP Professional that has an installation of Microsoft Internet Information Services (IIS), the Microsoft FrontPage 2000 Server Extensions, and the .NET Framework libraries. You need to verify that you have these components installed now, either locally on your own computer or through a server connection.

> **important**
>
> Windows XP Home Edition doesn't include or support IIS and the FrontPage 2000 Server Extensions, which means you cannot create ASP.NET Web applications **locally** using Windows XP Home Edition. However, it is possible to create ASP.NET Web applications using Windows XP Home Edition by accessing a properly configured remote Web server. This chapter assumes that you are using Windows 2000 or Windows XP Professional and that your Web server is local.

Fundamentally, this is a Visual Studio .NET Setup issue—during the installation of the Visual Studio .NET software, a setup routine called Windows Component Update analyzed your system to see if you had the capability to create local Web projects. If you didn't have the necessary support files, you were asked to install IIS and the FrontPage 2000 Server Extensions using your original Windows 2000 or Windows XP Professional setup CDs. If you ignored these messages at the time and didn't install the necessary support files, you will need to install the files now to enable your system for ASP.NET programming.

> **note**
>
> Microsoft recommends that you install IIS and the FrontPage 2000 Server Extensions **before** you install the .NET Framework and Visual Studio .NET because the .NET Framework must register extensions with IIS. If you install IIS and the FrontPage 2000 Server Extensions after the .NET Framework, you will need to repair the .NET Framework as described in the steps below to ensure that it is configured properly.

If you find that you don't have IIS and the FrontPage 2000 Server Extensions installed to start programming with ASP.NET, follow these steps:

Install IIS and the FrontPage 2000 Server Extensions

1   On the Windows Start menu, click Settings, and then click Control Panel.

2   Double-click Add/Remove Programs.

3   In the Add/Remove Programs dialog box, click Add/Remove Windows Components.

4   In the Windows Components Wizard, click Internet Information Services (IIS), and then click Details.

5   If FrontPage 2000 Server Extensions and World Wide Web Server aren't already selected, click these check boxes.

note

If the FrontPage 2000 Server Extensions and World Wide Web Server options are already checked, your computer is probably already configured for ASP.NET programming. You can cancel the installation and continue at the section "Create a new Web application".

6   Click OK.

7   Click Next to start your installation of the files and follow the instructions that appear.

   You might be prompted to insert your Windows 2000 or Windows XP Professional CD during the installation process.

If it was necessary to install IIS and the FrontPage 2000 Server Extensions, follow these steps to repair the .NET Framework:

Repair the .NET Framework

1   If you are using Visual Studio .NET CDs, insert the Windows Component Update CD. If you are using a Visual Studio. NET DVD, insert the DVD.

If you are using CDs, a message might be displayed to insert Disk 1. Ignore this message and click OK.

2 On the Windows Start menu, click Run.

The Run dialog box appears.

3 If you are using Visual Studio .NET CDs, type the following command in one long line in the Open text box, replacing *<CDdrive>* with your CD drive letter:

```
<CDdrive>:\dotNetFramework\dotnetfx.exe /t:c:\temp
/c:"msiexec.exe /fvecms c:\temp\netfx.msi"
```

If you are using a Visual Studio .NET DVD, type the following command in one long line in the Open text box, replacing *<DVDdrive>* with your DVD drive letter:

```
<DVDdrive>:\wcu\dotNetFramework\dotnetfx.exe /t:c:\temp
/c:"msiexec.exe /fvecms c:\temp\netfx.msi"
```

4 Click OK.

A message will appear asking you if you want to install the Microsoft .NET Framework Package.

5 Click Yes.

After you complete the .NET Framework repair process, your computer should be ready for ASP.NET programming.

note

Because the Visual Studio .NET software installation hasn't been performed in the order that Microsoft recommends, you still might encounter problems when creating Web applications. For example, you might not be able to create a new ASP.NET Web application project, or the Web application might not display properly in a Web browser. If you still encounter problems after performing the steps in this section, check out the following resources:

Setup\WebServer.htm and Setup\WebServerInfo.htm on Visual Studio .NET CD1 or DVD

"Visual Studio .NET Software Requirements" and "Troubleshooting Web Projects" topics in the Visual Studio online Help

After you have loaded the necessary support files, you're ready to build your first ASP.NET Web application.

Create a new Web application

1   Start Visual Studio and open the New Project dialog box.

2   In the New Project dialog box, click the ASP.NET Web Application icon in the Visual Basic Projects folder.

When you select this icon, Visual Studio will prepare the development environment and your program files for Internet programming.

Creating a new ASP.NET Web application project is similar to creating a Windows Application project. However, the Name text box is disabled and the Location text box is a different type of setting. In a Web application environment, you are directed to specify a specific Web server for your project, or accept the default value of http://localhost. As I mentioned earlier, you can choose a local or remote Web server (that has the .NET Framework and supporting files installed) for your project while it is under construction, and Visual Studio will use the specified Web server to place and organize your project files. The Web server isn't identified using a drive and folder names, but rather using a valid Internet address (URL).

3   Enter your Web server URL and the Web application name in the Location text box. Because these steps assume your Web server is on your local machine, type **http://localhost/MyWebCalculator**.

Your screen will look this:

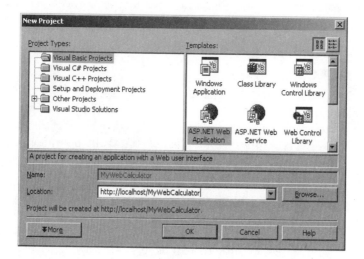

4   Click OK.

note

If Visual Studio displays an error while attempting to create a new ASP.NET Web application project, your setup isn't configured properly for ASP.NET programming. Review the steps in the section "Installing the Software for ASP.NET Programming" earlier in this chapter to make sure you have the proper software installed.

Visual Studio loads the Web Forms Designer and creates a Web Forms page (WebForm1.aspx) that will contain the user interface and a code-behind file (WebForm1.aspx.vb) that will contain the code for your Web application. Your screen will look like this:

Web Forms controls

Formatting toolbar   Web Forms Designer   WebForm1.aspx file

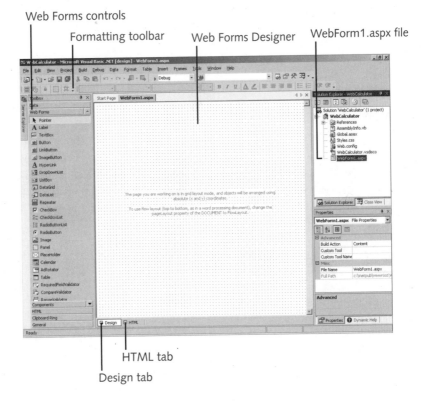

HTML tab

Design tab

Unlike the Windows Forms Designer, the Web Forms Designer displays the Web Forms page in the center of the development environment using a large white document window and a grid of tiny grey dots. Two tabs at the bottom of the designer (Design and HTML) allow you to change your view of this Web Forms page. The Design tab (the default view) shows you approximately how your Web Forms page will look when it is displayed by a Web browser. When the Design tab is selected, you can choose either grid layout mode or flow layout mode to control how the objects on your Web Forms page are arranged. The message you see on the Web Forms page describes these two modes. (You'll experiment with them in the next section.)

The HTML tab at the bottom of the designer lets you view and edit the HTML code that is used to display the Web Forms page in a Web browser. If you've used Microsoft Visual InterDev or Microsoft FrontPage in the past, you'll be familiar with these two ways of displaying a Web Forms page and perhaps with some of the HTML formatting codes that control how Web Forms pages are actually displayed.

A few additional changes in Visual Studio are also worth noting at this point. Below the Standard toolbar are new Design and Formatting toolbars, which contain design and formatting options for your Web Forms page. The Web Forms tab of the Toolbox is visible on the left side of the screen and offers the Web Forms controls that you can use to customize your ASP.NET Web applications. (If you don't see the Web Forms controls, click the Web Forms tab now.) Solution Explorer on the right side of the screen contains a different list of project files for the Web application you are building. In particular, note the WebForm1.aspx file in Solution Explorer, which contains the user interface code for this Web Forms page.

Now you're ready to add some text to the Web Forms page using the Web Forms Designer.

Using the Web Forms Designer

Unlike a Windows Form, you can add text directly to a Web Forms page when it is in flow layout mode in the Web Forms Designer. In flow layout mode, text appears in top-to-bottom fashion as it does in a word processor, such as Microsoft Word. You can type text in flow layout mode, edit it, and then make formatting changes using the Formatting toolbar. Manipulating text in this way is usually much faster than adding a Web Forms Label control to the Web page to contain the text. You'll practice entering the text for your car loan calculator in the following exercise.

Add text in flow layout mode

1   Click the Web Forms page in the Web Forms Designer, and then open the Properties window.

   You'll change the Web Forms Designer from grid layout mode to flow layout mode to facilitate text entry on the form, but before you do so you need to select the Web Forms page in the designer. When the Web Forms page is selected, the label DOCUMENT will appear in the Object drop-down list box of the Properties window.

2   Change the pageLayout property of the DOCUMENT object to FlowLayout.

   Visual Studio removes the grid from the Web Forms page. You can switch between flow layout and grid layout by changing the pageLayout property when the DOCUMENT object is selected.

3   Click the Web Forms page again.

   A blinking text cursor appears at the top of the Web Forms page.

4   Type **Car Loan Calculator,** and then press Enter.

   Visual Studio displays the title of your Web application on the Web Forms page, exactly as it will appear when you run the program in your browser.

5   Type the following sentence below the application title:

   Enter the required information and click Calculate!

   Now you'll format the title with bold formatting and a larger point size.

6   Select the Car Loan Calculator text.

   When you select text on the form, the Formatting toolbar displays font information for the text you selected.

7   Click the Bold button on the Formatting toolbar, and set the font size to 5.

   Font size isn't specified in points in Web applications, but in relative sizes. (Font size 5 is about 18-point type.) Your screen will look like this:

Formatting toolbar

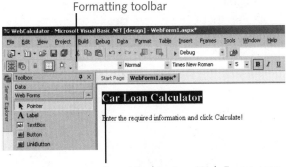

Formatted text on Web Forms page

Now you'll examine the HTML code for the text you entered.

View the HTML for a Web Forms page

1   Click the HTML tab at the bottom of the Web Forms Designer.

The HTML tab displays the actual HTML code for your Web Forms page. To see more of the code, you might want to temporarily close the Toolbox. The HTML code for the Web Forms page looks like this:

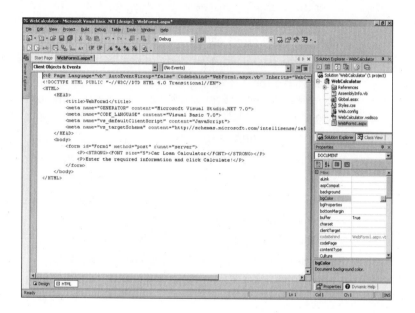

A Web Forms page is made up of file and document information, formatting codes called *HTML tags* that are enclosed in angle brackets, and the text and objects to be displayed by your Web Forms page. This Web Forms page is still rather short—it contains a header with information about the language you selected when creating the Web application, the name of any code-behind file, and any inherited forms.

The body tag identifies the beginning of the document; tags typically always appear in pairs so that you can see clearly where a section begins and ends. Notice that the "Car Loan Calculator" text appears within a line of HTML that formats the text as strong (bold) with font size 5. Below this text, the second line of text you entered is displayed.

tip

The HTML view is an actual editor, so you can change the text you entered now by using standard text editing techniques. If you know something about HTML, you can add additional formatting tags and content as well.

2   Click the Design tab to display your Web Forms page in Design view, and open the Toolbox if you closed it.

3   Select DOCUMENT in the Object drop-down list box of the Properties window.

4   Set the pageLayout property to GridLayout.

You're finished adding text to the Web Forms page, so you can switch from flow layout to grid layout.

Flow Layout vs. Grid Layout

Why are there two different layout modes, flow layout and grid layout? Each layout mode has advantages and disadvantages, but fundamentally, the choices are designed to give you, the Web application designer, different ways to control how a Web Form looks in a Web browser. Grid layout allows you to precisely position, size, and even overlap objects on a Web Form page. The drawback is that grid layout generates more complicated HTML to position the objects, which might not display as expected in different or older browsers. If you want your Web applications to display cleanly in the widest ranges of Web browsers, set the pageLayout property to FlowLayout and the targetSchema property to Internet Explorer 3.02 / Navigator 3.0.

Adding Web Forms Controls to a Web Application

Now you'll add TextBox, Label, and Button controls to the car loan calculator. Although these controls are located on the Web Forms tab of the Toolbox, they are very similar to the Windows Forms controls of the same name that you have used throughout this book. (I'll cover a few of the important differences coming up.) After you add the controls to the Web Forms page, you'll set property settings for the controls.

Use TextBox, Label, and Button controls

1   Display the Web Forms tab of the Toolbox if it isn't already visible, and verify that the Web Forms page is in grid layout mode. (The grid should be visible on the form.)

abl

TextBox control

2   Click the Web Forms TextBox control, and then create a text box object on the Web Forms page below the text you entered. Align the text box object along the left margin.

Visual Studio allows you to create Web Forms controls just like you create Windows Forms controls. Because the Web Forms page is in grid layout mode, you can size and position the controls precisely, just like you can fine-tune the placement of controls on a Windows Form.

Notice the small green icon that appears in the upper left corner of the control, which indicates that this control runs on the server.

3 Create two more text box objects below the first text box.

Now you'll create labels using the Web Forms Label control to identify the purpose of the text boxes.

A

Label control

4 Click the Web Forms Label control, and then draw a label object to the right of the first text box object.

5 Create two more label objects below the first label object and to the right of the second and third text box objects.

ab

Button control

6 Use the Web Forms Button control to draw a button object at the bottom of the Web Forms page.

The Button control, like the TextBox and Label controls, is very similar to its Windows Forms counterpart. Your screen should look like this:

Green icon indicates server control

Now you'll set a few properties for the seven new controls you created on the Web Forms page. As you set the properties, you'll notice one important difference between Web Forms and Windows Forms—the familiar Name property has been changed to ID in Web Forms. Despite their different names, the two properties perform the same function.

7 Set the following properties for the objects on the form:

Object	Property	Setting
TextBox1	ID	txtAmount
TextBox2	ID	txtInterest
TextBox3	ID	txtPayment
Label1	ID	lblAmount
	Text	"Loan Amount"
Label2	ID	lblInterest
	Text	"Interest Rate (for example, 0.09)"
Label3	ID	lblPayment
	Text	"Monthly Payment"
Button1	ID	btnCalculate
	Text	"Calculate"

Your Web Forms page will look like this:

Writing Event Procedures for Web Forms Controls

You write event procedures (or event handlers) for controls on a Web Forms page by double-clicking the objects on the Web Forms page and typing the necessary program code in the Code Editor. Although the user will see the controls on the Web Forms page in their own Web browser, the actual code that is executed is located on the Web server and is run by the Web server. When the user clicks a button, for example, the browser typically sends the button click event back to the server, which processes the event and sends a new Web page back to the browser. Although the process seems similar to Windows Forms, there is actually a lot going on behind the scenes when a control is used on a Web Forms page!

In the following exercise, you'll practice creating an event procedure for the btnCalculate object on the Web Forms page.

Create the btnCalculate_Click event procedure

1   Double-click the Calculate button on the Web Forms page.

The code-behind file (WebForm1.aspx.vb) is opened in the Code Editor and the btnCalculate_Click event procedure appears.

2   Type the following program code:

```
Dim LoanPayment As Single
'Use Pmt function to determine payment for 36 month loan
LoanPayment = Pmt(txtInterest.Text / 12, 36, txtAmount.Text)
txtPayment.Text = Format(Abs(LoanPayment), "$0.00")
```

This event procedure uses the Pmt function, a financial function that is part of the Visual Basic language, to determine what the monthly payment for a car loan would be using the specified interest rate (txtInterest.Text), a three-year (36-month) loan period, and the specified principal amount (txtAmount.Text). The result is stored in the LoanPayment single-precision variable, and then formatted with appropriate monetary formatting and displayed using the txtPayment text box object on the Web page. The Abs (absolute value) function is used to make the loan payment a positive number—the Pmt function returns a negative number by default (reflecting money that is owed), but I think this formatting looks strange when it isn't part of a balance sheet.

Notice that the program statements in the code-behind file are just regular Visual Basic code—the same stuff you've been using throughout this book. You'll even use an Imports statement. This process feels very similar to creating a Windows application.

3   Scroll to the top of the Code Editor, and enter the following program statement as the first line of the file:

```
Imports System.Math
```

As you learned in Chapter 5, the Abs function isn't included in Visual Basic by default, but it is part of the System.Math class in the .NET Framework, which can be included in your project via the Imports statement. Web applications can make use of the .NET Framework class libraries just like Windows applications can.

4   Click the Save All button on the Standard toolbar.

That's it! You've entered the program code necessary to run the car loan calculator and make your Web Forms page interactive. Now build the project and see how it works!

Build and run the Web application

1 Click the Start button on the Standard toolbar.

> **note**
>
> If an error displays here indicating that the Web server doesn't support debugging ASP.NET Web applications, this means that IIS, the FrontPage 2000 Server Extensions, and the .NET Framework aren't properly installed and configured. Review the section "Installing the Software for ASP.NET Programming" for recommendations on how to correct.

Visual Basic builds the project and runs it using Internet Explorer. The car loan calculator looks like this:

2 Type **18000** in the Loan Amount text box, and then type **0.09** in the Interest Rate text box.

You'll compute the monthly loan payment for an $18,000 loan at 9% interest for 36 months.

3 Click the Calculate button.

Visual Basic calculates the payment amount and displays $572.40 in the Monthly Payment text box. Your screen will look like this:

4   Close Internet Explorer.

You're finished testing your Web application for now. When Internet Explorer closes, your program is effectively ended. As you can see, building and running a Web application is basically the same as a Windows application, except that the final application is run in the browser. You can even set break points and debug your application just like it was a Windows application. To deploy a Web application, you would need to copy the .aspx file and any necessary support files for the project to a properly configured virtual directory on the Web server.

Validating Input Fields on a Web Forms Page

Although this Web application is useful, it runs into problems if the user forgets to enter a principal amount or interest rate, or specifies data in the wrong format. To make this Web application more robust, consider adding one or more *validator controls* to the Web Forms page that will require user input in the proper format. The validator controls are located on the Web Forms tab of the Toolbox and include controls that require data entry in important fields (RequiredFieldValidator), require entry in the proper range (RangeValidator), and so on. For information on the validator controls, search the Visual Studio online Help.

One Step Further: Creating a Link to Another Web Page

If your Web application will feature more than one Web page, you might want to use the HyperLink control on the Web Forms tab of the Toolbox to let your users jump from the current Web page to a new one. The HyperLink control places a hyperlink, which the user can click to display another Web page. When you use a HyperLink control, you specify the text that will be hyperlinked and you specify the desired resource to display (either a URL or a local path) by using the NavigateUrl property.

If you have already created the Web pages, you can add them to your Web application project and establish the proper links. If you want to create new Web pages, you can use Visual Studio .NET.

In the following exercise, you'll create a second Web page using Visual Studio, and you'll save it in HTML format along with your other project files. The document will be a Help file that users of your Web application can use to get more information. Next you'll add a HyperLink control to the WebCalculator project and set the HyperLink control's NavigateUrl property to the new HTML page.

Create an HTML Page

1   Click the Add HTML Page command on the Project menu.

    The Add New Item dialog box appears with the HTML Page template selected.

2   Type **WebCalculatorHelp.htm** in the Name text box and click Open.

    The WebCalculatorHelp.htm file is added to Solution Explorer and is opened in the HTML Designer in Design view.

    Notice that the Web Forms tab is no longer displayed in the Toolbox. Since this is an HTML page, the Web Forms controls aren't supported on this type of page.

3   Click the HTML page and change the pageLayout property in the Properties window to FlowLayout.

    Visual Studio removes the grid from the HTML page.

4   Click the HTML page to add your cursor and type the following text:

    Car Loan Calculator

    This Car Loan Calculator program was developed for the book *Microsoft Visual Basic .NET Step by Step*, by Michael Halvorson (Microsoft Press, 2002). The Web application is best viewed using Microsoft Internet Explorer version 5.0 or later. To learn more about how this application was created, read Chapter 22 in the book.

Operating instructions:

Type a loan amount, without dollar sign or commas, into the Loan Amount text box.

Type an interest rate in decimal format into the Interest Rate text box. Do not include the "%" sign. For example, to specify a 9% interest rate, type "0.09".

Note that this loan calculator assumes a three year, 36-month payment period.

Click the Calculate button to compute the basic monthly loan payment that does not include taxes or other bank fees.

5   Using the Formatting toolbar, add bold and italic as shown here:

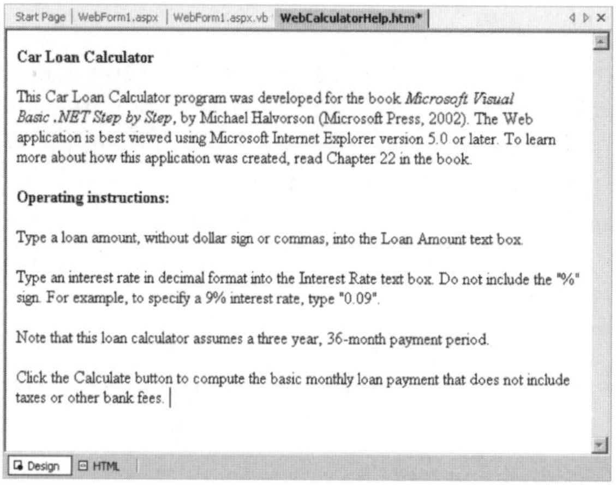

Now you'll use the HyperLink control to create a hyperlink on your Web Forms page that opens the WebCalculatorHelp.htm file.

Use the HyperLink control

1   Display the Web Forms page (WebForm1.aspx) in Design view.

A

*HyperLink
control*

2   Click the HyperLink control on the Web Forms tab of the Toolbox, and then draw a hyperlink object on the Web Forms page to the right of the Calculate button.

3   Set the Text property of the hyperlink object to **Get Help**.

The Text property contains the text that will appear underlined on the Web Forms page as the hyperlink. You want to use words here that will make it obvious there is a Web page available containing Help text if the user wants it.

4   Click the NavigateUrl property, and then click the ellipsis button in the second column.

Visual Studio opens the Select URL dialog box, which prompts you for the location of the Web page you want to link to.

5 Click the WebCalculatorHelp.htm file in the Contents pane.

The URL text box displays the name of the file you want to use as the hyperlink. Your dialog box will look like this:

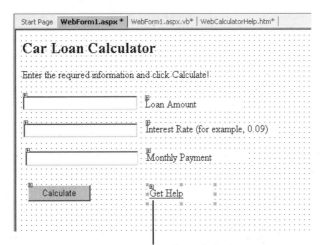

6 Click OK to set the NavigateUrl property.

Your Web page looks like this:

New hyperlink object

Your link is finished, and you're ready to run the WebCalculator application again.

The complete WebCalculator program is located in the c:\vbnetsbs\ chap22\ webcalculator folder. See the readme file in the chap22 folder for instructions on how to configure and test.

7   Click the Save All button on the Standard toolbar.

8   Click the Start button.

Visual Studio builds the Web application and runs it in Internet Explorer.

9   Compute another loan payment to verify that the original program is operating correctly (specify your own principal amount and interest rate this time).

10   Now click the Get Help hyperlink to see how the HyperLink control works.

After a moment, Internet Explorer displays the second Web page. Your screen looks like this:

11   Read the text, and then click the Back button in Internet Explorer.

Just like any Web application, you can click the Back and Forward buttons to jump from one Web page to the next.

12   When you're finished experimenting with the Web Calculator program, close Internet Explorer. You're finished working with Visual Basic .NET for now.

As you add additional HTML pages to your solution, feel free to add additional hyperlinks by using the handy HyperLink control. Although ASP.NET has many additional capabilities, you can see from these simple exercises how powerful Web Forms are and how similar the development process is to the Windows Forms techniques you have been learning.

Congratulations on completing the entire *Microsoft Visual Basic .NET Step by Step* programming course! You're ready for more sophisticated Visual Basic .NET challenges and programming techniques. Check out the resource list in Appendix B for a few ideas about continuing your learning.

Chapter 22 Quick Reference

To	Do this
Create a new Web application	Select the ASP.NET Web Application icon in the New Project dialog box, and then specify a Web server and a project name.
Enter text on a Web Forms page or an HTML page	Use the Properties window to change the DOCUMENT object's pageLayout property to FlowLayout, and then click the page and type the text you want to add.
Format text on a Web Forms page or an HTML page	In flow layout mode, select the text on the page that you want to format, and then click a button or control on the Formatting toolbar.
View the HTML code in your Web Forms page or HTML page	Click the HTML tab at the bottom of the designer.
Display the layout grid in the Web Forms Designer or HTML Designer	Use the Properties window to change the DOCUMENT object's pageLayout property to GridLayout.
Add controls to a Web Forms page	Display the HTML or Web Forms tabs of the Toolbox and drag controls to the Web Forms page in the Web Forms Designer.
Change the name of an object on a Web Forms page	Use the Properties window to change the object's ID property to a new name.
Write an event procedure for an object on a Web Forms page	Double-click the object to display the code-behind file and write the event procedure code for the object in the Code Editor.
Verify the format of the data entered by the user into a control on a Web Forms page	Use one or more validator controls from the Web Forms tab of the Toolbox to test the data entered in an input control.
Run a Web application in Visual Studio	Click the Start button on the Standard toolbar. Visual Studio will build the project and load the Web application into Internet Explorer.
Create an HTML page for a project	Click the Add HTML Page command on the Project menu, and then add the new HTML page to the project. Create and format the HTML page using the HTML Designer.
Create a link to other Web pages in your Web application	Add a Web Forms HyperLink control to your Web Forms page, and then set the control's NavigateUrl property to the address of the linked Web page.

PART 7

Appendixes

A

Upgrading Visual Basic 6 Programs to Visual Basic .NET

In this appendix you will learn how to:

✔ *Evaluate Visual Basic 6 programs for compatibility with Visual Basic .NET.*

✔ *Locate Internet resources for migrating applications.*

✔ *Run the Visual Basic Upgrade Wizard to upgrade Visual Basic 6 programs to Visual Basic .NET.*

This book teaches Visual Basic .NET programming techniques from scratch and assumes no previous programming experience. However, many users will be coming to Visual Basic .NET with significant development time in previous versions of Visual Basic, including Visual Basic 6. So what steps do you follow if you have older Visual Basic programs that you want to convert to Visual Basic .NET? Are there tools or resources that can assist in this upgrading, or *migration*, process?

This appendix identifies a few of your resources for analyzing and upgrading Visual Basic 6 programs to Visual Basic .NET. You'll learn some of the major features of Visual Basic 6 that are no longer supported in Visual Basic .NET, the strategies Microsoft recommends for migrating Visual Basic 6 applications, and the location of useful Internet resources that document the upgrading process in greater detail. You'll also learn how to use the Visual Basic Upgrade Wizard, which can automatically convert part or all of your Visual Basic 6 application to Visual Basic .NET.

Assessing Visual Basic 6 Programs for Compatibility

Visual Basic .NET is a very significant revision to the Visual Basic programming language and to Windows programming in general. This change brings numerous advantages: a revised Visual Basic language syntax, which emphasizes clear and maintainable code; the new .NET Framework class libraries, which add additional functionality and eliminate the hassle of calling Windows APIs; real object-oriented programming features, including inheritance; the new ADO.NET database programming model, which provides access to truly distributed data sources; and new controls in the Toolbox, including the Web Forms controls for Internet programming. However, these new features come at a cost—not all Visual Basic 6 code is supported in Visual Basic .NET, and in many cases you'll need to extensively revise existing Visual Basic 6 programs to make them compatible with Visual Basic .NET.

The decision is up to you—you can upgrade your existing Visual Basic 6 code or you can continue to maintain some of it in Visual Basic 6, which Microsoft has announced it will continue to sell and support. For each Visual Basic 6 application, you have three choices:

- Leave your programs in Visual Basic 6 format. Microsoft continues to support Visual Basic 6 and will do so for the foreseeable future.

- Upgrade part of your Visual Basic 6 program (for example, one or more components), and interoperate with COM components created using Visual Basic 6.

- Upgrade the entire Visual Basic 6 program to Visual Basic .NET.

Your decision will depend on the goals of your project. If your Visual Basic 6 application is basically complete, if you are in maintenance mode, or if your program relies on some older components that cannot easily be updated, you may wish to leave the program in Visual Basic 6 format. If your application is still in development, if it will make particular use of XML or Web pages, or if it will utilize distributed data sources, upgrading the program to Visual Basic .NET will likely be cost effective.

Problematic Issues

Microsoft has provided a list of unsupported or problematic features in Visual Basic 6 that will require special consideration when you upgrade your application to Visual Basic .NET. The list includes

- **OLE Container Control.** This ActiveX control isn't supported in Visual Basic .NET, and no replacement is available.

- **Dynamic Data Exchange.** Dynamic Data Exchange (DDE) methods are no longer supported. Applications that depend on DDE should be revised to use another method of inter-application communication, such as the SendMessage API.

- **DAO or RDO Data Binding.** Data binding to a DAO or an RDO data source isn't supported in Visual Basic .NET. The Data control and the RemoteData control are no longer available in Visual Basic .NET. Applications that rely on DAO or RDO data binding either should be updated to use ADO in Visual Basic 6 or should use ADO.NET after upgrading to Visual Basic .NET.

- **Visual Basic 5 Projects.** Visual Basic 5 projects should be upgraded to Visual Basic 6 projects before upgrading to Visual Basic .NET. To upgrade to Visual Basic 6, open the project in Visual Basic 6 and choose to upgrade controls. Then save the project in Visual Basic 6 before upgrading to Visual Basic .NET.

- **ActiveX DHTML Page Applications.** These are client-side Web technologies and cannot be automatically upgraded to Visual Basic .NET. These should be left in Visual Basic 6. These applications interoperate well with Visual Basic .NET technologies; you can navigate from an ActiveX DHTML page application to a Web Forms page and back.

- **ActiveX Documents.** Like ActiveX DHTML page applications, ActiveX documents cannot be automatically upgraded to Visual Basic .NET. Similarly, you can navigate from an ActiveX document to an ASP.NET Web page and back; so, you can leave these applications in Visual Basic 6.

- **Property Pages.** These aren't supported in Visual Basic .NET because the Windows Forms property browser is very flexible and can display and edit any classes, unlike the Visual Basic 6 property browser. You should reimplement the properties on property pages as standard control properties.

- **User Controls.** User controls created with Visual Basic 6 can be used in Visual Basic .NET. Currently, modifications to user controls should be done in Visual Basic 6.

- **WebClasses.** Visual Basic 6 WebClasses cannot be upgraded to Visual Basic .NET Web Forms. WebClasses can interoperate with Visual Basic .NET Web technologies, however—you can navigate from a Visual Basic 6 WebClass to an ASP.NET application or from an ASP.NET application to a Visual Basic 6 WebClass.

- **Visual Basic Add-Ins.** Because Visual Basic .NET uses the Visual Studio IDE, the object model for extensibility is significantly different from that of Visual Basic 6. Add-ins must be rewritten in Visual Basic. NET. The advantage in doing so is that the add-in will then be available to all languages.

- **Graphics.** The Visual Basic 6 forms graphics methods, such as Line and Circle, cannot be automatically upgraded by the Visual Basic Upgrade Wizard.

- **Drag-and-Drop Functionality.** Drag-and-drop functionality cannot be automatically upgraded by the Visual Basic Upgrade Wizard.

- **Variants.** Visual Basic .NET no longer supports the Variant data type in Visual Basic 6. When an application is upgraded using the Visual Basic Upgrade Wizard, the Variant data type is converted to Object.

- **Windows APIs.** It is still legitimate to call the Windows API directly in a Visual Basic .NET application, but many existing API calls are no longer necessary due to the increased functionality of the .NET Framework class libraries. Existing calls to the Windows API in Visual Basic 6 applications might need to be revised, although direct calls are still permissible.

Internet Resources for Migration

Microsoft is aware that upgrading existing code is an important priority, so it has assembled numerous resources on the Web to make the process easier, or at least more straightforward. The following Web site contains useful information for assessing existing Visual Basic 6 applications and converting them to Visual Basic .NET:

http://msdn.microsoft.com/vbasic/technical/upgrade/

On this site you'll find white papers about various aspects of upgrading Visual Basic 6 applications, technical sessions (multimedia presentations) describing important migration tools and issues, and checklists for planning the conversion process. This site changes periodically, so monitor it on a regular basis if you are upgrading one or more Visual Basic 6 applications to Visual Basic .NET.

Upgrade Steps

If you decide that upgrading your existing Visual Basic 6 applications to Visual Basic .NET is your best choice, here are the overall steps that Microsoft recommends:

1   Install Visual Basic 6 and Visual Basic .NET on the same computer.

    Installing Visual Basic 6 isn't a requirement, but if the project to be upgraded uses controls or components that don't have an upgrade equivalent in Visual Basic .NET, you might encounter additional upgrade errors and warnings.

2   Compile and run your application in Visual Basic 6 first to ensure it works correctly.

3   Run the Visual Basic Upgrade Wizard to upgrade.

4   Review the upgrade report and upgrade comments and make any necessary modifications.

Running the Visual Basic Upgrade Wizard

Visual Studio .NET includes a special program called the Visual Basic Upgrade Wizard that can assist you in upgrading your Visual Basic 6 applications to Visual Basic .NET. The Visual Basic Upgrade Wizard isn't a complete solution for migrating Visual Basic 6 applications—the tool can handle most repetitive code changes and can even swap Visual Basic 6 controls for .NET controls on forms. But in all except the most trivial applications, you'll have some hand coding to do when the wizard is complete.

The Visual Basic Upgrade Wizard starts automatically when you try to load a Visual Basic 6 application in Visual Studio .NET. It creates a new Visual Basic .NET project for the original application, and then migrates as much code as possible. When the wizard cannot upgrade a feature, it adds comments to the program code identifying issues that you will need to address later. The wizard also creates an upgrade report listing general issues related to the migration and any problems it wasn't able to fix.

The following exercise demonstrates how the Visual Basic Upgrade Wizard works. In the example, I'll open and upgrade a Visual Basic 6 project named Alarm.vbp, which uses a Timer control, TextBox controls, and Button controls to create a personal appointment reminder that notifies users when it is time for an important meeting. Because the program doesn't use features that aren't supported in Visual Basic .NET, the upgrade is relatively straightforward. Within Visual Basic 6, the Alarm project looks like this:

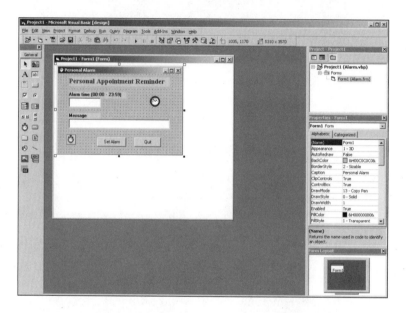

note

Because the Alarm Visual Basic 6 project doesn't use any unsupported features, it isn't necessary to have Visual Basic 6 installed to follow these upgrade steps.

Upgrade the Alarm program

1   Start Visual Studio .NET and open the Alarm.vbp project in the c:\vbnetsbs\appa\alarmvb6 folder.

Visual Studio recognizes that Alarm.vbp is a Visual Basic 6 project, and it starts the Visual Basic Upgrade Wizard to upgrade the project to Visual Basic .NET. You'll see this dialog box:

A

Upgrading

note

Visual Basic .NET Standard doesn't include the Visual Basic Upgrade Wizard. If your edition of Visual Studio .NET doesn't include the Visual Basic Upgrade Wizard, a message box will be displayed indicating that Visual Basic 6 migration isn't supported.

As the dialog box indicates, the Visual Basic Upgrade Wizard assists in the migration process by creating a new Visual Basic .NET project for the Visual Basic 6 application, copying form and class files to the project and converting them to the new format, and issuing an upgrade report that identifies additional work items. The upgrade report is added to the Visual Basic .NET project so that it is easy to locate and read.

2   Click Next to start the conversion.

The wizard asks you some questions about the format of your project and its component contents. Your screen will look like the illustration on the following page.

Visual Basic Upgrade Wizard - Page 2 of 5

Choose a Project Type
The wizard can upgrade your project to one of several new project types.

Your Visual Basic 6.0 project is a Windows Application.

What type of project would you like this to be upgraded to?

- ◉ EXE
- ○ DLL / custom control library

More Information

Cancel   < Back   Next >

In this example, EXE format was selected by default for the Alarm application because the tool is an application program and not a DLL (dynamic link library).

3   Click Next to continue the upgrade process.

The wizard prompts you for a location for the new Visual Basic .NET project. The default folder is a subfolder within your original project folder, as shown in this dialog box:

Visual Basic Upgrade Wizard - Page 3 of 5

Specify a Location for Your New Project
The wizard will place your new project files in a new folder.

Where do you want your new project created?

C:\vbnetsbs\appa\AlarmVB6\Project1.NET   Browse...

The project will be created as: C:\vbnetsbs\appa\AlarmVB6\Project1.NET\Alarm.vbproj

Cancel   < Back   Next >

4   Change the new project path to **c:\vbnetsbs\appa\my alarmvb.net**

This will place the upgraded Visual Basic .NET project in a new folder named My AlarmVB.NET in the appa folder.

5   Click the Next button, and then click Yes if you are prompted to create a new folder.

6   Click Next again to begin the upgrade process.

The Visual Basic Upgrade Wizard invokes the upgrade engine and steps through the Alarm project's form and code to convert the controls to .NET controls, to update the program code to conform to Visual Basic .NET specifications, and to create an upgrade report. The upgrade report is saved in HTML format and is named _UpgradeReport.htm.

After a few minutes, the wizard closes and the new Visual Basic .NET project appears in the Visual Studio development environment. The new project's contents are listed in Solution Explorer.

7   If the form isn't visible, select Alarm.vb now in Solution Explorer and click the View Designer button.

Your screen will look like this:

View Designer button

If you compare this figure to the first one in this appendix (the Alarm project loaded in Visual Basic 6), a few characteristics of the Visual Basic Upgrade Wizard are apparent. First, although the wizard accurately sized the form and its objects, the fonts used on the form aren't an exact match and will need to be adjusted in Visual Studio .NET to display the proper user interface. Second, the Visual Basic 6 controls were upgraded to .NET controls. The Label and TextBox controls were upgraded to their equivalent .NET versions. The CommandButton controls are now Button controls, even though they still have the "Command" name. The Image control showing the clock was upgraded to a .NET PictureBox control. Visual Studio doesn't have an Image control, and graphic files are now displayed using just the PictureBox control. The Timer control was upgraded to the .NET version, and it now appears in the component tray.

Finally, the wizard has added a ToolTip control to the component tray below the form. In Visual Basic 6, many controls had a ToolTipText property to display a tool tip for an individual control. Visual Studio .NET has a different mechanism to display tool tips and uses a single ToolTip control to manage tool tips for all the controls on a form. Since many Visual Basic 6 controls had the ToolTipText property, even if it was empty, the Visual Basic Upgrade Wizard adds it as a matter of course to upgraded Visual Basic 6 projects.

8   Double-click the _UpgradeReport.htm file in Solution Explorer.

Visual Studio displays the formatted upgrade report, giving you an opportunity to review the issues that remain in the migration of this application.

9   If necessary, close the Toolbox to get more space, and then open the Global Issues and Alarm.vb sections by clicking the plus signs (+) to read the detailed report.

Your screen will look like this:

The upgrade report describes any upgrade issues. For example, the PaletteMode property for the form wasn't upgraded and the default property for the Timer1 object couldn't be resolved. If you click on the Description hyperlinks, additional documentation about the issue is displayed.

10 Click Alarm.vb in Solution Explorer and click the View Code button to display the Alarm code in the Code Editor.

View Code button

Near the top of the Code Editor, you'll see a collapsed Upgrade Support section. This section includes code to assist in the Visual Basic 6 compatibility. As you scan through the program code, you'll see comments that flag potential issues as shown here:

Upgrade Support section

Upgrade comments

These upgrade comments describe the issue, and if you scroll the Code Editor to the right, the comments typically contain a hyperlink for additional documentation. For example:

```
'UPGRADE_WARNING: Couldn't resolve default property of object
   CurrentTime. Click for more:
   'ms-help://MS.VSCC/commoner/redir/redirect.htm?keyword="vbup1037"'
```

Realizing that some upgrade problems might be confusing, Microsoft has engineered the Visual Basic Upgrade Wizard to insert hyperlinks to where there is more information.

A

Upgrading

Run the upgraded Alarm program

The upgraded Alarm program is located in the c:\vbnetsbs\appa\ alarmvb.net folder.

1   Click the Start button on the Standard toolbar.

A Save File As dialog box appears asking for a location and a name for the Alarm solution file.

2   Click Save to accept the default name of Alarm.sln in the AlarmVB.NET folder.

The Personal Alarm form appears! Even though the upgrade included warnings, it didn't include errors that required modifications to the code.

3   Type a time in the Alarm Time text box that is a couple minutes in the future. Specify the time using a military format, where 8:00 am is specified as 08:00 and 1:00 pm is specified as 13:00.

4   Type a short message in the Message text box, such as **Upgraded to Visual Basic .NET!**, and then click the Set Alarm button.

Patiently wait for the time to expire, and you should see your message appear.

5   Click OK, and then click Quit to close the program.

In this simple case, the Visual Basic 6 project was upgraded, and it didn't require modifications to run. However, most upgrades will require some modifications to compile and run without error. You will also typically need to make some user interface adjustments and perform careful testing to ensure the program works the same. In my opinion, the benefits of upgrading most projects using the Visual Basic Upgrade Wizard outweigh the potential disadvantages, but you'll need to assess this for your own projects on a case-by-case basis. Best of luck!

B

Where to Go for More Information

In this appendix you will learn how to:

✔ *Search Web sites for information about Visual Basic .NET.*

✔ *Locate additional books about Visual Basic .NET programming.*

This book has presented beginning, intermediate, and advanced Visual Basic .NET programming techniques with the aim of making you a confident software developer and Windows programmer. Now that you have experimented with many of the tools and features in Visual Basic .NET, you are ready for more advanced topics and the full breadth of the Visual Studio .NET development suite. If you have your sights set on a career in Visual Basic programming, you may also wish to test your proficiency by preparing for a certified exam in Visual Basic .NET development. In this appendix, you'll learn about additional resources for Visual Basic .NET programming, including helpful Web sites on the Internet, a source for certification information, and books that you can use to expand your Visual Basic .NET programming skills.

Visual Basic .NET Web Sites

The Web is a boon to programmers and is definitely the fastest mechanism for gathering information about Visual Basic .NET and related technologies. In the following section, I list several of the Web sites that I use to learn about new products and services related to Visual Basic .NET. As you use this list, note that the Internet address and contents of each site changes from time to time, so things may not appear exactly as I have described. Considering the constant ebb and flow of the Internet, it is also a good idea to search for "visual basic" or "visual studio .net" occasionally to see what new information is available.

http://msdn.microsoft.com/vbasic/

The Microsoft Corporation Visual Basic home page is the best overall site for documentation, breaking news, conference information, and product support for Visual Basic .NET. This site will give you up-to-date information about the entire Visual Basic product line and will let you know how new operating systems, applications, and programming tools affect Visual Basic development. From the Visual Basic home page, you can also click on support links for the remaining Visual Studio .NET tools.

http://www.devx.com/

DevX is a commercial Web site devoted to numerous Windows development topics and issues, including Visual Studio .NET and Visual Basic .NET programming. Discussion groups among professional Visual Basic .NET programmers provide peer-to-peer interaction and feedback for many development issues. In addition, the DevX Marketplace offers books, controls, and third-party tools for sale.

http://www.microsoft.com/mspress/

The Microsoft Press home page offers the newest books on Visual Basic .NET programming from Microsoft Press authors. Check here for new books about Microsoft Visual C# .NET and Microsoft Visual C++ .NET as well. You can also download freebies and send mail to Microsoft Press.

http://www.microsoft.com/traincert/

The Microsoft Corporate Web site for software training and services, including testing and certification. Over the last few years, many Visual Basic programmers have found that they can better demonstrate their development skills to potential employers if they pass one or more certification examinations and earn a Microsoft certified credential, such as the MCP (Microsoft Certified

Professional), MCSE (Microsoft Certified Systems Engineer), or MCSA (Microsoft Certified Systems Administrator). Visit this Web site to learn more about your certification options.

http://communities.microsoft.com/home/

Newsgroup communities for many Microsoft software products, including the tools in the Visual Studio .NET family. Currently, Visual Studio .NET newsgroup topics are listed under the keywords "vb", "vc", "dotnet", "vsnet", and "vstudio".

Books for Visual Basic .NET Programming

Printed books about Visual Basic .NET programming provide in-depth sources of information and self-paced training that Web sites can supplement but not replace. As you seek to expand your Visual Basic .NET programming skills, I recommend that you consult the following sources of printed information (listed here by category). Note that this isn't a complete bibliography of Visual Basic .NET titles, but is a list that is representative of the books available in English within a few months of the original Visual Basic .NET software release.

Visual Basic .NET Programming

- *Programming Microsoft Visual Basic .NET*, by Francesco Balena (Microsoft Press, ISBN 0-7356-1375-3).
- *Coding Techniques for Microsoft Visual Basic .NET*, by John Connell (Microsoft Press, ISBN 0-7356-1254-4).
- *Professional VB .NET*, by Fred Barwell, Richard Blair, Richard Case, Jonathan Crossland, Bill Forgey, Whitney Hankison, Billy Hollis, Rockford Lhotka, Tim McCarthy, Jan D. Narkiewicz, Jonathan Pinnock, Rama Ramachandran, Matthew Reynolds, John Roth, Bill Sempf, Bill Sheldon, and Scott Short (Wrox Press, ISBN 1-8610-0497-4).
- *Upgrading Microsoft Visual Basic 6.0 to Microsoft Visual Basic .NET*, by Ed Robinson, Michael Bond, and Ian Oliver (Microsoft Press, ISBN 0-7356-1587-X).
- *Practical Standards for Microsoft Visual Basic .NET*, by James D. Foxall (Microsoft Press, ISBN 0-7356-1356-7).
- *Professional .NET Framework*, by Jeff Gabriel, Denise Gosnell, Jeffrey Hasan, Kevin Hoffman, Christian Holm, Ed Musters, Jan D. Narkiewicz, Jonothon Ortiz, John Schenken, Thiru Thangarathinam, and Scott Wylie (Wrox Press, ISBN 1-8610-0556-3).

■ OOP: *Building Reusable Components with Microsoft Visual Basic .NET*, by Kenneth L. Spencer and Tom Eberahrd (Microsoft Press, ISBN 0-7356-1379-6).

■ OOP *with Microsoft Visual Basic .NET and Microsoft Visual C# .NET*, by Robin A. Reynolds-Haertle (Microsoft Press, ISBN 0-7356-1568-3).

Web Programming with ASP.NET

■ *Building Web Solutions with ASP.NET and ADO.NET*, by Dino Esposito (Microsoft Press, ISBN 0-7356-1578-0).

■ *Beginning ASP.NET Using VB .NET*, by Rob Birdwell, Ollie Cornes, Chris Goode, John Kauffman, Ajoy Krishnamoorthy, Juan T. Llibre, Christopher L. Miller, Neil Raybould, David Sussman, and Chris Ullman (Wrox Press, ISBN 1-8610-0504-0).

■ *Teach Yourself ASP.NET in 21 Days*, by Chris Payne and Scott Mitchell (Sams, ISBN 0-6723-2168-8).

■ *Professional ASP.NET*, by Richard Anderson, Brian Francis, Alex Homer, Rob Howard, Dave Sussman, and Karli Watson (Wrox Press, ISBN 1-8610-0488-5).

Database Programming with ADO.NET

■ *Microsoft ADO.NET Step by Step*, by Rebecca M. Riordan (Microsoft Press, ISBN 0-7356-1236-6).

■ *Programming Microsoft SQL Server 2000 with Microsoft Visual Basic .NET*, by Rick Dobson (Microsoft Press, ISBN 0-7356-1535-7).

■ *Microsoft ADO.NET* (Core Reference), by David Sceppa (Microsoft Press, ISBN 0-7356-1423-7).

Visual Basic for Applications Programming

■ *Microsoft Excel 2002 Visual Basic for Applications Step by Step*, by Reed Jacobson (Microsoft Press, ISBN 0-7356-1359-1).

■ *Excel 2002 Power Programming with VBA*, by John Walkenbach (Hungry Minds, ISBN 0-7645-4799-2).

■ *Microsoft Access 2002 Visual Basic for Applications Step by Step*, by Evan Callahan (Microsoft Press, ISBN 0-7356-1358-3).

Upgrading Index

This index provides an alphabetical guide to many of the upgrading topics in this book. It is designed to help readers who are familiar with Visual Basic 6 identify the new features in Visual Basic .NET and use them to upgrade their applications. Scan both the Upgrade Topic and Description columns to find topics that you are curious about, and then turn to the page number indicated for a discussion of the upgrading material. Note that a comprehensive index following this table offers additional information about Visual Basic .NET features and programming skills.

Index

Send feedback about this index to *mspindex@microsoft.com*

About the Author

Michael Halvorson is the author or co-author of twenty computer books, including *Microsoft Office XP Inside Out*, *Visual Basic 6 Professional Step By Step*, *Learn Microsoft Visual Basic 6 Now*, *Running Microsoft Office 2000 Premium Edition*, and *Microsoft Word 97/Visual Basic Step by Step*. Michael earned a bachelor's degree in Computer Science from Pacific Lutheran University in Tacoma, Washington, and master's and doctoral degrees in History from the University of Washington in Seattle, Washington. He was employed at Microsoft Corporation as a technical editor, acquisitions editor, and localization manager from 1985 through 1993. Michael currently spends his time developing innovative software solutions for Microsoft Office and Microsoft Visual Basic .NET and teaching European history courses at colleges in the Pacific Northwest.

Photo by Kim Halvorson

Protractor Triangle

The word navigation traditionally meant the art or science of conducting ships and other watercraft from one place to another. A device commonly used in navigation is the protractor triangle. It plots courses accurately in tight spaces when used with a parallel rule or course plotter. It's essential for easily measuring right angles, celestial azimuth angles, and lines of position. With its protractor scales, the triangle is easily aligned in any direction with a chart meridian.

At Microsoft Press, we use tools to illustrate our books for software developers and IT professionals. Tools are an elegant symbol of human inventiveness and a powerful metaphor for how people can extend their capabilities, precision, and reach. From basic calipers and pliers to digital micrometers and lasers, our stylized illustrations of tools give each book a visual identity and each book series a personality. With tools and knowledge, there are no limits to creativity and innovation. Our tag line says it all: *The tools you need to put technology to work.*

The manuscript for this book was prepared and submitted to Microsoft Press in electronic form. Text files were prepared using Microsoft Word XP. Pages were composed by Microsoft Press using Adobe PageMaker 6.52 for Windows, with text set in Sabon and display type in Syntax and Syntax Black. Composed pages were delivered to the printer as electronic prepress files.

Interior Graphic Artist

Michael Kloepfer

Principal Compositor

Elizabeth Hansford

Principal Copy Editor

Patricia Masserman

Indexer

Bill Myers

MICROSOFT LICENSE AGREEMENT
Book Companion CD

IMPORTANT—READ CAREFULLY: This Microsoft End-User License Agreement ("EULA") is a legal agreement between you (either an individual or an entity) and Microsoft Corporation for the Microsoft product identified above, which includes computer software and may include associated media, printed materials, and "online" or electronic documentation ("SOFTWARE PROD-UCT"). Any component included within the SOFTWARE PRODUCT that is accompanied by a separate End-User License Agreement shall be governed by such agreement and not the terms set forth below. By installing, copying, or otherwise using the SOFTWARE PRODUCT, you agree to be bound by the terms of this EULA. If you do not agree to the terms of this EULA, you are not authorized to install, copy, or otherwise use the SOFTWARE PRODUCT; you may, however, return the SOFTWARE PROD-UCT, along with all printed materials and other items that form a part of the Microsoft product that includes the SOFTWARE PRODUCT, to the place you obtained them for a full refund.

SOFTWARE PRODUCT LICENSE

The SOFTWARE PRODUCT is protected by United States copyright laws and international copyright treaties, as well as other intellectual property laws and treaties. The SOFTWARE PRODUCT is licensed, not sold.

1. **GRANT OF LICENSE.** This EULA grants you the following rights:

   a. **Software Product.** You may install and use one copy of the SOFTWARE PRODUCT on a single computer. The primary user of the computer on which the SOFTWARE PRODUCT is installed may make a second copy for his or her exclusive use on a portable computer.

   b. **Storage/Network Use.** You may also store or install a copy of the SOFTWARE PRODUCT on a storage device, such as a network server, used only to install or run the SOFTWARE PRODUCT on your other computers over an internal network; however, you must acquire and dedicate a license for each separate computer on which the SOFTWARE PRODUCT is installed or run from the storage device. A license for the SOFTWARE PRODUCT may not be shared or used concurrently on different computers.

   c. **License Pak.** If you have acquired this EULA in a Microsoft License Pak, you may make the number of additional copies of the computer software portion of the SOFTWARE PRODUCT authorized on the printed copy of this EULA, and you may use each copy in the manner specified above. You are also entitled to make a corresponding number of secondary copies for portable computer use as specified above.

   d. **Sample Code.** Solely with respect to portions, if any, of the SOFTWARE PRODUCT that are identified within the SOFT-WARE PRODUCT as sample code (the "SAMPLE CODE"):

      i. **Use and Modification.** Microsoft grants you the right to use and modify the source code version of the SAMPLE CODE, *provided* you comply with subsection (d)(iii) below. You may not distribute the SAMPLE CODE, or any modified version of the SAMPLE CODE, in source code form.

      ii. **Redistributable Files.** Provided you comply with subsection (d)(iii) below, Microsoft grants you a nonexclusive, royalty-free right to reproduce and distribute the object code version of the SAMPLE CODE and of any modified SAMPLE CODE, other than SAMPLE CODE, or any modified version thereof, designated as not redistributable in the Readme file that forms a part of the SOFTWARE PRODUCT (the "Non-Redistributable Sample Code"). All SAMPLE CODE other than the Non-Redistributable Sample Code is collectively referred to as the "REDISTRIBUTABLES."

      iii. **Redistribution Requirements.** If you redistribute the REDISTRIBUTABLES, you agree to: (i) distribute the REDISTRIBUTABLES in object code form only in conjunction with and as a part of your software application product; (ii) not use Microsoft's name, logo, or trademarks to market your software application product; (iii) include a valid copyright notice on your software application product; (iv) indemnify, hold harmless, and defend Microsoft from and against any claims or lawsuits, including attorney's fees, that arise or result from the use or distribution of your software application product; and (v) not permit further distribution of the REDISTRIBUTABLES by your end user. Contact Microsoft for the applicable royalties due and other licensing terms for all other uses and/or distribution of the REDISTRIBUTABLES.

2. **DESCRIPTION OF OTHER RIGHTS AND LIMITATIONS.**

   - **Limitations on Reverse Engineering, Decompilation, and Disassembly.** You may not reverse engineer, decompile, or disassemble the SOFTWARE PRODUCT, except and only to the extent that such activity is expressly permitted by applicable law notwithstanding this limitation.

   - **Separation of Components.** The SOFTWARE PRODUCT is licensed as a single product. Its component parts may not be separated for use on more than one computer.

   - **Rental.** You may not rent, lease, or lend the SOFTWARE PRODUCT.

   - **Support Services.** Microsoft may, but is not obligated to, provide you with support services related to the SOFTWARE PRODUCT ("Support Services"). Use of Support Services is governed by the Microsoft policies and programs described in the user manual, in "online" documentation, and/or in other Microsoft-provided materials. Any supplemental software code provided to you as part of the Support Services shall be considered part of the SOFTWARE PRODUCT and subject to the terms and conditions of this EULA. With respect to technical information you provide to Microsoft as part of the Support Services, Microsoft may use such information for its business purposes, including for product support and development. Microsoft will not utilize such technical information in a form that personally identifies you.

- **Software Transfer.** You may permanently transfer all of your rights under this EULA, provided you retain no copies, you transfer all of the SOFTWARE PRODUCT (including all component parts, the media and printed materials, any upgrades, this EULA, and, if applicable, the Certificate of Authenticity), **and** the recipient agrees to the terms of this EULA.

- **Termination.** Without prejudice to any other rights, Microsoft may terminate this EULA if you fail to comply with the terms and conditions of this EULA. In such event, you must destroy all copies of the SOFTWARE PRODUCT and all of its component parts.

3. **COPYRIGHT.** All title and copyrights in and to the SOFTWARE PRODUCT (including but not limited to any images, photographs, animations, video, audio, music, text, SAMPLE CODE, REDISTRIBUTABLES, and "applets" incorporated into the SOFTWARE PRODUCT) and any copies of the SOFTWARE PRODUCT are owned by Microsoft or its suppliers. The SOFTWARE PRODUCT is protected by copyright laws and international treaty provisions. Therefore, you must treat the SOFTWARE PRODUCT like any other copyrighted material **except** that you may install the SOFTWARE PRODUCT on a single computer provided you keep the original solely for backup or archival purposes. You may not copy the printed materials accompanying the SOFTWARE PRODUCT.

4. **U.S. GOVERNMENT RESTRICTED RIGHTS.** The SOFTWARE PRODUCT and documentation are provided with RESTRICTED RIGHTS. Use, duplication, or disclosure by the Government is subject to restrictions as set forth in subparagraph (c)(1)(ii) of the Rights in Technical Data and Computer Software clause at DFARS 252.227-7013 or subparagraphs (c)(1) and (2) of the Commercial Computer Software—Restricted Rights at 48 CFR 52.227-19, as applicable. Manufacturer is Microsoft Corporation/One Microsoft Way/Redmond, WA 98052-6399.

5. **EXPORT RESTRICTIONS.** You agree that you will not export or re-export the SOFTWARE PRODUCT, any part thereof, or any process or service that is the direct product of the SOFTWARE PRODUCT (the foregoing collectively referred to as the "Restricted Components"), to any country, person, entity, or end user subject to U.S. export restrictions. You specifically agree not to export or re-export any of the Restricted Components (i) to any country to which the U.S. has embargoed or restricted the export of goods or services, which currently include, but are not necessarily limited to, Cuba, Iran, Iraq, Libya, North Korea, Sudan, and Syria, or to any national of any such country, wherever located, who intends to transmit or transport the Restricted Components back to such country; (ii) to any end user who you know or have reason to know will utilize the Restricted Components in the design, development, or production of nuclear, chemical, or biological weapons; or (iii) to any end user who has been prohibited from participating in U.S. export transactions by any federal agency of the U.S. government. You warrant and represent that neither the BXA nor any other U.S. federal agency has suspended, revoked, or denied your export privileges.

DISCLAIMER OF WARRANTY

NO WARRANTIES OR CONDITIONS. MICROSOFT EXPRESSLY DISCLAIMS ANY WARRANTY OR CONDITION FOR THE SOFTWARE PRODUCT. THE SOFTWARE PRODUCT AND ANY RELATED DOCUMENTATION ARE PROVIDED "AS IS" WITHOUT WARRANTY OR CONDITION OF ANY KIND, EITHER EXPRESS OR IMPLIED, INCLUDING, WITHOUT LIMITATION, THE IMPLIED WARRANTIES OF MERCHANTABILITY, FITNESS FOR A PARTICULAR PURPOSE, OR NONINFRINGEMENT. THE ENTIRE RISK ARISING OUT OF USE OR PERFORMANCE OF THE SOFTWARE PRODUCT REMAINS WITH YOU.

LIMITATION OF LIABILITY. TO THE MAXIMUM EXTENT PERMITTED BY APPLICABLE LAW, IN NO EVENT SHALL MICROSOFT OR ITS SUPPLIERS BE LIABLE FOR ANY SPECIAL, INCIDENTAL, INDIRECT, OR CONSEQUENTIAL DAMAGES WHATSOEVER (INCLUDING, WITHOUT LIMITATION, DAMAGES FOR LOSS OF BUSINESS PROFITS, BUSINESS INTERRUPTION, LOSS OF BUSINESS INFORMATION, OR ANY OTHER PECUNIARY LOSS) ARISING OUT OF THE USE OF OR INABILITY TO USE THE SOFTWARE PRODUCT OR THE PROVISION OF OR FAILURE TO PROVIDE SUPPORT SERVICES, EVEN IF MICROSOFT HAS BEEN ADVISED OF THE POSSIBILITY OF SUCH DAMAGES. IN ANY CASE, MICROSOFT'S ENTIRE LIABILITY UNDER ANY PROVISION OF THIS EULA SHALL BE LIMITED TO THE GREATER OF THE AMOUNT ACTUALLY PAID BY YOU FOR THE SOFTWARE PRODUCT OR US$5.00; PROVIDED, HOWEVER, IF YOU HAVE ENTERED INTO A MICROSOFT SUPPORT SERVICES AGREEMENT, MICROSOFT'S ENTIRE LIABILITY REGARDING SUPPORT SERVICES SHALL BE GOVERNED BY THE TERMS OF THAT AGREEMENT. BECAUSE SOME STATES AND JURISDICTIONS DO NOT ALLOW THE EXCLUSION OR LIMITATION OF LIABILITY, THE ABOVE LIMITATION MAY NOT APPLY TO YOU.

MISCELLANEOUS

This EULA is governed by the laws of the State of Washington USA, except and only to the extent that applicable law mandates governing law of a different jurisdiction.

Should you have any questions concerning this EULA, or if you desire to contact Microsoft for any reason, please contact the Microsoft subsidiary serving your country, or write: Microsoft Sales Information Center/One Microsoft Way/Redmond, WA 98052-6399.

PN 097-0002296

Get a **Free**
e-mail newsletter, updates,
special offers, links to related books,
and more when you

register on line!

Register your Microsoft Press® title on our Web site and you'll get a FREE subscription to our e-mail newsletter, *Microsoft Press Book Connections.* You'll find out about newly released and upcoming books and learning tools, online events, software downloads, special offers and coupons for Microsoft Press customers, and information about major Microsoft® product releases. You can also read useful additional information about all the titles we publish, such as detailed book descriptions, tables of contents and indexes, sample chapters, links to related books and book series, author biographies, and reviews by other customers.

Registration is easy. Just visit this Web page and fill in your information:

http://www.microsoft.com/mspress/register

Microsoft®

Proof of Purchase

Use this page as proof of purchase if participating in a promotion or rebate offer on this title. Proof of purchase must be used in conjunction with other proof(s) of payment such as your dated sales receipt—see offer details.

Microsoft® Visual Basic® .NET Step by Step

0-7356-1374-5

CUSTOMER NAME

Microsoft Press, PO Box 97017, Redmond, WA 98073-9830